Japan Advances

AF785356

Japan Advances

A GEOGRAPHICAL STUDY

Prue Dempster

Cartography by K. J. Wass

METHUEN & CO LTD
11 NEW FETTER LANE · LONDON EC4

First published in Great Britain 1967
by Methuen & Co Ltd, London
Second Edition 1969
© Prue Dempster 1967 and 1969
Printed in Great Britain by
Butler & Tanner Ltd, Frome and London
SBN 416 13290 1

Distributed in the U.S.A. by
Barnes & Noble, Inc

Contents

TO MY PARENTS
with thanks for all their help and encouragement

Preface

The emphasis in these pages is on the rapidly changing economic geography of Japan which has transformed both the way of life of the individual and the urban and rural landscape during the past century. The story involves not only the part played by many aspects of physical geography in this relatively small area but also that played by the people who, under circumstances that are by no means favourable ones, have continued to improve farm productivity, develop industry and raise the standard of living of the population, so that the country can now compete in world markets with the most highly developed countries. This process is intrinsically an interesting one and the results are worth describing. How this happened and the methods used are also of world significance both to the Western countries with whom she now competes and to the under-developed countries who may hope to develop in a similar way.

In the study of a European or 'Western' country much of the background can be assumed from a conscious Western tradition but Japanese development has its roots in a different historical and social setting with people motivated by attitudes, desires and aims different from those activating Westerners. To understand Japanese geography and development it is necessary to understand the Japanese outlook as well as the physical background. The high regard for duty to State as well as family at the expense of the individual who counts for relatively nothing, has played a great part in the rapid advance during which individual loyalty to the State has helped Japan to become a political and economic world power. The custom that the eldest has a duty to look after the family land has checked the development of farming, keeping it on a small scale.

This book attempts to describe and illuminate this story and these facets of Japan and the Japanese, using detailed studies of farms, factories, villages and towns to build up a realistic picture of the rapidly changing Japanese scene.

Preface to the Second Edition

The preparation of a second edition has made it possible to bring up to date figures showing the rapidly changing economic scene. When the maps and diagrams were drawn for the first edition only 1962 figures were available but now 1966 figures have been used in most cases and in some places those for 1967. Few changes have been made in the first five chapters other than minor corrections but the chapters on farming, population, industry, transport and trade have been thoroughly revised using more recent figures. In some cases sections have been rewritten and new material added. Maps and diagrams have been redrawn where a changed pattern makes this necessary but not where the pattern remains similar.

The farming chapter has been revised to show the effects of the increasing shortage of labour resulting from the increasing demands of expanding industries, the sharp fall in the agricultural labour force in 1966–7 and its influence on farming. The section on government policy has been expanded.

In the industrial chapter material has been added on the growth of large scale industry in the sixties through mergers and the building of large factories and the concentration of ownership into a few hands in many industries. A section has been added on the development of industry and mining abroad by many of the large firms. The section on the motor vehicle industry has been rewritten to show its recent rapid growth which has made Japan the third largest world car producer and a growing exporter. The increased size of ships has given Japan's system of building ships in dry docks a great advantage. The new chemical industry map shows the petro-chemical plants established up to 1967.

The chapters on population have been revised drawing on the 1965 census and bringing out the reasons for the very marked change in regional birth rates and the growth of conurbations especially that centred on Tokyo with its resultant problems of housing, transport congestion and a shortage of public services.

The transport and trade chapters show the growing dependence on Australia for raw materials including coal, and iron and food especially meat, dairy produce and cereals and the general increase in trade with the highly developed nations.

There is a supplementary bibliography.

I am most grateful to the many people who have made comments and suggestions on the first edition many of which have been used in the preparation of this edition.

Kidderminster, October 1968

Acknowledgments

I should like to acknowledge the help of a great many people in providing material, ideas and encouragement in writing this book. While I was in Japan during 1959–60 the Ministry of Foreign Affairs, Asia Kyokai and the Ministry of Agriculture arranged for me to stay with many Japanese families in town and country all over Japan and to visit farms, workshops and factories. I am especially grateful to the many Japanese families who allowed me to become part of their households.

Professor Tada and Professor Kobori, of the Geography Department of Tokyo University, were especially helpful, as were Professor Ishizuka and Professor Inouye of the University of Hokkaido, Dr R. Hall, the International Society for Educational Information in Tokyo, the Japanese Information Bureau in London and the staff of the library at the London School of Economics. Mr Wass has taken a great deal of trouble in drawing the maps and diagrams.

Mr A. Walton of the University of Keele and Mr M. Robertson of Avery Hill College have read the manuscript and given much helpful advice. Among others who have helped and encouraged me are Professor Kiuchi of Tokyo University, Professor Allen of University College, London, Professor Dore and Professor Buchanan of the London School of Economics, Mr Storry of St Anthony's College, Oxford, and Miss A. Campbell of Birkbeck College, London. Many ideas have arisen from discussions with my students at Whitelands College, London, and Summerfield College, Kidderminster. Professor G. Trewartha's work is acknowledged in the text.

My thanks for the use of plates to

Asahi Evening News 5
Fuji Iron and Steel Co. 43
John Getrup 37
Hosoe Town Office 38
International Society for Educational Information, Tokyo 2, 13, 56, 58
Japanese Embassy 3, 11, 14, 18, 34, 36, 39, 41, 46, 47, 48, 49, 51, 54
Japan Tourist Association 57
Ministry of Agriculture 19, 20, 30
Mitsui Co. 48
Orion Press 7, 8
Wild Heerbrug 6, 28
Yawata Iron and Steel Co. 45
Others are by the author 1, 4, 10, 12, 15, 16, 22, 23, 24, 25, 26, 27, 29, 31, 32, 33, 42, 50, 52, 53, 55

Maps and Figures

Plates

Japan Advances

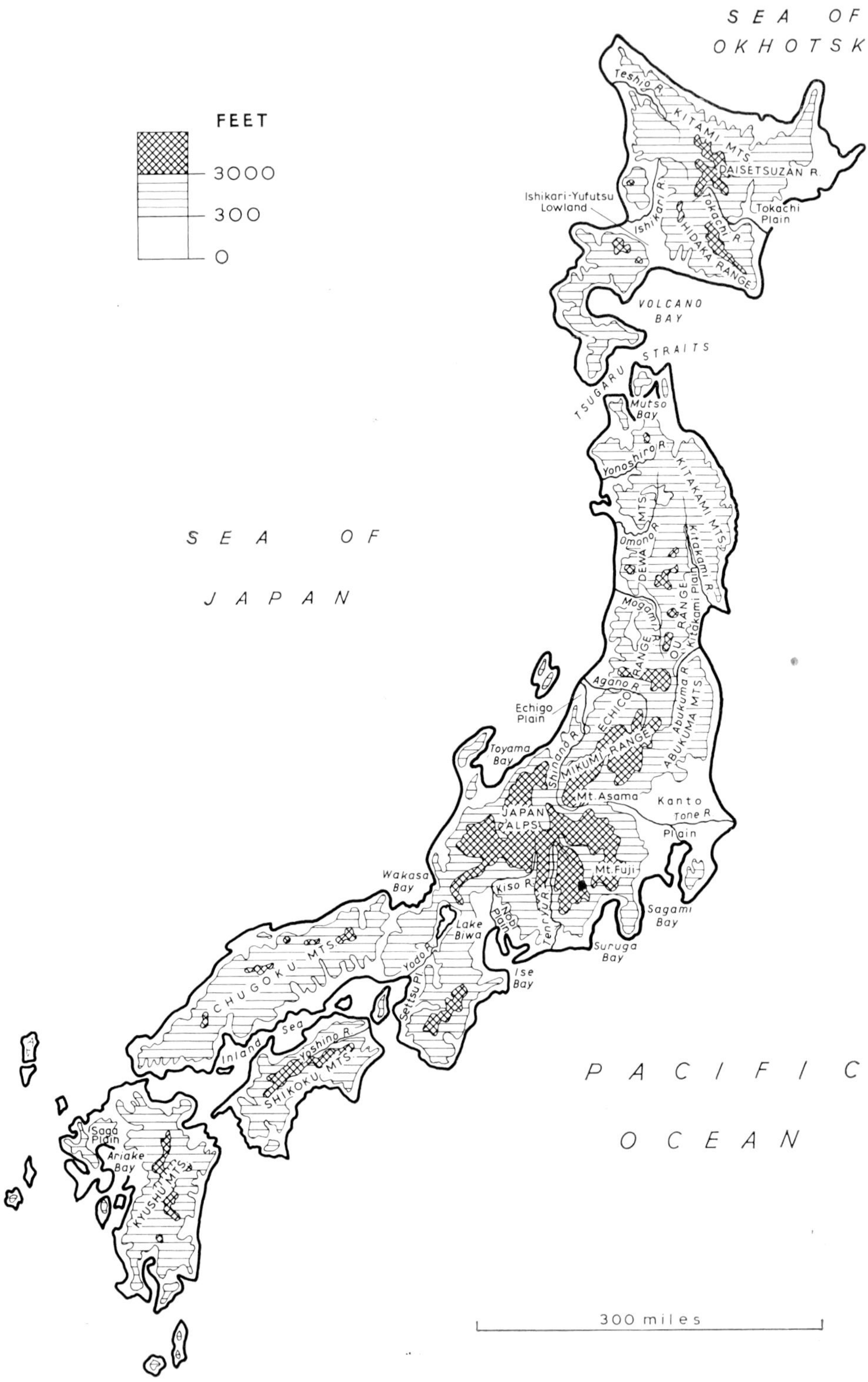

FIG. 1. Main relief features and rivers (219).

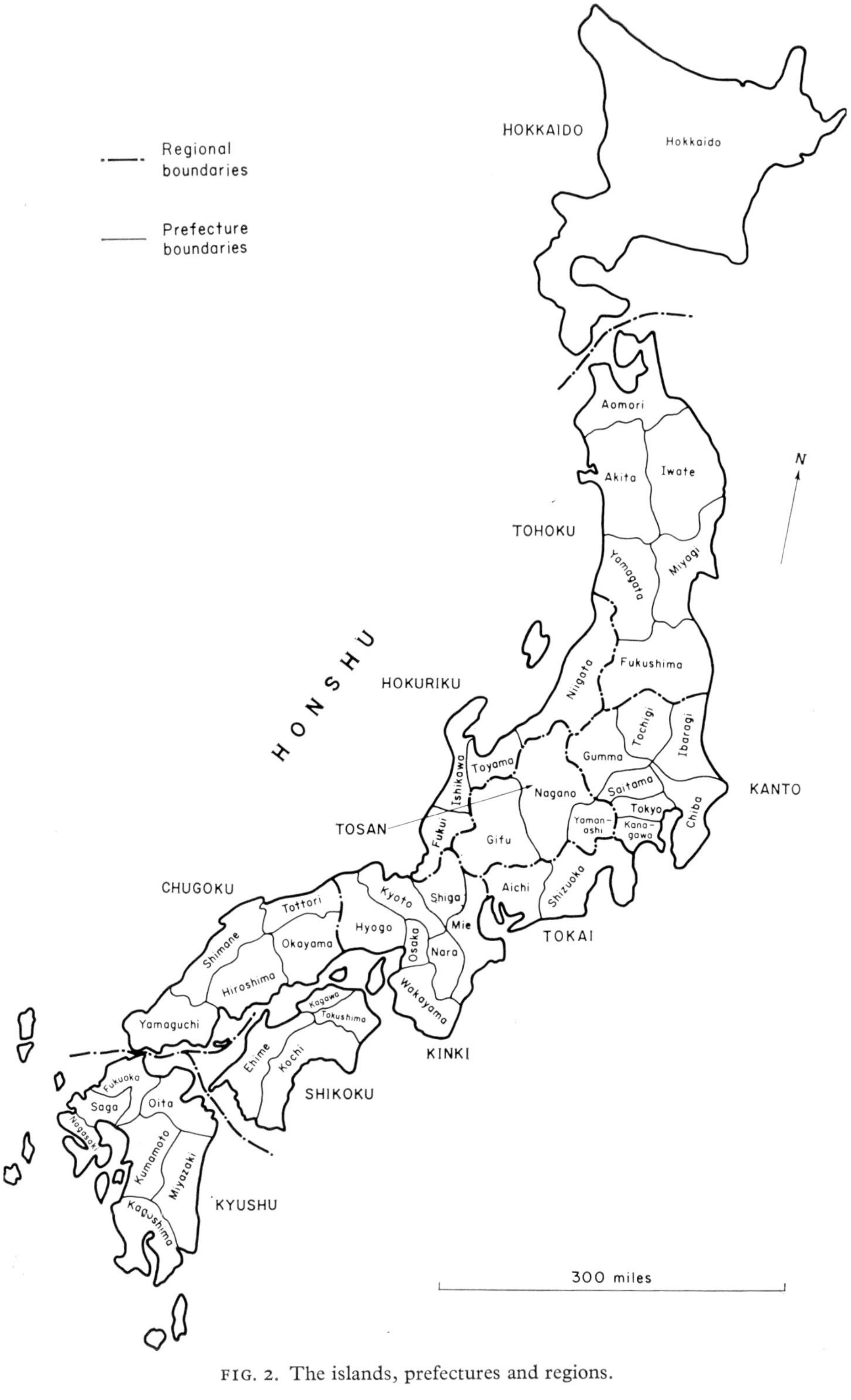

FIG. 2. The islands, prefectures and regions.

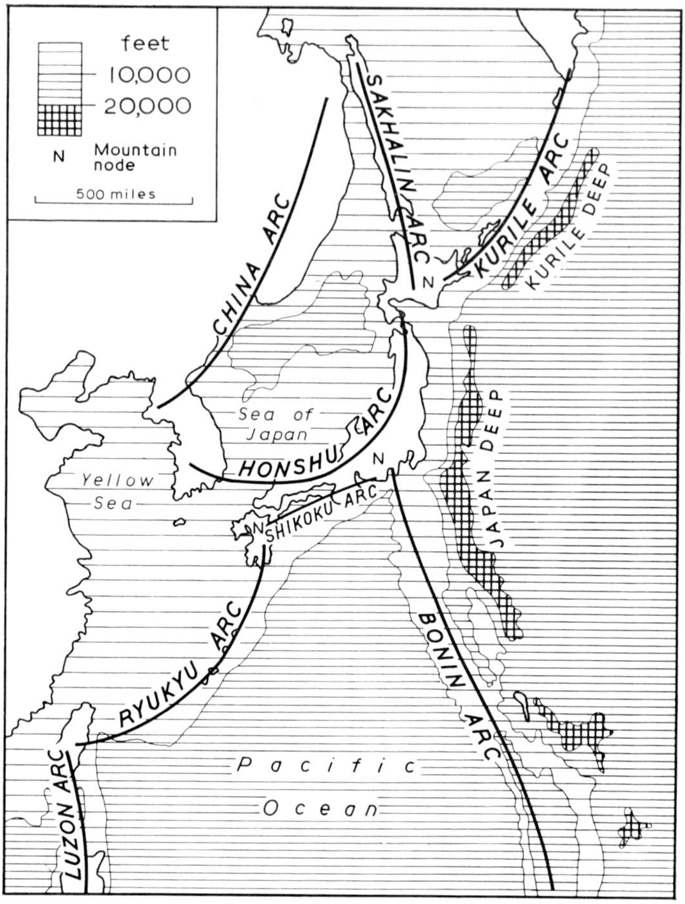

FIG. 3. Mountain arcs and ocean deeps.

Figures in brackets refer to the bibliography.

CHAPTER ONE

The Physical Landscape

The Japanese islands are at the junction of four main, geologically recent, unstable mountain arcs (fig. 3). The Honshu Arc follows the line of the main islands. The Ryukyu Arc runs south-west with a few peaks above the surface of the sea forming the Ryukyu Islands that join the Luzon Arc in Formosa. The Kurile Arc stretches through Hokkaido and the Kurile Islands to Kamchatka. A third runs from Hokkaido northwards through Sakhalin, a fourth, the Bonin Arc, stretches southward from central Japan, breaks the surface in the Bonin Islands, and continues towards New Guinea through the Mariana Islands and Guam.

The Japanese archipelago forming the easternmost limit of Asia is separated from the mainland by the Sea of Japan, which is over 10,000 feet deep and was an ocean trough even in Pleistocene times when Japan was probably linked to the continent by a land bridge leading to Korea in the west. Each of the island arcs is bordered to the east by an ocean trench. Unlike the coast of south and central China, which is bordered by a continental shelf, to the east of Japan the trench runs close to the coast and the slope of the ocean bed plunges from the 8,000-feet peaks of the Japanese mountains to the deeps nearly 28,000 feet below sea level. The trenches lie along the andesite line where the thicker predominantly acidic rocks of the continental mass meet the thinner, denser basic rocks of the Pacific Ocean floor. They coincide with the outcrops of the major thrust planes where the crust below the ocean seems to be thrust beneath the continental mass, forming a deep marginal trench. The crust on the continental side of the trench has been upwarped, producing a high edge where the crust is thicker. There are two seismic arcs (fig. 4) associated with lines of weakness on either side of this edge. Deep-seated earthquakes are associated with the outer arc which lies along the ocean trench east of Japan. The inner one is subject to volcanic and tectonic activity.

The structure of Japan is determined by the complex folding of these mountain arcs torn by faults. Mountains are aligned along the arcs and complex mountain nodes have been formed where two or more of these arcs meet (fig. 3). In the north the Kurile and Sakhalin arcs meet in the Hokkaido node forming the Daisetsuzan Range. The Honshu Arc meets the Bonin Arc in central Honshu to form Japan's highest mountain complex, the Chubu node, that includes the Japan Alps. The Ryukyu and Shikoku-Kii arcs meet to form the Kyushu node.

By the geological time scale the Japanese islands are young (fig. 5), as two-

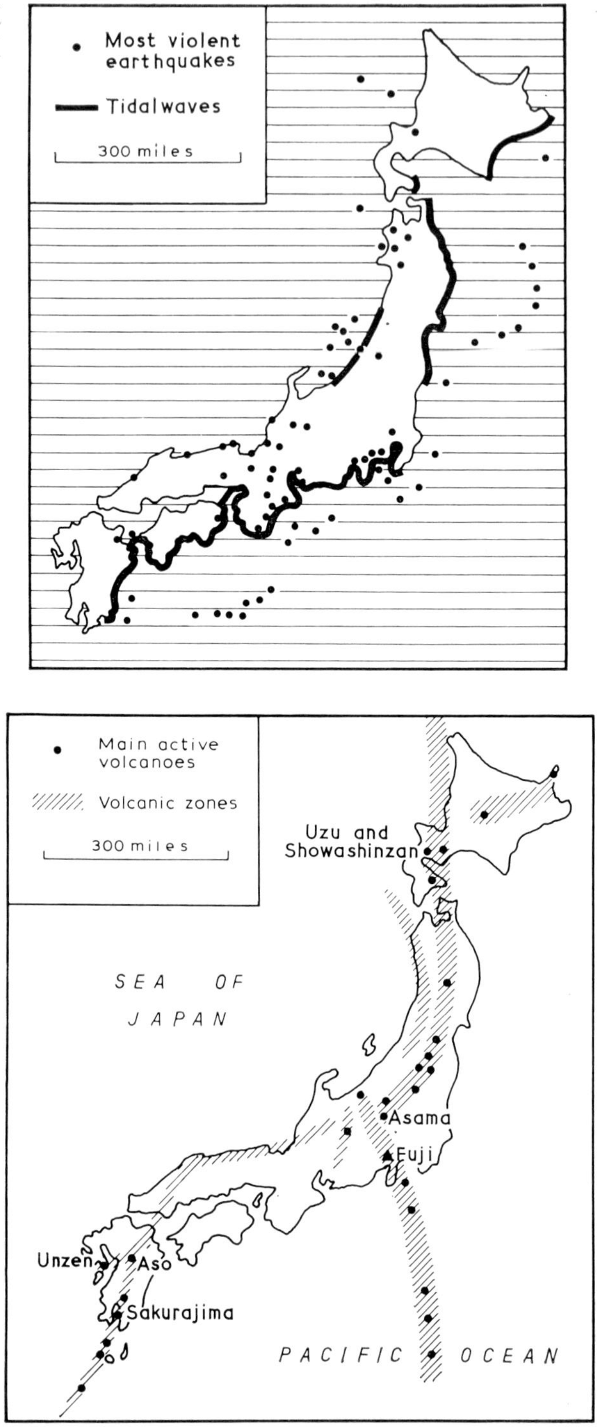

FIG. 4. Earthquakes and *tsunami* (tidal waves) (2) and volcanic zones and main active volcanoes (15).

thirds of the surface rocks including many volcanic rocks are of Tertiary or more recent age. There are few rocks proved to be older than Palaeozoic. Japan forms

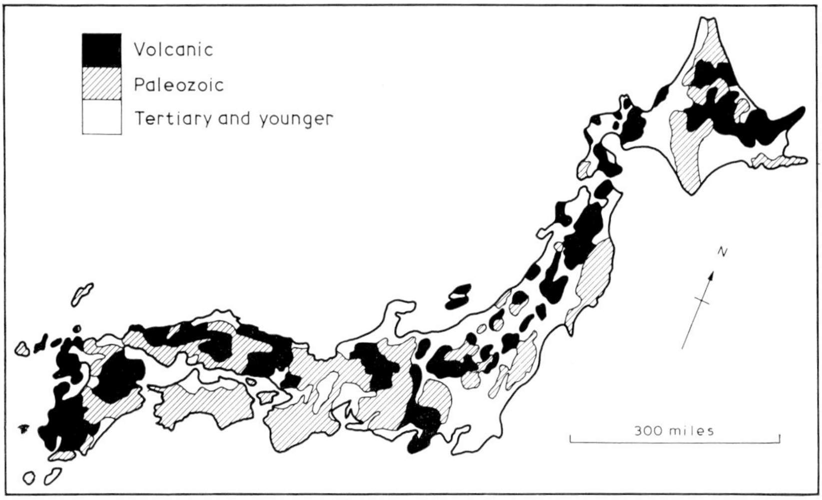

FIG. 5. Main rock types (6).

PLATE I. This is the view from the Makinohara Plateau in Shizuoka across the Oi Valley to Mount Fuji. The Makinohara Plateau is famous for its tea grown in long rounded hedges. The Oi Valley is filled with a wide braided stream which was almost dry in December when this photograph was taken. The deeply ravined forested hills fall abruptly to a broad diluvial terrace. Above rises the snow-covered peak of Mount Fuji. Kanaya lies at the bridging point for both road and railway on the Tokaido route. This landscape is typical of Japan, where hills predominate rising above small valleys while volcanoes tower over all (220).

part of the 'Fiery Ring' which runs round the Pacific and 35% of its surface is formed of volcanic materials (15). The steaming and sometimes rumbling volcanoes and bubbling hot springs indicate the instability of the earth's crust in this geologically young country.

Throughout its geological history Japan has been the site of folding, faulting and intensive intrusive and extrusive volcanic activity because of its position in relation to the andesite line. Folding and faulting have broken up sedimentary, igneous and metamorphic formations alike, so that it is hard to trace the history of the country in the mosaic of fragmented rocks. Young granites in the mountains of Tohoku and Chugoku (fig. 5) have been exposed by rapid erosion.

Because of recent and continuing volcanic activity, tectonic movements and rapid denudation by heavy seasonal rainfall and rejuvenated streams, accompanied by much deposition, Japan's landforms have an outstandingly youthful, varied, rapidly changing character (pl. 1) with steep, freshly made slopes and ungraded streams and fans of detritus. The deeply dissected block mountains, crowned by newly built volcanic peaks, are broken by a multitude of small plains, narrow valleys and small tectonic basins.

Tectonic Regions

Similar landscapes are found all over Japan with variations which form the basis for regional sub-division (fig. 6). The alignment of formations in Japan

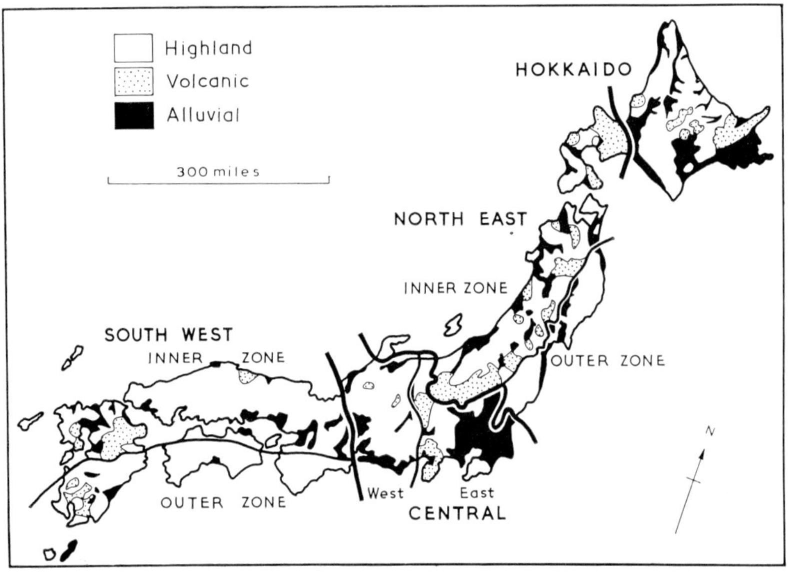

FIG. 6. Tectonic regions and landscape types (20).

following the trend of the arcs, stands out clearly in the complex topographic pattern. In Tohoku and Hokkaido the trend is from north to south, and in the south-western half of Japan from north-east to south-west. Between these two regions is the central region, central Honshu, where the arcs meet in the Chubu node. Here the great faulted trench, the Fossa Magna, divides the younger Tertiary sedimentary and volcanic formations of northern Japan from the mainly Palaeozoic rocks of the south-west. Hokkaido with its complex of mountain areas forms a separate region though its structure in the west is like that of Tohoku.

These north-east and south-west regions can be sub-divided into an *inner zone* on the Japan Sea side and an *outer zone* on the Pacific border. The median tectonic line separates the two sub-regions. Each of these six major regions has its own character. They are Hokkaido, the inner and outer northern regions, the central Fossa Magna–Kanto region, and the inner and outer south-west regions.

HOKKAIDO

Two mountain systems make up the foundation of Hokkaido's physiography (fig. 1). To the east of the Ishikari–Yufutsu Lowland, running north–south, is the Kitami–Hidaka chain of mountains, which is rather similar in structure to western Tohoku (see below). Two parallel north–south ranges, broken by antecedent rivers, are separated by a series of five basins, including the Kamikawa Basin drained by the upper Ishikari. Running east from this range is the broad Chishima Range, with its many volcanoes, which extend to the Shiretoko Peninsula. The Chishima and Kitami–Hidaka Ranges meet in the central node, forming the Daisetsuzan Mountains. Between these three mountain chains lie the three main plain areas of Hokkaido, each formed of detritus from the mountains around. The Tokachi Plain to the south-east is the largest, with broad terraced fans in four main steps rising to 1,500 feet. These have been overlaid with volcanic ash which is very deep on the older terraces. The Ishikari–Yufutsu Plain has more alluvial land than any other plain in Hokkaido but drainage is poor and extensive areas of peat have formed. There are smaller plains in the north. The Konsen Plain in eastern Hokkaido is a marine platform with a deep mantle of volcanic ash incised with shallow valleys made marshy by recent subsidence. None of Hokkaido has very high relief and the mountain areas are characterized by level summits which are relics of erosion surfaces. All are penetrated by valleys which provide easy routes for communication. The coastline is angular and faulted (220) with a striking series of coastal terraces almost everywhere. These rise to their highest at Cape Erimo, where they reach over 1,000 feet above sea level. These relatively continuous level marine benches make convenient lines of communication.

NORTHERN JAPAN

Northern Japan is formed mainly of younger Tertiary rocks. The western, inner zone has been subjected to folding as well as faulting but the main features are two parallel ranges of block mountains (fig. 1), the Ou and the Uetsu (Echigo–Dewa) Ranges, stretching from north to south. In the east of the zone the Ou Mountains form the backbone of Tohoku and extend into southern Hokkaido, forming much beautiful scenery. They rise to a fairly continuous summit line ranging from 5,000–7,000 feet with a few high passes, and are formed of

Palaeozoic rocks overlaid with Tertiaries and topped by cone-shaped volcanic peaks, including Mount Asama which rises to over 6,000 feet in the south, and Mount Nantai near Nikko. The volcanoes and the forested area round the caldera, Lake Towada, in the north are particularly attractive to holidaymakers. The Ou Mountains are divided from the Uetsu Range to the west by a line of weakness along which a series of six tectonic basins (220) has developed, each basin having steep fault scarps rising to east and west and a floor choked with river detritus. The Uetsu Range is divided into two parts, the Dewa Ranges north of the River Mogami and the Echigo Ranges in the south. Rivers rising in the Ou Ranges to the east gather tributaries developed along the line of basins and cut through these coastal ranges in great antecedent clefts. The coastal ranges are deeply dissected but have a fairly level skyline, rising sharply to still higher summits in the volcanic peaks of Tsugaru Fuji, the 'Fuji of Hirosaki', and Mounts Chokai, Gassan and Iide.

The coastline of western Tohoku is faulted and has changed rapidly even during historic time. Tectonic bays have been filled by material brought down by swift streams which have rapidly eroded the uplifted mountains and carried vast quantities of material down to the sea. They have built out marshy plains to fill the lagoons that once lay behind the lines of sand dunes that have been piled up by wind and sea action at the mouth of each river. Today the west coast alternates between precipitous faulted cliffs and smoothly curving dunes with, especially in the north, terraces and old sea cliffs at several levels where uplift has taken place (220).

The Pacific or outer northern zone sub-region in eastern Tohoku is divided from the inner sub-region by a tectonic trench. East of this the ancient sedimentary Kitakami Plateau and the crystalline Abukuma Plateau are resistant to erosion. Rising above their generally peneplained surfaces are monadnocks like Mount Hayachine on the Kitakami Plateau. The coastline of the southern Kitakami region has been deeply dissected by river erosion and subsidence has led to the development of an impressively beautiful coastline of deep rias (pl. 42) (220). In contrast the northern Kitakami and the Abukuma Highlands are bordered by an unbroken elevated coastline with a raised coastal plain. To the west these highland areas end abruptly in a fault scarp that drops to the wide valleys of the Kitakami and Abukuma rivers that drain the great tectonic corridor of northern Honshu which continues into the Ishikari valley in western Hokkaido.

SOUTH-WESTERN JAPAN

Much of south-western Japan is formed of older, Palaeozoic rock. *The Japan Sea or inner sub-region of western Japan* comprises Chugoku and the parts of Shikoku and Kyushu which are north of the median dislocation line. This is a complex region where granite and folded sedimentary rocks have been eroded to form marine platforms, fractured and uplifted to form block mountains broken by strikingly rectangular basins in the east and south like the Kyoto,

Nara and Biwa basins and the five drowned basins of the Inland Sea (figs. 7 & 8, pl. 2) (220). In Chugoku away from the Inland Sea the area has been faulted but there are few basins. The landscape is more mature with low rounded hills and fewer volcanoes than are found in most other regions of Japan. Relief in the area varies according to the character of the underlying rock. Many of the hills are rounded, being formed of granite or gneiss which has been maturely dissected;

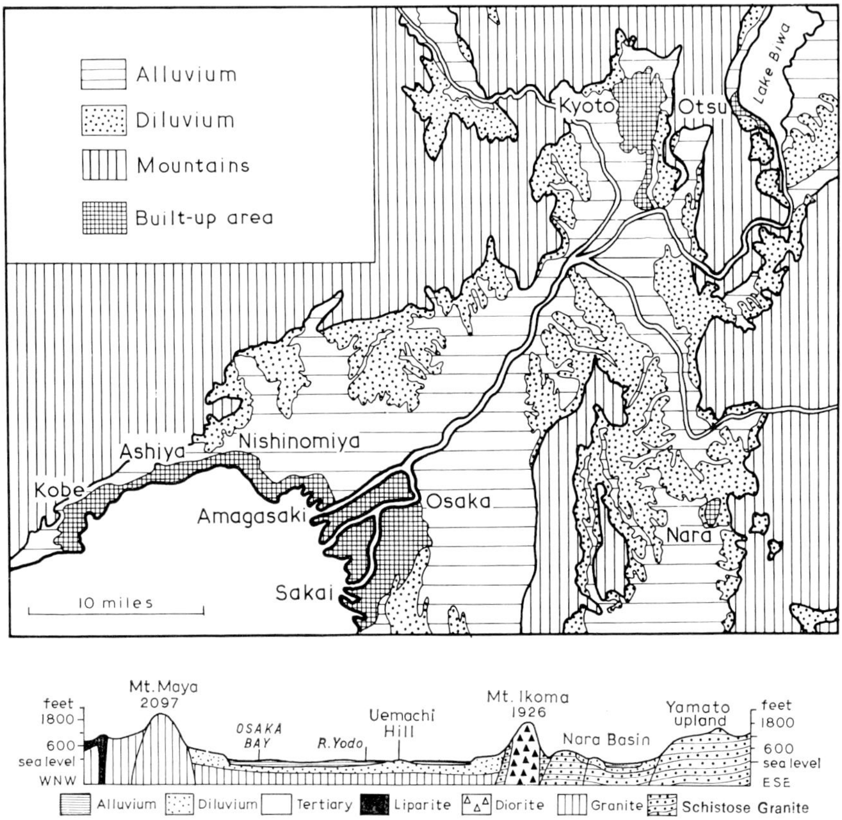

FIG. 7. The rectangular tectonic basins in Kinki are shown by the heavier line marking the edge of surrounding horsts. The basins are filled with diluvial terraces and alluvial plains (8).

there are limestone plateaux and very broken schist and slate country. Frequently faulting has interrupted the drainage pattern, ponding up the drainage to form lakes like Lake Biwa. Overflowing rivers have carved youthful valleys through intervening blocks to link one rectangular flat-floored basin with another, choking the basins with wide stepped piedmont terraces that have been built at the foot of fault scarps and with cones and fans of diluvium and poorly drained alluvium. Distinct steps in the terraces mark the stages of uplift.

天理市
大三輪町
櫻井市
天理教會
高等女學校

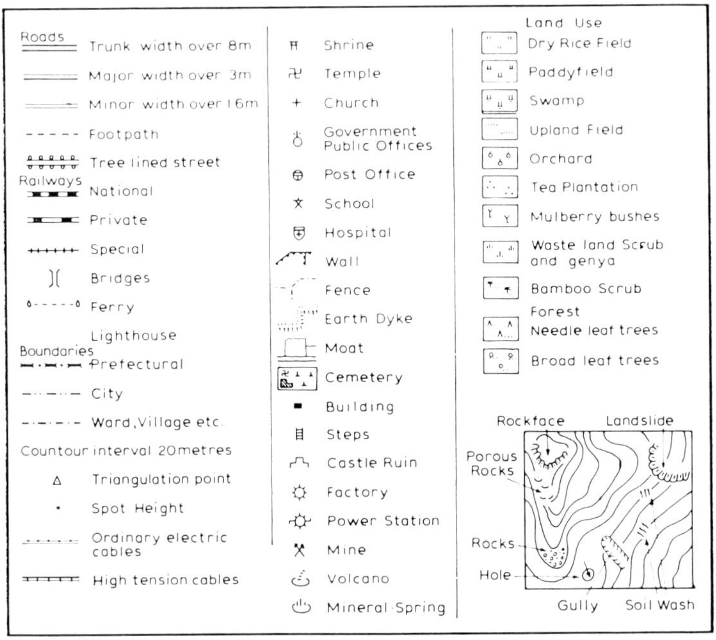

FIG. 8. Key to Nara Basin 1 : 50,000 map (*opposite*).

The shallow Inland Sea (pl. 3) is a series of five rectangular basins or *nada* which have been formed by the submergence of a horst and graben landscape (220). From it innumerable ancient denuded hills rise to form low, often flat-topped barren rock or forested islands. The islands and rugged indented coast make the scenery very attractive and the waters provide a valuable sheltered and an almost landlocked seaway. In Chugoku the valleys between the barren, inhospitable mountains have been filled with long narrow strips of fertile alluvium which swell to form wider plains where larger rivers have built out deltas into the shallow parts of the Inland Sea, as for example at Osaka on the Yodo River and at Hiroshima. Bays are being silted up, notably Kojima Bay in Okayama (figs. 9, 80 & 81) and Ariake Bay (fig. 82) in western Kyushu. In spring the denuded brown hills rise like islands out of the plains, formed by the infilling of old valleys, their gullied slopes contrasting sharply with the level and relatively fertile soils of the green valleys.

The Pacific or outer sub-region of western Japan is formed largely of uplifted folded mountains and, in contrast to other regions, is characterized by the relative absence of faults and the clear alignment of the resistant Palaeozoic formations in a north-east to south-west trend, following the line of the Shikoku Arc from south Kyushu in the west through Shikoku to the Kii Peninsula. Active volcanoes occur only in southern Kyushu. Resistant metamorphic rocks form rugged inhospitable highland left largely in its natural forested state. There is little lowland

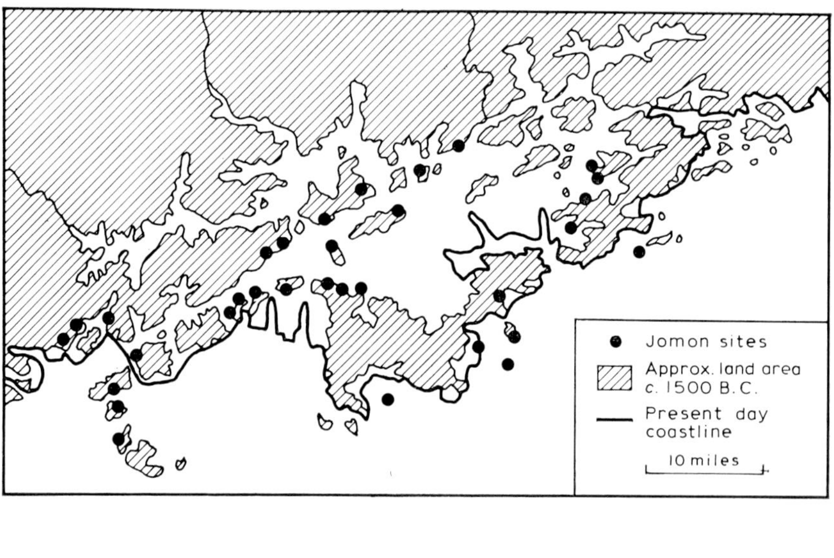
Jomon sites
Approx. land area c. 1500 B.C.
Present day coastline
10 miles

in the region as the valleys are not sufficiently wide or mature for the development of alluvial plains and the coast is subject to drowning by the down warping that

PLATE 3. The Inland Sea looking south-east from the coast of south Okayama towards Kagawa Prefecture in northern Shikoku (220).

characterizes the region. This has created a typical ria coastline on the east and west coasts of Kyushu, Shikoku and the Kii Peninsula where the mountains run at right angles to the coast.

CENTRAL JAPAN

In Central Japan the Honshu, Shikoku and Bonin arcs meet to form the Chubu node, which is the highest area of block mountains in Japan. It includes the Japan Alps, which rise to over 10,000 feet on the upwarped eastern edge, and include the Hida Ranges (pl. 44). Here the Fossa Magna, breaking across the trend of all the other regions, is a major tectonic line. It is a deep structural trench about

---

Opposite above
PLATE 2. The Nara Basin is tectonic. The fretted fault scarp on the western edge of the Basin shows clearly in the photograph, on the 1 : 50,000 map overleaf and in plate 32. The steep forested ridges of the highland area and deep youthful valleys drained by rushing streams contrast markedly with the diluvial terraces and alluvial plains crossed by meandering braided streams bounded by tree-covered levees. This shows clearly the abrupt contrasts characteristic of Japanese landforms.

Opposite below
FIG. 9. The coast of Okayama prefecture on the Inland Sea showing its rectangular faulted character. Alluvial plains now fill the basins between land masses that formed islands about 1500 BC (see fig. 80). Jomon settlements were close to the old coastline (120).

30 miles wide bounded to the west by the high, faulted scarp of the Japan Alps (220). The trench runs from the Japan Sea coast in Toyama in the north along the line of the Hime, Upper Shinano and Tenryu rivers to the Pacific coast in Shizuoka (fig. 1). To the west of it lie the Japan Alps and to the east the Joshin

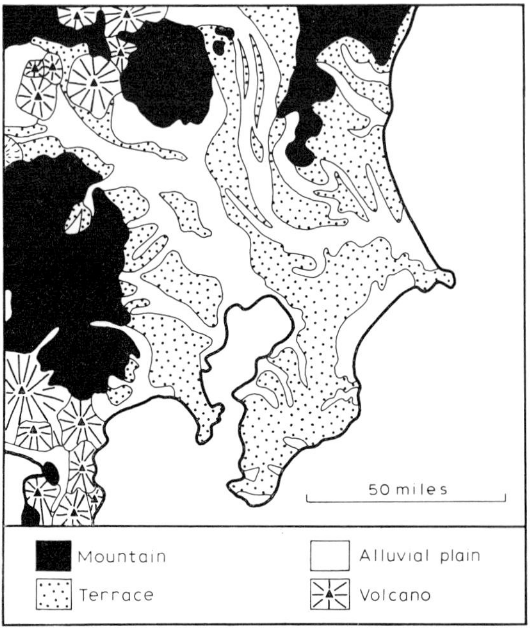

FIG. 10. The Kanto Plain showing the large area of diluvial terraces, the alluvial plain and some of the volcanoes associated with the Fossa Magna to the west (8).

Etsu Plateau. The trench is no longer clearly discernible as the area was under the sea in Miocene times when it was partially filled with Miocene rocks. The great bulk of several large Quaternary volcanoes, including the towering masses of Mount Fuji in the south and, further north, those of Mount Yatsu and Mount Myoko, fill it in many places. Between the volcanoes are tectonic basins, notably the Matsumoto, Suwa and Kofu Basins on the western edge of the trench and the Nagano and Ueda basins near the eastern fault scarp. These basins, like those in the Kinki and in the north-west, have been partially filled by cones of coarse detritus and alluvium forming slopes and terraces and plains. The tectonic line of the Fossa Magna is continued in the Bonin–Mariana Arc.

The *Kanto Plain* sub-region (fig. 10, pl. 25) (220) is an upland plain two-thirds of which is formed of a series of sloping diluvial terraces much like the Tokachi Plain in Hokkaido. At each uplift rejuvenation has formed a new terrace; some of these terraces fall as much as 50–150 feet to the level below. The Tone and other rivers are building the plain out into the Pacific and into Tokyo Bay. The older higher areas to the west have fans of coarser material which are dissected by deep gullies floored with newer alluvium. The lower terraces are flat or undulating, cut by valleys. The marshes along the lower Tone are still swampy and difficult to drain. The terraces have been covered by acid volcanic ash from Mount Fuji. It lies up to 140 feet thick on the older terraces.

Hills, Plains and Rivers

In spite of the structural contrasts between the five regions the features are similar throughout Japan. Three characteristic landforms – the hills and mountains, volcanoes and plains – everywhere have a common character. *Hills and mountains*, including all land sloping at more than 15°, form about 75% of the surface area of Japan (fig. 11) and are always in sight.

The view of the western edge of the Tenryu Valley near Ina (pl. 4) is typical of the higher mountain areas and is part of the western fault scarp of the Fossa Magna. Most of the mountains were formed by uplift as recently as Pleistocene times and the relics of earlier erosion surfaces often remain as level hill summits.

The heavy snowfall, spring melt and the violent summer storms cause vigorous erosion by short, swift streams that are able to roll and bump large boulders along their beds at flood time and cause landslides to be very common on the steep slopes. Loosely consolidated volcanic rocks and shattered sedimentary rocks are easily eroded. The short streams have steep courses and considerable volume and velocity which combine to cause great vertical erosion. Waterfalls are found where streams cross fault lines or at the junction between volcanic and less resistant rock. Steep-sided narrow valleys, gorges and gullies, are characteristic of rejuvenation. These, with incised meanders, are all dramatic features of the youthful scenery (220). Soil erosion is so rapid and landslides so common on many of the steep slopes, that thin lithosols support little vegetation or at most poor forest land. Many of the higher slopes are without vegetation, their bare slopes scored by deep ravines. Steep fault scarps (pl. 2) have been fretted into ridges and ravines. Where tributary valleys reach the floor of a larger, flatter valley vast quantities of coarse detritus are deposited to form cones and fans (pl. 4). These are often left as terraces as the landscape is rejuvenated by uplift. The older alluvium forming these terraces is called diluvium.

Some mountains in the Japan Alps compare in size and grandeur with the European Alps but, despite the prevalence of steep slopes and rugged interfluves, Japanese mountains on the whole lack the grandeur of the peaks, serrated edges, arêtes and cirques that are characteristic of glaciated mountains like the Alps. Only small areas of the higher mountains in Honshu and the higher parts of Hokkaido have been glaciated. The dominant impression of Japanese mountain scenery, apart from the volcanoes, is of tectonic blocks that have been subjected to violent dissection into knife-edged ridges topped by the even summits of an erosion surface and cut by incised rivers in deep V-shaped valleys (pl. 44).

There are many *plains*. The mountains end abruptly in the level surface of diluvial terraces and alluvial floors of coastal plain and inland basins. Here streams are forced to drop much of their load, so that along the border of all the Japanese mountains steeply sloping cones and fans have been built up of the coarser diluvial material carried by the streams. In places the diluvium chokes the whole valley as it does along parts of the Tenryu Valley. As in the Kanto Plain the wide areas of diluvium have been uplifted several times and each successive terrace has been dissected by the rivers, forming a series of well-developed

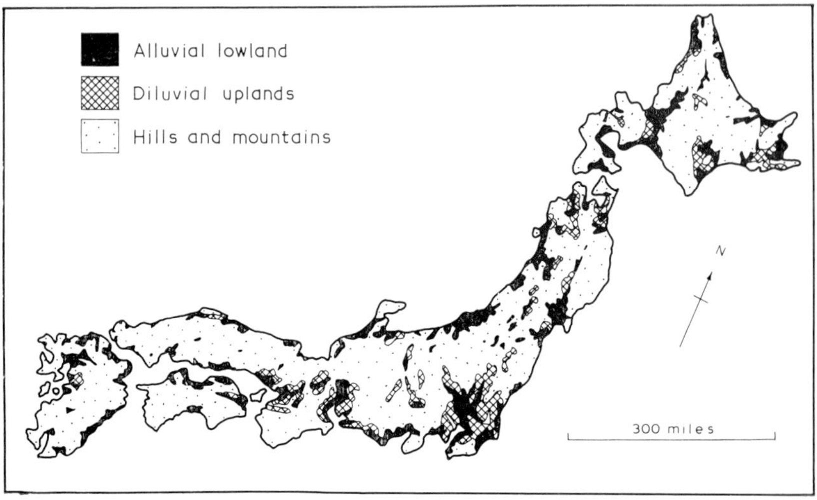

FIG. 11. Landforms. Hills and mountains form three-quarters of Japan, the diluvial uplands and the alluvial plains are small. 12).

PLATE 4. The fault scarp on the western edge of the Fossa Magna near Ina in December. A tributary of the Tenryu River has built a fan of coarse gravel where it leaves the highland. Many valleys in Japan are choked by detritus. Some of the mixed forest in the photograph has been cleared and conifers planted by many different landowners.

steps (fig. 10, pl. 16) (220) as much as 100 feet high in some places. During recent times there have been many general upthrusts but two stand out particularly strongly and they have left their mark in the development of terraces in the diluvium all over Japan. With rejuvenation the fans and cones have been dissected and the streams run in deep canyons. In many places the coarse gravel is exposed in eroded river cliffs as along the Tenryu River, where they are 60–120 feet high. The clearly defined terraces which border the steep mountain slopes

PLATE 5. Coastal terraces on the Inland Sea. The coast of the Inland Sea has been subject to subsidence and hills fall steeply to the sea. Here a small stream has built out a plain into the sea and reclamation has added to the land area. The region has long been inhabited and there has been great population pressure until recently. The hillsides have been terraced almost to their summits. Sweet potatoes can be seen growing on the left. This summer crop is followed by winter crops of wheat or barley. On the small plain crops of vegetables are intensively grown on tiny plots between the farmhouses.

are similar to those in the South Island of New Zealand, and the huge terraces on the northern edge of the Ganges Valley, which are other areas of deposition at the foot of high mountains with heavy precipitation.

Diluvial terraces are often difficult to irrigate because they are formed of coarse porous material with rivers running in gullies far below the terrace level. The surface is often too broken for irrigation and the leached soils are too porous for good farming. Good examples of alluvial fans are to be found in the area near Obihiro on the Tokachi Plain (fig. 58) (220) and in the basins in the Kinki. It

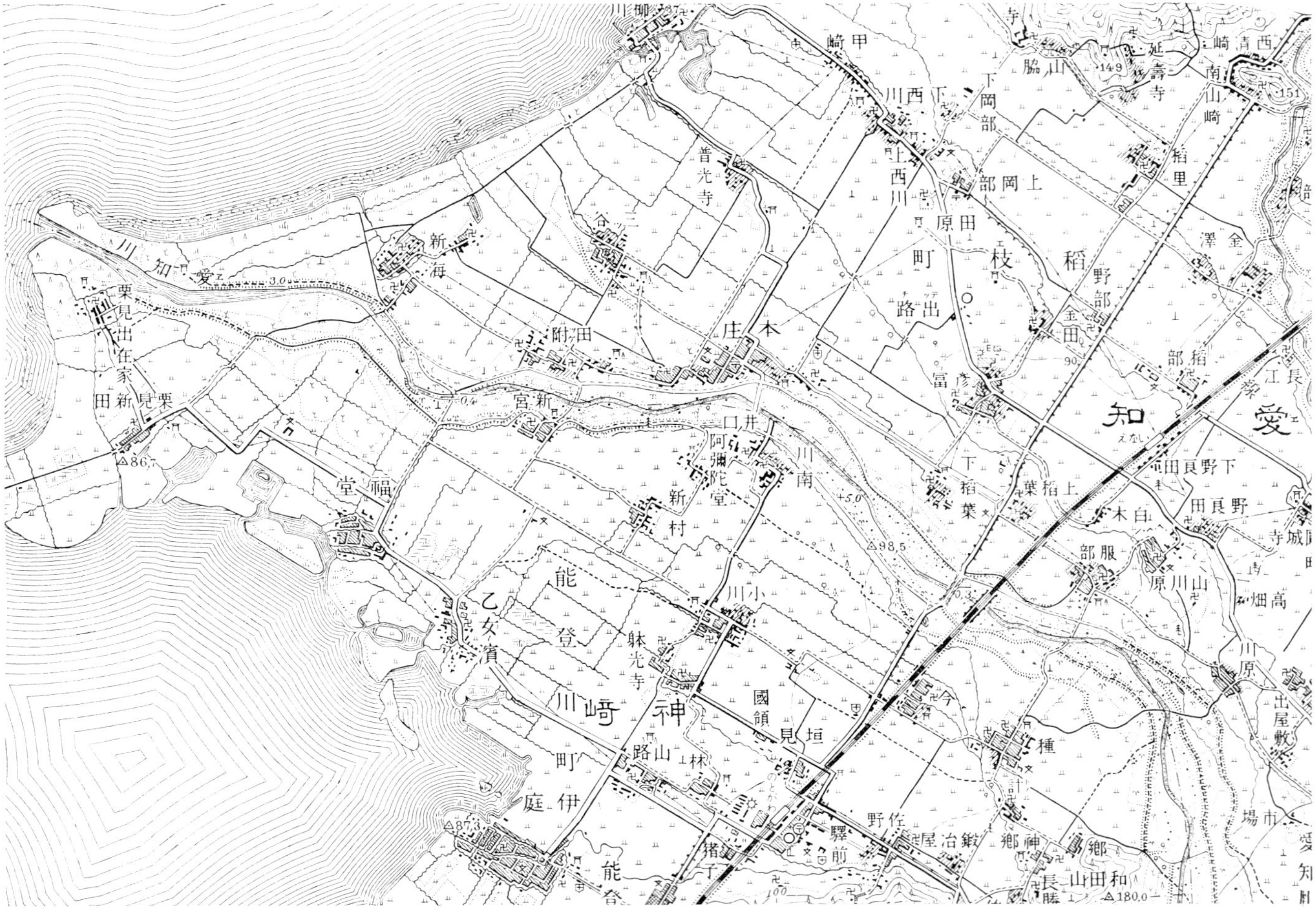

FIG. 12. Map of Echigo River 1 : 50,000.

PLATE 6. The wide braided River Echigo with its gravel bed and wooded levees is also shown in the map opposite. In summer when the river is full the water is above the level of the nearby houses. The width of the river makes bridging costly and bridges are often washed away in spring and summer floods. The square *jori* grid pattern stands out clearly here, each square of land being divided into many small strips. The photograph was taken in the spring. Rice plants still in the seedbeds show as small dark plots. Other fields have not yet been ploughed after the harvest of wheat and barley and the light coloured stubble remains in the fields. The grid pattern is not dominant on the more recently reclaimed fields in the woodland near the river (220).

is these fan and terrace areas that form the unirrigated upland fields of Japan that contrast strongly with the paddylands of the alluvial valley floors.

Below the dissected diluvial terraces the alluvium of coastal plains and valley floors is usually formed of finer clay and silt but sometimes of gravel laid down by the occasional or seasonal floodwaters of meandering, braided streams that flow across the plains. Despite short length, shallow depth and seasonal flow (fig. 111), Japanese rivers are powerful agents of erosion when swollen by heavy summer rain, autumn typhoons and snow melt. In the spring, steep slopes, earthquakes and landslides of loose volcanic material, combine to provide large quantities of terrigenous material for the development of plains round the margins of Japan (pl. 5). These plains are small and marshy and form only 12% of Japan's area. They are of recent origin, filling only shallow inlets and basins, as the sea round Japan is too deep for rapid accumulation and for the growth of large coastal plains, especially where there has been recent submergence, as for example in southern Shikoku. Plains including the larger Kanto, Nobi, Tokachi, Kitakami, Settsu, Echigo and Saga plains have been formed by the infilling of sheltered bays by the accumulation of fluvial deposits in a shallow sea between higher land areas under natural conditions aided by general uplift. Conditions in the Inland Sea are particularly suitable for the growth of delta plains as the water is sheltered and the tidal range is only about 10 feet. There are marshy areas along the sea, but most of these have been drained during the last 2,000 years to add to Japan's scarce area of flatland both for paddyland and, more recently, to provide valuable tidewater industrial sites. Unfortunately the sea beside the plains is shallowed by constant silting and this makes navigation difficult. All these plains are traversed by the wide gravelly beds of braided streams, bounded by high levees. These streams are often *tenjogawa* (rivers above the ceiling), running on a bed raised high above the surrounding countryside (pl. 6, fig. 12). They threaten floods in time of storm and snow melt (pls. 13 & 31).

The plains of the Japan Sea coast differ in formation from those of the Pacific coast as they have pronounced coastal spits. The coast is exposed to the northwest winds from Asia in winter and currents pile up sand spits, smoothing off the indentations of the many faulted bays. They often extend like the spits in the Ishikawa Prefecture, across the mouth of a bay and in the shallow still water behind the bar rivers deposit their load, building up many small plains all along the Japan Sea coast of Honshu.

THE COAST

The coastline of Japan is extremely long in proportion to its area (pl. 3). There is one mile of coast to every 14 square miles of land, whereas even in Britain with her long coastline the proportion is only one to every 20 square miles. Nowhere is one far from the sea and the vast majority of the Japanese people live on plains within easy reach of it. Many are dependent on it for a livelihood as sailors or fishermen. The diversity of coastal form is of interest to tourist and physiographer alike (fig. 13). The coastline runs roughly parallel to the trend of the axis of the fold mountains, so in general Japan's coastline may be classified as of the Pacific type with some deep indentations like those of Ise and Sagami Bays (fig. 1). In detail there is great variety caused by the elevation or subsidence of the coastline in relation to the sea, by tectonic movements and by erosion and deposition by the sea and rivers.

The *north-east region* including Honshu from the Kanto Plain northwards and most of Hokkaido has an elevated coastline. Throughout these coastal areas marine terraces are widespread and vary in height from marine platforms covered by high tides to those that form steps rising to over 1,000 feet above the sea at Cape Erimo in southern Hokkaido (220 Toya). Where there has been elevation the growth of coastal plains filling bays and smoothing the coast has been facilitated. In contrast with the elevated coasts of Japan which are relatively smooth, in

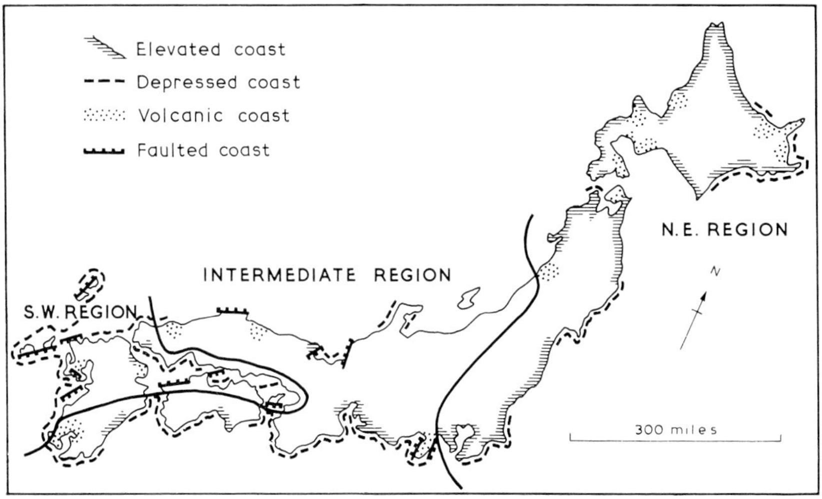

FIG. 13. Coastal regions showing the mainly elevated coasts in the north-east, the drowned coasts of the south-west and the intermediate region with both drowning and elevation (21).

the *south-west region* there has been subsidence and, especially where the land is hilly as it is around the Inland Sea, highly indented coastlines have been created where drowned valleys form rias and drowned tectonic basins form rectangular bays. The whole of the Inland Sea area has subsided, forming rocky inlets and rectangular faulted basins, and isolating many hilltops as islands (pl. 3). Long inlets have been formed in the outer zone of western Japan where the grain of the country runs discordantly across the line of the coast, and subsidence has allowed the sea to flow inland up long valleys like that of Nagasaki Harbour (220) and Yatsushiro Bay in Kyushu. There are long promontories in western Shikoku where the geological formations and the axis of structure run at right angles to the coast, making resistant ridges that form long peninsulas like the Sada Misaki Peninsula in north-west Shikoku (fig. 1) which extends more than twenty miles out to sea.

In the *intermediate region* there has been uplift and subsidence. There have also been many local tectonic movements which are the result of the complex twisting and buckling taking place along the major arcs of structure. The coast of the southern Kitakami Highland (fig. 1) (pls. 7 & 42) is broken by deep rias as a result of local drowning. The bays of the south coast of central Honshu,

PLATE 7. Matsushima Bay 10 miles north of Sendai in eastern Tohoku. A marine platform of Tertiary tuff has been uplifted, dissected and then drowned to form long shallow rias, up to 10 feet deep, between low pine-clad hills. The blue sea, green pines and white cliffs of tuff make this one of the three most famous beauty spots in Japan. This is a miniature version of the large rias to the north along the coast of Iwate (plate 42).

The more fertile soils in the narrow valleys have been cultivated to grow rice. Some of the shallow bays are being reclaimed, some for industry. On the right is the Shiogama, the electric power station which uses Hokkaido coal. *Nori* (seaweed) and pearl oysters are grown in square beds in the shallow water and rafts are also used for oyster culture (220).

notably Tokyo, Sagami and Suruga bays (220), have been formed by the down faulting of the whole sea floor along fault lines that cut across the trend of the mountain arc and break the line of the coast, forming sheltered, though shallow, harbours. Even on a small-scale map (fig. 1) many rectangular coastal forms are obvious, especially in Hokkaido, Kyushu and central Honshu. On the Japan Sea coast many faulted areas have been downthrust to form small bays or lifted to form promontories like the Shimane Peninsula and the peninsulas round

Wakasa Bay. On the Pacific coast there has been warping; for example, the Makinohara Plateau in Shizuoka, famous for its tea growing, is being upwarped at its northern end.

Fluvial and marine deposits are modifying the Japan Sea coastline where the forces of sea, wind and river have worked together to smooth off faulted promontories and fill in faulted bays. The northward-moving current has built out spits from the south side of bays with the aid of wind and waves, cutting off the bays from the open sea. On the other hand some parts of the coast are becoming more indented where submergence is forming inlets. All these features show even more clearly on larger scale maps (220).

SEISMIC ZONES AND ASSOCIATED VOLCANIC ACTIVITY

EARTHQUAKES

Tectonic movement and volcanic activity have taken place in Japan throughout geological time. The movements that were taking place in Palaeozoic, Mesozoic and Tertiary times are still proceeding today, and volcanic and igneous rocks form 35% of Japan's surface (fig. 5). Earthquakes are felt in every part of the country as they accompany movement along fault lines and volcanic activity. It is not uncommon to be wakened in the night with the sensation of being shaken, but violent earthquakes are relatively rare.

There are three seismic zones (fig. 4) with associated earth movements and volcanoes. One follows the inner tectonic zone with a double belt in western Tohoku and a branch through eastern Hokkaido to the Kurile Islands, another lies in the sea along the edge of the ocean deeps, and the third cuts across Japan along the Fossa Magna, extending into the sea in the Bonin Islands. The epicentres of the most violent disturbances lie offshore to the east of Japan and these are related to the andesite line where the crust is weak as the continental mass is being underthrust by the ocean floor. Undersea earthquakes bring *tsunami* or tidal waves to the Pacific coast from Kyushu to Tokyo and to eastern Tohoku and south-east Hokkaido and to the Japan Sea coast of southern Tohoku (fig. 4). The waves often break the dykes on artificially drained land and sweep inland, causing great damage to crops. The seismic activity of the inner zone is associated with the line of weakness west of the edge of the continental land mass. Most earthquakes with their epicentres on land occur in the inner zone and the Kinki, as both areas are faulted in a very complex pattern. Frequent slight earthquakes result from movements along these minor fault lines. Gifu in central Honshu holds the record of 516 noticeable earthquakes in one year. Outside the seismic zones, in the Pacific outer zone, movements take place mainly by gradual warping.

One of the most destructive earthquakes this century was the Great Kanto earthquake of 1923 when the floor of Sagami Bay moved several feet. The south coast of Sagami Bay at Kanagawa was uplifted by 6 feet, while in the north it was thrown down by 5 feet. At Tokyo, 57 miles from the epicentre of the earthquake, the uplift was fortunately only a few inches. Besides the vertical movement there was horizontal displacement. The peninsulas at the southern end of the

Sagami Bay area moved south-south-east up to 12 feet 5 inches at the maximum, but only 7 inches at Tokyo. *Tsunami* swept inland rising to 36 feet, washing ships inland, and homes and people out to sea. The worst loss of life was caused in Tokyo not by the actual shocks and falling houses, but by fire which spread rapidly from cooking stoves. The closely packed houses were built of wood and burned for three days. Over 100,000 victims were trapped and burned before they could escape. Tokyo is particularly liable to earthquakes, as it lies on a line of instability running along the edge of the Kitakami Valley northwards through Tohoku and Hokkaido. However, compared with Gifu's record of 516 sensible shocks a year Tokyo has only 150. *Tsunami* are a growing danger to Tokyo as the level of the lower parts of the city is sinking. As more and more underground water is being pumped for household and industrial use the level of the water table is falling in the Ara Valley, and the land is being increasingly compacted and lowered.

The Nankaido earthquake in southern Kyushu in 1946 was of a different type. It was caused by warping rather than faulting. The south-easterly tip of Shikoku rose 3 feet and Kochi on the central south bay sank 2 feet. Sometimes the movement along a fault can be clearly seen. After the Tango earthquake in 1927 it was observed that the west side of the fault had moved over 3 feet south relative to the east side.

VOLCANOES

Most of the volcanoes lie in the Honshu Arc, in the mountains of the eastern belt of the inner Japan Sea zone, in Tohoku and Hokkaido (fig. 4), in the Chishima Range of eastern Hokkaido and in the Kyushu and Fossa Magna–Bonin arcs. There are over 160 volcanoes in the main Japanese islands and the Kurile, Bonin and Ryukyu arcs, 54 of which are active. Most of the active, or recently active, volcanoes are in four main regions. First, in the Chishima Arc in eastern Hokkaido there are two main active centres and many extinct cones; second, in western Hokkaido the Honshu Arc is particularly active in the south around Volcano Bay and includes strongly active Mount Azuma in the south; third, in the Fossa Magna–Bonin Arc area which includes dormant Mount Fuji; and fourth, in the Kyushu–Ryukyu Arc, which includes the active volcanoes Aso, Sakurajima and Unzen. Western Honshu and Shikoku have no active volcanoes.

Most Japanese volcanoes are composite in type, being formed of both lava and ash. Some are cone-shaped like Fuji, others are large calderas. The composite cone reaches near perfection in Mount Fuji (pl. 8, fig. 14) (220). Viewed from the south-east its concave slopes sweep up to over 12,000 feet above sea level in an almost perfect cone topped by a relatively small crater. The slopes are much admired for their curves, gentle on finer material accumulated at the base, steeper near the summit where coarser ash has collected. From a distance the cone is deceptively smooth. It is smoothest to the south-west. The north face is broken by secondary cones and lava flows which reach to the foot of the mountain and dam surface drainage in the Five Lakes, in which reflections add to Fuji's beauty. The largest secondary cone is the triple-headed Mount Ashitake on the south-east slope formed of deeply dissected lava. Being formed of porous ash Mount Fuji has little surface drainage and its smooth curving slopes are little eroded. It has been dormant since 1708. When cones are formed of both ash and lava, like Mount Nantai near Nikko, they are dissected by radial streams that expose the layers of ash interspersed with lava. Basalt sills and dykes give rise to

PLATE 8. This photograph of the complex volcanic area of Mount Fuji and the Hakone National Park was taken from the east in January. It shows the smooth curve of the ash cone of Fuji which dams up streams to form the 'Five Lakes' against the hills behind the mountain on the right. On the left is the dissected secondary lava cone of Mount Ashitaka. In the foreground are the lava cones of the smaller volcanoes in Hakone National Park. These lie inside a caldera with steep infacing slopes. Lake Ashi lies between the caldera rim and the newer volcanic cones. The many hot springs that support spas and striking scenery of this National Park only 50 miles south of Tokyo make this one of the most popular tourist areas in Japan. On a clear day Mount Fuji itself can be seen from the higher parts of Tokyo (219 & 220).

waterfalls, like the Kegon Falls on the slopes of Mount Nantai at Nikko, where water drops 330 feet over a ledge of basalt.

Contrasting with the simpler cone-shaped volcanoes are those with wide calderas, like Mount Aso in Kyushu, Mount Akan in Hokkaido, and the Toya caldera in southern Hokkaido (pl. 10) (220). Lake Toya was formed when the volcano erupted, flinging out masses of rock and forming a huge crater inside which water has collected to form the lake. New cones arise out of the lake, which is about 600 feet deep; its floor, 300 feet below sea level, is about the same depth as Volcano Bay nearby. Mount Uzu, which rises on the southern edge of the caldera, is itself a very complex mountain with many parasitic cones. On the

西八代郡
富士郡
巨摩郡
庵原郡
安倍郡
富士宮市
吉原市
富士市
清水市
由比町
蒲原町
富士川町
興津町
鷹岡町
芝富村
内房村
松野村
小島村
両河内村
富士根村
上野村
柚野村
白糸村
上井出村
北山村
大淵村
富河村
万沢村
原田村
元吉原村
大河内村
庵原村
有度村
清水港
三保
富士川

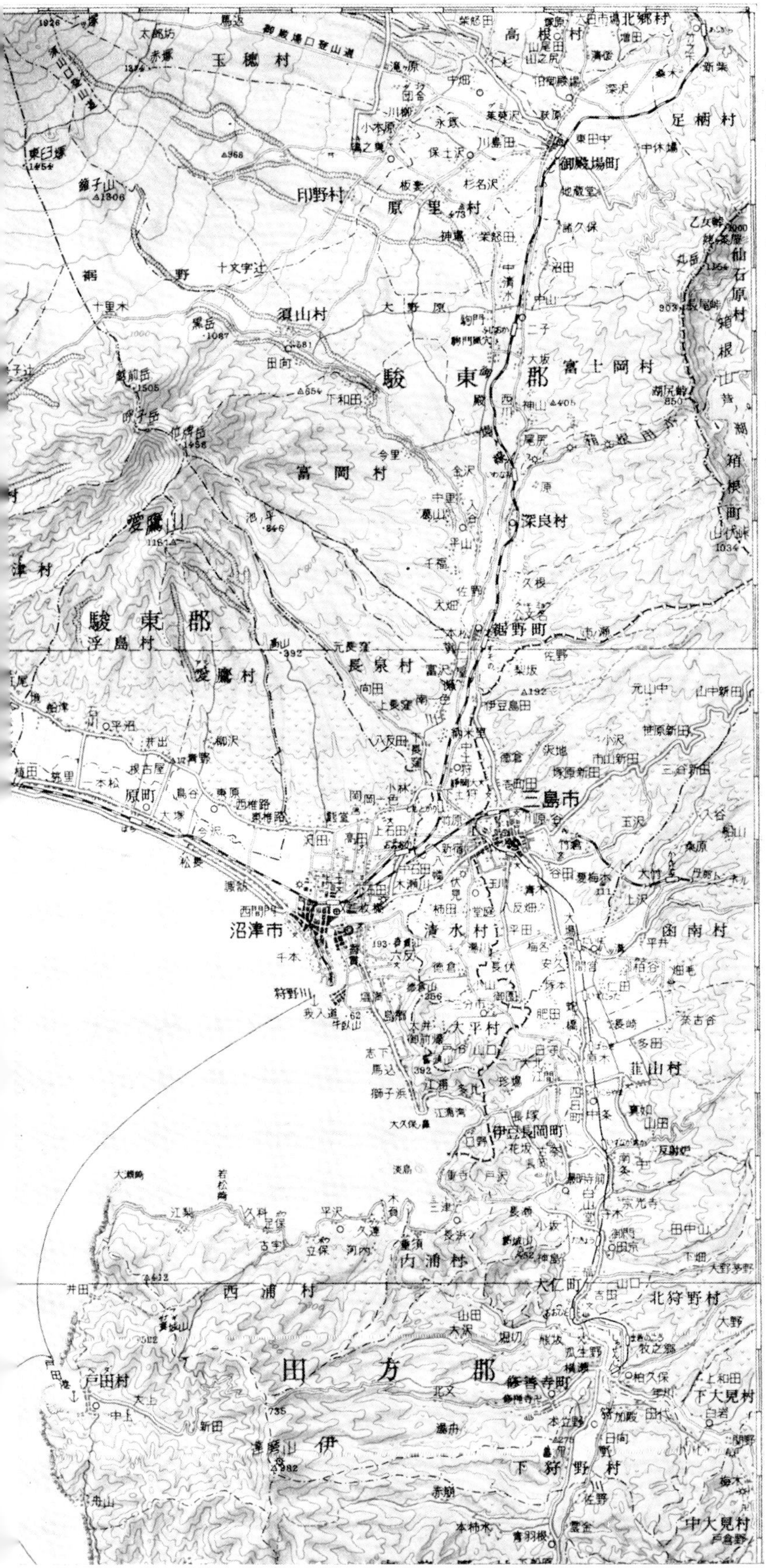

Key to 1:200,000 maps.

Roads
- Width over 5·5 m.
- Width over 4·5 m.
- Width over 3·0 m.
- Track or Footpath

Railways
- National
- Private
- Special
- Dyke
- Sea Route (red)

Boundaries
- Prefectural
- National
- City or Ward

- County Hall
- Town Hall
- Local Government Offices
- Police Station
- Post Office
- School
- Factory
- Electricity Generator
- Mine
- Coalmine
- Oil field (red)
- Natural Gas field
- Airfield
- Shrine
- Temple
- Historical Site
- Emperor's Tomb
- Castle Ruin
- Hot Spring
- Active Volcano (red)
- Triangulation Point
- Spot Height
- Important Port
- Local Port
- Lighthouse (red)
- Direction of flow
- Paddyfield
- Dry field
- mud shoal
- sand shoal

Oblique illumination.
Contour interval 100 metres - over 100 m. green.
Height taken from datum at Tokyo Bay.

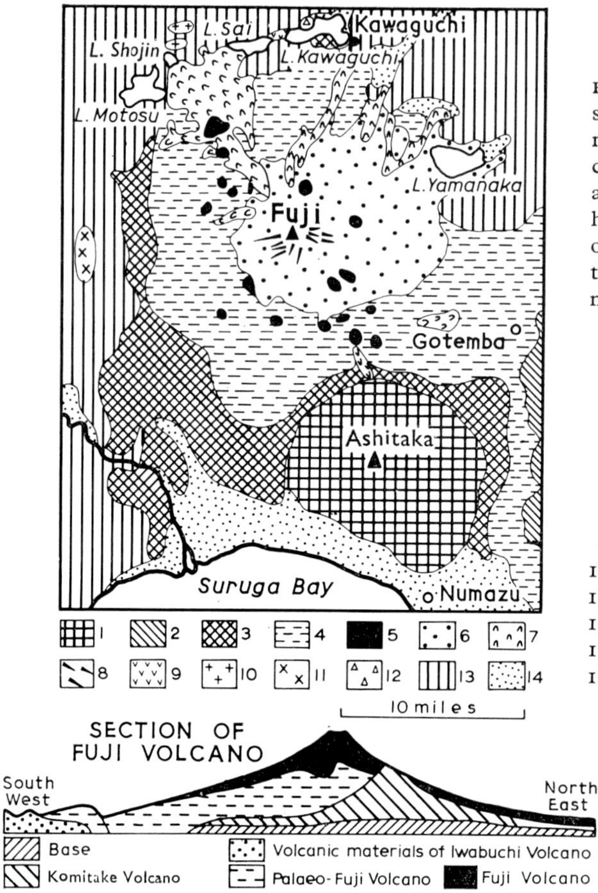

FIG. 14. Mount Fuji showing the build of the mountain, its subsidiary cone, Mount Ashitaka, and the lava flows which have dammed the waters of the Five Lakes against the Tertiary hills to the north

1 Ashitaka lava
2 Hakone lava
3 Fuji lava and Palaeo Fuji agglomerate
4 Fuji ejecta (fine)
5 Fuji ejecta (coarse)
6 Parasitic cone ejecta
7 & 8 New lava flows
9 Dacite
10 Porphyrite
11 Diabase
12 Limestone
13 Tertiary sediments
14 Alluvium (8).

Overleaf

PLATE 9. This map of Fuji area 1 : 200,000 shows many of the features in plate 8 including the smooth curve of Mount Fuji, the dissected cone of Mount Ashitaka and the Hakone Caldera. The coastline of Suruga Bay has many features typical of Japan's coasts. It has been formed by complex faulting and sheer cliffs line the many bays along the coast of the Izu Peninsula in the south-east. The braided river Fuji has built out a stony delta into the bay. A sand bar has developed off the coast south of Mount Fuji and the lagoon behind has silted up leaving marsh, some of which has been reclaimed for rice paddies. In the east there is a small rectangular tectonic basin. Apart from the volcanic areas deeply dissected plateaux are the dominant feature. The river pattern has been influenced by north–south faulting and there are both youthful valleys and incised meanders. On the porous ash of Mount Fuji there is little surface drainage and consequently little dissection in contrast with the incised radial streams on Mount Ashitaka.

Settlement is characterized by small towns on delta plains and small centres, often at bridging points. Farmhouses often lie in a linear pattern along the edge of wetter ground and along coastal sandbars as they do south of Fuji. A larger scale map is necessary to see the settlement detail clearly.

summit two spines rise to nearly 2,000 feet. In 1910 there was activity on the northern slope and forty-five vents opened. The most recent phase of activity in December 1944 culminated in the formation of a new parasitic cone, Mount Showashinzan (pl. 11) on its eastern flank. The eruption started with frequent earthquakes under the upland fields and the arching up of the area to form a dome. Explosions broke this up and formed a cone about a mile across and 500 feet high. By the end of 1945, a 1,300 foot peak of lava had been built at one

PLATE 10. Lake Toya in early November with the first snow of the winter, from the foot of Mount Uzu near Mount Showashinzan looking north across the lake, with several cones rising above the water, their slopes clothed in deciduous birch, alder and willow. In the background on the right another volcano, Mount Yotei, disappears into the clouds (220).

end of the dome. This peak, though no longer growing, still emits steam, sulphur and carbon gases through piles of boulders that form it.

Mount Asama is the most active of Japan's volcanoes and one of the most violent. In 1912 some of the blocks ejected measured 150 feet across and rocks landed as much as 10 miles away. In 1783 12,000 lives were lost as a result of one eruption, although few people lived near the mountain.

Sakurajima, in Kyushu, though less violent, frequently showers ash over Kagoshima across the narrow 3-mile strait. The triple peaks of Sakurajima rise from Kagoshima Bay, which is itself a caldera filled with sea water. The whole area is very unstable and islands in the bay are gradually being submerged. Since 1914 Sakurajima (Cherry Blossom Island) has no longer been an island, as a mass of scoria and ash, built out to the south-east, now links the island to the mainland by a narrow neck of loose ejecta. Lava flows have built the volcano out into the sea on all but the north-west side. One of the most recent flows to the west poured blocks of lava into the sea. Despite its activity, the land at the foot of Sakurajima is farmed, though in the last few years farming has become increasingly difficult, as ash has buried the fields and glowing lumps of lava and ash are liable to set light to the wood and thatch houses. Its beauty, volcanic interest and spas bring tourists to Kagoshima. This has helped the local farmers who still manage to grow the largest, round, turnip-like radishes in Japan, often weighing as much

PLATE 11. Mount Showashinzan is a jumble of blocks of rock and ash with steam rising from many fissures. A light fall of snow covers the ground below the birch and alder trees which have lost their summer foliage (220).

as 6 lb. Unfortunately Japan's largely acidic lava and ash is not helpful to the farmer. Soils on the volcanic materials are too porous to hold water and they lack the necessary mineral nutrients and organic matter.

Mount Aso (fig. 15) in central Kyushu is a fine example of the caldera type of volcano. Its caldera is 16 miles across, with 40,000 people living within its walls. The volcano has spread its mud flows over a radius of 40 miles and ash over a much wider area. The steep inner caldera slopes are drained by streams which have joined to cut a deep gorge through the caldera lip to the west at Tateno. In the centre of the caldera are five peaks, only one of which is active at present. The highest cone rises to 5,257 feet. Nakadake or the 'middle peak' has a deep smouldering crater that frequently ejects ash.

Calderas are most common in Hokkaido, and the volcanoes of Akan National Park in north-east Hokkaido are fine examples of the complexities of the composite volcanoes. The Akan area in eastern Hokkaido is a museum of volcanic types (fig. 16) (220). There are two main calderas, Akan and Kutcharo. Kutcharo caldera is as large as Aso and 16 miles across from east to west. After erupting the whole area collapsed to form the caldera and many parasitic cones have grown. The largest and most impressive of them is the subsidiary Mashu

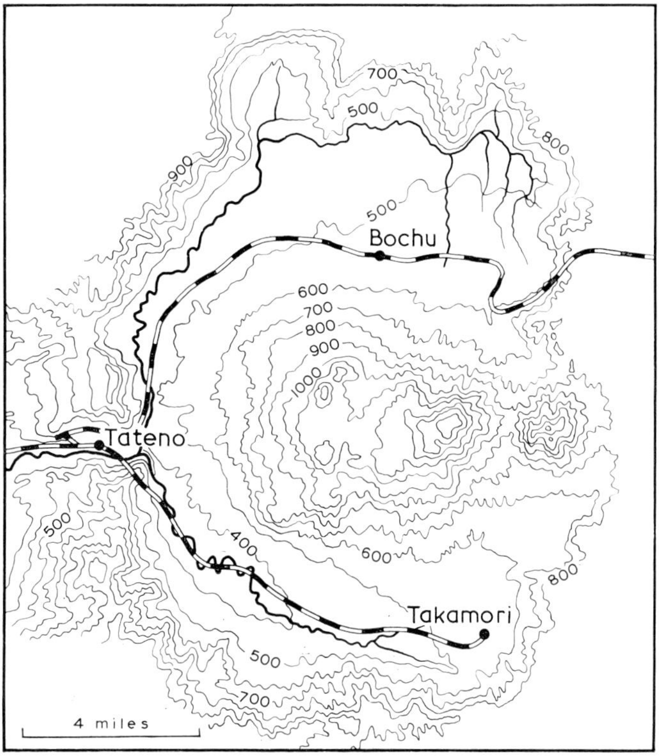

FIG. 15. Mount Aso showing its five peaks in a great caldera now drained westward through the rim (8).

caldera to the east (pl. 12). Its steep inner cliffs fall over 600 feet to the deep waters of Lake Mashu and a rocky spine rises out of the clear water. The rugged crater of Kamuinupuri rises on the eastern side of the lake, making this one of the most beautiful sights in Japan. From the lip of the Mashu caldera to the west can be seen the six cones of Makuwanchisapu, with steam rising from associated solfatara and hot springs. The springs feed Lake Kutcharo, which has yet another cone forming an island in the lake. To the south-west is the Akan caldera with a smaller lake and a line of four cones, including Me Akan with its plume of steam and its parasite Fuji-like Akan Fuji. In many volcanic areas there is other thermal activity. At Noboribetsu on Volcano Bay there are very active solfatara where steam escapes with the noise of an express train, leaving yellow

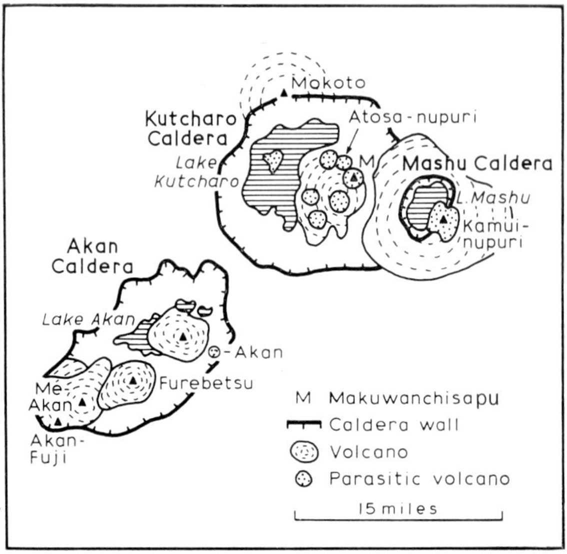

FIG. 16. Calderas in Akan National Park in eastern Hokkaido showing the three main calderas, crater lakes and associated volcanoes (after Watanabe, 8).

PLATE 12. The Mashu caldera looking north with the parasitic cone of Mount Kamuinupuri rising to the east. The inner walls of the caldera fall steeply to the lake, which is unusually clear so that the spine rising above the surface of the water can be seen far down into the clear water. In early December there is a light covering of snow on the rhododendrons and frost coats the birch trees (220).

sulphur round the orifice. Water escapes to form small geysers and there are lakes of boiling water. Similar phenomena are found in Kyushu and elsewhere

There are over a thousand *hot spring* areas in the volcanic zone and many of them have been developed as resorts, as taking hot baths is one of the favourite pastimes of the Japanese. Each hotel has its large hot pools 2 feet 6 inches deep where bathers lie and chat. Each spa has its own character and its medicinal value varies according to the chemical content of the water. Springs associated with Mount Aso in Kyushu have a high sulphur content; Arima springs near Osaka are slightly radioactive with radon and radium. Towns like Beppu in eastern Kyushu and Atami on the coast near Mount Fuji (pl. 9) have developed with hundreds of hotels round some of the most accessible and pleasantly situated spas. Tokyo people go for the weekend to Atami or to one of the many resorts in the beautiful Hakone area south-east of Fuji. In southern Hokkaido, Noboribetsu is famous. Osaka people go to nearby Arima, and many people holiday in Beppu in Kyushu. The water and the heat is often used commercially. In Beppu it is used for heating glasshouses and growing flowers and vegetables, along the Inland Sea for evaporating salt, drying fish or fermenting bean paste, but the most lucrative of its uses is the hot spring resort.

The physical geography of Japan is youthful, complex and rapidly changing. It provides a difficult terrain for the farmers, as mountains predominate and only the small plains are hospitable. It spite of this the Japanese now grow three quarters of the food needed for 100 million people on small peripheral plains and in basins and valleys in the mountains.

CHAPTER TWO

The Climate

Characteristics and Climatic Factors

The Japanese climate is characterized by regional contrasts and seasonal changeability which make it even more varied and complex than that of Britain. With a greater latitudinal extent than Britain it varies from Sapporo in Hokkaido in the north that has a winter with four months of snow, to Kagoshima in Kyushu in the south-west of Japan that has subtropical winter temperatures averaging 7°C (45°F) in January (fig. 19). On the Japan Sea coast winters are grey and gloomy, while on the Pacific side they are clear and sunny. There are more extreme climates in the mountain basins; Nagano in Tosan has an annual range of 28°C (51°F), while Tokyo on the coast has a more equable climate with an annual range of only 23°C (41°F).

As is the case in Britain, Japan is subject to the influences of air masses. Tropical and polar air masses (fig. 17) in their maritime and continental forms, each has its own character and associated weather. Three air masses predominate. Tropical maritime air brings hot, humid conditions; polar maritime air, cool wet weather and continental air crossing the Japan Sea brings cold, relatively wet weather in winter and hot dry weather in the summer to the Japan Sea coast.

Japan's position, on the east side of the world's greatest land mass in middle latitudes, and north-west of the world's greatest area of ocean in tropical and equatorial latitudes, gives the country a unique position at the junction of the world's most strongly developed continental and maritime variants of the polar and tropical air masses and makes the influence of air masses the most important factor in her climate.

The most striking weather elements are the raw, biting north-west winds which blow in winter across the Sea of Japan from the Asiatic thermal high pressure bringing cold, humid polar continental air, and the fierce storms in hot, wet tropical maritime air which come from southern seas in the summer. The tropical and polar air masses meet along a well-marked frontal zone within which typical depressional storms develop. The front lies over Japan in spring and autumn, bringing wet muggy weather. In summer and autumn there are many typhoons. For an island country Japan has a climate of extraordinary extremes, ranging from the sultry heat of summer when Tokyo's daily maxima reach 40°C (104°F) to the icy winter when the average daily minima at Asahigawa in Hokkaido drop to −41°C (−42°F).

Japan stretches over 1,000 miles of latitude between 30° and 45° north of the

Equator, a range similar to that of the Mediterranean from North Africa to the plains of northern Italy. The hot, dry summer of the Mediterranean contrasts strikingly with the humid heat of Japan, as does the rainy winter with Japan's relatively dry continental cold (fig. 18).

The proximity of the vast continental mass causes polar influences to extend unusually far south in the winter (fig. 19) bringing average February temperatures

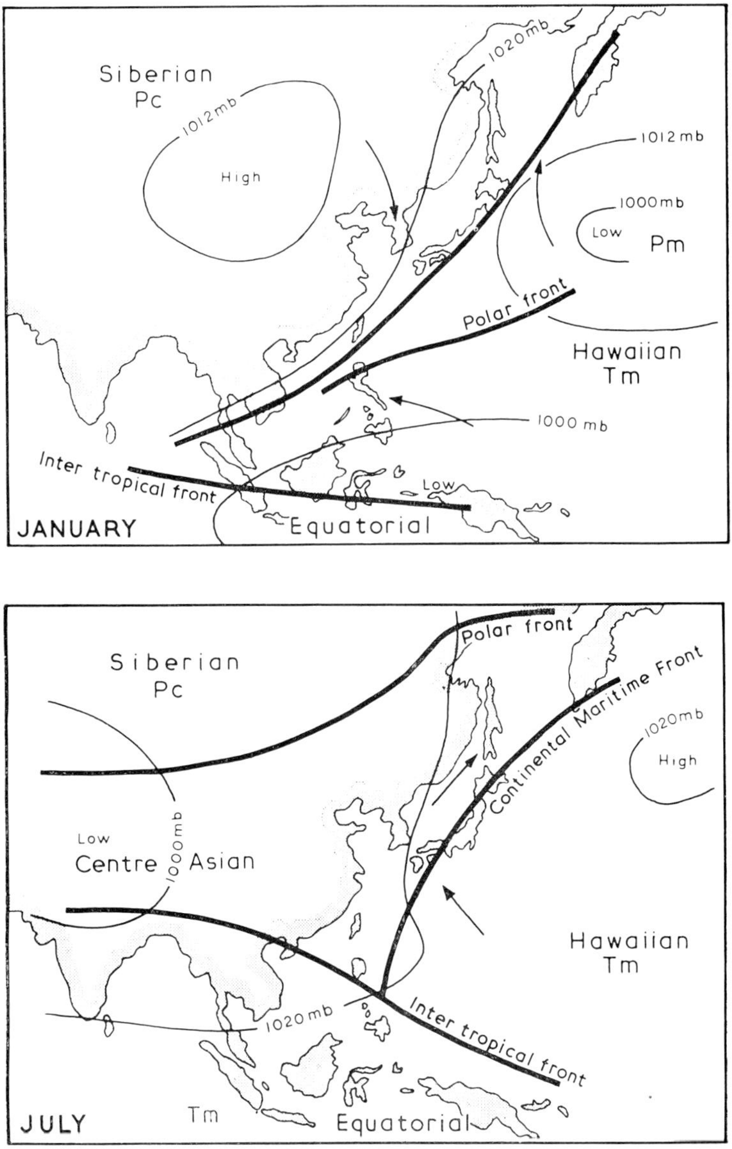

FIG. 17. Air masses in Eastern Asia in January and July.

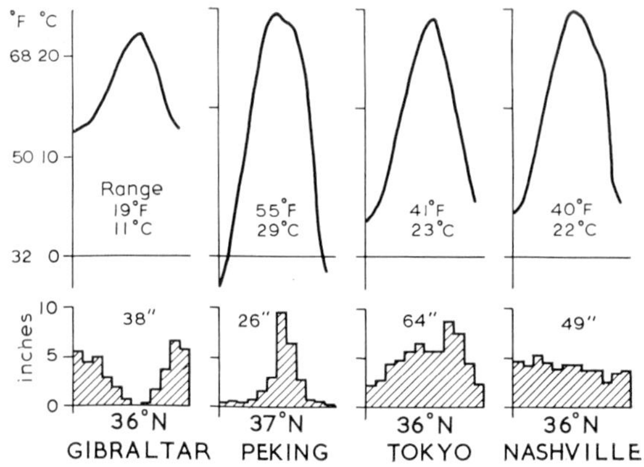

FIG. 18. Contrasting climates in warm temperate latitudes: representative examples of western margin, continental and eastern margin types.

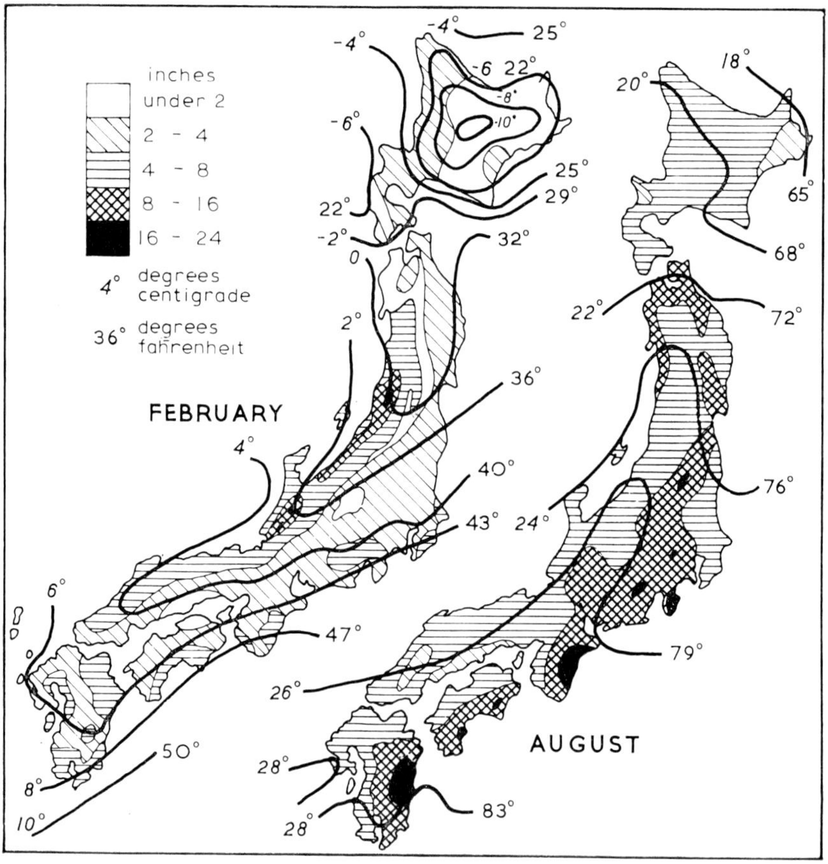

FIG. 19. Temperatures and rainfall distribution in February and August (22).

to freezing point as far south as central Tohoku. In summer the hot maritime air from the wide tropical and equatorial areas of the Pacific Ocean lift Tokyo's mean temperature for July to 26°C (79°F). Middle latitude temperatures are thus modified by both the continental and maritime air masses. Latitude affects Japan's climate most markedly in the winter when Hokkaido has an arctic winter with snow deep on the ground from November until April, but Kagoshima's palm trees rarely experience icy winds and with average monthly temperatures over 6°C (43°F) crops grow throughout the year. These warm winter temperatures above 6°C (43°F) make two crops possible in lowland areas of Japan south of

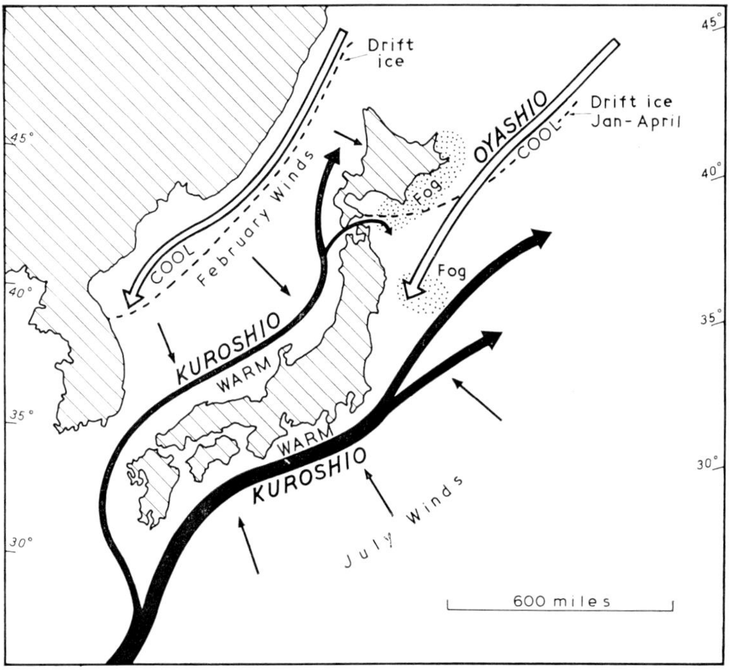

FIG. 20. Factors affecting Japan's climate.

Tokyo. In the summer variations are less significant and there is only 6°C (11°F) difference between the August temperature of Kagoshima 27°C (81°F) and that of Sapporo 21°C (70°F), compared with 13°C (24°F) difference, −6°C (21°F) to 7°C (45°F), in January.

The island nature of Japan modifies the temperatures so that the islands are neither as cold in winter nor as warm in summer as nearby China. Although the Sea of Japan is narrow it modifies the climate. Warm and cold ocean currents influence Japan (fig. 20). The Kuroshio current brings warm water flowing from the south warming especially the Pacific coast south of Tokyo and less strongly the Japan Sea coast. The Oyashio current from the north cools the coasts of Hokkaido and eastern Tohoku but less than the Labrador current cools the

North American coast, as little water from the Arctic passes through the shallow and narrow Behring Strait between Asia and America.

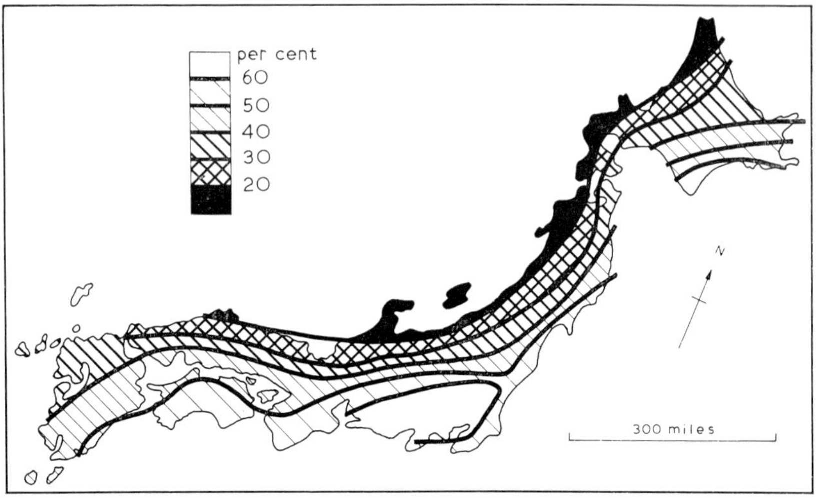

FIG. 21. The percentage of possible January sunshine showing the sunny Pacific coast and the cloudy Japan Sea coast (22).

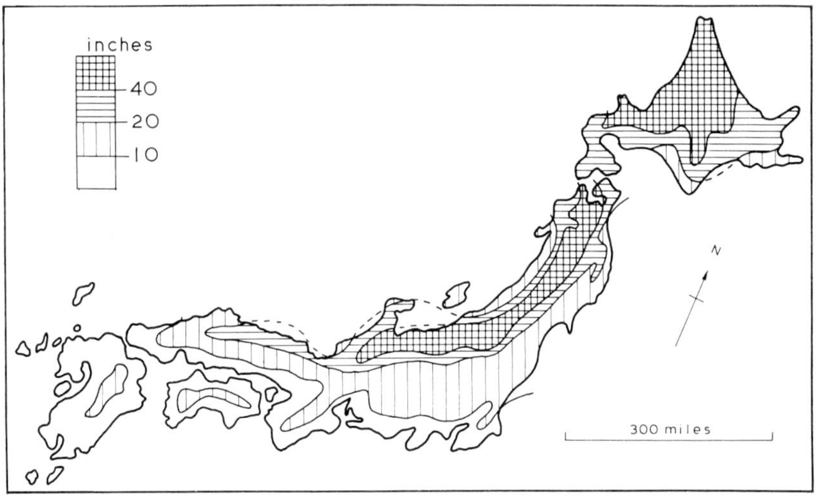

FIG. 22. Mean annual maximum depths of snow showing the contrast between the inner and outer coasts, and the north and the south-west (22).

The north-east to south-west trend of the relief tends to restrict the continental influences to the Japan Sea coast (figs. 21 & 22), which has a cold, cloudy, raw winter with snow often over 6 feet deep. In summer it is drier than the Pacific coast when it is in the rain shadow from the south-east winds. The maritime influences are more marked on the Pacific side of Japan except in Hokkaido, where the mountains do not form a significant barrier. The Pacific coast is warmer and wetter in summer when the south-east wind blows, and warmer and drier in winter as it is sheltered from the north-west wind. In February the 6°C (43°F) isotherm follows the Pacific coast from Kyushu to Tokyo. The mountains, lying across the track of the prevailing winds, cause the moisture-laden winds from the warmer sea to bring precipitation from the north-west to the Japan Sea coast in winter and from the south-east to the Pacific coast in summer. The mountains isolate inland basins from the influence of the sea and more extreme temperatures occur. For instance Asahigawa in central Hokkaido, only 40 miles from the sea, has an average July temperature of 21°C (70°F) and the temperature drops to an average of −10°C (14°F) in January when it has an average minimum of −41°C (−42°F). Its range of temperature is 31°C (36°F) compared with 27°C (49°F) at Sapporo. Local variations of temperature and rainfall are great and depend on the relief and the exposure of the slope to the prevailing wind and to the sun.

The Seasons

There are seven periods of contrasting weather. The cold dry winter when the winds blow from the continent and the hot wet summer when the winds blow from the ocean are the main ones. Between these there is a period of depressions in early spring when the polar front lies across Japan. More settled anticyclonic weather in April and May is followed by the *Bai-u* rains in June and July. After the wet summer there is an unsettled autumn when the polar front returns, until, in the late autumn, the continental thermal anticyclone expands over Japan heralding the return of winter.

In *winter* from late November to February (fig. 23*a*) the polar continental air mass prevails. Asia is the largest of the land masses and its vast area causes the development of an intensely cold air mass within which the hemisphere's lowest winter temperatures occur. Verkhoyansk has an average January temperature of −51°C (−60°F). The resulting air pressure is very high. For example on 10 December 1964 at −34°C the pressure was 1064 mbs. Cold dry winds blow outwards strongly from the high-pressure centre towards the lower-pressure, less stable area over the relatively warm North Pacific (fig. 17). The narrow Sea of Japan modifies the temperature and humidity of the lower layers of the air slightly, so that winters in Japan are 4°C (8°F) colder than those of corresponding latitudes in eastern United States (fig. 18). January mean temperatures range from 7°C (45°F) in Kagoshima to — 10°C (14°F) in Obihiro. In February Hokkaido has temperatures of − 2°C to − 10°C (25°F to 14°F). Tohoku and the mountains of Tosan are under 0°C (32°F) and the Pacific coast south of Tokyo is the warmest part of Japan with over 6°C (43°F).

The north-west winter wind (fig. 17) picks up moisture as it passes across the relatively warm Sea of Japan and brings gloomy weather with snow from

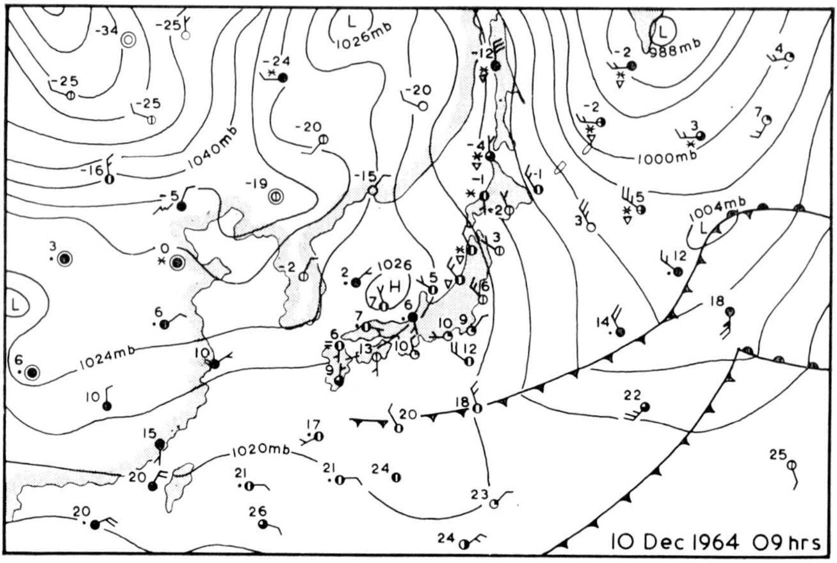

FIG. 23a

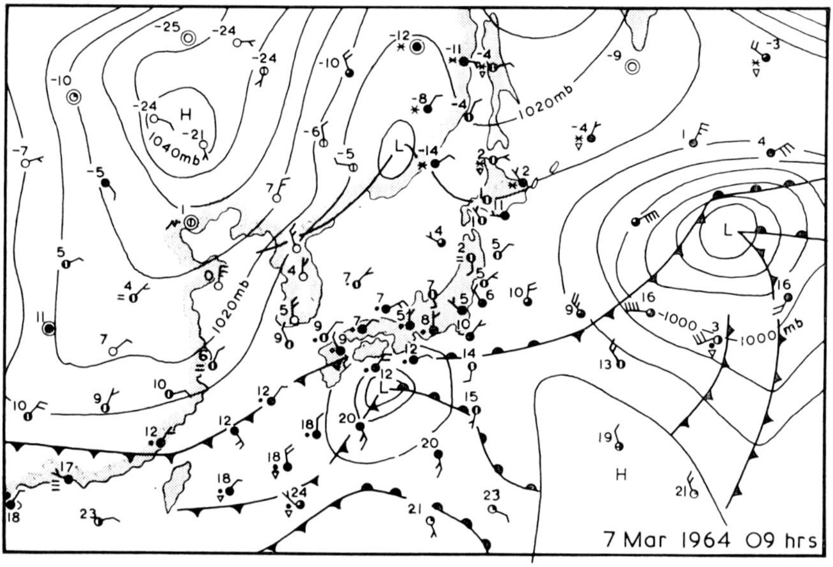

FIG. 23b

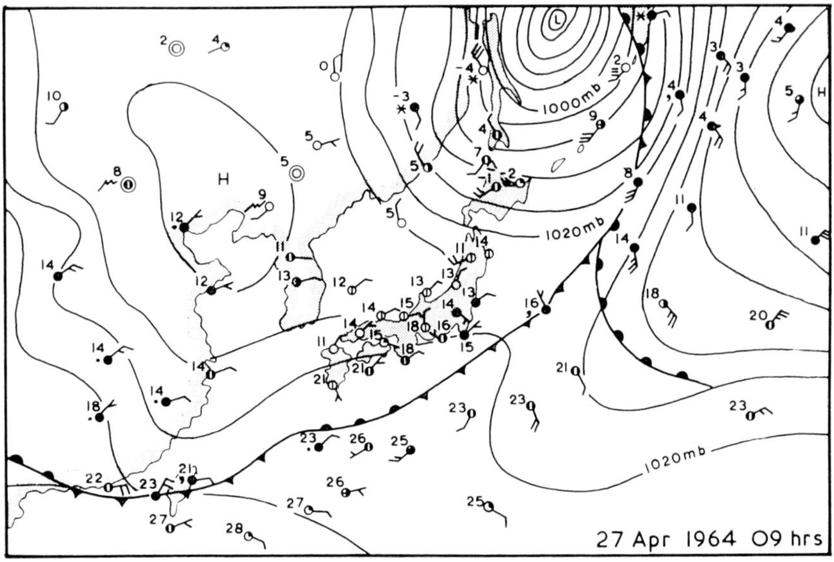

FIG. 23C

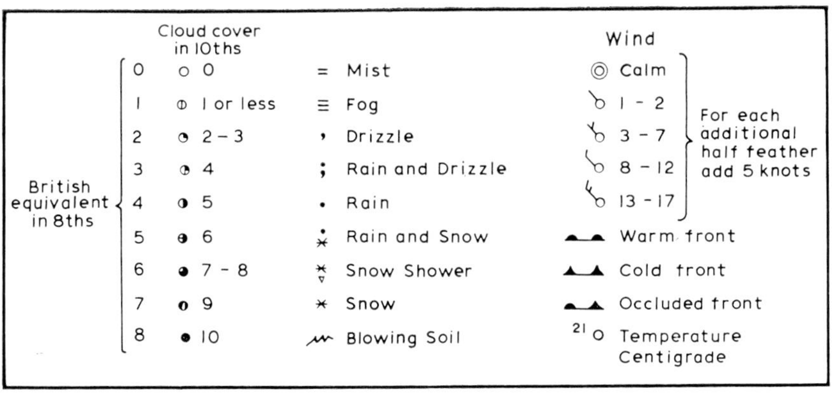

FIG. 23. Seasonal weather maps (*Central Meteorological Office*)—*continued overleaf.*

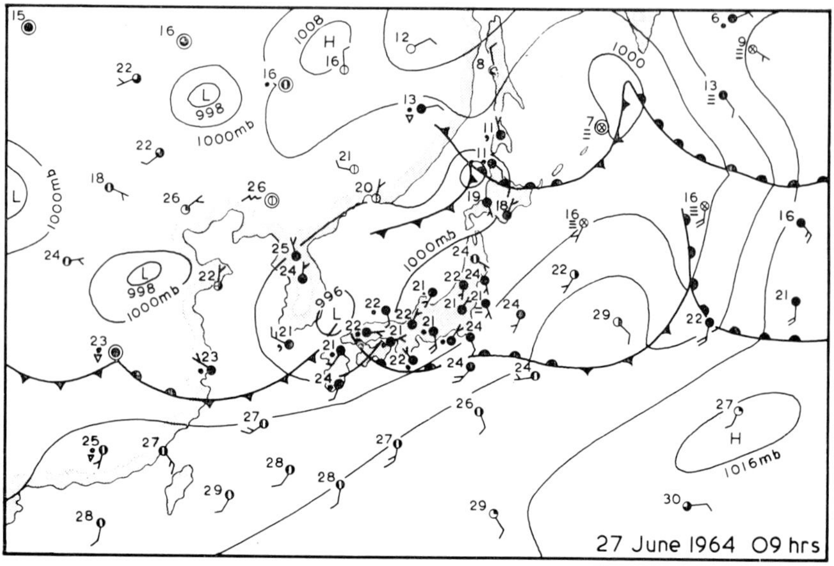

FIG. 23d

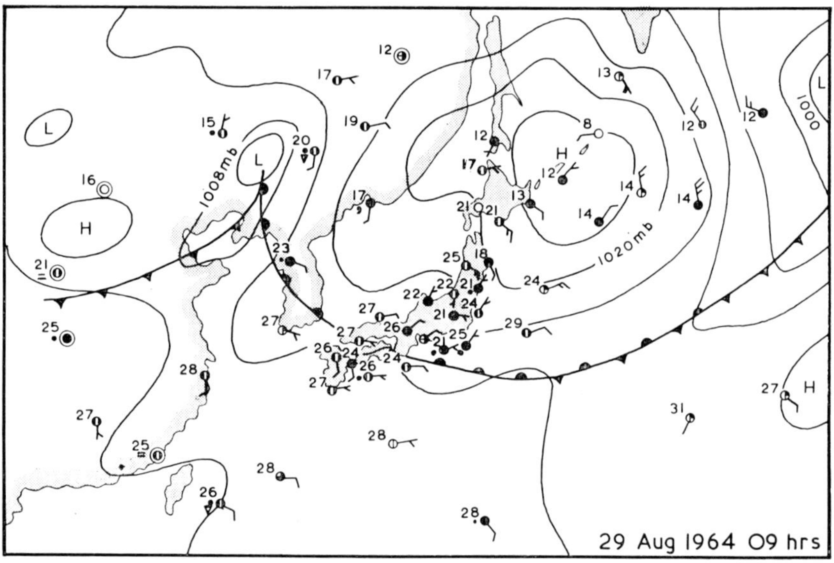

FIG. 23e

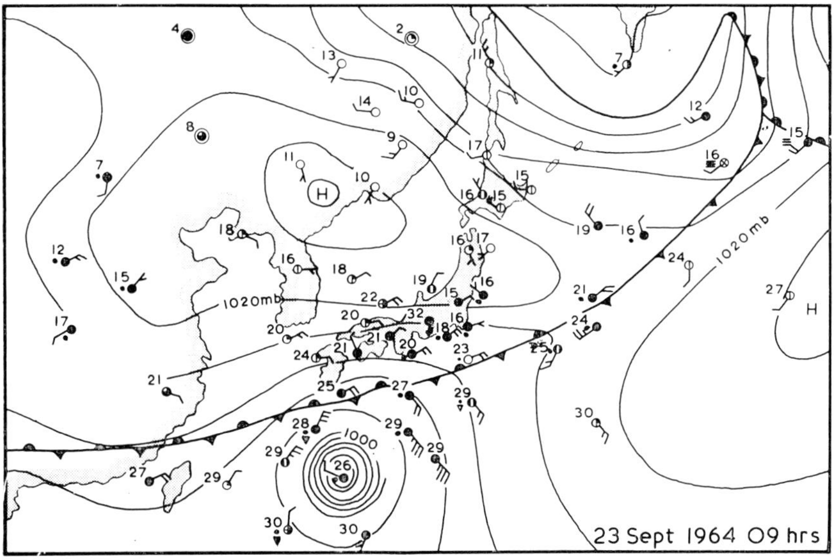

FIG. 23f

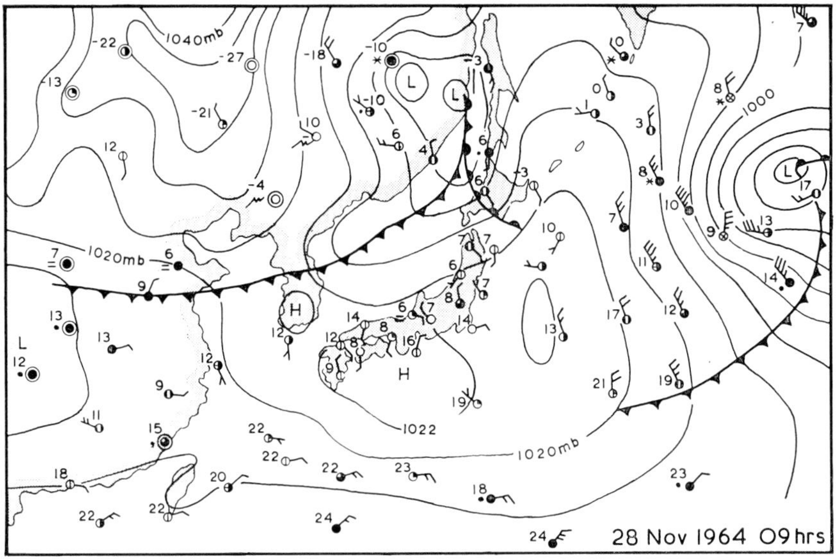

FIG. 23g

an overcast sky to the Japan Sea coast. Strong, cold, westerly winds prevail over Japan, west of the mountain backbone, during most of the winter. This is very different from the clear, sunny days of the east coast on the leeward side of the mountains. Niigata has 15 inches of precipitation and only 56 hours of sunshine in January, compared with only 2 inches of precipitation and 189 hours of sunshine in Tokyo on the Pacific side.

Early spring is an unsettled time. In late February the Siberian anticyclone weakens and the Pacific air becomes warmer. Depressions (fig. 23*b*) develop over the Japan Sea along the front between the still cold Siberian Pc air and the warmer Okhotsk Pm air (fig. 17), bringing very variable, unsettled weather and storms. The cold winds that blow from the west into the depressions occasionally bring dust from the dry plains of Mongolia to darken the sky and shower yellow sand on to the Japan Sea coast. The southerly winds of the warm front bring warmer weather and, as the air passes over the mountains, become a warm, dry foehn wind melting the snow on the eastern, leeward side of the mountains and bringing a danger of fire, as do the Alpine foehn winds of Europe.

In *late spring* in April and May (fig. 23*c*) anticyclonic conditions with high pressure spreading across from the continent bring more settled conditions and a period of still, sunny days and calm, starlight nights. The radiation on cold, clear nights brings the danger of frost damage to the young shoots of tea and mulberry bushes, especially in Tohoku and in the inland basins in central Honshu.

The fourth period (fig. 23*d*), the *Bai-u* period, begins in mid-June and lasts until mid-July. At this time the Hawaiian high-pressure area is expanding its influence over the seas to the south-east of Japan. The front between Tm air from this source and Okhotsk Pm air tends to lie along the Japanese divide bringing the *Bai-u* or 'plum rains' period. Warm moist air flowing north-east from the Hawaiian air mass meets the denser, colder Okhotsk air in a frontal zone, rises over it along the frontal surface and also over the mountains, bringing gloomy, overcast, humid, drizzly weather, especially to outer Japan south of Tohoku, and fog to eastern Tohoku and Hokkaido. There is ample rain for starting the rice crops though storms sometimes break the bunds and cause flooding.

By middle July the *summer* season (figs. 17 & 23*e*) has started. The Hawaiian air mass has developed strongly and the heating of the continental land mass has developed a deep low-pressure area over Asia. In the summer south-east winds prevail over the whole of Japan as air flows from the unstable side of the expanded Hawaiian high-pressure cell over the ocean towards the continental thermal low pressure, bringing a stream of hot, humid tropical maritime air which rises and cools under orographic influence and produces cloud and heavy precipitation on the windward slopes of south-western Japan. The range of temperature in August is relatively small (fig. 14). Kagoshima has an average of 28°C (83°F) and Obihiro 20°C (68°F). Hokkaido is mainly under 22°C (72°F), Tohoku 22°C (72°F) to 26°C (79°F), and south-western Japan over 26°C (79°F). Kagoshima is exposed to the winds and has 13 inches of rain in July, compared with 6 inches in Osaka in the shelter of Shikoku and 7 inches at Niigata on the Japan Sea coast. Summer, the period of maximum rainfall, is not a pleasant season in Japan. Humidity and heat combine to produce sultry weather, enervating, oppressive and trying for the Japanese but ideal for the rice crop. The Japanese house with its removable walls is designed to promote what circulation of air is possible at this season.

Early autumn (fig. 23*f*) in Japan is rather like the period of the 'plum rains'. As the Siberian high pressure grows more intense and extends the influence of its air mass in September, the front between it and the warmer oceanic Hawaiian air mass lies over Japan. It brings drizzle from overcast skies. This is followed by *autumn anticyclones* (fig. 23*g*) when the continental high spreads over Japan giving fine, dry, sunny weather, especially on the Pacific coast, before winter sets in with the intensification and spread of the Siberian air mass in November (fig. 23*a*).

TYPHOONS

Typhoons cut across the normal weather conditions in summer and autumn in violent and often disastrous bursts, perhaps 20 times a year between July

PLATE 13. These blocks of flats on the Nobi Plain near Nagoya were isolated by the 'tidal waves' and river floods brought by the typhoon 'Georgia' in 1959. The small distributaries with wooded levées are above the level of the surrounding country. The area is difficult for settlement and communications. Houses are sometimes built in linear villages along levées, as is the one in the right background (220).

and November (fig. 23*e*). The number may vary from as few as 15 in 1960 to as many as 31 in 1958. Typhoon 'Wilda' in September 1964 is typical of many of these tropical revolving storms. Pressure in her fell to below 970 mbs as she moved across Japan, bringing rain and winds in excess of 70 knots.

Typhoons develop to the south-east of Japan near the Marshall, Mariana and Caroline Islands, where the sea surface temperature is over 82°F and where the

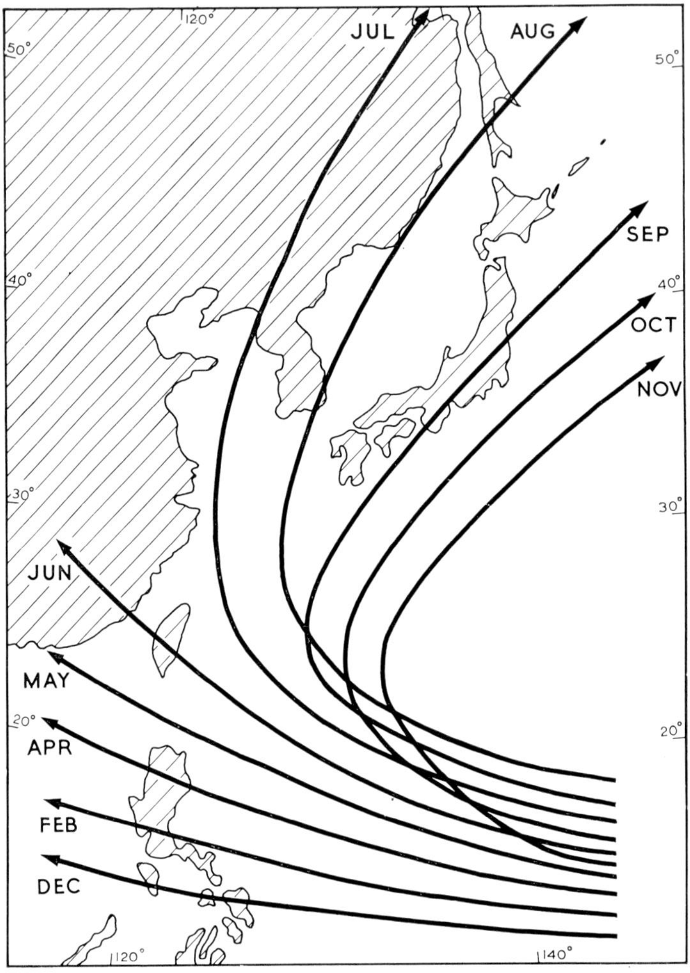

FIG. 24. The main typhoon paths (2).

equatorial air meets tropical maritime air and the polar continental air in a three-cornered pattern of fronts (fig. 17). The typhoons move along arcuate tracks (fig. 24) curving first west and then northwards. Half of them die out over the continent but the other half curve north-eastwards over the sea towards Japan. They bring with them lashing wind and rain (fig. 23*f*), whipping up 'tidal waves' and causing widespread damage, especially in south-west Japan where they are most frequent and most fierce. They come at a time when the rice is tall and about to ripen and the strong winds bend and batter the heads, bringing disaster to some areas every year. Further north they may blow the apple crop from the trees and break off branches. Typhoons cause more damage in Japan than rain, drought, frost and floods put together.

The Nagoya typhoon 'Georgia' of 26 September 1959 was typical of many but more intense than most. She left a trail of destruction from Ise Bay through Tosan to the Japan Sea coast. The typhoon hit the coast from the south-west, coming up Ise Bay at the same time as the high spring tide. It caused a 'tidal wave' that swept up the bay and on to the Nobi Plain (pl. 13), to cause both sea and river floods. Fishing villages, barely above sea level, were swept into the sea as the waves retreated, leaving no sign of either the people or their houses. It took 5,000 lives and destroyed 35,000 homes. In Nagoya itself the south and west of the town were under water and waves pounded at the houses, using stocks of timber as battering rams. Boats were left high and dry far above the normal sea level. Inland, the whole countryside seemed to lean drunkenly in the direction of the wind's passing – houses, telegraph poles and trees alike. Many huge cedars round the ancient Ise shrines were snapped off and splintered to matchwood, and whole forests were combed flat against the hillsides. On the plains the sea water burst over the dykes and flooded many hundreds of acres of rice land. Six weeks later, when the water drained away, there was a line of barnacles left sometimes 4 feet up the walls of houses, and salt from the sea water made much of the soil sterile for the following year's crops. Further inland the rivers, ponded back by the sea water, formed a huge lake engulfing the rice crop, which was ready for harvest, and stranding many a farm family on its rooftop in the middle of the night. Fortunately most of the typhoons that reach Japan are not as strong as this one.

Climate Regions

Japan can be divided into four main climatic regions (fig. 25): Hokkaido, Tohoku, the Japan Sea coast of south-western Japan and the Pacific side of south-western Japan. These are distinguished by the season of maximum rainfall which divides inner from outer Japan south of Tohoku, and the summer temperature which serves to divide the northern regions.

Hokkaido (1), in spite of being an island, has a cool-summer continental climate. The influence of high latitude is paramount. It is the coldest part of Japan with an average temperature for four months below freezing point and over 130 days with crisp snow. In winter the winds from Siberia bring cloudy, snowy weather to the whole island but especially to the west. Summers in Hokkaido come suddenly as the continental air mass gives way to maritime air. They are pleasantly cool compared with the rest of Japan. In inland Sapporo the average August temperature is as high as 21°C (70°F). The south-east coast is cooler; Nemuro 17°C (63°F) is chilled by the cool Oyashio current which causes coastal fog. This brings the temperature down below the 20°C (68°F) average for July and August which is necessary for rice growing. Relief in Hokkaido is not high, so there is no barrier to Siberian or Pacific influences. Because of this low relief rainfall is only about 40 inches, the west coast having more precipitation as snow in winter and the east coast as rain in summer.

Tohoku (*2*) climate is warmer than Hokkaido. The August temperature average is over 25°C (77°F). The difference between east and west, e.g. Akita and Sendai,

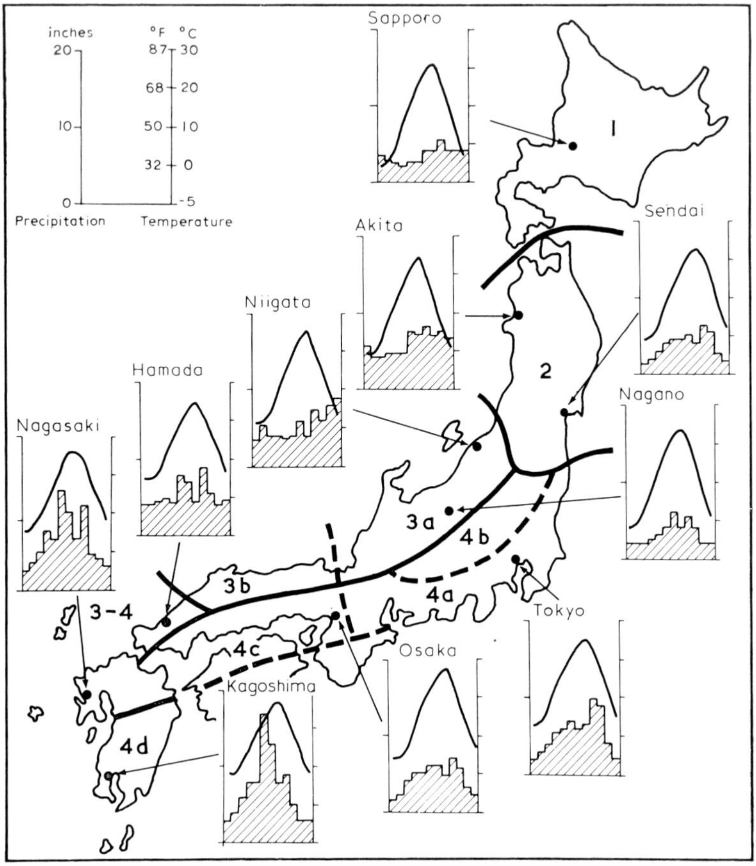

FIG. 25. Climate regions and representative stations (7 & 8).

is more marked as the mountains are higher. Western Tohoku has a winter precipitation maximum, up to 15 feet of snow, and much cloud, the east coast a summer maximum. There is little difference in temperature between the two coasts in winter though the raw westerlies are sensibly colder on the west coast, but in summer the east coast is cooled by the Oyashio current and coastal fog.

In western Japan the major climatic divide follows the watershed. *Inner Japan* (*3*) has a marked winter precipitation maximum, but there is considerable rain in summer as well. It is cooler in winter but warmer in summer than outer southern Japan. In February San In has a temperature of 4°C (40°F) compared with 8°C (47°F) in southern Shikoku, and in summer San In's 25°C (78°F) compares with Shikoku's 27°C (81°F). The region may be sub-divided according to the importance of the winter rain maximum which decreases to the south. Region *3a* (Niigata) has a greater maximum in winter than region *3b* (Hamada).

The climate of *outer southern Japan* (*4*) is characterized by very heavy summer rains, frequent typhoons and clear, sunny, winter days. The yearly rainfall distribution is markedly seasonal. There is relatively little range of temperature. There are four sub-divisions. The northern coastal area (*4a*) has a very mild dry winter, when Tokyo has a January average temperature of 4°C (40°F), and a hot summer with 26°C (79°F) in August, most rain falls in the summer and there is danger of typhoons in the autumn. The mountain area (*4b*) has great local variations in both temperature and rainfall because of variations in altitude and aspect. The interior basins have a more extreme and drier climate, for example Nagano has −2°C (29°F) in January and 24°C (76°F) in July and has only 40 inches of rain in local rain shadow areas. The Inland Sea area (*4c*) is the driest in Japan because it is sheltered from rain-bearing winds to the north and south. Osaka has only 53 inches of rain compared with 89 inches in Kagoshima. It also tends to have more extreme temperatures. Osaka has a range of 23°C (42°F) compared with 20°C (36°F) in Kagoshima, in spite of the moderating influence of the Inland Sea.

The southern parts of Kyushu, Shikoku and the Kii Peninsula (*4d*) are the most nearly tropical in Japan. It is only there that the very mild winters allow palms to grow. Everywhere temperatures average over 6°C (43°F) in January, so plant growth is possible all the year. Summer temperatures are much like the rest of the southern area but the climate is rather wetter, with 17 inches of rain in June in Kagoshima compared with 8 inches in Osaka. Typhoons come each year and there is a very striking summer rainfall maximum.

Northern Kyushu (*3–4*) is intermediate in character. It differs from the rest of southern Japan because it has both the winter rains of the Japan Sea coast and the summer rains and typhoons of the Pacific, and it is rather more equable than either east or west, with winters warmed by the influence of the Kuroshio current and summers cooled by maritime influences.

Japan's climate with its ample rainfall in the growing season, a growing season of twelve months in the south-west, and a large area with more than 200 frost-free days, is favourable to farming on the whole, but there are climatic difficulties. Apart from the very severe winters of the northern half of Japan, by far the greatest and most intractable problem is the typhoon with devastating winds and floods that do such great damage to crops. Also summer storms and the *Bai-u* rains during the early summer fill the rivers. On the Japan Sea coast, the warm mountain winds in March thaw the snow rapidly and release destructive floodwaters and rivers easily overflow and burst their banks, for their channels are often above the level of the surrounding flat plains.

Low temperatures are a problem in winter and summer. In the north the rice crop is damaged if July and August temperatures average less than 20°C (68°F). In Hokkaido and Tohoku frost damages crops in the winter by heaving, especially in the light volcanic soils; early spring frosts may damage crops during anti-cyclones in April. Droughts are caused by the occasional expansion of the Hawaiian high-pressure system into Japan in June.

CHAPTER THREE

The Vegetation

Forests are of great importance in Japan. They cover 65% of the total area. In temperate latitudes only Finland can equal this. After 2,000 years of occupation most of the forest is no longer virgin, but it is important in the economy of Japan. Wood-based industries, using mainly home-produced wood, form 5% of the total value of Japanese industry, especially in the form of rayon, paper, furniture, plywood and veneer, as well as charcoal and other fuel which forms 1% of the energy supply. Most houses are still built of wood and most cooking and heating is done by wood fuel. Many farms own a small area of forest which they use to provide fuel and humus. Forests add beauty to the landscape on hill and coastland, especially in the autumn when vivid reds, oranges and yellows blaze out from a sombre green background, and they protect steep hill slopes from the ravages of streams.

In Neolithic times Japan was completely forested but for the small area above the tree line that drops from about 9,500 feet on Mount Fuji to 5,000 feet in Hokkaido. Even today only 20% of the land has been cleared for farming and 65% of Japan is still clothed in forest (fig. 30). Over much of the country the soil is so thin that the land is only capable of supporting forest. The large mountain area with its steep slopes and swift streams, and the loose nature of much of the volcanic rock, combine with severe storms to make erosion so rapid that it is imperative that the slopes are left under forest or are reafforested when timber is cut (pls. 4 & 28). If the vegetation cover is removed erosion is accelerated and soil and rock debris removed to be redeposited lower down the river, causing disastrous flooding. The need to maintain a forest cover in these topographic and climatic conditions is particularly great.

Japanese forests are characterized by their mixed stands of a large variety of deciduous and coniferous trees of both Asian and North American species which have spread by way of the island chains linking Japan with Asia and North America. Because of the heavy rainfall, especially in the growing season on the Pacific coast, the forests are very dense with heavy undergrowth on better soils.

The forests vary in species according to latitude and altitude (fig. 26). They can be divided into three major *types*; subarctic coniferous forest in the north and at higher altitudes, cool temperate deciduous broadleaved hardwood forests in northern Honshu; and subtropical evergreen broadleaved hardwood forests in western Japan.

There is *coniferous* forest in central and eastern Hokkaido where the climate is colder, and at higher altitudes as far south as Tokyo where it is found above 6,000 feet on Mount Fuji. The forest is predominantly of fir and spruce with some deciduous trees, mainly hardy birch, alder, aspen and willow (pl. 4), that

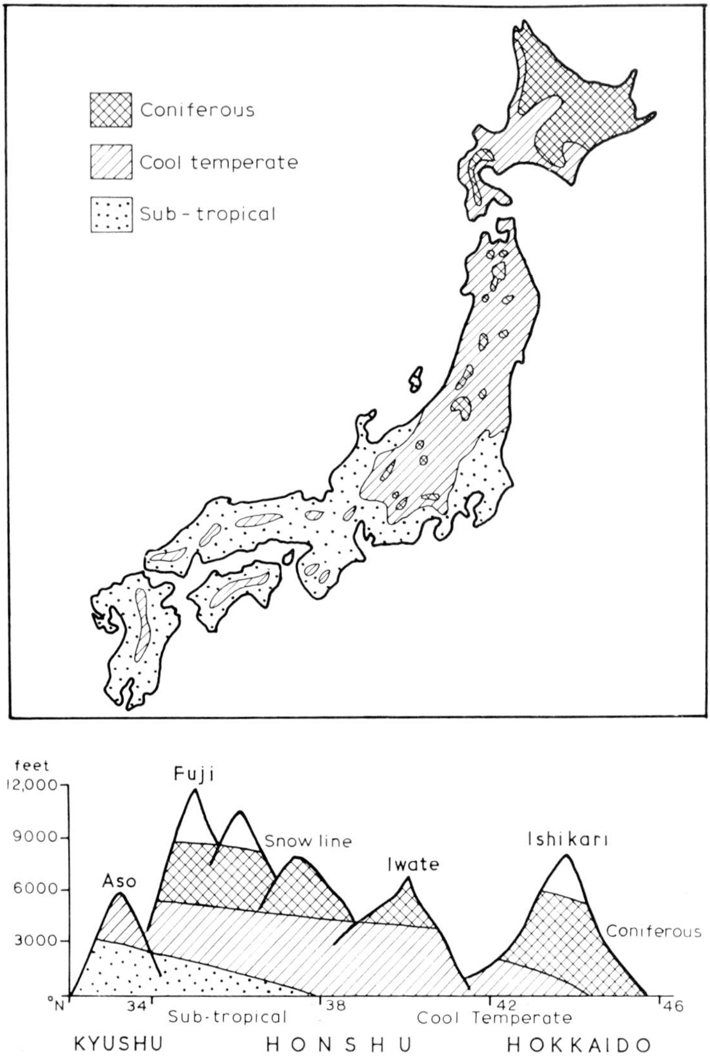

FIG. 26. Vegetation regions and altitude zones (2).

stand out in marked contrast to the dull, dark green conifers when their leaves turn golden, red and bronze in the autumn.

The *cool temperate* deciduous hardwood forest extends from western Hokkaido south to central Honshu and occurs too on the higher mountains in the whole of south-west Japan. Here there are beech, ash, chestnut, poplar and oak trees, with walnut, alder, bamboo and cherry, and some conifers. The broadleaved hardwood trees are increasingly being replaced by more useful fast-growing coniferous plantations of cedar, pine, larch, fir and spruce (fig. 27). Both coniferous and deciduous trees do well in the climate of central Japan and central Honshu is the main source of Japanese timber.

The lower coastal areas of central Honshu and all but the higher areas over 3,000 feet in the west are forested with *sub tropical* broadleaved evergreen hardwoods. There is evergreen oak, laurel, camphor, camellia and myrtle, as well as pine, fir, hemlock and cedar. The original vegetation was evergreen with

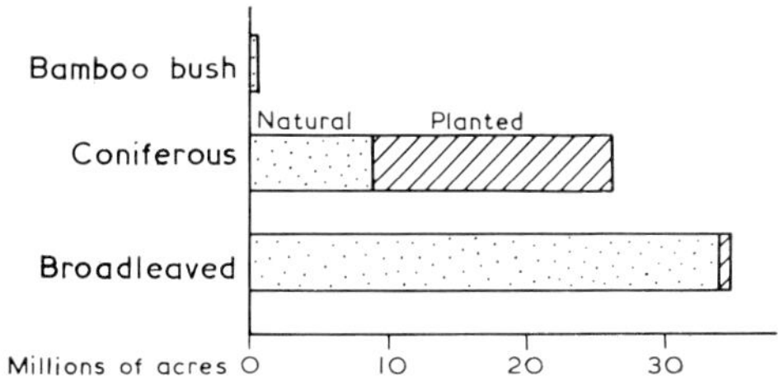

FIG. 27. Proportion of forest types showing the increasing area of coniferous forest (91).

heavy undergrowth because of the high rainfall. The timber was not very useful but more useful cedars, cypresses and pines are being planted to replace the original forest.

Forests are of great importance to the Japanese economy. They supply lumber, fuel, building materials, woodpulp and food. Only 27% of the forest is saw timber, mainly in Hokkaido, the mountains of Honshu and the south-west. Wood and charcoal supplies for fuel for heating and cooking formed 1% of Japan's total fuel supply in 1966 in spite of the increased use of gas and electricity. Houses are mainly built of timber. Wood pulp is used to make rayon in the south-west, especially in Chugoku and Shikoku. The forest provides humus for the farmer too. Many foods including walnuts and fruits, mushrooms, bamboo shoots, camphor for medical purposes and bamboo for baskets, furniture, building and paper are all forest products. Also important is the function of the forest in adding beauty to the scenery, acting as a windbreak, preventing soil erosion, conserving water for irrigation and hydroelectric power, and preventing the rapid run-off from carrying materials that choke rivers and cause flooding.

By 1966 the total cutting in Japan was treble the pre-war figure. Timber was needed for construction and pulp for paper and textile fibres in an expanding economy. The demand for pulp alone has increased fourfold since the war. A plywood industry has developed for home sales and for export. To meet these needs Japanese forests are being over-cut, leading to erosion and flooding. In 1966 the growth of timber was only 60 million cubic metres but 75 million cubic metres of timber were cut. Only a quarter of Japan's forest land is accessible and produces timber. The more accessible areas have already been very much depleted. The rest is either inaccessible or only provides fuel. The growth rate of the forest is only 2·7% per annum. This is much lower than most European forests, for example Norway's is 4·1%. This is because much of Japanese forests are poor regrowth with a growth rate of only 2% (fig. 27). Only the afforested area forming 27% of the total, and mainly conifer–cypress, cedar and pine, has a growth rate of over 6% and this area needs to be increased. The reafforestation of cut-over areas and the extension of the cultivated forest area is necessary to check the present consumption of capital forest resources and to ensure Japan's timber supply. In 1954 a ten-year plan was formulated to preserve 1¼ million acres of forest, to develop forest reserves, and to restore 1 million acres of devastated and/or deforested area. Most of the afforestation is softwood plantations to meet the growing demand for this type of timber, which covers only 39% of the area but supplies 85% of the timber for construction, paper and rayon. Half Japan's timber resources are nationally owned and it is on this land, mainly in Hokkaido and in the mountains in the other islands, that much of the large-scale planting is taking place. There are 2½ million small owners of forest land in Japan. Three-fifths of them own less than 2½ acres and 90% own under 10 acres. These are often farmers who draw upon it for their own supply of fuel and compost rather than for timber.

In Japan's highly developed economy there is a large and growing need for timber especially for pulping to make paper and rayon and for making an increasing amount of furniture for the more prosperous community. Her paper industry is now third to USA and Canada. Her own forests can supply most of the timber for pulp and she only imports 12% of her consumption but she needs to import 26% of the timber for making furniture and for plywood which has become a useful export. Before the war 65% of her imports came from America but these have become too costly so now south-east Asia supplies hardwood timber suitable for making plywood and veneers. The Philippines supplies 30% of her needs but much of the best timber has been used so that she has turned to Indonesia where she is working with the Indonesian government to develop the timber resources.

CHAPTER FOUR

The Soil

Three-quarters of Japan is mountain with thin lithosols that are unsuited to cultivation. Of the rest much of the soil is poor, being immature, easily leached soil on recently formed porous diluvial terraces or on infertile acid volcanic ash. Only the alluvium of plains and valley floors is naturally quite fertile, and in most areas this land suffers from having been cultivated to grow monoculture rice, or rice followed by a winter crop of cereals, for hundreds of years. In spite of limited and poor soil resources Japan manages to produce 77% of the food needed for 100 million people.

World Types

Until 1930 Japanese pedologists believed that the soils of Japan did not fit into the world pattern of soil classification developed by Russian soil scientists. They

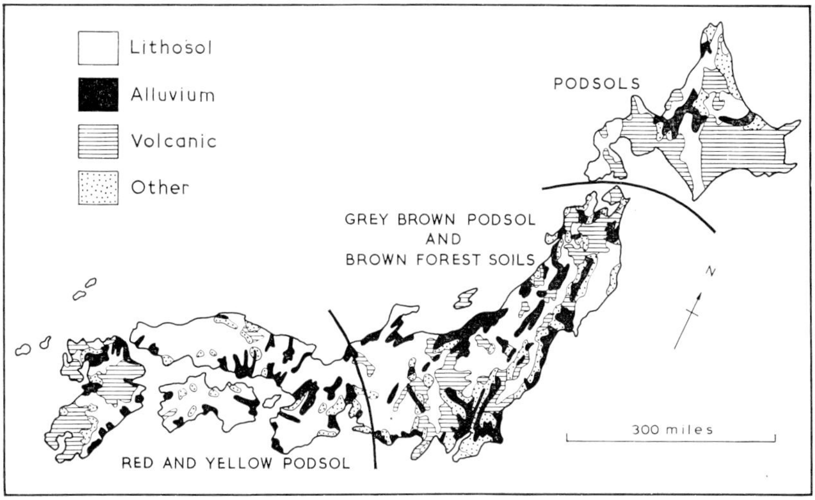

FIG. 28. World soil regions and intrazonal and azonal soil types. 'Other' is mainly soil on diluvium (28).

classified Japanese soils by particle size, except for peaty, alluvial and volcanic soils, and overprinted soil maps on top of the geological map showing the importance they attached to the relationship between geology and soil. Since then

Japanese soils have been found to fall into world soil types (fig. 28) based on the influence of climate and vegetation and classified by the chemical composition of the soil and its profile. It is possible to recognize in Japan three major world soil types: podsols, brown forest soils and red and yellow soils. The azonal soils of the earlier classification that cut across this tripartite division have more significance for the Japanese farmer.

Climate, vegetation and physiography all influence soil character. As rainfall is heavy all over the country, all the soils are either leached or podsolized. Soils may be divided into three main types which correlate closely with the three main types of vegetation, as both are influenced by the temperature variation between northern and south-western Japan. The podsol region corresponds approximately with the coniferous forest area, the brown forest soils are found where the temperate deciduous hardwoods grow, and the red and yellow laterized soils predominate in the warm evergreen hardwood area (fig. 26).

Podsols are found over the whole of Hokkaido with its cold climate. The heavy rainfall has leached the soil of its soluble mineral content so that it is poor in plant food. The coniferous forest provides little organic matter and, in the cool climate, this largely remains as raw humus in the shallow topsoil and is not available as plant food. These grey, shallow, leached soils, poor in soluble minerals and decayed humus, are acid and relatively infertile. The *brown forest soils* found in northern Honshu are only slightly podsolized. They are less subject to leaching in the flatter areas and where the rainfall is less but in the higher, more exposed areas, where there is more rain, leaching is more marked. Their organic content is higher because the deciduous hardwoods are a better source of organic matter which decomposes more rapidly in the warmer climate. Brown forest soils are therefore more fertile, though still not rich in organic and mineral plant food. The *red and yellow soil* region covers the whole of Kyushu, Shikoku and western Honshu, except for areas of brown forest soil at higher altitudes. This is the wettest and the warmest region in Japan, so that the soils are intensely leached and lacking in soluble minerals and humus. Not one of these three major soil types is naturally very fertile but upland soils are generally light and easily worked and often well drained while valley floor soils are much more fertile alluvium so that with the addition of fertilizers it is possible to grow two or more crops a year on both types of soil.

Azonal Types

An azonal classification of soils is more relevant for farming than the classification into world soil types for, as 75% of the country is steep, rugged, mountainous, and rainfall is heavy, erosion is very rapid and there is little time for mature soils to develop except on the limited lowland. Soils are largely immature and so are closely related to the underlying geological strata. Of azonal and intrazonal soils six types are of great significance. Most widespread over the greater part of Japan's mountain areas and covering 68% of Japan are the *lithosols*. These thin, stony, immature soils are formed on slopes greater than 15%. Here the heavy rainfall and steep slopes combine to cause rapid soil erosion, especially where there is little vegetation cover, and to prevent the development of a mature soil profile. Finer particles are washed away leaving almost bare rock surfaces and patches of thin stony soil leached of its soluble mineral and organic content, and often lacking in water supply, as the run-off is very rapid.

Soils developed on young *volcanic* ejecta are generally acid and relatively infertile. They cover 35% of the total area of Japan and are particularly widespread in Kagoshima Prefecture in southern Kyushu, on the Kanto Plain in east-central Honshu and in south-east Hokkaido, where volcanic ash is still being deposited today by such volcanoes as Sakurajima, Mount Azuma, and others. Near Neshime (p. 103) in Kagoshima, for example, the ash is as much as 100 feet deep, and fossilized soil profiles can be seen in the almost vertical gully sides where new deposits of ash have covered layers of soil. As recently as 1960 Sakurajima ejected vast quantities of ash which covered the surrounding area to a depth of several inches. Between 1707 and 1709 Mount Fuji covered the whole of the Kanto Plain with a mantle of ash 3 inches thick. The soils developed on this light, porous material resemble the loess soils of China in structure. The volcanic fallout is acidic and porous, so that the soils, unlike those developed on the ash of Mount Vesuvius and in Java which have good supplies of iron, potash and phosphorous, are very infertile. They are easily leached, but their high colloidal content makes them heavy in wet seasons. They lack organic matter and need humus to improve them. Minerals leached from the topsoil sometimes collect in the subsoil to form iron pan 2 feet below the surface, which hampers drainage and prevents root growth. When they are cultivated the powdery texture makes them readily subject to rapid and excessive erosion by water and wind. It is common to see a sloping plot that has been cultivated for only a few years with black soil at the bottom of the slope and white ash at the top devoid of all organic matter and soluble minerals. Despite attempts at bunding and furrowing, to divert the water along rather than down the slopes, soil wash and gullying are very common. When the wind blows on a dry day there is ample evidence of wind erosion both in the dust in the air and the collection of finer particles in hollows in the fields. Walking down a steep slope on this powdery soil, it slips like scree at every step. In northern Japan and on the mountains further south frost heaving on volcanic soils is a problem. On the Tokachi Plain young roots are severed as the surface ½ inch of soil is lifted often 3 inches or more by long slender ice crystals. These soils retain what fertility they have only for a short time. Without forest cover leaching, run-off, and erosion are extremely rapid.

Less widespread are soils derived from *sand and silt* deposits along the coast. The loose, dry, sandy soils are often also strongly leached, of poor structure and lack organic matter. In many coastal and some inland plain areas in Japan, rivers have brought down silt and deposited it in shallow bays or on flat plains. Reeds have grown and *bog and marsh* soils have been formed in these extremely wet areas of lowland. Many of these bogs have been drained to form some of the most fertile land in Japan. Hachiro Lake in Akita and the Ishikari Plain in Hokkaido (p. 150) are being developed in this way. Shrinkage following the process of drainage makes it necessary to build strong embankments and to protect the area from floods by river and sea and to control the water table carefully. These peaty soils lack inorganic minerals and need marling to improve them.

Most Japanese farmland is on *alluvial or diluvial soils* which together comprise 18% of Japan's total area. The richest soils in Japan are those developed on the alluvium spread over the many small plains scattered round the periphery and in the tectonic basins in the mountains, which sometimes contain drained lake floors. Nutrients are concentrated in these soils which have a high water table. It is only on this relatively level land, near to the local base level of river work and so not easily eroded, that mature slightly leached soils develop with a high silt or clay content to form the most fertile soils in Japan. The diluvial soils are derived from coarser and more porous terrace materials. On fig. 28 'other' is mainly diluvial soil (fig. 11) which is easily leached and lacks organic matter. The alluvial soil forms 12% of the total area and the diluvial 6%.

On some of these lowland areas *planosols* with poor drainage and clay pan have been produced, largely as a result of man's terracing and bunding for rice paddies which prevents natural run-off. The fine clay particles have been washed from the topsoil and have collected in the subsoil to form an impermeable layer, which has the advantage of keeping irrigation water in the paddyfields from seeping away but is difficult to drain well enough in the winter, when good drainage is needed for a wheat or barley crop. Deep furrows must be dug to drain off the excess water. This requires a huge amount of labour and is often not an economic proposition, as for instance on the Nobi Plain near Nagoya, where few winter crops can be grown. Poor drainage in this area made it very difficult to wash away the salt left after the sea flooding by the typhoon in September 1959.

The relative infertility, except of the alluvial soils, limits farming mainly to these, and about three-quarters of all the land cultivated in Japan is alluvium or diluvium. This represents only 14% of the whole surface of Japan and of the rest, most of the land is mountainous. No less than 39% of Japan is composed of hard granite. Palaeozoic and Mesozoic rocks are often metamorphosed and resistant to erosion so that they only allow the formation of thin lithosols which are easily washed away by the heavy rainfall. Throughout Japan soils suffer from leaching by excessive rainfall and rapid erosion on steep slopes. Volcanic soils have poor structure and are porous and easily leached, as are the diluvial soils on fans and coarse stony cones. Bog soils are poorly drained. All these soils need the addition of organic and other fertilizers if they are to be productive.

Soil erosion is a major problem in Japan in all but the small plain area. The steep slopes of the youthful mountains combined with the rushing ungraded streams and the poor soil structure of the light ash soils make a soil conservation policy a national necessity. Where the soil is left unprotected by trees from the torrential rains, as in parts of Hiroshima Prefecture, a badland topography has developed. The land is denuded of soil and the topography makes cultivation impossible. Fortunately the Japanese preference for rice has led to farmland being terraced and this has reduced erosion of the more valuable soil.

Today soil can be greatly improved by the addition of fertilizers. For generations farmers in Japan have used human excrement and humus from the forest to improve their heavy alluvial soils. Many farmers own several acres of forest land which supply humus as well as fuel. In Meiji times the use of night-soil was one of the main factors in raising the yields by 80% between 1880 and 1920. Since the war chemical fertilizers have been an important factor in raising rice yields by a further third between 1945 and 1955. Fertilizer is particularly necessary in Japan where often two or more crops are grown per year. Only Netherlands farmers use more fertilizer per acre than those in Japan, and this, rather than the original fertility of the soil, is the reason for rice yields in Japan being three times those in India. Japan used 125 kilograms of fertilizer per hectare in 1965 compared with Britain's 78 kilograms, the USA 23 and India 3 (156).

CHAPTER FIVE

The Historical Geography

The island nature of Japan close to the shore of a great continent has influenced her history in much the same way that Britain's similar position has influenced hers. Both were close enough to their respective continents to allow waves of people to reach them but each has been distant enough to develop its own individuality. The greater distance between Japan and her continental neighbours made it easier for her to isolate herself from them as she did for over 200 years during the Tokugawa period.

Settlement in Japan was difficult. Mountainous and forest-covered, she offered little foothold to the pioneer. Little land was easily cleared and, even when improving techniques enabled the shore dwellers to move inland, it was not easy to travel from one small lowland area to the next except by sea nor to link isolated pockets of settlement under a unified control.

Against this background Japanese history can be pictured as a series of waves of foreign influence, from Korea, China and the West, each followed by a period of calm isolation during which the foreign intruders or their ideas have been assimilated and become an integral part of the Japanese way of life. The Japanese are often said to be a nation of copyists. At first glance the man in the street appears to be completely westernized: in his western dress he travels in a modern bus or train to work in a factory that uses the latest methods of automation, but if you follow him home you will probably find him in his simple wooden home, sitting in his kimono on the *tatami*-covered floor eating a rice meal with chopsticks. Even the most casual visitor is soon struck by the distinctive way of life so obvious in Japanese houses, dress, manners, religion and outlook, that lies behind this western façade.

Early Settlement

Until about AD 400 myth and fact are inextricably mixed in Japanese history. In Japanese legend 'Toyo-ashi-no-hara-no-chio-aki-no-mizu-ho-no-kuni', 'Land of fertile reed plains, of bounteous harvests and full rice ears', now known by the Japanese as *Nippon* ('sun origin'), was founded at the command of the Sun Goddess by her grandson. The emperor is regarded in legend as his descendant.

It seems probable from geological evidence that in Pleistocene times Japan was linked to the mainland and possibly to the Philippines and Java. Although there is no positive proof of the existence of *early Stone Age* man in Japan he probably came, in small numbers, along these land links and lived near the sea

BC	*Pre 3500*	*Old Stone or Palaeolithic Age* probably a land link to Asia and some settlement.
	3500–300	*Jomon culture* – Mesolithic or Middle Stone Age – tribes of hunters.
	300 BC–200 AD	*Yayoi culture* probably came to Japan from south China bringing rice and settled farming, bronze and iron.
	100	Political centre probably moved from Kyushu to Kinki.
AD	*3rd–9th century*	*Yamato state.* Tomb Culture. 6th–9th century of great Chinese influence, introducing Buddhism, new ideas on administration, settlement patterns, and the arts. 710 Nara capital. 784 Kyoto capital and seat of Emperor to 1869.
	9th century to 1867	*Feudal Era* – war and unrest. 14th century–1639 Japanese merchants and pirates active in east Asia, South Pacific and Indian Ocean. 1543–1649 First period of European influence. 1543 Portuguese arrived finding industrial development similar to that in contemporary Europe except for navigation, firearms and medicine. 1549 St Francis Xavier brought Christianity. 1600 Dutch traders arrived. 1600–1854 Tokugawa Shogunate country united. Yedo (Tokyo) capital. Climax of the feudal era. 1639–1854 Closed period except to Dutch and Chinese merchants at Nagasaki. 1854 Japan reopened.
	1868 Modern Era	Meiji period and rapid industrialization. 1894–1945 Expansionist era. Empire building. 1894–1895 Sino-Japanese war – Taiwan ceded to Japan. 1904–1905 Russo-Japanese war – S. Sakhalin ceded to Japan. 1910 Korea annexed. 1914–1918 World War I – mandate over Mariana, Caroline and Marshall Isles. 1931 annexed Manchuria. 1941 (Dec.)–1945 World War II.
	1945 Post War Era	Japan lost her colonies and was occupied under the Supreme Commander, Allied Powers. 1945–1948 Years of acute shortage. 1949 Increasingly rapid industrial development. 1951 Success assured by Korean war. 1952 Sovereignty regained.

TABLE I Historical Table

at the edge of the forested and marshy plains. Subsequently the relative levels of sea and land changed, making Japan an island, and drowning the plains where these people had settled, wiping out all evidence of them. Remains of elephants from this era have been found on the floor of the Inland Sea.

The Jomon or Mesolithic era has left abundant remains. During this period a wave of migrants came probably across the then narrower straits from northern and southern Asia, mainly through Karafuto to the north but also through Korea (fig. 96). Japanese myths, dress, homes, food, language and customs can be traced to sources in both northern and southern Asia. The early pit dwellings in the islands are like those of north-east Asia and the present-day raised houses are reminiscent of those of Malaysia, Indonesia and the Philippines. There has been much speculation as to what these people were like. Since they came from northern and southern Asia and had already intermarried during the course of centuries, they were almost as mixed as the people of Japan are today; some were fairer, some more Caucasian and some more Mongoloid, but on the whole they were probably less Monogoloid in appearance than the Japanese are now. The modern Japanese and the few thousand Ainu who today live in Hokkaido and differ from other Japanese in their prolific body hair, probably evolved from these people.

These tribes lived in the islands from about 3500 BC to 300 BC, living by hunting and fishing. Their pit dwellings with shell mounds and the distinctive pottery, that gives the name of *Jomon* to the era, have been found from the north of Hokkaido to the south of Kyushu. They hunted wild boars, fished and collected wild plants and fruits from the forests. Many lived on the Kanto and other plains on the edge of the sea and round the river estuaries. The level of the sea was falling during this period and, as successive generations followed the retreating water, moving closer to the present sea coast, they left behind them evidence of their occupation in the form of shell mounds and pit dwellings (pl. 14) on diluvial plains.

After about 300 BC the culture of the Mesolithic hunters was gradually overlaid by a wave of more advanced culture coming from the continent by way of Korea. Stone was superseded by bronze and then by iron in the more advanced *Yayoi* culture. It was a great step forward. The many migrants brought with them the techniques of cultivation, including the growing of irrigated rice, and they could work metals and throw pots on a wheel. Social organization was transformed into a stratified hereditary society, the elements of which persisted in Japan in modified form until the late nineteenth century. In Yayoi society the migrants formed the dominant class with earlier people in hereditary classes specializing in pottery, metalwork or farming, with a few slaves making up the lowest class. The migrants probably came from China and South-east Asia, most were Mongoloid and, as they were assimilated into the community, the more Mongoloid Japanese characteristics that we know today were developed. The Mongoloid characteristics are short stature, small bones, round heads, flat faces with eyes with epicanthic folds, and dark straight hair.

Early centres of Yayoi culture were probably in north-west and south-east Kyushu and San In (fig. 29), where contact with Korea was closest. To push the frontier from here northwards a warrior class developed, and throughout the period the Yayoi culture gradually spread north until by 200 BC it had reached the Kinki. It was in Shizuoka by 100 BC, the Kanto Plain by the beginning of the

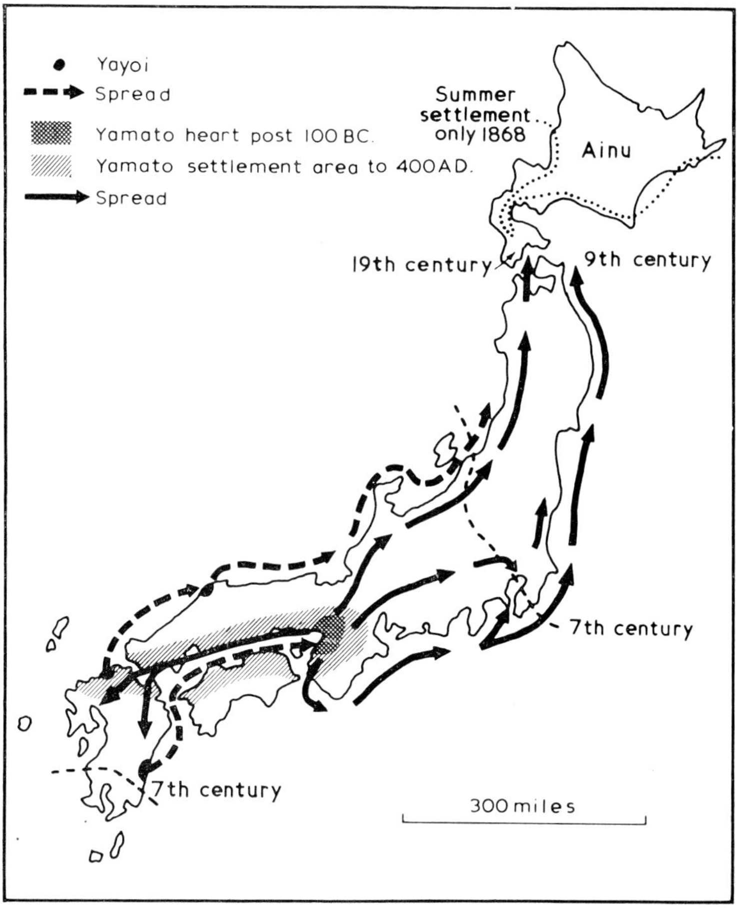

FIG. 29. The spread of the Yayoi culture and the Yamato state from the early sites to the heartland and from there to the whole of Japan.

Christian era and by AD 100 those Jomon people who had not already been assimilated had been forced into the less attractive mountain areas of Tohoku and the inhospitable island of Hokkaido.

The people who spread this culture lived as autonomous clans and tribes on plains separated by mountains and gradually became loosely organized to form the Yamato state. Legends say that about 100 BC the first emperor, Jimmu, went by sea from south-east Kyushu to Kinki which became the Yamato heartland and the centre of an empire which by the fourth century had a foothold in Korea and spread from Nagasaki to Shizuoka in Tokai. During this long, relatively calm period successive capitals were built including Kyoto and Nara. The huge tombs built for the Yamato rulers suggest that this was a highly aristocratic society.

The Development of the Heartland and Yamato State

During the sixth century there began another strong wave of Chinese influence. The Imperial Japanese court, realizing the great potentialities of the culture of the Chinese Tang dynasty which was then at its peak, sent emissaries to China to learn all they could and bring back their knowledge to be used in Japan. In just the same way in the late nineteenth century, in the Meiji era, representatives were sent to Europe and America to learn, and advisers were sought, in a second period of planned modernization. Both were periods of rapid and purposeful change.

From the sixth until the ninth century there was a constant flow of knowledge from China. Chinese techniques were selected and adapted to suit Japanese ways. The Japanese adopted the Chinese system of centralized political organiza-

PLATE 14. Japanese characters make Japanese office work highly complex. It takes two years to learn to use a typewriter efficiently. These girls are typical of many young office workers.

tion, though they used hereditary lords as local administrators rather than the system of bureaucrats appointed after examination that was employed by the Chinese. The Chinese grid pattern was adopted in planning the first capital in 710 near the modern town of Nara, and the new capital at Kyoto in 784 where it remained until 1868. The influence of the Chinese grid pattern can still be seen in Kyoto and in rural and urban settlement patterns today. Buddhism was adopted as were elements of Confucianism which form the basis for the development of the Japanese belief in duty to the family and to the country that is embodied in the Shinto faith and is the core of the Japanese moral code.

Chinese poetry, painting, literature, philosophy, ceramics and architecture have all left their mark in Japan, but the strong love of the simple beauty to be found in nature during the ever-changing seasons distinguishes Japanese art and has helped to develop throughout all classes a deep appreciation of beauty in all its forms. Landscape gardens, flower arrangements and *bonsai* growing are all related to natural beauty. Many arts are popular, the cult of the tea ceremony, woodblock printing and the use of the graceful kimono. Even in the simplest of farmhouses there is some ornament that is prized for its beauty.

The Chinese method of writing came to Japan with Chinese philosophy, poetry and literature. Just as in medieval Europe Latin was the language of learning, so in Japan Chinese was used until Japanese came to be written using a mixture of *kanji* characters and *hiragana.* Often kanji characters can be interpreted in many ways, giving great scope for complex literary word juggling that is ideally suited to the Japanese desire not to commit themselves to a definite idea. With such a multitude of characters commercial correspondence must be written by hand or typed on very complex machines. A child is faced with the need to learn at least 3,000 kanji characters as well as the *katagana* and *hiragana* syllabary and the Roman alphabet to be fully literate. In spite of this Japan has a literacy rate of 98%, similar to that in the United States and Britain.

Feudal Japan

For the next 800 years, from the ninth century to 1590 when power became centralized again under Hideyoshi and the Tokugawa Shogunate was established in 1600, there was a period of civil strife, during which the emperor had little control. For most of this period, culminating in the Age of the Country at War, power lay with the feudal lords. The characteristic pattern of small lowlands divided from each other by mountain ridges influenced the political pattern. Almost every peripheral plain and inland basin, conveniently isolated by mountains, was controlled by a different lord. There were frequent battles for power between the lords.

In spite of this industry and trade developed, so that by the time Portuguese traders arrived in Japan in 1543 its industrial development could compare with that of Europe, but the Japanese lagged behind the Portuguese in the knowledge of navigation, firearms and medicine. Many of the lords already sponsored industry, and trade and guilds were formed among such craftsmen as weavers, metalsmiths and paper makers. Some cities specialized in particular products; for instance, Seto and Arita in ceramics, Kyoto in silk and lacquerware and Osaka in cotton goods.

Many Japanese travelled abroad during this time and some mixed piracy with trade. Some settled and founded trading posts in the Philippines, Malaya and India as early as the fourteenth century before the first Europeans reached the Indian Ocean or the Pacific. Had it not been for the arrival of the Portuguese with superior arms the development of these settlements might have made the political pattern of the Far East very different today.

The first wave of European influence was heralded by the arrival in Japan of Portuguese traders in 1543, closely followed by missionaries led by St Francis Xavier, who landed at Kagoshima in 1549. Later, in 1600, Dutch traders came. A Portuguese, Organtino, in 1577 said of the Japanese: 'These people are in no sense barbarians. Excluding the advantages of religion we ourselves in comparison are most barbarous.' The Portuguese found the Japanese friendly and eager to learn. Each lord was anxious for them to settle in his domain so that he could learn from them to further his struggles against other lords. Realizing that where the missionaries settled traders came too, some lords even ordered their subjects to become Christians.

The Tokugawa Shogunate

In 1600 the Tokugawa family inaugurated a new era ending the long period of civil wars and uniting Japan by securing power over the whole country, which they ruled from Yedo (Tokyo). They held sway for over two and a half centuries until the Meiji restoration in 1868. The period was one of isolation and consolidation. To maintain control they regulated social and political organization. They saw in the Portuguese a danger to their power and as they suspected that the foreigners were ambitious to interfere in local power politics, they cut all contacts with the outside world except through the open port of Nagasaki. They froze the feudal social structure that consisted of a hierarchy of four hereditary classes. At the top were *daimyo* or lords, under them *samurai* or warriors, followed by farmers, then artisans and merchants and, at the bottom of the scale, the outcast classless *eta*. Each class owed respect to those above and above all to the emperor. Duty to the feudal lord came even before duty to the family and conflicting loyalties are the theme of many Japanese plays. The Tokugawas feared the power of local lords and organized a complex system of control to prevent subversion. Each lord had to spend part of the year in Yedo and when he went home to his lands he had to leave his family in Yedo as hostages. There was strict control of movement along all the highways to prevent any military coup.

There was need to unite the country and make communications easier, so that the lords could get to their lands from Yedo and growing trade could be carried on. Roads were improved and developed linking the settlements on many small isolated plains. Many roads used today were built or improved in Tokugawa times. The great *Tokaido* (fig. 134) from Kyoto, the old capital, to the new capital Yedo was the most important road in Japan from the beginning of the Tokugawa period, when the capital was moved to Yedo (Tokyo). The road along the Inland Sea through San Yo and Kyushu to the open port of Nagasaki was also much frequented. Towns grew up along the roads where people could get food and spend the night. This led to a growing sale for farm and craft products and the population of the Tokai–Kinki region grew between the two main centres of population. Road transport remained in a very primitive state and was mainly used by people travelling rather than for goods. With wide, gravelly river beds to cross, wheeled traffic was at a disadvantage and most goods were carried on horseback or by men, while the more important passengers were carried in palanquins, like those in Hiroshige's pictures of scenes on the Tokaido towards the end of Tokugawa times (pl. 35).

Sea transport was much more important than the roads for carrying goods. In spite of the fact that to maintain the isolation of the country the Tokugawas forbad the building of ships of more than 50 tons, merchants made use of the easy access to the sea of almost all the settled areas of Japan and by the end of the period small boats carried most of Japan's trade, especially bulky rice and textiles.

During the Tokugawa period industry became far more important and special local crafts and industrial workshops prospered. There were three types of industry; village industry for local needs, domestic industry in specialist towns and workshop industry. In most villages such things as lacquer bowls and chopsticks were made for local use. In the towns many of the people were artisans working in guilds through the domestic system which was organized by merchants to produce such things as cotton and metal goods and paper. Some towns specialized in certain products. Kyoto had many very special craft industries making luxury goods, such as silk, lacquerware and pottery. Fine silk brocades were woven for men's costumes and elegant women's kimonos. Many of Japan's best craftsmen served the needs of the emperor's court and the noble families who gathered round it, as happened in Paris during the reign of Louis XIV. By the late seventeenth century many craftsmen had moved to Yedo to serve *daimyo* families but this industry continued in Kyoto. Much of the silk used in Kyoto was produced on the upland farms of the Kinki.

The ceramics industry grew in many places where there were supplies of clay, but Seto near Nagoya and Arita in western Kyushu were among the most important producers, since leading craftsmen emerged there and their families carried on the skills that they developed. Osaka was a newer town. Its cotton industry depended less on inherited skills than on the growing of cotton and indigo round the nearby Inland Sea.

A third type of industry was organized on a larger scale by more progressive lords. Workshops processed copper, gold and silver, and mines produced coal and iron. Some of these employed more than a hundred men and were very profitable. The lord of Satsuma in southern Kyushu established an iron foundry in

1852, using local iron ore and drawing upon the plentiful supply of local wood for fuel.

The Tokugawa period was one of great stability but bred within it the seeds of social and economic discontent which led to its downfall. One of the most dissatisfied groups was the samurai. By the Meiji period there were probably 2 million of them forming about 6% of the population. They were parasites living on the productive efforts of the rest of the people, for with peaceful conditions they had no fighting function. The samurai were paid in rice and so their incomes depended on rice prices which fluctuated greatly. As these gradually declined, their incomes fell.

The peasants, who formed about three-quarters of the population, were oppressed by the high rents and taxes needed to support the feudal rulers who often took 30–40% of their crops. They also suffered from a period of droughts and cool summers that caused famine during the latter half of the eighteenth century.

One of the most significant changes that led to the downfall of the Tokugawa regime was the growth of industry and trade, which was accompanied by the rise of a middle class of merchants in the cities. By tradition these people were in the lowest class, severely controlled by the sumptuary laws and taxed by the authorities. As they became richer they were no longer willing to accept their inferior social position, so the struggle of conflicting interests between feudalism and capitalism, between status and wealth, helped to undermine the stability of the Tokugawa regime. The growth of industry and trade led to a growing demand for food for the cities and, despite a doubling of the cultivated area between 1600 and 1730, and rising yields, the country could not meet the needs of the increasing urban population.

Both internal and external pressures led to the reopening of Japan to the world. On the one hand many Japanese were keen to have contact with foreigners so that they could learn new western techniques, while on the other hand certain nations, especially Russia and the USA, were anxious to use Japanese ports for supplies during the long Pacific Ocean crossing. The arrival of Admiral Perry leading an American naval force in 1853 and 1854 provided the final thrust necessary to make the Japanese realize that they could no longer isolate themselves and must open their ports to international trade. The Tokugawa regime with its rigid organization was unsuited to lead Japan into this new phase of development and it fell when warriors from fiefs in western Japan, notably Choshu and Satsuma, in Southern Kyushu, restored the emperor Meiji to power in 1868. So began the modern era for Japan and the most recent wave of foreign influence, which is dealt with in subsequent chapters.

CHAPTER SIX

The Farming

Characteristics and Regional Contrasts

Japanese farming is on a very small scale but it is very intensive and highly productive. Rice is the dominant crop and covers nearly half the farmland (fig. 44). Many farmers grow wheat, barley, soya beans, apples, oranges, mulberry and vegetables, and an increasing number rear beef and dairy cattle and keep chickens. As in mainland Asia farms are small, their average of 2·7 acres comparing with about 50 acres in Britain. Few farmers have more than 5 acres and 69% 2½ acres or less. Better seed, more fertilizer and more advanced techniques of cultivation give Japan rice yields that are three times those of India.

Though prosperous compared with peasant farmers in Asia, Japanese farm incomes are very much lower than those in any western country. In spite of rice yields of 60 bushels an acre compared with 40 for wheat in Britain, the small size of Japanese farms limits the productivity per farm worker to only a fifth of that in Britain (fig. 84). This is because farm size is small and this makes mechanization difficult and costly. By 1966 only one farmer in three owned even a mechanized cultivator, although many more hired one from time to time. Poor soil, which requires a great deal of fertilizer, and small farms, that make the economic use of labour difficult, make the products of Japanese farms expensive. Government policy protects farmers from the competition of foreign rice, wheat, sugar and dairy and other produce, which, with world surpluses, sells in the world market at about two thirds the price of home produce in Japan. This encourages farmers to produce enough food to meet the needs of the growing population and avoids the use of much-needed foreign currency to buy food abroad. The policy is fairly successful and Japan is nearly self-supporting in rice production but has to import 23% of her total food needs. This act of feather-bedding *par excellence* protects inefficient farming and food is more expensive than it need be. If protection were reduced, as it may well be, it would stimulate farming to become more competitive and concentrate on the more profitable fruit and vegetable crops instead of rice and wheat which could be imported more cheaply. There is need for some farmers to sell their land so that those who remain can crop larger areas using more machinery, and so earn higher incomes.

Since 1959 there have been signs of fundamental changes taking place in farm structure. The eldest son, who has always had a duty to take on the family farm, has begun to neglect this and take a job in the city. This could herald a new era in Japanese farming. The number of farms has at last begun to decline. It fell from

6 million in 1960 to 5·5 million in 1966, and the number engaged in farming fell from 13·7 million to 9·4 million in 1967 but the size of farms rose only slightly from 2·1 to 2·7 acres between 1960 and 1966.

Two-thirds of Japan is forested mountain land (fig. 30) and only 20% can be farmed compared with 80% of England and Wales. Farms are mainly in the narrow valleys and on small plains (pl. 31), and with so little land available rural population densities are the highest in the world with 1,340 people per square kilometre of cultivated land nearly three times that of the Netherlands (495) the next highest. Farms are necessarily very small, averaging only 2·7 acres, and so they must be farmed very intensively, often with two or more crops grown on the land each year, especially in warmer south-west Japan. Farmers meticulously

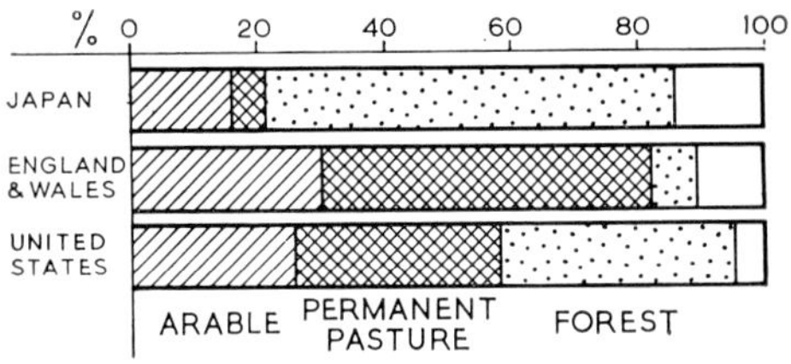

FIG. 30. Comparative land use 1966, showing the small proportion of farmland and of pasture and the high proportion of forest (156).

cultivate their small plots either with a power cultivator, with a horse- or ox-drawn plough, or by hand. Inter-cultivation with, for example, vegetables between rows of wheat, is a common practice and even the bunds between the fields are cropped. There is little pasture.

Rice is grown on 44% of Japan's cultivated land and accounts for 42% of farm production (fig. 44). It is grown on all the paddyland, and on some of the upland fields. The farmer's first aim is to grow at least enough rice for his family, and most farms do this. Commercial crops are of growing importance. Many farmers have both paddyland and uplands fields and grow a variety of crops – rice on the paddyland in summer followed by wheat, barley, and vegetables in winter, and wheat, barley, fruit and vegetables on the unirrigated upland fields. Few farmers specialize in one crop so that mixed farming predominates and 60% of the crops are grown for home use. Few animals are kept in Japan. In 1966 there were still only 1·3 million dairy cows in Japan. Up to a hundred years ago the Japanese did not kill four-footed animals and there is no tradition of animal rearing. On such tiny holdings little land can be devoted to fodder crops or pasture, but recently the number of pigs, chickens and dairy cattle has increased.

Farming in Japan is no longer the main activity of the people as it is in the other countries of Asia. In 1967 only 19% of the work force was engaged in agriculture and forestry (fig. 31) and brought in only 12% (fig. 95) of the total national income. This decline from 82% of the work force since 1880 is the effect of the growing relative importance of industry. The number of people employed in farming has fallen by 4 million, from 14 to 9·7 million, since 1958; the surplus

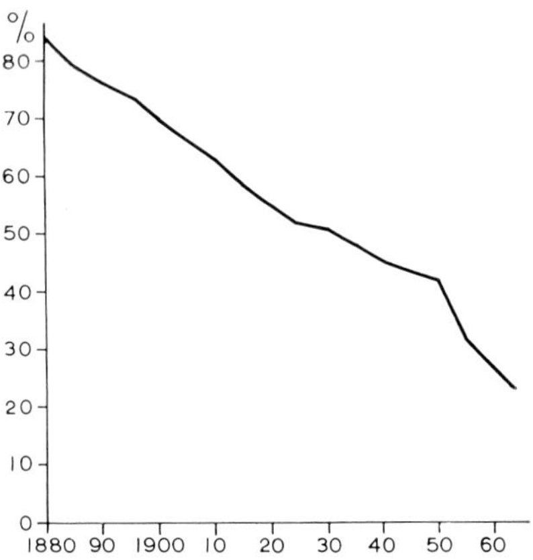

FIG. 31. The percentage of the labour force in farming since 1880 (85 & 91).

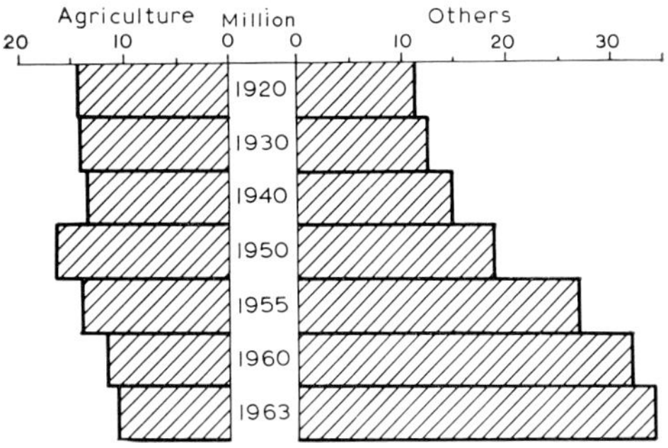

FIG. 32. The labour force since 1920, showing the relative stability and recent decline in farm numbers and the growth of non-agricultural labour force (85 & 182).

Key Farm Statistics 1966.

Area: Area of Japan farmed 21%. Area cultivated 16% – 4·7 million hectares.

Land use rate 123%.

Farm size: Average 1955 2·1 acres, 1966 2·7 acres. Under 2·5 acres 68%.

Work force: 1966 11·1 million, 1967 9·7 million, men 4·4 million, women 5·3 million.

19% of total work force (UK 4%, US 11%).

5·5 million farm families (1955 6·1 million).

Income: 12% of national income 1967 (1966 9%).

Part time farm families are those with income from outside farming.

Farm family income from outside farming 52%. Income from farming 48%.

'Part time' farm families 79%, farming only 21%.

Of part time families most income from farming 33%.

Of part time families most income from other sources 46%.

Commercialization: 73% of produce sold, 20% of farmers sold under 45% of produce.

A farm household is classified as such if it has 0·1 of a hectare of land, 1 cow, horse or pig or 30 hens, whether or not it has more income from outside farming.

A first class household has more than 1·25 hectares of land (2·5 in Hokkaido) or less than this if it is intensively farmed with hot houses, stock, poultry or sericulture.

Dependance on imports. 23% of food including 7% of rice needed.

farm population has moved into other work, but farm production has increased. The 13 million acres of land cultivated has changed little in total because land reclamation has almost equalled the loss of farmland to the growing industrial cities (fig. 77). Rice production has increased by a third since before the war and, whereas before World War II Japan imported 16% of the rice and a third of the food she needed to feed 70 million people, in 1966 she imported only 7% of the rice and 24% of the food to feed 100 million, more than a third above the pre-war population (fig. 61).

Farm families have recently become much less dependent on farming. Before World War II farmers depended largely on subsistence crops of rice, cereals, vegetables and fruit, but now half of farm family incomes come from employment outside farming by some family members.

Many Japanese farms, of which 68% have less than 2½ acres (fig. 33) of land,

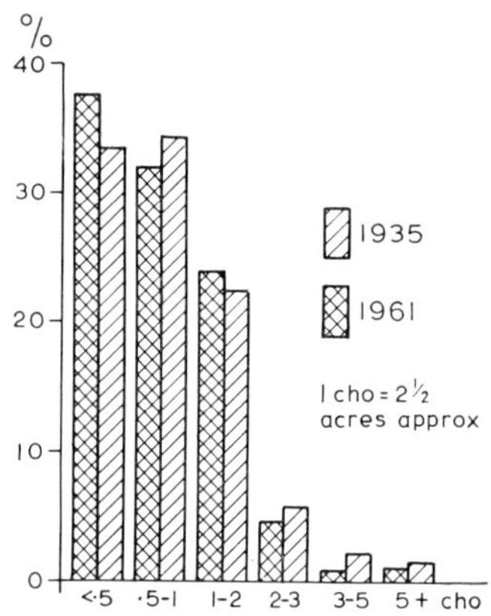

FIG. 33. Farms by size: distribution in 1935 and 1961 (91).

are too small to occupy the whole family. The wife grows enough rice and vegetables for the family, helped by her husband at weekends. During the week her husband and children work in shops or factories in the local town. This part time or 'weekend and womenfolk' farming is becoming increasingly common in Japan

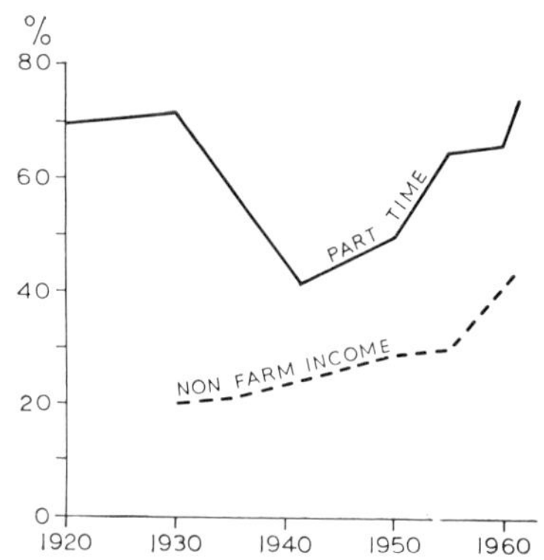

FIG. 34. The percentage of part-time farm households and their non-farm incomes showing the high proportion of part-time farming and the increase in non-farm incomes (91).

(fig. 34) especially where farms are small, on the Japan Sea coast where there is no work to do on the farm during the winter (fig. 35). In 1966 79% of farm families had other sources of income which brought in 52% of all farm house-

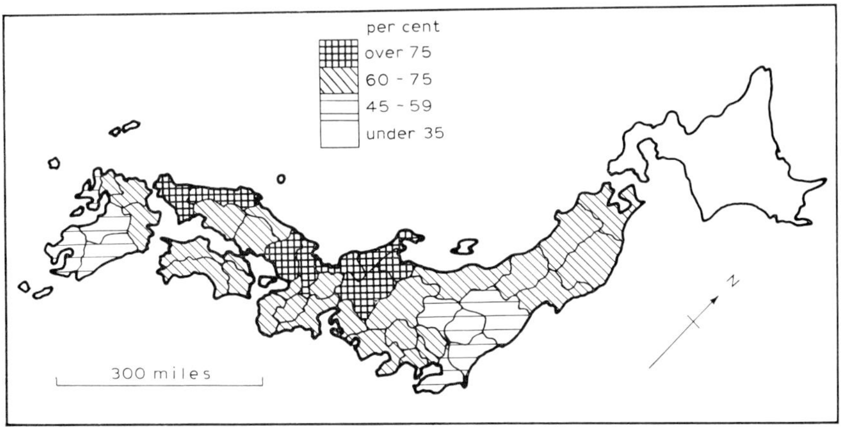

FIG. 35. The percentage of part-time farm households. Regional variations are related to the size of farms and the amount of winter cropping. Where farms are small and where few winter crops can be grown farm families take other jobs if they are available, 1962 (91).

hold incomes (fig. 36), and only 33% of farm families earned most of their income from their land. Many farms of under half an acre are the equivalent of a large British garden.

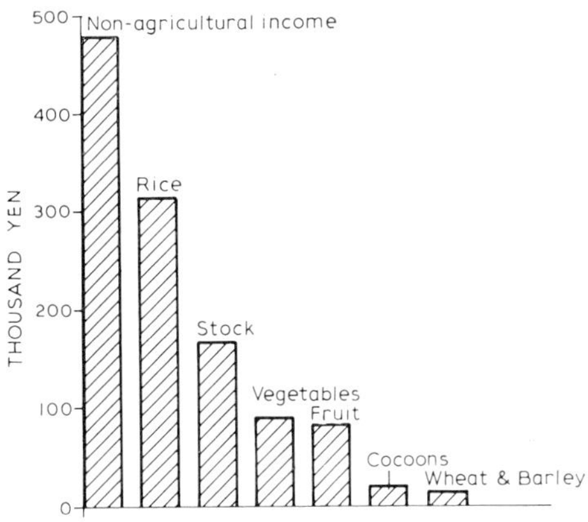

FIG. 36. The main sources of farm family income in 1965 (88).

Though most crops are grown for use in the home, an increasing number of more profitable cash crops are being produced to meet the growing needs of an urban population that is steadily becoming more prosperous, and has more money to spend on fruit, vegetables, meat and dairy produce. Japanese farmers today are more prosperous than any in mainland Asia. They usually use a power cultivator to cultivate their land and yields are high, new crops are profitable and

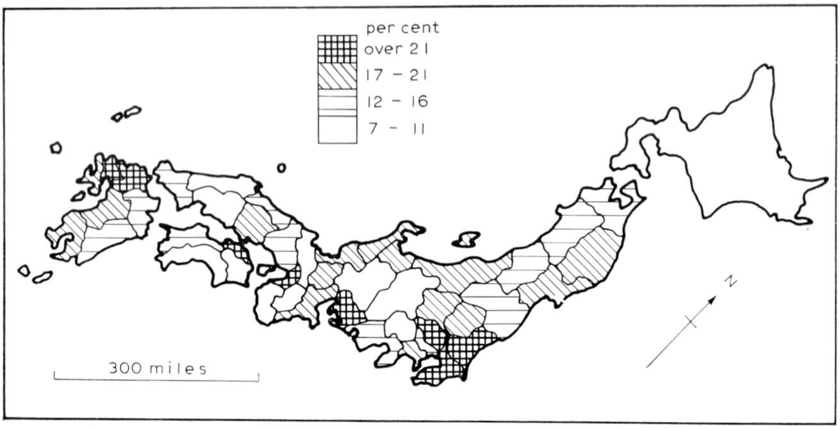

FIG. 37. The percentage of the land cultivated in each prefecture, 1962. This is much influenced by the amount of lowland and the date of settlement (91).

work off the farm doubles the family income. In 1966 no less than 94% of farmers had a television set, 76% had a washing machine and 62% owned a refrigerator. In 1963 19% of farmers' children went to college at eighteen.

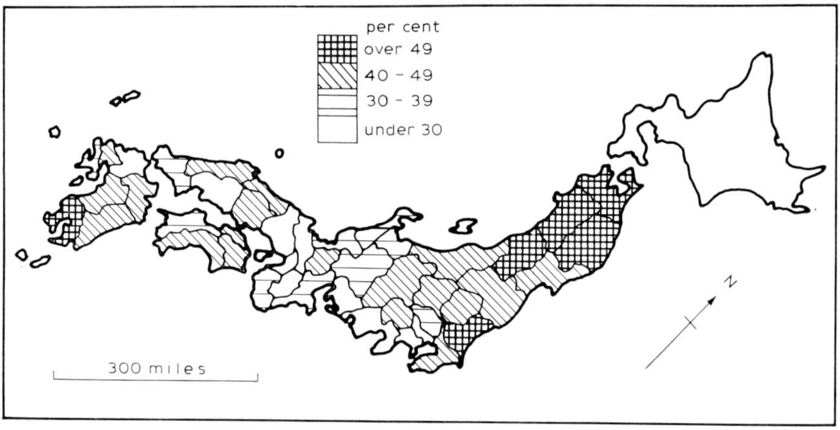

FIG. 38. Map to show the proportion of the labour force in farming in 1962 showing the high proportion in the 'frontier' areas of Tohoku and southern Kyushu and the small proportion in industrial areas and in Hokkaido where forestry, fishing and other industry employs many people (91). The pattern in 1966 was similar with lower percentages.

The importance of farming varies very much from one part of Japan to another (figs. 37 & 38). It is most important in the isolated 'frontier' zone of Tohoku and

Kyushu (fig. 52) where more than 20% of the labour force was engaged in farming, and least important in the industrial zone stretching from Tokyo to north Kyushu (fig. 102) where less than 16% of the labour force were farmers in 1966.

AN EXAMPLE TO SHOW THE CHARACTERISTICS OF JAPANESE FARMING

The main characteristics of farming are illustrated by Mr Morita's farm in Tanaka hamlet (220), which is a small group of houses near Shizui town in Kumamoto Prefecture in the island of Kyushu (fig. 52 no. 12). The Morita household in Tanaka (fig. 40) is unusually large for Japan. Usually there are three generations living at home, the old, perhaps retired, grandparents, the

PLATE 15. This farmhouse is like the Moritas' with its paper *shoji* and thatched roof. Notice the hole in the paper, the persimmons drying and the shoes carefully left outside. The family is typical with three generations living in one farmhouse.

head of the household and his wife and their children. Mr Ichiro Morita is head of the house, but since he is busy working as a farm adviser his younger brother lives at home to help to run the farm. There are ten people in the household. There is grandmother Morita who looks after the house and two of her sons and their wives, Kumiko who has three children and Masako who has two.

Their house has four big rooms (fig. 39, pl. 15) which are divided from one another by sliding partitions or *fusuma*, made of a framework of wood covered with thin but tough paper. The house is bare of furniture except for a foot-high table in the room where they entertain their guests, and another in the kitchen where they eat. All the rooms have two uses for when Kumiko takes the mattresses and blankets from a built-in cupboard and spreads them on the floor, all the rooms are used for sleeping. At the back of the house is the kitchen with a new, tiled, wood-fired range for cooking and water from a pump over the sink. Like

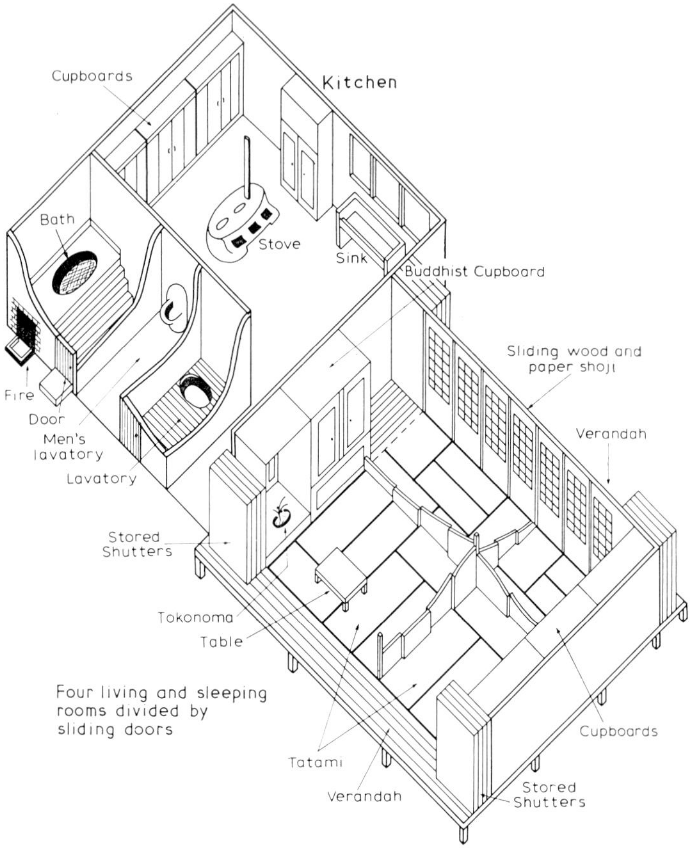

FIG. 39. Inside a Japanese farmhouse (see plate 15).

almost all Japanese homes the Moritas' have electricity to light the house and for the television. The four main rooms of the house are floored with *tatami*. These are pads of compressed rice straw, 3 feet by 6 feet, and 2 inches thick, with a thin woven rush mat stitched over the top of each. Every room is built so that it can be completely covered with these thick mats, which are comfortable to sit on, and, with bedding, comfortable to sleep on too (pl. 39). The main room of the house has an alcove where a scroll is hung and a bowl of flowers is set. Beside this is a black cupboard with the family record inside on black and white tablets.

The outer walls of the house are *shoji*, paper-covered screens which slide aside to show the highly polished wooden verandah all round the house. There are shutters too that are pulled along the outer edge of the verandah at night or during storms. The whole house is raised about 18 inches above the ground. This raised style of house is similar to those in Malaysia, Indonesia and other parts of south-east Asia, and more suitable for a tropical than a temperate climate such as that in Tohoku, where the average January temperature is below freezing point and the wind whistles under the floor and through the cracks in the paper screens. These conditions make heating a problem, and the temperature inside the house cannot be raised sufficiently since the insulation is so poor. The Japanese heat themselves rather than their rooms by wearing heavy woollen or padded cotton kimonos and using a *hibachi*. The Moritas' *hibachi* is a round blue pot about 2 feet across and 2 feet deep, which they half fill with ash on top of

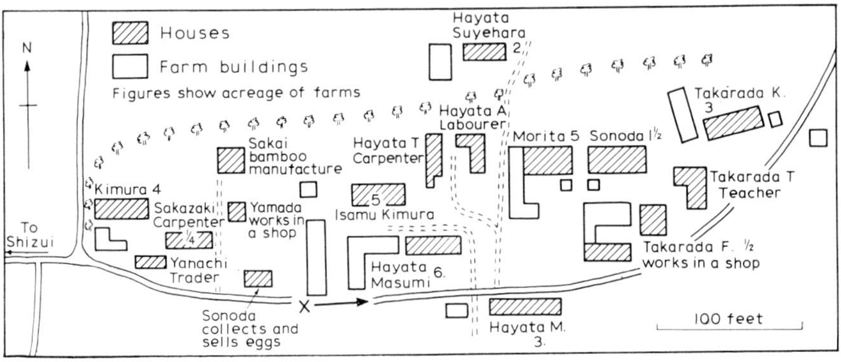

FIG. 40. Tanaka *buraku* showing the houses, land owned and other jobs done by each family.

which they put glowing charcoal. The family crowd around and hold their fingers over the heat, but it warms little more than their hands.

The Moritas usually eat in the kitchen from a western-style table. The rice they grow is their staple diet and they eat it at all the three main meals. For breakfast they have bowls of boiled rice with small squares of omelette, a bowl of tasty soup made from soya beans, and tea. The men and children like to have bread sometimes for a change, and the children drink hot milk from the home cow. They have rice with pieces of fish, vegetables and perhaps an egg, fruit and tea for their lunch, and their evening meal is much the same. When visitors come they serve tea and sweet rice cakes in the best room, kneeling or sitting on flat cushions round the low table.

Tanaka is a small *buraku* with a group of seventeen houses (fig. 40, pl. 16) in the valley of the river Koshi at a point where it is a mile wide. There are more details about the *buraku* on page 60. Tanaka homes are on the alluvial plain very little above the level of the carefully embanked river (fig. 41, pl. 17). To the north is the sharp edge of the diluvial terrace that rises steeply about 15 feet

PLATE 16. The track from Shizui arrives at Tanaka hamlet (figure 52 no. 2, figure 40). In January there is young wheat and barley growing on the paddyland. The diluvial terrace on which the Moritas' upland fields lie shows clearly in the background with the dissected mountains beyond.

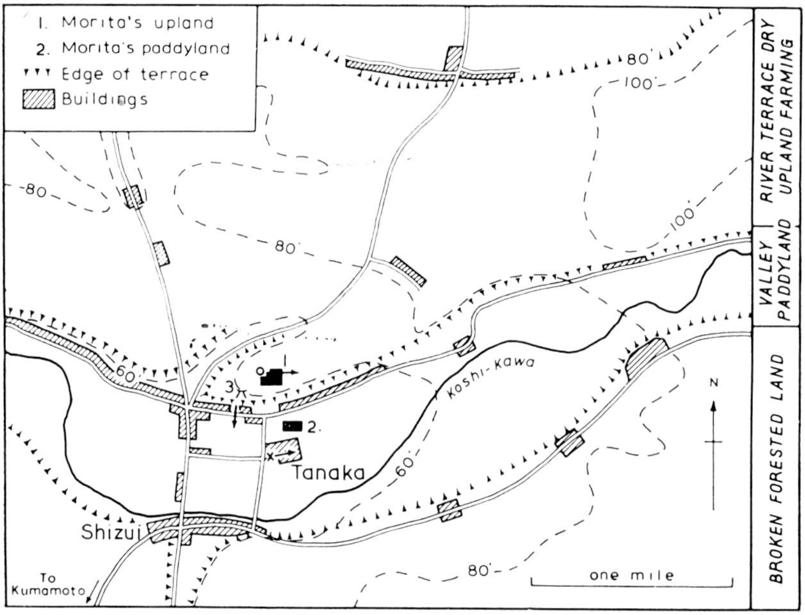

FIG. 41. The area around Tanaka showing the valley, the diluvial terrace and hills. Plate 22 was taken from 1, Plate 16 from 2 and plate 17 from 3 (220).

above the valley floor. Southwards and across the river from Tanaka the valley gives way to low, broken, wooded, hilly country. Not far away to the east are the forested mountains with their thin soil and precipitous slopes, and above these rises the cone of Mount Aso with its plume of dust, gases and steam. This volcano has a diameter of 40 miles and spreads over a greater area than any other in Japan.

Mr Morita has land in all three parts of the valley. As everywhere in Japan his paddyland and upland crops differ (fig. 42) so that he can grow a wide variety on his scattered plots. He has 2¾ acres of land on the valley floor near the *buraku*

PLATE 17. The view across the Koshi Kawa-Valley from the shrine on the edge of the diluvial terrace (fig. 41). The wheat and barley are neatly aligned in the paddifields, and the irrigation ditches and the raised road can be seen in the middle distance. A track climbs the slope of the levee beyond. In the background are the hills where the Moritas have their woodland (220).

(pl. 17) and 2¼ on the diluvial terrace upland to the north (pl. 22), and he also has rights in the forest on the hills to the south. Of all the cultivated land in Japan about 44% is upland, that is land on which water cannot be held even though some of it is irrigated. On this land wheat, barley, fruit and vegetables are grown. The rest of the farmlands, where water can be held, are paddyland growing rice in summer and, in some places, wheat, barley and vegetables in winter.

Altogether the Moritas have only 5 acres of land, but this is double the 2·7 acres average for Japan. Because of their very small size, Japanese farms are worked extremely intensively and Mr Morita grows not one but several crops on his land during the year. This means that although he cultivates 5 acres he takes crops from 11 acres and so has a land use rate of 220%. He grows two crops a year on most of the paddyland and sometimes three, and three crops on some of the upland fields. He grows rice on the alluvial paddyland (fig. 42) in the summer and follows this with a crop of wheat or barley in the winter. Before the rice is harvested clover seed is sown under some of the rice so that he can cut a catch crop of hay before the wheat or barley is planted. Similarly, before the wheat and barley are harvested he plants beans between some of the

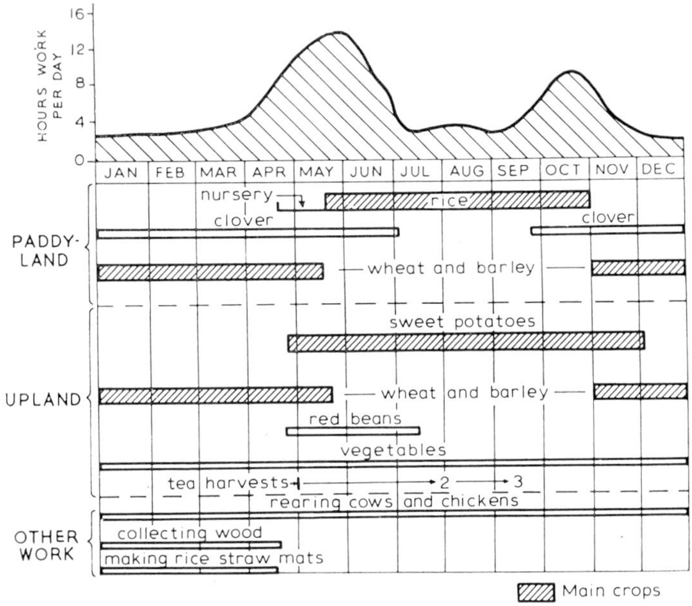

FIG. 42. The farm year in Tanaka.

rows and harvests these before the land has to be prepared for planting out the rice seedlings. This multicropping is only possible in southern Japan, where there is a long warm growing season and where the paddyland is well drained.

In Kumamoto 74% of the paddyfields are cropped more than once (fig. 43) and 62% of the upland fields. The latter often grow several crops. The overall land use rate in Japan, including the cold north where only one crop can be grown on the paddyfields, was 123% in 1965. The Moritas have little room for fodder on their precious land and have only two cows and one calf, a horse, one sheep and twenty chickens.

As in every prefecture in Japan, rice is the Moritas' most important crop (fig. 44). It takes up more than half their land in summer and brings in most of their income, though they also sell small quantities of eggs, milk, wheat, barley, potatoes, vegetables and wood. The farmers in Tanaka co-operate to prepare the rice nursery in a sheltered place near the *buraku*, adding fertilizer and manure to the soil and breaking it down into a fine loam. Then they vernalize the seeds by chilling them to make them sprout earlier, soak them for a week and then scatter them over the beds, which they cover with sheets of plastic to help to keep the ground warm. This makes the seeds germinate so rapidly that soon they are

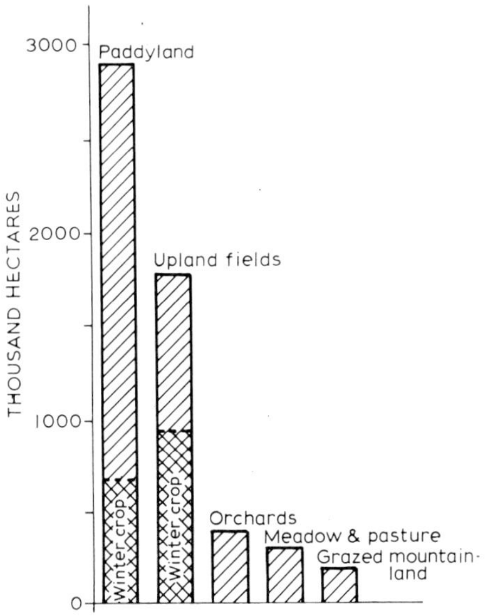

FIG. 43. Types of land use and winter cropping, 1965 (91).

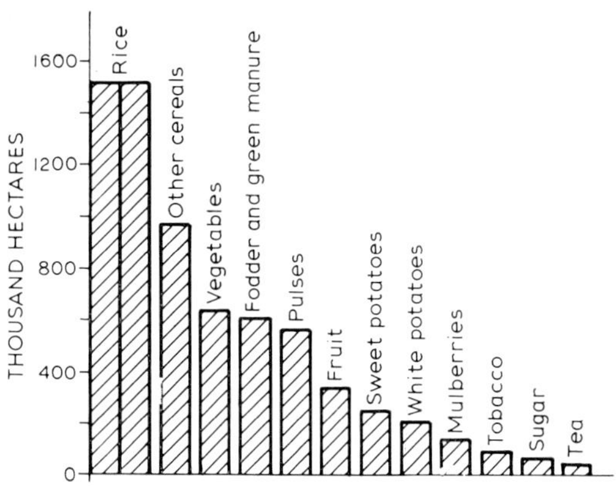

FIG. 44. The main crops grown in 1966 (91).

ready for thinning and, after only forty days, instead of the fifty for uncovered seedlings, they are ready to be transplanted. Meanwhile the Moritas plough their land (pl. 18) with a small power cultivator and break up the clods into fine particles to reduce seepage from the paddies. They flood the field to a depth of 1 or 2 inches with water from the river raised by a motor pump (fig. 46*a*), smooth over the mud and mark out the planting pattern with string ready to transplant the young plants. The men of the *buraku* pull up the young plants from the nursery beds, tie them into bundles and carry them to the carefully prepared paddyfields. Everyone who is free helps as the planting must be done quickly (pl. 19). Eight people can plant an acre in a day and it is a backbreaking job. Standing in the water they push clumps of three or four plants into the mud, following the marked pattern so that each is exactly in line both ways and 9 inches from its neighbours,

PLATE 18. The rural landscape is a busy one when the farmers prepare the riceland with hand cultivators in April. Bunds hold the irrigation water on the fields.

to ensure that the rotary hoe (fig. 45*f*) which is used for weeding, can easily be pushed through the mud between the rows.

In Japan today most rice is transplanted, since to grow it in a well-protected nursery saves water and leaves the main fields available for other crops while the seedlings are growing. The transplanted crop grows more evenly. After planting the field is hoed four times, at fortnightly intervals, with a rotary hoe. During this period the water on the fields is carefully controlled so that at night, or on cold days, the soil is covered by 2 or 3 inches of water to keep up the temperature. Everyone in Tanaka plays a part in keeping the irrigation channel from the nearby stream open and in controlling the water that flows from it on to the fields. When the plants are large enough they get together and spray all the *buraku* fields with

PLATE 19. Transplanting rice in May is women's work. The plants are carefully aligned so that a rotary hoe can be run between the rows to weed the crop and aerate the soil. The winter wheat and barley harvest has been hung up to dry on the racks behind as spring is not a dry season. The hills are terraced to grow upland crops.

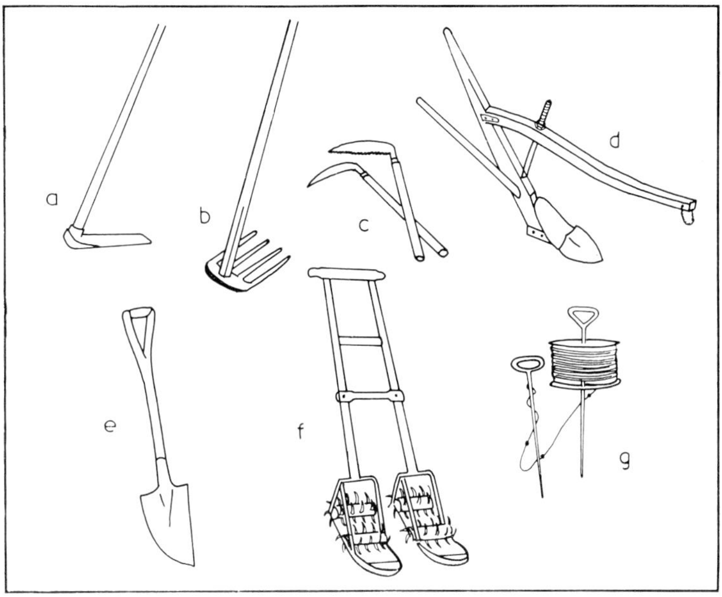

FIG. 45. Farm tools: (a) mattock, (b) fork, (c) sickle for harvesting, (d) plough drawn by horse or ox, (e) spade, (f) rotary hoe, (g) liner.

insecticide (pl. 20) and weed killer using new power sprays capable of treating all the fields in one day. Chemical fertilizer and night-soil is applied twice while the crop is growing. Tanaka has heavy rain in summer brought by the south-east monsoon, and this is supplemented with irrigation water, lifted by foot and motor pump, so that the rice gets 2 to 4 feet of water during the time it is growing. Three weeks before the harvest the fields are drained while the crop ripens and clover seed is undersown.

By mid-October, when the golden heads of rice hang heavily on the stalk,

PLATE 20. Spraying the ricefields with insecticide on the flat Nobi Plain.

harvesting (pl. 21) is a task for the whole family. As soon as the older children arrive home from school they go out to the fields and help to cut the crop with small sickles (fig. 45*c*) and lay it on the ground ready to be tied into bundles. Japan is very humid at harvest time and the rice is not dry enough to be threshed when it is cut, so it is tied into bundles and hung on racks round the fields to dry. The Moritas use a petrol-driven threshing machine in the field. Mr Morita feeds the head of each sheaf into the machine and his wife collects the grain in rice-straw sacks and piles up the bundles of straw. The grain is spread on mats in the yard by the house for three or four days to dry, and the straw is stored in the barn ready for bedding the animals, for making mats, bags for rice, *tatami* and many other things. Any that is left is chopped up and used on the fields as compost. The grain is packed in round, rice straw bags to go to the co-operative. The government controls the sale of rice and subsidizes the farmers who grow it, acting through the co-operative. Today much of the grain is hulled in local mills. The end of the harvest is marked by a joyous feast.

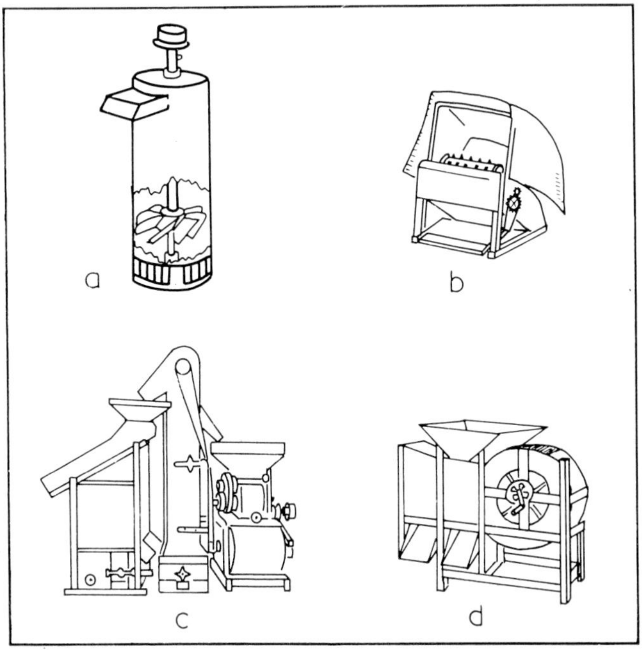

FIG. 46. Farm machinery: (a) irrigation pump, (b) pedal thresher (which are powered now), (c) huller, (d) winnower.

PLATE 21. The ears of rice are heavy. Each clump of rice plants is cut in October with a long-handled sickle and laid ready to be tied into sheaves. Autumn is a wet season and the ground is wet on the Nobi Plain. The sheaves are hung up to dry before being threshed.

As soon as the land is clear of the rice crop it is ploughed and ridged with a power cultivator to help drainage while the young wheat and barley are growing. The ridges, 15 inches high, run across the fields and two rows of seeds are sown in each (pls. 16 & 17). As soon as they are growing strongly the young plants are trampled by foot to compress the soil and encourage tillering. When the crop is nearly ripe beans are planted between some of the rows.

December, January and February are quiet months on the farm. Humus is collected from the forest and spread with farm manure, night-soil and artificial fertilizer on the fields; machines and implements are repaired and irrigation ditches, bunds and tractors made ready for the busy season beginning in March.

Farming in Japan uses a great deal of labour, and the cultivation of rice required about 320 man and 100 animal days per acre in 1958. The planting and harvesting that are the main jobs are only beginning to be mechanized effectively and, since there must be enough family labour available for these peak periods, there is under-employment at other seasons.

Much of the work on Japanese farms must still be done by hand and many Japanese implements (fig. 45) are pulled instead of pushed, so that much of a Japanese farmer's working time is spent in a doubled-up position. The mattock used for digging is raised above the head and then brought down into the earth, which is then pulled over; hoeing is done with a draw hoe. The increasing use of machinery has reduced the hard physical work required of the younger generation.

The Morita family has 2¼ acres of upland (pl. 22) that is too high above the river and covered by a diluvial soil that is too porous to be irrigated, so the crops grown there are quite different from those on the paddyland. They are more varied, including wheat, barley, fruit, vegetables, fodder crops and tea.

As the main summer crop on their upland fields they grow 1½ acres of sweet potatoes to feed their animals. With growing prosperity there is a good sale for milk in the towns, and more fodder is grown to feed livestock instead of mulberries to feed silkworms, as the price of silk has dropped with the advent of cheaper chemical fibres. Tea has replaced mulberry as it needs little looking after. Other summer crops include a wide variety of vegetables, such as giant radishes called *daikon* that grow up to 3 feet long and 3 or 4 inches thick and are pickled and eaten with almost every meal. Daikon takes up 15% of the whole vegetable area in Japan. Japanese cabbage, peas, soya and red beans and ground nuts are also grown. In the winter there is also a great variety of crops including cabbages, onions and potatoes, with clover and rape for fodder. All these crops thrive on the poorer soil and do not need irrigating.

The crops grown on the Moritas' farm, the use of upland and paddylands, the intensive multicropping and intercultivation practised, the small number of animals kept, and the methods used are typical of Japanese farms. It differs from farming in other areas by being more intensive and smaller than farms in the colder area north of Tokyo and larger than many farms in western Japan.

PLATE 22. The Moritas' upland fields on the diluvial terrace in January. Mr Morita's neighbour, beyond the persimmon tree, grows mulberries, but the Moritas have replaced theirs with young tea bushes interspersed with cabbages. Beyond the persimmon tree rise the clouds of steam from Mount Aso (220).

Farming Regions

Japan can be divided into farming regions based on three main criteria: the crops grown, the intensity of cropping and the size of farms. These are determined by variations in the climate, the period in which the area was first settled, the proximity of markets and the availability of other work.

It is much more difficult to divide Japan into farming regions than it is in most countries for, although there are climatic differences, the most important crops vary little from the north to the west. Their love of rice has led the Japanese to use great ingenuity in adapting its cultivation to their full range of climatic variation, so that everywhere in Japan, even in Hokkaido, rice is the dominant crop (fig. 47). The less important crops differ. In the north more beans, oats, pasture, white potatoes and cabbages are grown and farming is closer to the north-west European type. In the warmer west oranges, tea, mulberry and sweet potatoes can be grown. Wheat, barley, beans, vegetables and fruit are grown in addition to rice in every prefecture.

Since there are no major physiographic contrasts, as there are, for example, in the United States between the mountains of the west and the central plains, the local differences in mountains and plains, alluvial and diluvial land, rather than regional differences influence the crops grown. Most significant are three contrasting areas: first the alluvial paddyland in valleys and on plains which can be irrigated to grow rice, secondly the dry diluvial river terraces and other upland, where wheat, barley, fruit and vegetables are grown, and thirdly the steep mountains which remain forested. The relief of Japan is fragmented and there is paddyland, upland and forest in every prefecture. Ginsberg has (fig. 48) used the varying proportion of paddyland, upland and forest as a basis for agricultural divisions. This criterion shows how the pattern of land uses varies with physiography rather than regionally. It gives local fragments rather than large regions. Paddyland is dominant where there are large areas of alluvium; equal paddyland

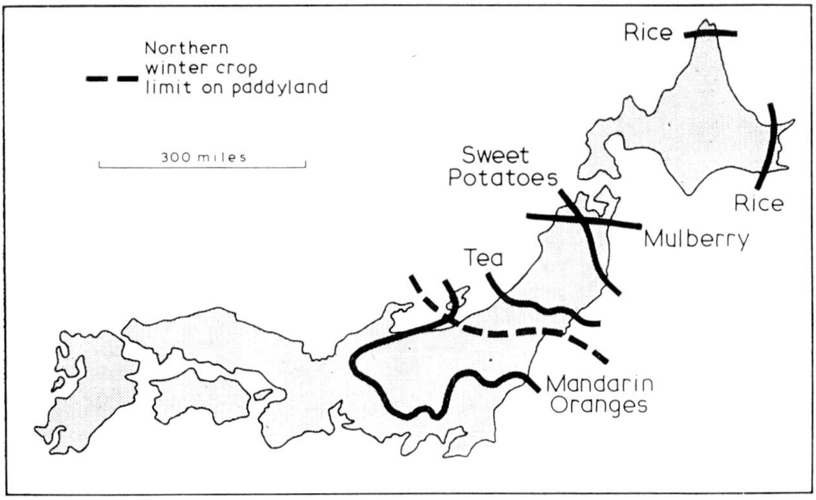

FIG. 47. The northern limits of some crops (12).

and upland areas occur where there are alluvial valleys bordered by diluvial terraces; upland exceeds paddyland on the volcanic land of south Kyushu, and in similar areas in Kanto where there is a limited area of alluvium; the mountains are forested.

To arrive at *regional divisions* one must consider other characteristics of the farming as well as its products. The size of farms (fig. 49), the intensity of farming (fig. 50) and the time of settlement (figs. 29 & 51) are all significant. South of Tokyo (36°N) the climate is warm enough for two crops a year to be grown on the rice fields (fig. 75). A summer crop of rice is followed by a winter crop of wheat, barley or vegetables. Farming is more intensive and a smaller farm will feed a family. This area was settled early (fig. 29) and in areas near the main industrial centres many farm people work in the cities. North of 37°N the winter is too cold for another crop after the rice harvest and more land is needed to feed a family, so that there farms are larger and farming is less intensive, especially in Hokkaido, which has been settled mainly since 1900.

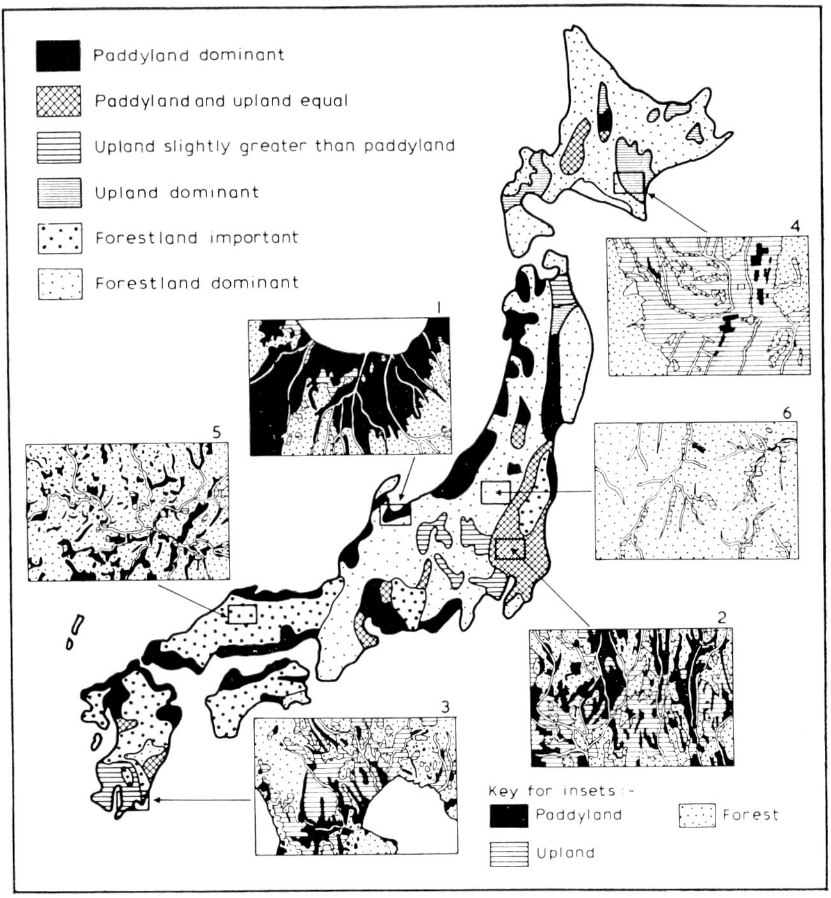

FIG. 48. Ginsberg's farming regions based on the proportion of paddyland, upland and forest (3).

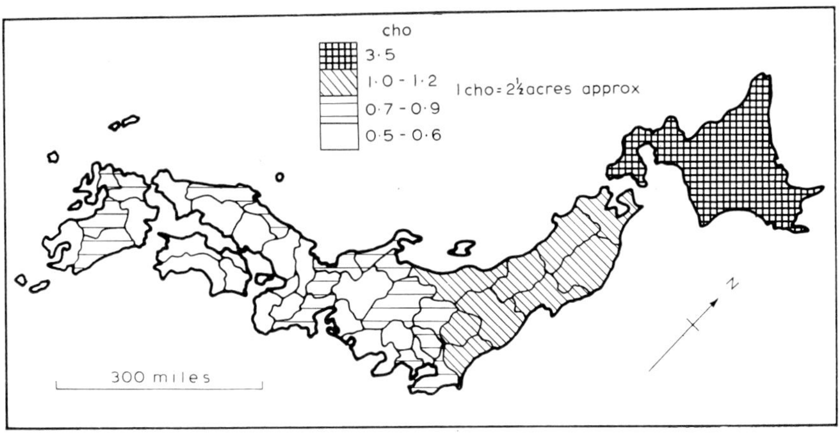

FIG. 49. Average farm size, 1965 (91).

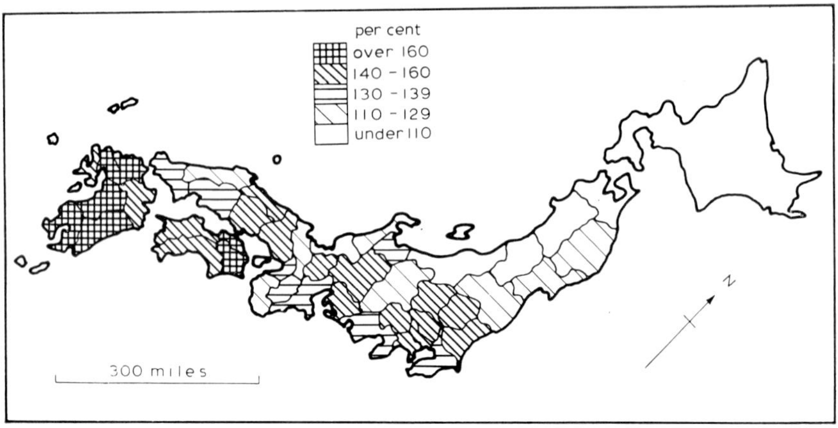

FIG. 50. Land use rate in 1961. Ratio of cropped to farmed area (91).

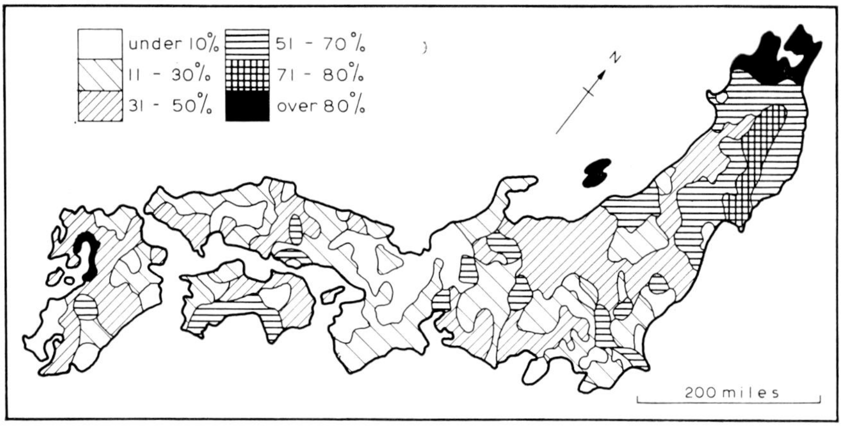

FIG. 51. The percentage of the cultivated area newly settled during Tokugawa times (Toshio Kikuchi).

The major division (146) therefore is into *Old Japan* (fig. 52 region 1) and colder *Hokkaido*, which has been more recently developed (region 2). Old Japan can be sub-divided into the Central Zone (1A) which was developed before Tokugawa times, and is farmed more intensively, and the Frontier Zone (1B), which is much less developed than the Central Zone because of its relative isolation and where there was much settlement in Tokugawa times and where new farmland is still being developed. The Central Zone can be further divided into the Core (1Aa) and the Peripheral (1Ab) Zones. The Core Zone was settled first and has the smallest farms which have been farmed for over a thousand years.

Hokkaido can be divided into the west where rice farming is important, the centre where a north-west European type of farming is dominant, and the newly developed eastern area.

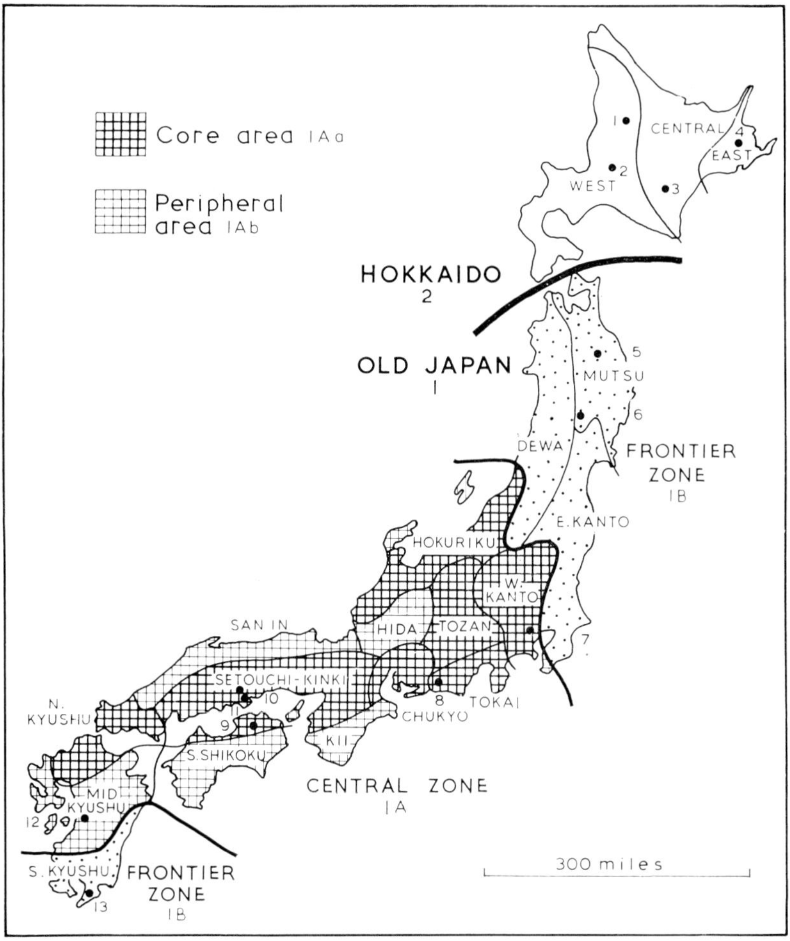

FIG. 52. Ogasawara's farming regions based on farm size, intensity of land use and crops grown.

Sample farms in text: 1 *page* 111, 2 *page* 112, 3 *page* 115, 4 *page* 151, 5 *page* 106, 6 *page* 106, 7 *page* 98, 8 *page* 125, 9 *page* 94, 10 *page* 149, 11 *page* 97, 12 *page* 77, 13 *page* 103 (146).

REGION 1. OLD JAPAN

The Core Zone

The Core Zone (1Aa) is the heartland of Japan and was the first area to be developed (fig. 29) and farms have been so sub-divided that they are now the smallest in Japan, averaging only $1\frac{1}{4}$ acres. Where there has been much pressure on the land and the climate allows it, two or more crops are grown each year, so that the land use rates are among the highest in Japan. Because most of Japan's great centres of population are in this area farmers grow fruit, vegetables and flowers and rear animals to supply meat and dairy produce. Great pressure on farmland has caused hillsides to be terraced (pl. 31) to increase the farming area, and many farmers supplement their incomes by working in the cities.

The Core Zone can be sub-divided into (*a*) Setouchi-Kinki, (*b*) north Kyushu, (*c*) Chukyo, (*d*) Tokai, (*e*) west Kanto, (*f*) Tosan and (*g*) Hokuriku.

Setouchi-Kinki includes the main centre of the ancient heartland of Japan round the Inland Sea. It is a region of small, intensive, diversified farms in scattered basins and on small plains with 80% of the paddyland winter cropped. Here fruit, vegetables and animals for supplying the cities are particularly important. Fruit grows well on upland fields in the relatively hot, dry summer away from maritime influences, and the northern shores of the Inland Sea are especially famed for their beef cattle.

Over many hundreds of years every possible piece of cultivable land has been brought into use. Many hillsides are terraced and, with the increased demand for mandarin oranges and other fruits, orchards are creeping up the hillsides so that in western Shikoku, and on islands in the Inland Sea, terracing now stretches from sea level to the tops of the hills (pl. 5). The most fantastic terraces are near Uwajima where, in the summer, farmers grow sweet potatoes on terraces that are often only a foot wide, with a 6-foot drop, faced with a stone wall, to the terrace below. In the winter rows of wheat fill these narrow shelves. Terraces like this are rare in Japan for most farmland is on plains or diluvial terraces.

Two examples from Setouchi-Kinki

Bocho buraku (pl. 23, fig. 53) in Kagawa Prefecture in the Setouchi-Kinki area (fig. 52 no. 9) (220) is in the crowded Sanuki Plain of northern Shikoku. Farming in Bocho is among the most intensive and diversified in Japan, for multicropping and interculture are made possible by the warm climate. Today its long, dry summer is assisted by the increasing use of plastic to bring on young seedlings. The use of machinery also makes rapid preparation of the ground possible and this lifted the land use rate to 162%, one of the highest in Japan in 1965.

Bocho has been settled for over a thousand years. Farms were set up under the *Jori* system (p. 160) and its square field pattern is very clear today, even though some *buraku*, such as Bocho, have overlapped their original rectangular boundaries. Farmhouses in most Japanese *burakus* are grouped, but in Bocho they are scattered through the *buraku* land.

Two-thirds of Japan's irrigation water comes from diverted streams, but in Bocho the streams coming from the nearby hills have very small drainage basins and the gradients are steep, so that the small amount of rain that falls runs off rapidly. Farmers therefore store water by damming the small streams in the hills and building square ponds among the paddyfields where the scant water supply is carefully conserved. These take up a sixth of the paddyland area. Artesian water is used for irrigation on many alluvial plains.

Farms in Bocho are very small, averaging only 2 acres, though they are above the $1\frac{1}{4}$ acres average for the whole of Kagawa, where more than 90% of the farms have less than $2\frac{1}{2}$ acres of land. Mr Fujisawa has a farm of 3 acres. His land is in four blocks near his house.

PLATE 23. *Jori* grid on the Sanuki Plain. The *buraku* just to the east of Bocho from the south-east showing the *jori* grid and tiled, prosperous and scattered farmhouses and barns. The paddyland has a winter cereal crop and there are fruit trees on the slope in the foreground. Forest has been cleared from the lower slopes of the hills and orchards have been planted (220).

The Fujisawas farm very intensively, taking two crops from two-thirds of their land and three from the other third. Some of the fast-maturing rice that they plant on all their 3 acres in May is harvested in August or early September, in time for them to plant sugar beet and vegetables. They harvest the later varieties of rice in late October, and the wheat seedlings, that have already been sprouted, are planted out. A month before the wheat harvest in May the heads are tied up in bunches to make room for young melon, tomato and pumpkin plants, which have been brought on under plastic sheeting.

In addition to the rice and wheat that everyone grows, farmers in Kagawa specialize in growing melons, tobacco, *igusa*, young trees or the gnarled *bonsai* trees, grapes, tomatoes, chickens, cucumbers, pumpkins, flowers or peaches. Farming is becoming increasingly intensive as the area under wheat falls and is replaced by more fruit, vegetables and flowers and the fodder crops that are fed to the growing number of dairy* cattle that supply the cities in the Hanshin

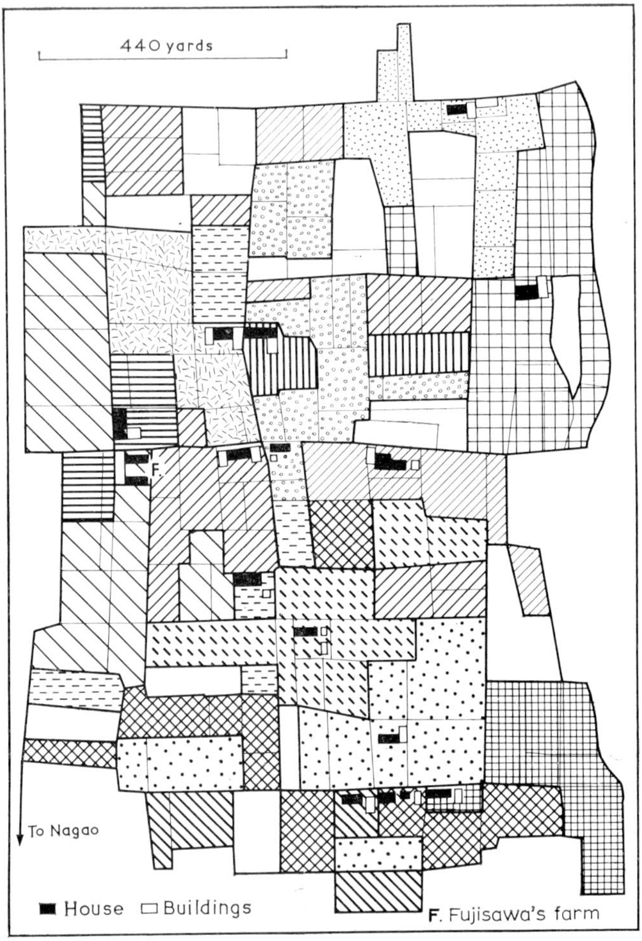

FIG. 53. Bocho *buraku* showing the *jori* grid and scattered farm-houses with their farmland.

region. Bocho farmers mainly depend on their farm incomes and these intensive crops keep them fully occupied. Only two have a large percentage of their incomes from other sources.

Even where more intensive and more remunerative cropping is possible each farmer in Bocho usually continues to grow some rice, relying on the security

* By 1968 the Fujisawas had 27 dairy cows.

of guaranteed rice prices. There is a deep-rooted feeling in Japan that a farmer should grow the rice his family needs. This subsistence attitude to farming for life, rather than for profit, holds back progress in mainland Asia. Sometimes by growing crops for sale and buying food for the family, incomes could be raised and prosperity increased. There are still some relics of this attitude in Japan.

Bocho is advanced in farm mechanization. Prosperity and close contact with city life is helping in this, as is the need for speedy cultivation to succeed in growing a number of crops during the year. Farmers here have had irrigation pumps for thirty years; by 1960 five power cultivators were shared between the fifteen houses and each of three co-operative working groups owned a huller and power spray, though they still had ten working cattle.

Farmers in Bocho are relatively progressive. Some have constructed easily maintained cement bunds to increase their field area and prevent seepage, while one has built himself a concrete, western-style farmhouse, which is unusual in rural Japan. Some take advantage of the sunny climate to heat their domestic water supply in a glass-covered tank on the roof, raising the temperature of the water several degrees even in the winter and so saving fuel. The co-operative runs a telephone service which gives a news bulletin each morning. Incomes from the intensive, efficiently grown crops are high enough to enable them to buy cameras, watches, electrical goods and motor-bicycles (seven in Bocho) in the shops in Nagao half a mile away.

Niiike buraku (220) in Okayama Prefecture (fig. 52 no. 11) is a second example. It lies to the north of the Inland Sea and has been very fully described by Beardsley, Hall and Ward in their book *Village Japan* (120). It is typical of many Japanese *buraku* in its upland and paddyland crops (pl. 24).

Their maps (figs. 54 & 55) show very clearly the contrast between the summer and winter crop patterns. In summer the small bunded paddyfields are almost entirely devoted to rice, all the upland is used for vegetables or fruit and the steeper hills are forested, providing fuels and humus.

There is a wide variety of winter crops, except in the east where the land is poorly drained. Upland fields grow vegetables, wheat or barley, and paddyland is used predominantly for wheat, barley and *igusa* (p. 149). See also pages 155 and 158 for further details about Niiike.

(*b*) In *north Kyushu* farming is less diversified than in Setouchi-Kinki. More rice is cultivated than in other parts of the Core Zone as there is a larger area of plain. Incomes are high, as there is opportunity for farm families to work in factories in Kitakyushu.

(*c*) In *Chukyo* farming differs because there is a very large area of paddyland surrounded by diluvial upland. There is opportunity for farm families to earn an income outside farming.

(*d*) *Tokai* lies along the great routeway from Kyoto to Tokyo and is crushed between the mountains and the sea. It is warmed by offshore currents and so particularly well suited to the growing of mandarin oranges. Valleys are narrow and 45% of the area cultivated is upland fields, where the warm sandy soils and the easy access to markets have led to the development of market gardening. Fruit, especially mandarins, peaches, grapes and strawberries, are grown as well as tea and all sorts of vegetables; animals are reared. An example of farming in Tokai will be found on page 125.

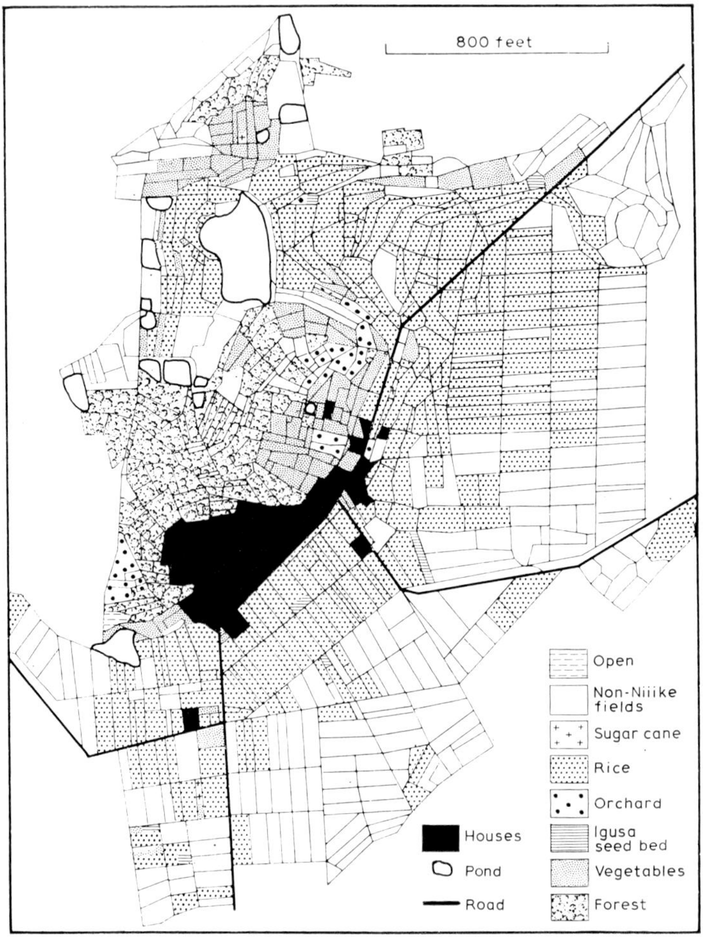

FIG. 54. Summer crops in Niiike *buraku* (120).

(*e*) *West Kanto* has a high proportion of plain and therefore of cultivated land, 70% of which is diluvial terrace (fig. 11) cropped twice a year. This area is one of the largest areas of upland farming in Japan (pl. 25) but there are many alluvial valleys (fig. 48 no. 2) (220). A third of Japan's wheat and half her barley is grown here on the porous diluvial soils. They do not need a great deal of water, but other crops suffer in the droughts that affect the Kanto area about every three years. The leached soil has an impervious iron pan about 2 feet below the surface which can cause waterlogging after heavy rain, and prevents soil water from coming to the surface in dry periods. This hinders the full development of the root system of deep-rooted plants but is not of great importance

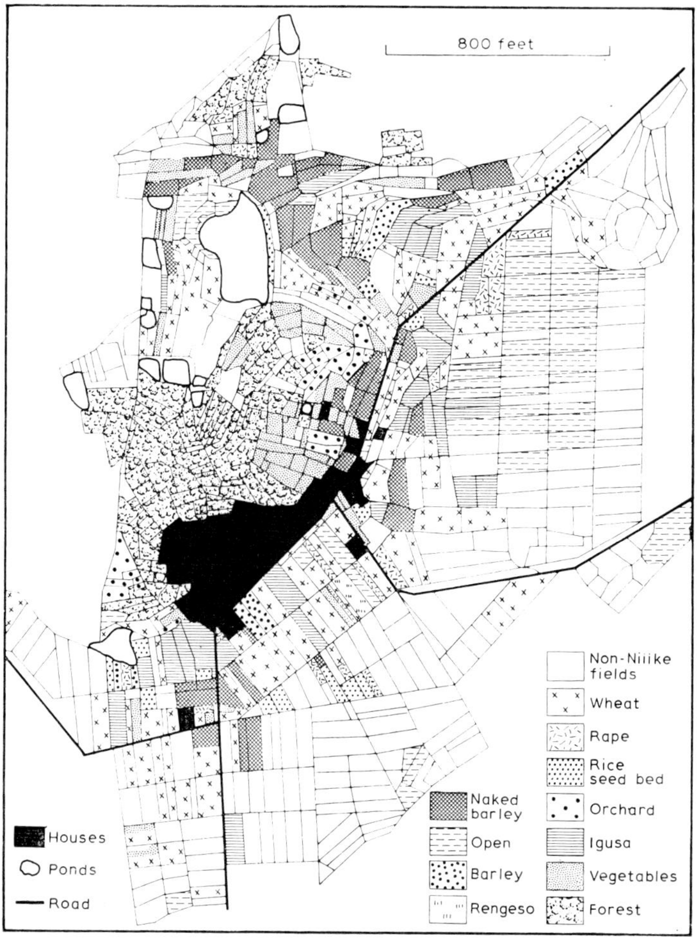

FIG. 55. Winter crops in Niiike *buraku* (120).

for the shallow-rooted cereal crops. It is an important area for mulberries, and the warm, light, early upland soils are well suited to soya beans and vegetables for the Tokyo market. Upland rice is widely grown here and milk, meat and eggs are also important. Small farms are often very intensive (pl. 33).

(*f*) *Tosan* is a high mountainous area cut by such deep narrow trenches that little of the area can be cultivated (fig. 48 no. 6) (220) and most is still forested (pl. 28). Rice is grown on the narrow valley floors but most of the farmland is upland fields on river terraces and mountain slopes. In the more accessible areas farms are progressive and prosperous and yields are high. Fruit, vegetables and animal products are sent to the nearby cities. Mulberry bushes feed the worms that produce over half Japan's silk in Tosan and west Kanto.

Above the paddyfields on the valley floor and the better upland fields with their fruit, mulberries, vegetables and flowers, cultivation is less intensive and there is poor subsistence farming (fig. 56). Crops of wheat, barley, potatoes, soya beans

PLATE 24. Niiike (220) from the south in February shows the many small bunded plots of ridged paddyland under winter crops scattered with rice-straw ricks. Behind, like so many *burakus*, Niiike clusters at the foot of the hills which are covered with woods and orchards.

and maize are grown in a two-year rotation with three crops in each two-year period. This is the common system in mountain areas (see p. 106). Above 3,000 feet, where the winter is too cold for crops to be in the ground all the year and the growing season is shorter, crops of potatoes, barley, and higher up of buck-wheat or rye are grown. In some of the larger plateau areas the government is experimenting in pasture development, but in most places the forest comes down to the edge of the cultivated area at about 4,000 feet and there is no Alpine meadowland above the tree line as there is in Europe.

(*g*) The coastal plains of northern *Hokuriku* are important rice-producing areas where yields are high, and farms relatively large. There is much mechanization,

PLATE 25. Sugaya (220), on a diluvial terrace on the Kanto Plain, is typical of upland farming in this area. The land is all cropped in the winter with wheat, barley and vegetables. These are sheltered by surrounding hedges of tea and mulberries from cold north winds. In the summer sweet potatoes, soya beans and upland rice are grown. In the narrow valleys there are paddyfields.

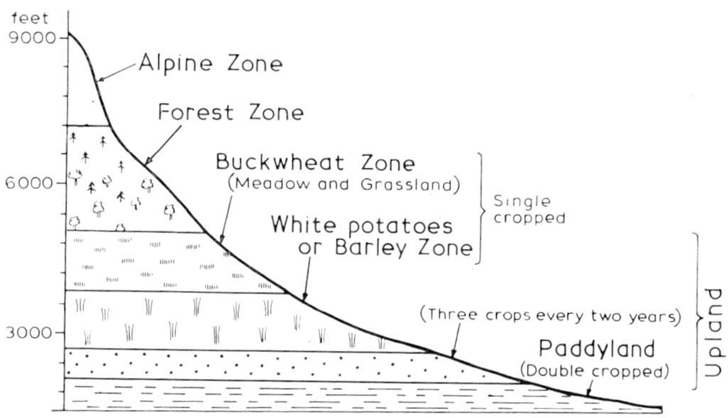

FIG. 56. The zonation of crops near Nagano in Tosan. The same pattern is found in other mountain areas (8).

and large surpluses of rice are produced. In spite of the cold winters 45% of the paddyland is cropped in winter but mainly with green manure crops. More than 75% of the farmers earn income from doing other work.

The Peripheral Zone

The Peripheral Zone (1Ab), including the mountains of south Shikoku and Kii and the Japan Sea coast, is more isolated than the Core Zone and some of it was only developed during early Tokugawa times. Farms are slightly larger and farming is less progressive and less intensive with less double cropping than in the Core Zone. Most of Japanese shifting agriculture is in this area. Farmers are less influenced by the cities and yields are lower with many poor crops of corn, millet and buckwheat. Mountain grasslands are used for beef rearing and most of Japan's soft timber is produced in this area. This zone can be sub-divided into four areas (*a*) mid-Kyushu, (*b*) San In, (*c*) southern Shikoku and Kii, (*d*) Hida.

(*a*) *Mid-Kyushu* is the most accessible and most prosperous area in the zone. Farms are somewhat larger than elsewhere in the zone and crops are varied. Fruit, mulberries and vegetables are grown, as well as rice. In central Kyushu, on the slopes of Mount Aso, there is a large area of pasture used as grazing for cattle. An example of farming in mid-Kyushu is the Moritas' farm (page 77).

(*b*) *San In* is much like the rest of the Japan Sea coast. In spite of being so far south there is little winter cultivation because drainage is poor and there is heavy winter precipitation. Draught and beef-cattle are important. It was one of the centres of Yayoi culture but the mountains of Chugoku isolated it from the nearby Yamato heartland.

(*c*) In the *Shikoku* mountains there is still some shifting cultivation in which the forest is burned and *mitsumata* for Japanese paper is grown as well as poor crops of maize, beans, buckwheat and millet.

(*d*) *Hida* is the most inhospitable, isolated, mountain area with few fertile valleys, a very sparse population and a high degree of subsistence farming. Forestry is important.

THE FRONTIER ZONE

The Frontier Zone (1B) includes (*a*) Southern Kyushu and (*b*) Tohoku. These areas were settled more recently than the Central Zone, mainly during and since Tokugawa times (fig. 51), and are still less fully developed than the Central Zone and less intensively cultivated. They are isolated from the main centres of population and are relatively backward, so that yields are low, incomes are the lowest in Japan and there is a large proportion of subsistence farmers who have few outside jobs.

South Kyushu

(*a*) In subtropical South Kyushu (fig. 52 no. 13) farming is among the most intensive in Japan with 151% land use rate but farms are so small, averaging only $1\frac{1}{2}$ acres, methods so backward, and so much of the farmed land has a thin soil on granite, or an infertile, light volcanic upland soil, that yields are low. Since there is little other work in this area 45% of the working population are farmers, more than anywhere else in Japan. The warm climate in south Kyushu makes it possible to grow oranges, lemons and sugar cane as well as early vegetables, fruit and flowers; but although these fetch high prices farms are so small that the average income for the farmers here is the lowest in Japan. Most farmers grow cereals and sweet and white potatoes on their upland fields to feed their families.

Fruit and vegetable growing and stock rearing are only slowly becoming more important.

An example from South Kyushu

Farming in Minamidani *buraku* (fig. 52 no. 13) in Neshime town on the east side of Kagoshima Bay is representative of the small-scale, poor upland farming in Kagoshima Prefecture in the Frontier Zone of south Kyushu. Kagoshima Bay is formed by two great calderas, mainly drowned by the sea. The town of Neshime lies on an alluvial plain inside the eastern edge of the southern caldera and behind it the caldera rim rises precipitously to north, south and east (pl. 26), and is capped by a resistant layer of basalt. Through this hard layer, deep, steep-sided, narrow canyons have been eroded in thick white, powdery ash. The basalt plateau on top is covered with black ash.

Minamidani *buraku* (pl. 27) lies in a narrow valley cut into a platform 200 feet above Neshime. It is less prosperous than most Japanese *burakus* but the houses are quite large, with four raised, *tatami*-covered rooms and a mud-floored kitchen with a wood-fired mud stove next to the working space where tools are mended and other household jobs done. Above, on the rafters, the family rice, barley and home-made soya sauce are stored under the dilapidated, thatched roof.

Farm incomes are low in Minamidani as in the whole of Kagoshima because farms average only 1¾ acres and ¾ acre of this consists mainly of very poor upland fields. There are few jobs away from the land to supplement farm incomes. From Minamidani some people work in the local rice mill, the starch-extracting plant, the tea-processing factory and the timber mill. Some are road builders, one is an insurance agent, another an electrician, there is an office worker and the secretary of a co-operative.

Isolation has hindered the spread of the knowledge of new farming methods, and the great distance from city markets, combined with poor soil and a lack of capital, have prevented progress and kept incomes low. Farmers concentrate on growing rice, barley and small quantities of fruit and vegetables to feed the family, producing very little for sale. Yields of rice and most other crops are below the national average.

Mr Tomita's farm is typical of this region. He has 2½ acres of paddyland and 3¾ acres of upland and on most of this he produces at least two crops a year to give a land use rate of 230%. He has two working cows and sells the calves for meat. He plants rice on his 2½ acres of paddyland in summer, but yields are low as the soil is poor and disease spreads easily in the hot climate. Typhoons in August and September frequently damage the crop while it is heading. In winter almost all this land is under barley. In the spring five neighbours, who have spare time, pay rent and plant a crop of tobacco between the rows of barley that is growing on 1¼ acres of the paddyland. Together with eastern Kanto this is the most important tobacco-growing area in Japan.

The upland crops on poor ash soil are more varied. In summer sweet potatoes, low-yielding upland rice and small quantities of ground nuts and vegetables are grown. Orange and persimmon trees fruit in the autumn and in winter there are crops of rape, barley, oats and fodder.

Mr Tomita has 16 acres of land on the plateau where he clears 4 acres at a time and then crops the land for ten years with sweet potatoes, rape and barley. It is then reafforested with pines, which are large enough after thirty years to be cut for

PLATE 26. Paddyfields in Neshime growing cereals and vegetables inside the wall of the caldera (220). There are upland fields on the highland to the right.

pulp. Then the land is cropped for another ten years. This system helps to prevent excessive erosion of the light powdery soils. Mr Tomita's farm is unusual in also having as many as 60 acres of pine, cypress and bamboo forest on the slopes of the plateau, which provide the main part of the family income. The choice of a cash crop on a Minamidani farm depends on its size and the size of the family. Mr Tomita, who has a relatively large farm on which he and his wife and parents do all the work, farms less intensively than other farmers. After timber, rice is his main source of income, followed by the sweet potatoes that go to the starch factory in the valley, rape seed for oil, and barley. All the other full-time farmers use their land more intensively and tobacco is their main source of income, followed by rice. The smaller, part-time farmers either put all their land under rice, barley and sweet potatoes, which require relatively little work and supply their food needs, and concentrate on their work off the farm, or they farm intensively, growing vegetables including cucumbers, peas and tomatoes, sometimes covering them with plastic sheeting to get an earlier crop.

PLATE 27. Ploughing with an ox in Minamidani which lies above the valley in plate 26. Most farmers in Minamidani *buraku* still use animals to pull the plough.

Minamidani incomes are very low, as methods are poor and vegetable crops are open to the competitition of those grown nearer the cities. They could be raised by improving farming methods and growing more profitable products including fruit and sugar beet, and rearing cattle for meat.

Tohoku

(*b*) Tohoku is colder and has larger, less intensive farms averaging over $2\frac{1}{2}$ acres. Only one crop a year can be grown on the paddyfields and the land use rate is less than 120%. There are three sub-regions in Tohoku: Mutsu, Dewa and east Kanto. *Mutsu* in eastern Tohoku is one of the poorest regions in Japan. The isolated upland area is backward and little developed. Summers are too cool for rice, so subsistence farmers grow only poor crops of millet, buckwheat, oats and potatoes on unirrigated land. Shifting agriculture and horse breeding were important before the war; recently dairying has increased.

Two examples from Tohoku

On the *Kitakami Plateau*, despite the large average size of farms of 5 to 7 acres, yields are so low that farmers are very poor. The plateau is sometimes called the 'Tibet' of Japan because its poor communications isolate it from the lowland areas. Buses have only served this area for the last ten years and some of the homes still have no electricity. Much of the cultivation is still done with a spade and new farming methods spread very slowly. Conditions for farming on the plateau are not easy, as the granite is often covered with bog or poor volcanic ash which is rapidly eroded on the steep valley sides leaving bare rock. Only the network of narrow valley floors can be used as paddyland (pl. 28, fig. 48 no. 6, fig. 52 no. 5) (220). Yields are low because the soil is poor and easily eroded, there is little water for irrigation, the winter is cold and long and the summer is chilled by fog that drifts inland from the sea where the warm Kuroshio meets the cold Kurile Current offshore. About every third year the fog reduces the temperature to below an average of 20°C in July and halves the rice crop, which in any case yields only half the average Japanese figure. On the upland fields crops are planted in a rotation to give three crops in two years. Usually wheat and barley are planted in the winter followed the next summer with soya beans, which are the main cash crop, and then by millet. In some parts of the plateau, as in other mountainous areas in Japan, shifting cultivation is practised.

Army horses were raised on the plateau before the war and Iwate is still second to Hokkaido in the size of its horse population. Cattle are increasing especially for beef as milk collection is difficult from the scattered farms. Maize and rape are grown as fodder. There is little that farmers can do to supplement their incomes but make charcoal from the forests that still clothe most of the plateau. Better communications are important for any further development but it is expensive to serve such a widely scattered population.

There is a great contrast between upland and valley farming in Tohoku. In the valleys and on the coastal plains rice farms are large and relatively prosperous, though it is too cold in winter to grow a second crop on the paddyland.

Teramukai buraku near Maezawa (fig. 52 no. 6) is representative of the paddy-farming areas. It lies in a small tributary valley of the Kitakami River near Maezawa in southern Iwate Prefecture, where the climate is intermediate between that of Kagoshima in the south and Hokkaido in the north. The winters are cold with the temperature in January averaging −2°C (28°F) and snow usually lies from late November until the end of March.

The valley floor at Teramukai slopes down to the river, so that to make more profitable paddyland much of the ground has been levelled and baulked to form broad terraces. About a third of the slopes are still covered with unirrigated upland fields. Farmers grow rice in the paddyfields in the summer, but the growing season is too short for a winter crop. Two crops a year can be planted on the upland fields: soya beans and vegetables in summer and wheat, barley and vegetables in winter.

Teramukai *buraku* is made up of thirteen houses, but unlike Tanaka, where the

PLATE 28. Mount Takeo 25 miles west of Tokyo is dissected by deep valleys into sharp ridges. Most of the land is still forested, some is in its virgin state but most has been replanted. The narrow valleys are the only area flat enough for cultivation (220).

houses are grouped, here they are scattered across the *buraku* lands. In spite of this the *buraku* is socially very closely knit. There are only two main families in the *buraku*, the Kikuchis and the Chibas, and in each group the head house owns the allegiance of four branch houses. Before the post-war land reform was carried out these head households were often the landlords. There are three unrelated families in the *buraku*: one a Chiba and another a Kikuchi whose land is apart from the rest of the *buraku*, and the Sakazaki family who run the small village store.

Before the war a farmer's land here was scattered in anything from five to twenty holdings, but now farmlands in Teramukai have been consolidated. It took three years and much discussion to reach the agreement that made each farm into a convenient, compact block near its farmhouse.

Tohoku is less progressive than other parts of Japan. There is very little farm machinery in eastern Tohoku and horses are being replaced only very slowly. Maezawa has a Meiji milk-processing factory and Teramukai's four milk cows are a new departure and add to the farm income. In winter they are fed on clover grass and silage of corn, grass and turnips supplemented by the purchase of beans and wheat.

Many people in Iwate supplement their farm income during the winter, some working in the forests, others building roads, constructing dams, terracing land and building new irrigation and drainage canals and ditches, while the rest work in their homes making baskets and preparing tobacco leaves, but jobs are not easy to find and no one is well paid.

In contrast, *Dewa* on the west coast of Tohoku has relatively large mechanized farms on the heavy fertile soil of the narrow coastal plain, which is well irrigated in spring by melt water from snow on the mountains and is the most important rice-growing area in Japan producing a large surplus for sale. Farmers depend almost entirely on the rice that ripens well in the hot summer, since the winter is too cold and the fields too wet for a winter crop and there are few other jobs available.

In spite of its nearness to Tokyo, *East Kanto* is cut off from the city influence by the frequent flooding of the lower Tone and farming has only recently begun to improve. The large area of diluvial terrace is used to grow subsistence crops in both summer and winter, but there is marshland and diluvium which could be reclaimed to grow vegetables for the Tokyo market.

REGION 2. HOKKAIDO

Farming in Hokkaido has been developed since 1869, when the island had only 58,000 inhabitants mainly on the coasts of the southern peninsula (fig. 29) engaged in fishing and subsistence farming. The Meiji government began large-scale development of Hokkaido in 1869, with military settlements as a strategic measure against the expansion of Russia from the islands to the north, and to make use of Hokkaido's resources for the growing population. The military settlements were mainly in the Ishikari Valley and were laid out with houses along either side of a road and square fields. The army proved to be not altogether successful as farmers, and after 1895 Hokkaido was developed by subsidizing colonists who wished to emigrate. The development extended rapidly eastwards after 1890 and new lands were laid out on the American homesteading system with a grid of 12½ acre plots each with its own farmhouse. This area was regarded as adequate for a family. Thus there were the four phases of development: first the coastal fishing and poor farming in the south, next military and later development of the riceland in the western half of the island, and thirdly, especially between 1910 and 1930, the development of the eastern upland farming area with beans, pastures, oats and many crops new to Japan. Finally the present stage of colonization further east for stock farming in an area with poorer soils and a cool climate.

Farms in Hokkaido are six times the average size in Old Japan and less intensively cultivated; with such a cold winter the land use rate is only 100% (that is one crop a year). Even in the colder climate of Hokkaido, rice takes up the largest area of any crop in spite of alluvial land being limited (fig. 57). It is grown whereever irrigation is possible, except in the far north and east where the summer is too cold for it to ripen. It occupies 20% of the farmed land compared with 44% for Japan as a whole. In the east, where the upland fields are dominant, farming is much more like that of western Europe than in other parts of Japan. Horses plough the fields and crops of beans, potatoes, oats and sugar beet are grown. Of Japan's pasture land 90% is in Hokkaido as is a third of her forage crop. Pasture and forage crops are used to feed cows, which produce 26% of Japan's milk supply and 80% of her processed dairy products. Pigs, sheep and chickens are also important. Farming is more commercialized than in most parts of Japan.

Most of the soil in Hokkaido is poor and yields are low. There is little alluvium except in the west, and bog and diluvial and volcanic soils are poor. To the north of the mountains the soil is heavy clay, while to the south much of it has developed on recent deposits of volcanic ash so it is light and lacks humus. In the valleys of the Ishikari, Teisho, Tokachi and Kushiro rivers there are large areas of peat soil. Because of the poor acid soil and cold climate farming is difficult, though rice yields are now above the average and oats, potatoes and beans do well. Further reclamation of marsh and forest land could double the cultivated area in Hokkaido.

Unlike farmers in Old Japan, many of whom earn much of their incomes from non-agricultural work, most Hokkaido farmers are more fully occupied with their larger farms and only 16% of their income is earned from outside farming. Farmers made up 16% of the work force here compared with 19% for Japan as a whole in 1967. Fishing, forestry, iron and steel and mining are all important.

Hokkaido can be divided into three regions. The *west* was developed earliest and most of Hokkaido's paddyland is here in the Ishikari Valley and the Kamikawa and other basins. Farms are smaller than in other parts of Hokkaido. The *central* area was developed especially between 1910 and 1920. Most of the land is upland and the farms are larger, three or four times the average for Hokkaido. The larger

25-acre, west European style farms rear stock and grow pasture, fodder and cash crops. In the colder *eastern* pioneering area farms are large but poor, as the cold climate and poor volcanic soil are only suitable for growing potatoes, oats and buckwheat, and pasturing animals.

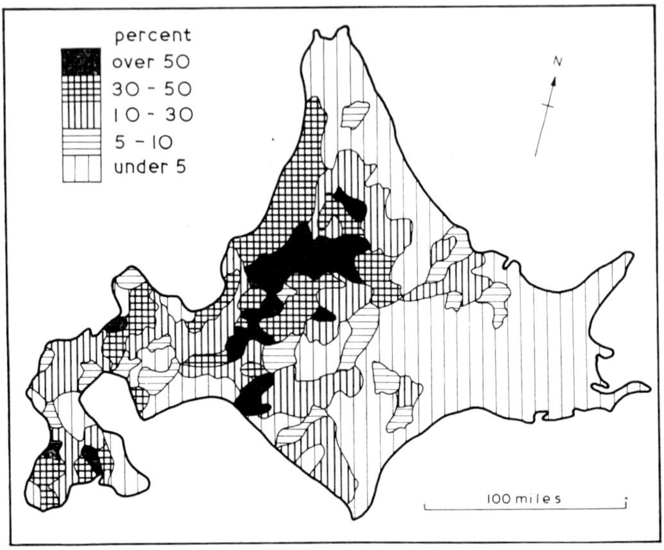

FIG. 57. Paddyland in Hokkaido in 1957 (*after Hideo Fukui*).

(a) The West

The first settlement in Hokkaido was in the Oshima Peninsula, where the climate is not very different from that in Old Japan and subsistence rice farming could be carried on, but further north the rice crops failed and farmers were forced to turn to potatoes, oats and hay and to develop the type of west European farming that is found on the Tokachi Plain. It was not until new cold-resistant and fast-maturing varieties of rice were developed after 1893 that rice became a successful crop in Hokkaido. It spread to its present limits by 1930.

Hokkaido rice production is now centred in the Kamikawa Basin where, sheltered from maritime influences, the summer temperatures are high, averaging 20°C–22°C (68°F–72°F) in July and August which suits rice very well. In 1896 an irrigation association was formed in Kamikawa and, with government encouragement, rice growing became widespread. By the end of the 1920's varieties of rice were developed that could be grown everywhere in Hokkaido except the cold north and the east coast where fog reduces the July temperature to 18°C (65°F). Present varieties still need an average temperature of at least 20°C (68°F) in July and August. During the decade up to 1930 the rice area in Hokkaido doubled and yields increased, so that rice became the most important crop. It now occupies 20% of Hokkaido's cultivated area and produces about 55% of farm products and its yields are among the highest in Japan. Fruit, especially apples, are also important.

An example from Western Hokkaido

Mr Saito's farm near Aibetsu (fig. 52 no. 1) in the Kamikawa Basin is like many rice farms in western Hokkaido; his house is adapted from the normal Japanese pattern to withstand the extreme cold of the winter for temperatures in January average −10°C (14°F). To shelter themselves from the strong cold winds from Siberia the Saitos have a cypress windbreak along the west and north sides of their house and instead of *shoji* they have solid walls and double sliding glass windows. Inside the house their thin metal stove roars as the wood burns, making the rooms cosier in winter than anywhere else in Japan. This is only a winter concession to the Hokkaido climate, for in summer the stove, and the metal pipe that leads the smoke away across the ceiling, is stored away. Some people use a Russian type *petchka* in which the hot air from the fire is led through flues in a brick wall so that the warm wall radiates heat to the room.

Mr Saito's farm differs from those in Old Japan because it is in a larger compact unit near his house. There are 10 acres of riceland, which is about the usual size in this area, and he has ¾ acre of upland where beans are grown for sale and dent corn to feed the animals. Since there are only three workers in the family they need to employ a woman from Tohoku for eight months in the summer. With his horse, four Corridale sheep and forty chickens he has more livestock than most paddyfarmers in Old Japan. Recently he planted 30 acres of fir trees on the mountainside nearby. He will sell the timber in due course.

As on other farms on Hokkaido Mr Saito's rice yield has increased very rapidly during the last decade, because his farming methods and seeds have improved. Before the war Hokkaido farmers used to sow their seed directly in the paddyfields using an implement with a row of evenly spaced tubes. Because of the low germination rate, they put thirty seeds in each group. Two-thirds of Hokkaido rice was sown in this way because it saved the labour of transplanting where farms were so much larger than in Old Japan. Since the war it has become usual to sow seeds in nursery beds and cover them with plastic sheeting. This makes it possible to sow seeds earlier and bring the plants along more quickly. Some of the nursery beds are even heated by electric wires buried under the soil. The seedlings from the nursery beds make an early start and are transplanted in long rows 16 inches apart running north–south, allowing 5 inches between the groups in the rows. The combination of relatively newly cultivated soil, the extra heat gained from the close planting of the seedlings and the north–south alignment, which maximizes the sun's warmth, gives yields that are usually above the average for Japan. However, about every fourth year the average temperature falls below 20°C (68°F) in July or August and the harvest is poor. Though yields are normally high the quality of the rice is not as acceptable to the Japanese as is 'mainland' rice from Old Japan.

There is not much that the Saitos can do in the long winter, when little work can be done on the farm and jobs are scarce elsewhere. They do odd jobs on the farm and make matting and rope from rice straw which they sell through the co-operative in Aibetsu. Co-operatives are very well developed in Hokkaido where, from the first, farmers have needed to co-operate in large numbers to clear and irrigate the land and to market their produce. The co-operative owns the largest shop in Aibetsu which has three branches and more than fifty employees.

In other parts of the western region farming is less concentrated on rice cultivation. In the Ishikari valley the upland area is about equal to the area of paddy-land in the valley. Mr Machimura's farm at Ebetsu (fig. 52 no. 2) is typical of many (220). He concentrates on dairying and half his land is under pasture, so that it looks rather like parts of Midland England. Near Sapporo and on the slopes in the warmer Yoichi area apples, cherries, vines, flowers and vegetables are grown. Along the Pacific coast there is little farming, as the summer fog makes it too cold for crops to mature. In some places windbreaks have been planted in an effort to keep the fog from the rice areas.

(*b*) *Central Hokkaido*

From the air, the rectangular pattern of upland farms on the volcanic soils of the terraced diluvial fans of the Tokachi Plain (fig. 52 no. 3, and fig. 48 no. 4) looks like the farms of the American middle west because the land was divided after 1900, using the American homesteading system.

During the first decade of settlement from 1910 to 1920 in the Tokachi Plain the farmers who came from Old Japan grew potatoes, wheat and barley, and beans to feed their families. When communications improved and the prices of crops rose due to shortages during World War I they started to grow beans and potatoes on a commercial scale. By the thirties the continued cultivation of row crops with little fertilizer and manure had led increasingly to erosion, and to the impoverishment of the poor volcanic ash soil accompanied by falling yields. Moreover the prices of these crops fell during the Depression of the 1930's. All these circumstances combined to force farmers to change their cropping. They began to rotate their cash crops with pasture and with fodder crops, which protected the soil from erosion and improved its structure. Livestock became important on upland farms especially in the Tokachi Plain area. Now, farming on the Tokachi Plain includes fodder crops of oats, maize, potatoes, hay and barley, and cash crops of beans, flax and sugar beet. Most farmers keep two or three horses to help to cultivate the land. The rotation of crops and pasture provides fodder for animals, especially dairy cows and horses, but also sheep, pigs and chickens, so that livestock produces 30% of incomes from farm products. Cash crops are important, especially beans, which yield over half of the farmers' incomes, with flax, sugar beet and potatoes bringing in most of the rest.

Since the war dairy farming has expanded rapidly. Many prime animals have been brought from abroad. The number of dairy cows in Japan increased three times between 1955 and 1966, and in 1959 40% of the farms on the Tokachi Plain kept dairy cows. A quarter of Japan's dairy cows are reared in Hokkaido,

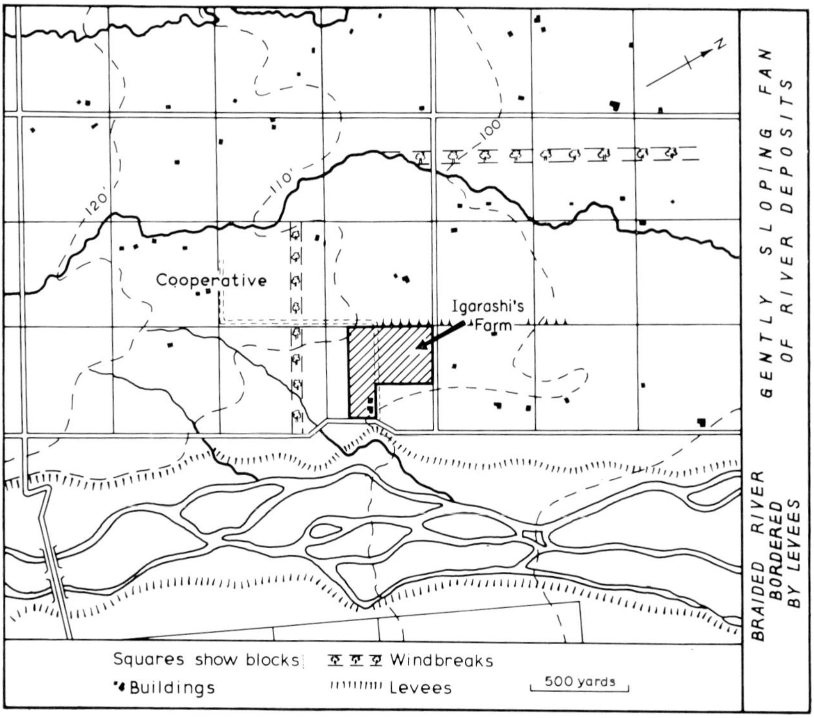

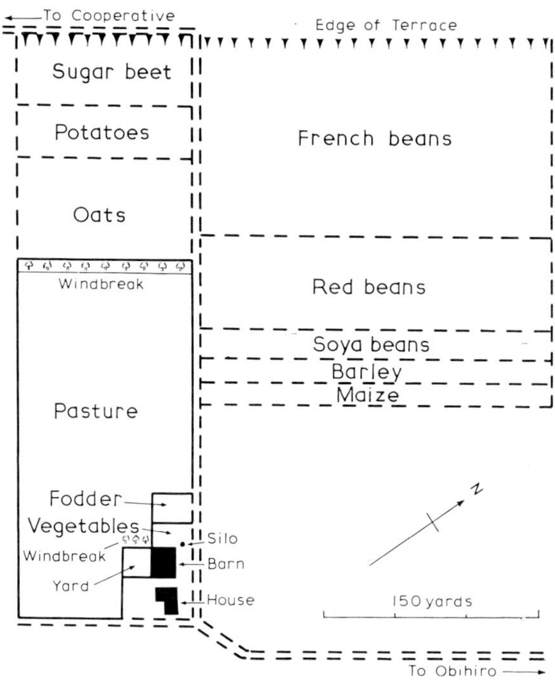

FIG. 58. Farmland near Obihiro on the Tokachi plain in Central Hokkaido showing a braided river, a fan sloping eastwards and the square settlement pattern with scattered houses and windbreaks (see fig. 48 no. 4).

Mr Igarashi's farm near Obihiro showing the crops grown.

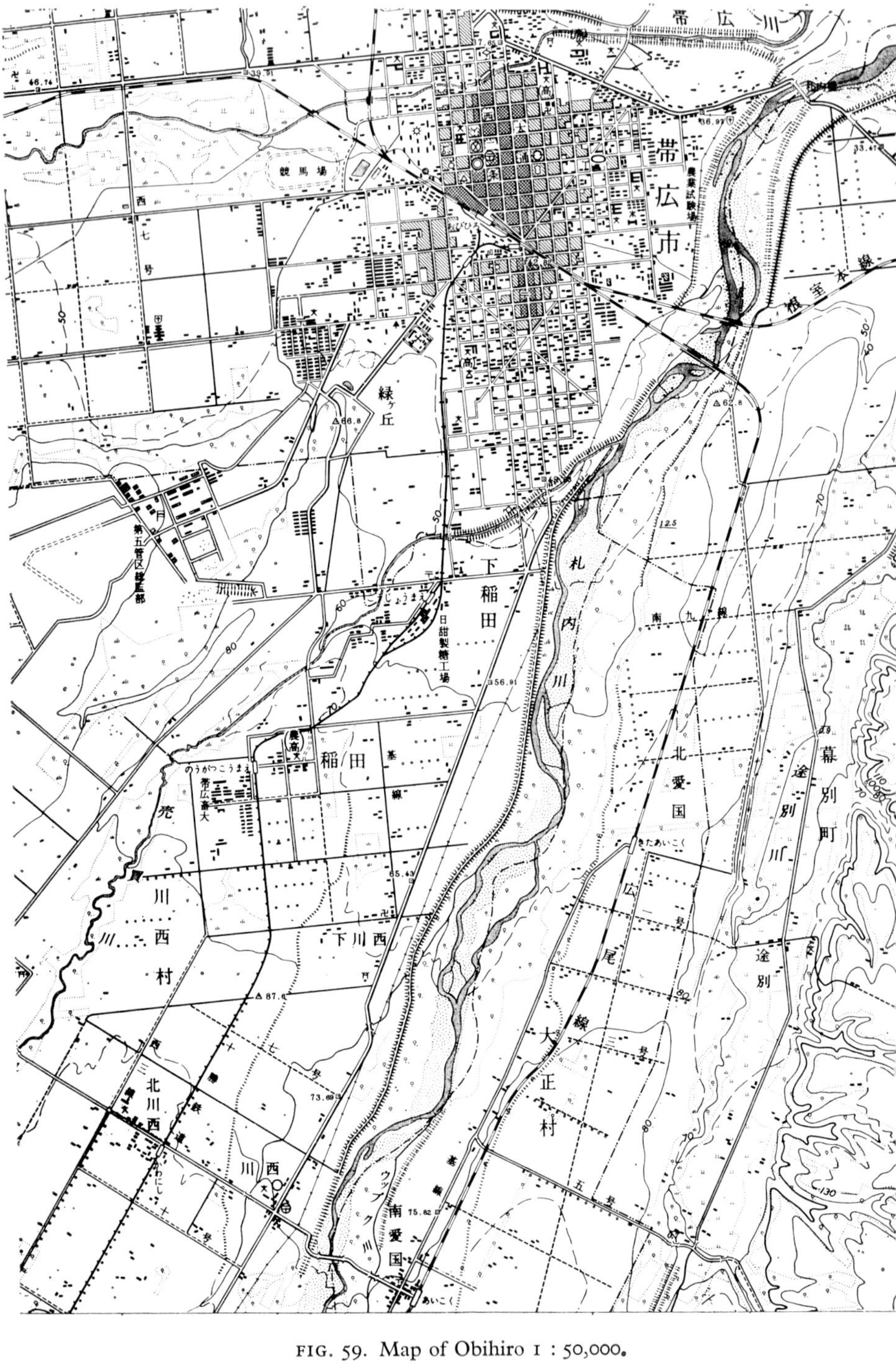

FIG. 59. Map of Obihiro 1 : 50,000.

but in 1966 dairy farmers only average a herd of 7 cows. These small numbers are uneconomic, since the labour and machinery required for feeding and milking a few cows could be used for more. Dairy farming in Japan tends to be over-capitalized and wasteful of labour. Fodder crops and pastures in Hokkaido have increased a great deal in recent years except for oats, which have declined because there are fewer horses. Hokkaido now has 90% of Japan's pastures and a third of her fodder crops. Beans are still the most important income-producing crop for most Tokachi farmers. A third of Japan's bean production is grown here and most of the rest comes from Tohoku. Beans took up nearly half the cultivated area on the Tokachi Plain, fixing nitrogen in the soil and increasing its fertility. They produced half the farm incomes in 1960 but this was before the import of beans was freed in 1961. Since then cheaper imported beans have forced farmers to reduce their acreage. Ninety per cent of the soya beans are now imported, mainly from USA Kidney, soya and *azuki* beans are all important. Azuki beans are often pounded up and mixed with sugar as a filling for rice cakes. Soya beans are used with barley to make the soya sauce that is used in every Japanese meal, and fermented to make *miso*, which is bean paste used to pickle vegetables and to flavour foods, especially the favourite breakfast soup *miso shiru*. In all these forms they are a source of protein to supplement fish and meat in the Japanese diet.

An example from Central Hokkaido

The Igarashis' farm near Obihiro (fig. 52 no. 3) (220) is like many of the mixed farms in south central Hokkaido (figs. 58 & 59). The farmhouse is at one end of the block of 38 acres of farmland and several fields away from his nearest neighbour. Most of the farms in the district are between 25 and 50 acres. The hip-roofed dairy barn with its corrugated iron roof, the silo (pl. 29) and the six Holstein cows in the yard make the scene look like one in the middle west of the United States. The Tokachi Plain was not settled until the first decades of this century mainly between 1900 and 1920 and American farmers advised on the development of the land, since the conditions on the upland fields, with snow lying for four months, are more like those in New England than northern Honshu and not suited to the monsoon rice farming of Old Japan.

The farm is on one of the gently sloping dissected fans of coarse material that have been built out by the rivers that rush down from the mountains to the west and north of the plain when the snow melts in spring. The wide gravel-covered bed of the braided tributary of the Tokachi River flows a hundred yards from the farm, and dykes have been built along it to prevent it from flooding the fields. Porous, powdery, acid volcanic ash from the Me-Akan and Tarumae volcanoes to the north has been deposited on top of the coarse material of the fan. The farm stretches from the river bank in the south-east to the cliff of the river terrace in the north-west. The farm on the terrace has extremely fine volcanic soil, as it has not been mixed with any of the recent river deposits. The light soil on the farms is rapidly leached and, since there is little humus to give it a

PLATE 29. A modern farmhouse among the birch trees on the Tokachi Plain in Hokkaido with hip-roofed barn and silo.

PLATE 30. Using a horse to cultivate in between the rows of summer beans on the light soil in Hokkaido and the Tokachi Plain. The windbreaks between the fields are of cupressus. This is a very different landscape from that in Old Japan.

good structure, it needs constant applications of fertilizer to maintain its fertility. It is readily eroded by the rain throughout the year, by melt water in the spring which removes the topsoil while the subsoil is still frozen, and by wind despite the many windbreaks that have been planted. The west wind which blows during ploughing time in the spring does most damage.

Unlike most of Japanese farms all Mr Igarashi's land is cultivated under a rotation system (pl. 30) which provides fodder for the cows and crops for sale. More than a quarter of the farm is under pasture made up of clover, timothy and rape, which he cuts three times during the summer months. He makes silage from 2 acres of dent corn and 3 acres of oats and his 2 acres of sugar beet provide tops and pulp for the animals as well as cash. Milk from his six cows goes to the Snow Brand factory in Obihiro to be made into butter and dried milk for city consumption, providing 40% of his income. Most of the rest comes from almost half the farm (16 acres) that is under french, red and soya beans, and from 2 acres of potatoes.

Mr Igarashi has a milking machine but often only two of his six cows are in milk, so he could milk more cows without buying more machinery. He aims to have fifteen but cannot afford to buy stock and can only increase his herd when a good heifer calf is born.

The two busiest periods in the growing season are in the spring when the ground must be prepared and the seeds sown, and in the autumn when the crops must be harvested, the beans threshed and the manure spread and ploughed in before the snow comes. During the summer the crops are cultivated and weeded every two weeks or so and sprayed as necessary, and the hay is cut three times. Mr Igarashi has his son and his son's wife to help him on the farm but this is not enough labour during the busy season, so from April to November he hires help from Tohoku.

Since World War II Hokkaido farming has become increasingly mechanized. The comparatively large size of farms and the shortage of farm labour has hastened the replacement of horses by tractors, though most farms are still too small, for in Hokkaido 50 acres are needed to make the smallest tractor an economic proposition. Even if farmers do have a tractor they usually keep a horse for cultivating between rows and to pull sledges for transport during the long snowy winter.

Mr Igarashi has two horses and the local co-operative, which owns tractors, ploughs for him on contract if he is short of time in the spring, when the fields must be prepared as soon as the ground thaws. Crops must be planted very early if they are to mature during the short summer that ends with the first snow in November. Some of the farmers on the Tokachi Plain work in the forests during the winter, but the need for constant care of the animals ties many of them to their farms.

(c) *Eastern Hokkaido*

The farming in the newly developed region is discussed on page 151 where land reclamation is dealt with.

Although there are contrasts between farming in Hokkaido and in other parts of Japan, since World War II similar changes have been taking place all over the country.

Changes in Farming

In spite of the upheavals of the last hundred years in Japan, including an industrial revolution and a doubling of the population, Japanese farms have remained small and little mechanized. In Britain one of the results of the Industrial and Agrarian Revolutions was that many farmers and farm workers left the land and farms became larger and more mechanized. This has not yet happened in Japan, where the tradition that the eldest son has the right and the duty to take over the farm and to look after his parents, has held families to the land, so that today, as in 1880, there are still 5·6 million farms but on 15 million acres, compared with 12½ million in 1880. Farms still average only 2·7 acres of cultivated land. The small size of farms has hampered farm mechanization and in 1966 only one farmer in three owned even a power cultivator.

Farming has become relatively less important in the Japanese economy as industry has developed during the last hundred years, although the number of people working on the land has only fallen from 14 million in 1880 to 9·7 million (fig. 32). In 1880 farmers formed 83% of the labour force, but by 1967 they formed only 19% (fig. 31). The percentage has been declining more rapidly since 1959. This is still a high percentage of people in agriculture compared with industrial countries. The UK has only 4% and USA 11% in agriculture (fig. 98). In Japan the percentage varies very much from region to region (fig. 38). It is highest in the less developed frontier zones of Tohoku and southern Kyushu and in San In and Tosan, where there is little industrial development and where several prefectures had over 40% of the working population in farming; it is lowest near the industrial centres, where less than 20% were farmers in 1965.

Until 1959 almost every eldest son stayed on the farm and only daughters and younger sons left to work in the towns. The demand for labour in an expanding economy has grown rapidly and there has been a labour shortage since 1959. This has forced wages up and many eldest sons are now being enticed from the and by the high wages that industry offers. At last the number of people in farming is falling. In 1958 there were 14 million people on the land as there were in 1880, but by 1967 this had fallen to 9·7 million (fig. 32). In Tanaka (p. 177) there are no men under thirty working on the land. They are already earning relatively high wages in the city and it is unlikely that they will sacrifice these to return, when their fathers retire, to their traditional duty on the land. Some will rent or sell their farms and those who buy them may begin to add farm to farm thus building up larger farms that lend themselves more easily to mechanization; but this is in the future.

Within this continuing pattern of small intensive farms, farm prosperity has increased since World War II. Farmers' real incomes rose by about a third in the decade up to 1966 but were only a third of those in industry, and farm production rose by a third between 1955 and 1966. This was the result of increasing yields, growing more profitable crops and Land Reform and also of farm families doing more work off the farm (fig. 34). Of the income of farm families in 1966 52% was earned by family members who worked in shops, offices and factories or made things at home. In 1966 79% of farm families had some non-farm income. Improved communications since the war have made it possible for more people to take jobs off the farm, so that now only 54% of farm families earn most of their income from farming. Farm families have easier access to more profitable city jobs and more factories have been established in rural areas to take advantage of rural labour supply. Industrial wages have risen and this has been an added attraction, but farm family workers still tend to work in the more poorly paid jobs, though even in these wages have risen substantially with the labour shortage since 1959. Most of the men and girls working off the farm are under thirty. The men work in construction, food industries, fishing and shops, the girls on other farms, in food industries, textile workshops and shops. Three-quarters of a million people work in industry during the winter and return to their farms to work in the summer.

In the industrial zone from the Inland Sea to Tokyo farms are very small and other jobs are available. Many people do jobs off the farm and over half of farm family incomes come from outside work. Few people work off the farm in Hokkaido and Tohoku where farms are large enough to employ the family full-time, and southern Kyushu where there is little industry and so few jobs are available and less than a third of farm family incomes come from outside sources. On the Japan Sea coast many people take jobs in the cold winter since there is little winter work on the farm.

Farming is increasingly becoming a part-time job. The work is being left to women and elderly people as school leavers take city jobs. In 1967 there were 5·3 million women farm workers and only 4·4 million men. 'Weekend and women-folk' farming on farms of about an acre provides food for the family while the men and girls work away from the farm.

The increased production of more profitable crops and animals (fig. 60) has raised farm incomes. Farmers are growing more apples, oranges and vegetables and rearing more cows, pigs and chickens, which yield quite high returns at the expense of less profitable crops of wheat, barley and beans and mulberries for feeding silkworms. Since Land Reform in 1947 when most tenants bought their land most of the increased income from higher yields and high income products has gone to the farmers where before this often half the crop went to the landlord.

All these changes have made farmers far more prosperous in Japan than in any other Asian country and raised their incomes to 50% above the pre-war level, although they still do much of their farm work by hand. Only one in three farmers own even a power cultivator. Without machinery each farmer can cultivate only a small area and his income must remain far below that of farmers in western countries. Farm incomes are only a third as much as the incomes earned in Japan's highly mechanized industry. In spite of the progress made during the last century the great problem facing farming in Japan the small size of farms, still

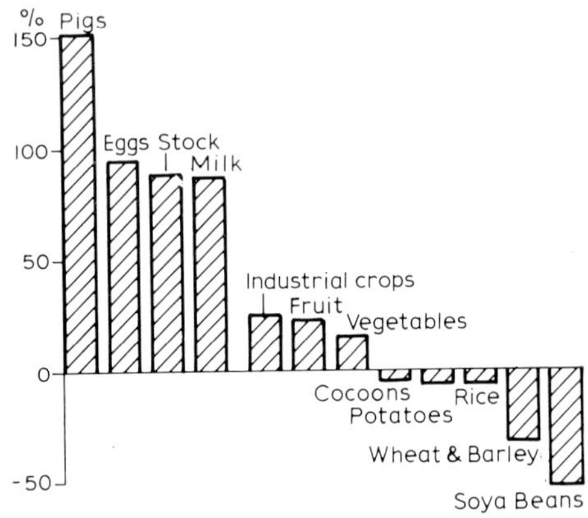

FIG. 60. Changes in quantity of farm produce between 1960 and 1966 showing the great increase in animal products, fruit and vegetables (90).

remains. This hampers mechanization and makes Japanese farm products so costly that most Japanese crops cost much more than those from other countries, so Japanese farmers depend for their livelihood on a home market which is protected by high tariffs.

Changing Farm Production

Since 1945 there have been important changes in Japan's farm products, though rice, grown on 44% of the land, still holds its leading place and is grown wherever irrigation is possible. As urban incomes have risen the demand for fruit, vegetables, eggs, meat, butter and milk have increased and more fruit and vegetables are being grown and more dairy cows, pigs and chickens reared (fig. 60). With the growing importance of nylon and other man-made materials mulberries and silk production have declined. Wheat and barley have become less important as farmers replace them with more intensive crops giving higher returns. The area of soya beans has declined as cheaper foreign beans have been freely imported since 1961 and 90% of the beans used are now imported.

RICE

Rice is the dominant crop in Japan (fig. 44). In 1966 it was grown on 92% of farms and on 44% of farmland yielding 42% of income from farm products, and with guaranteed prices, and greatly increased yields, it brings in the highest income per acre except for fruit and vegetables. It is a matter of pride for farmers to grow enough to feed their families, and about 80% of farmers are self-sufficient in rice. The government aims at self-sufficiency and has encouraged the production of rice wherever possible by giving guaranteed prices, and by providing loans and grants for paddyland development.

The loss of riceland near the spreading cities since the war has barely been counterbalanced by the extension of paddyland by terracing and irrigating upland fields and by reclaiming marshes, shallow bays and lakes (fig. 61). Although most

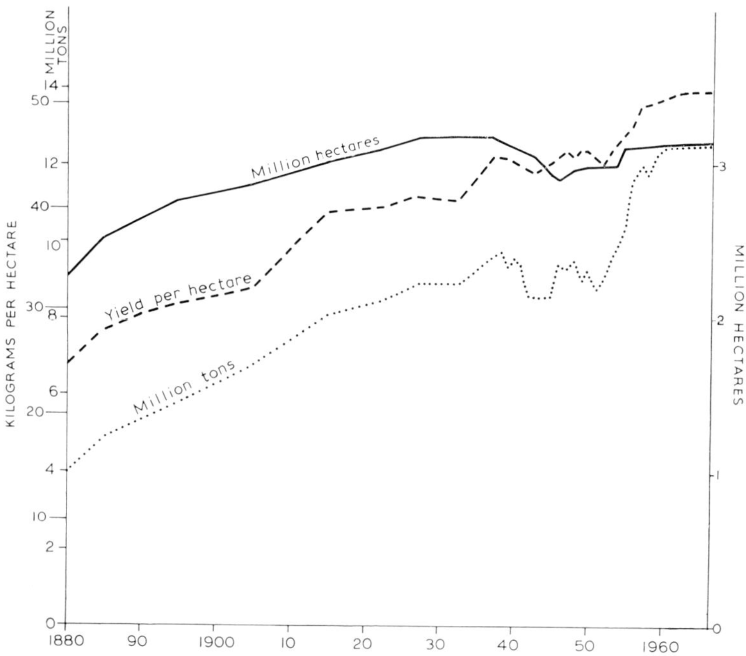

FIG. 61. Trends in rice area, production and yield on a five-year moving average since 1880 (9 & 91).

of the new paddyland is not as good as the land lost to farming, improved techniques increased yields rapidly until 1955 so that rice production nearly met home needs. In 1966 only 7% of Japan's rice requirements were imported compared with 16% before the war, but the cost of producing rice in Japan is at least 50% more than the cost of imported rice. Home-grown rice is protected by tariffs and by the fact that imported rice is not as acceptable to the Japanese palate.

Rice was first brought to Japan from China over 2,000 years ago and for centuries it was the form of currency. The samurai were paid in rice in Tokugawa times. Japanese village life revolves around the cycle of rice growing and rice is almost deified. Festivals and weddings are all arranged to fit in with rice growing. Almost all Japanese meals are based on rice, and the word *gohan* is used both for cooked rice and for a meal, which indicates the importance of rice in the Japanese diet. Since the war wheat bread has become popular for breakfast among city people, and as people can now afford more meat, fruit and vegetables, so the consumption of rice per head has fallen from 154 kilograms per head in 1935 to 139 in 1965.

Rice is grown on all the paddyfields and some of the upland fields as well (fig. 62). It is fairly well suited to the Japanese climate; the *Bai-u* rains during the spring start the rice growing, the summer rains can be supplemented by irrigation water, 74% of which comes from rivers and 18% from reservoirs and

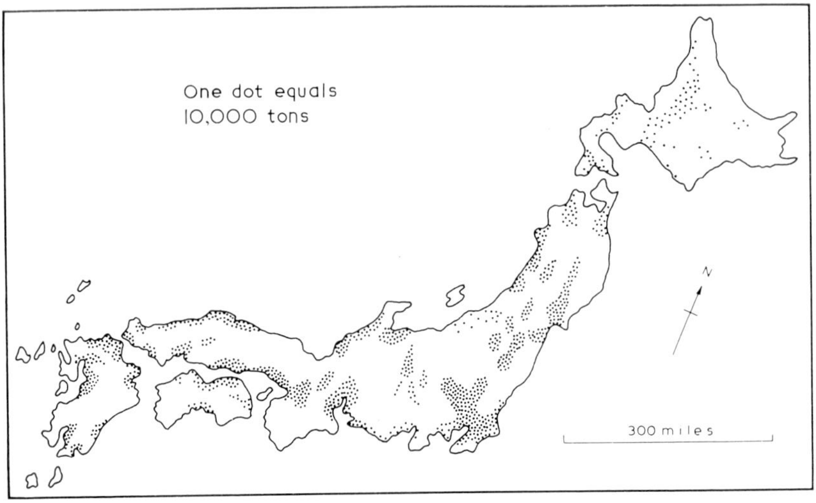

FIG. 62. The distribution of rice production showing the close correlation with the alluvial area (fig. 28) (91).

ponds and 8% from underground sources. The wet summer is followed by a drier period in the autumn when the crop ripens. The crop can be endangered by typhoons in the west, by a cold summer in the north, or a wet harvest time in the autumn. Rice has advantages where land is scarce, as it is in Japan, since it has a greater calorie yield per acre than any other cereal crop, its protein content of 7% is high, and its yield of 60 bushels per acre compares with about 40 bushels of wheat in Britain.

Rice has the great advantage that it can be planted in nursery beds and planted out in the fields with forty days' growth in hand. It does not need to occupy the land for as long as other crops and a crop of wheat or barley can follow the rice crop in well-drained paddyfields south of Tokyo.

Rice has been cultivated in Japan since Yayoi times. At first in subtropical south-west Japan in marshy areas, which closely resemble its natural habitat, paddies were laid out on the agricultural pattern of the *jori* system. Then, as population grew and farmers became more expert in controlling irrigation water, rice cultivation spread to less easily irrigated alluvial plains. During the last century varieties have been developed that will mature more rapidly. The frontier of rice cultivation was pushed gradually further north and higher into the mountains between 1890 and 1930 and now, even in Hokkaido, rice occupies 20% of the cultivated area (fig. 57). It is only in a very small part of cold northern Hokkaido, and eastern Hokkaido, where fog keeps summer temperatures below the necessary 20°C average in July and August and makes the growing season short, that rice cultivation is not possible (fig. 47). Rice can be grown in a colder climate here than in other countries because special varieties of seed and special techniques have been developed. Latitude 44° 10′ is one of the furthest north that rice is grown anywhere in the world, and in some mountain areas rice is grown up to 4,400 feet. Not only have new types of rice been bred but techniques of cultivation have been introduced that aimed to grow rice as rapidly as possible to make full use of the short growing season. With machinery to prepare the soil rapidly, seeds are planted in the seed beds early, after being vernalized to make them germinate quickly. Every effort is made to keep the seeds warm so they will grow rapidly. Plastic sheeting is spread over the nursery beds to raise the temperature of the soil which brings transplanting forward ten days. Water is run round the raised seed beds to keep the temperature up, especially at night. In Tosan irrigation water is first run along shallow channels where the sun warms it. In exceptional cases rice fields are heated by relatively cheap hydroelectricity using wires buried in the soil, or by geothermal heat from hot springs. Cetyl alcohol is sometimes sprayed on to the water in paddyfields to reduce evaporation and so keep up the temperature. The lengths to which the Japanese go to produce rice is an indication of the importance they attach to it. It is more than a food: it has a symbolic importance to them.

FRUIT, VEGETABLES AND FLOWERS

The production of fruit, vegetables and flowers has increased rapidly with the rising standard of living since the war (fig. 60). Between 1955 and 1966 fruit production, especially of oranges and apples, doubled and vegetable production increased by 40%. In 1965 fruit and vegetables formed 23% of the value of farm products. The fruit acreage far exceeds that of mulberries. Few farmers specialize in fruit or vegetable growing, many grow only enough for their home needs, but in a few areas like warm Tokai, around the sunny Inland Sea and in north Tohoku, more specialist commercial production of fruit has developed (fig. 63). Guaranteed rice prices bring a reliable income which is at least as great as that from fruit, so that farmers tend to grow rice wherever possible and limit fruit and vegetable growing to poorer marginal land.

Oranges

The two most important fruit crops in Japan are mandarin oranges and apples. Warm, sunny, terraced hill slopes in Shizuoka Prefecture in Tokai produce a third of Japan's mandarin oranges and they are also grown on terraces in the dry sunny Inland Sea area. Between 1956 and 1966 the production of mandarins

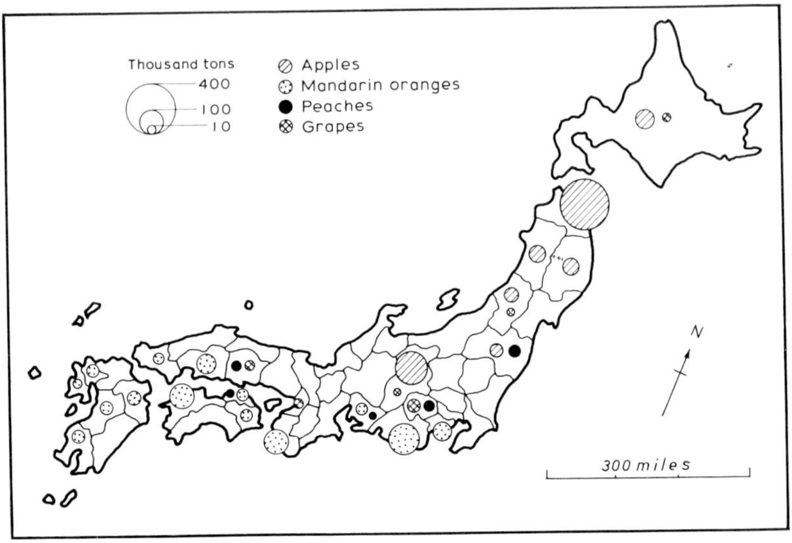

FIG. 63. The distribution of fruit production, 1962 (156).

PLATE 31. The Inoya valley (220) from ○→ on fig. 64 shows the flat valley floor with its small paddyfields arranged in a *jori* grid pattern crossed by the river – a *tenjogawa*. The steep terraced hillsides have recently been cleared for new mandarin orange orchards. Mount Fuji rises above the wooded hill slopes. This is a very typical Japanese scene.

quadrupled and with better trees, more irrigation, the use of fertilizers and modern insecticides, yields are rising rapidly.

Through the whole length of Shizuoka Prefecture the mountains come very close to the sea and are cut by narrow valleys whose floors are often almost wholly filled by the wide stony river bed. The steep hillsides have been terraced

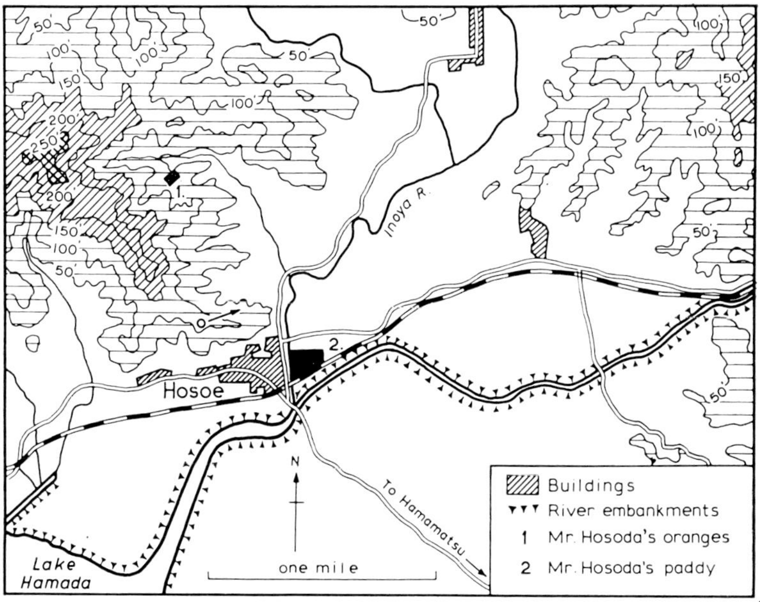

FIG. 64. Hosoe showing the valley floor and steep hills. Plate 31 is from ○→ looking east and plate 38 is a photograph of the High Street.

for oranges (pl. 31, fig. 64). The Hosodas' farm in Hosoe on the edge of Lake Hamada in Shizuoka (fig. 52 no. 8) (220) is typical of many of the farms growing mandarins. Mr Hosoda runs a co-operative which markets oranges from 50 acres of local orchards, owned by about 100 farmers. He also works on their 4-acre farm.

An Example – the Hosodas' Farm

The Hosodas have $3\frac{1}{4}$ acres of paddyland down by Lake Hamada. It is protected by high embankments from the lake and from the river which rushes down from the nearby hills. When the snow melts in the spring and during the summer rain, like other Tokai rivers it often overflows and floods the paddyfields. Near the lake the paddyfields are too wet for winter wheat, barley and vegetables, and so they can only grow these on the higher paddyland.

The Hosodas have $\frac{3}{4}$ acre of mandarin oranges on the steep hillsides north of the lake. Before the war a few oranges were grown just behind the town; but recently the demand for canned mandarin oranges in America and Europe has grown rapidly as has the demand for fresh fruit at Christmas on the Canadian and American west coast. Exports rose by a half between 1959 and 1966. With high prices for oranges it has been worth while carving the hillsides into steep terraces, and here in Hosoe new orchards are creeping up the hillsides. Many farmers grow peaches and a few rows of tea bushes as well to spread the risk of being dependent on the one crop. It is very expensive in labour and capital to develop these new orchards and only larger farms can afford to do so, for the forest must be cleared, the terraces built and after the young orange trees have been planted it is five years before they begin to yield a reasonable crop.

The Hosodas' orchard is terraced on the slope of a small valley. The stream has been diverted to store its water to irrigate the light porous soil. They spray the oranges eight times while they are maturing and employ eight women from local families in November and December to help them harvest the fruit with sharp cutters so that it is not injured. People come to help with the harvest in Shizuoka from Hokuriku and Tohoku where they are free at this time as it is too cold to grow winter crops. After the harvest the trees on the north-facing slopes are covered with rice straw matting to protect them from frost, and the oranges are kept in shallow boxes in a storehouse in the orchard until after Christmas when the glut has passed and prices have risen. In Shizuoka most oranges are sold through co-operatives such as the one Mr Hosoda runs. He collects the oranges in a three-wheel truck and takes them to market in one of the nearby cities.

The large number of three-wheeled trucks owned by the orange growers in Hosoe indicates their very high income from orange growing. The income per day's work from oranges is over five times that from wheat and barley and it is among the highest incomes per acre, only being surpassed by some very intensive crops like strawberries and vegetables.

Apples

Hirosaki in Aomori Prefecture in northern Tohoku was the first area in Japan to grow apples with the local lord's encouragement in the 1870's. Half Japan's production still comes from Aomori Prefecture (fig. 63), but the more recently planted orchards in mountain valleys of Nagano, Fukushima and Yamaguchi in Tosan with their young trees and more popular varieties, especially Golden Delicious, Red Delicious and Jonathan, are becoming more important. Both in Nagano and near Hirosaki, upland and paddyland are in close proximity, so farmers often have some of each. Some farmers have converted paddyfields to orchards and in some areas over half the farmland is planted to fruit. Farmers do not usually specialize in fruit growing but grow fruit in conjunction with other crops, and they often grow a small acreage of several kinds of fruit to spread the labour needed and the risks involved. About two-thirds of the fruit area in Nagano is under apples but persimmons, pears, grapes and peaches are also grown.

Fruit demands a great deal of labour; apples require even more work than rice.

A great deal of work goes into getting the greatest possible number of the largest possible apples. In March the trees are pruned and later they are pollinated, often by hand, and the blossoms thinned. To get the largest fruit they leave the strongest central, or king fruit, in each bunch. The apples must be sprayed frequently, and in June they are put into paper bags on the tree to protect them from insects and help them to colour evenly. It takes a whole day to bag 3,000 fruit. The bags must be removed two or three weeks before the harvest, which lasts from August, for the earlier varieties, until November.

Other fruit and vegetables

Other fruits of increasing importance in Japan include peaches which are grown both outside and under glass throughout most of Honshu, especially in the Okayama, Fukushima and Saitama Prefectures. Grapes are grown outside in Saitama and Nagano and under glass for the early market in Okayama. Japanese and European type pears, and persimmons are also widely grown.

Vegetables are of growing importance. They formed 12% of the total farm production by value in 1965. They are grown near urban centres often under plastic (pls. 32 & 33) and early crops are grown in the south-west.

WHEAT

The demand for wheat products in Japan has doubled since 1945. Rice supplies were short after the war and children were given wheaten bread in school and many young people developed a taste for it. Many families, especially in the cities, now have an easily prepared breakfast using bread instead of rice, and western-style cakes using wheat flour have also become popular. Despite the increasing demand for wheat, production has fallen since 1960 and farmers in 1966 grew only 55% of the production in 1960 in spite of increased yields (fig. 60). It formed only 1% of farm production. Barley production was only 60% of that in 1960. Without protection Japanese wheat could not compete with imports, which are of better quality and cost only about two-thirds the price of the home-produced grain. The area under wheat in Japan is supported by subsidy because, although the yield is still low, it is grown as a second crop on upland fields throughout the country (fig. 65) and on well-drained, often ridged paddyfields south of Tokyo (fig. 47, pl. 17). This brings in some small return in the winter when farmers would be idle.

With so little return from wheat, farmers have been encouraged to experiment with ways of reducing the work in growing it. Some wheat is planted after the rice harvest without cultivating the fields, sowing the wheat seeds in holes 10 inches apart and covering them with soil and a straw mulch. With this method yields can be increased by 20% and the amount of work in planting, cultivating and harvesting reduced from 108 to 40 work days per acre, but this only works well where the fields are very well drained and in many fields it is necessary to dig drainage channels and build ridges on which to plant the wheat.

PLATE 32. Winter vegetables are being grown in plastic tunnels between cereals in the Nara Basin. The faulted edge of the basin shown in plate 2 is seen clearly here. On the right is one of the many new factories which have been built in rural areas in the Kinki.

PLATE 33. Intensive farming in Sugaya on the Kanto Plain shows the great variety of vegetables grown by farmers with very little land. The milk from the Holstein cows is sold in Tokyo. The farmer living in the thatched house is prosperous enough to own a three-wheel truck on the road. Behind the pylon is his new barn (*see plate* 24).

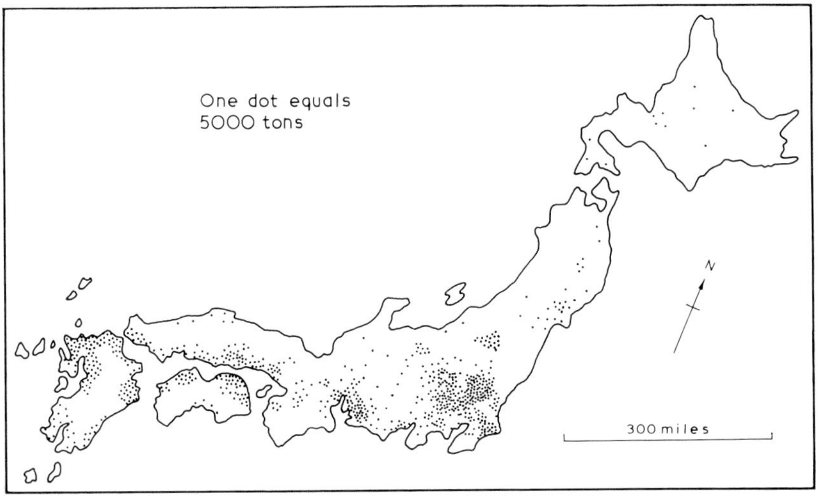

FIG. 65. The distribution of wheat and barley showing their importance as a winter crop on upland fields on the Kanto Plain and in Aichi and on both well-drained paddyland and upland fields round the Inland Sea (91).

ANIMALS

The number of animals reared for food production in Japan nearly doubled 1960–6 (fig. 60). In 1966 there were 1·3 million dairy and 1·6 million beef (and draft) cattle, 5 million pigs and 109 million chickens; but in spite of this fish still provided half of the animal protein consumed. Beans form an important source of the second class protein. There have been relatively few animals in Japan until recently because only during the last century have the Japanese killed four-footed animals, so there is no tradition of animal rearing. The small farms need to produce a maximum bulk of food; since crops produce more weight of food per acre than stock. The farmer has no land to spare for fodder crops. Rice straw does not provide suitable winter fodder but maize is being imported for fodder and since import restrictions were removed in 1960 imports have trebled. High guaranteed prices for rice have not encouraged farmers to turn to animal rearing. Japan lacks mountain pastures since, when forest is cleared, *genya* develops with unnutritious and unpalatable bamboo grass, and clearing the steep mountain slopes of this causes soil erosion. Only in south Hokkaido, north Tohoku, central Chugoku and central Kyushu is pasture growing at all important (fig. 66). The Japanese farmer does not take readily to rearing animals which he is not used to; they need such different attitudes and skills, in fact they demand a new way of life. Before the war animals were reared mainly for farm work and transport purposes and to supply manure, but since the war work animals are being replaced by machines and animals for meat and milk are of increasing

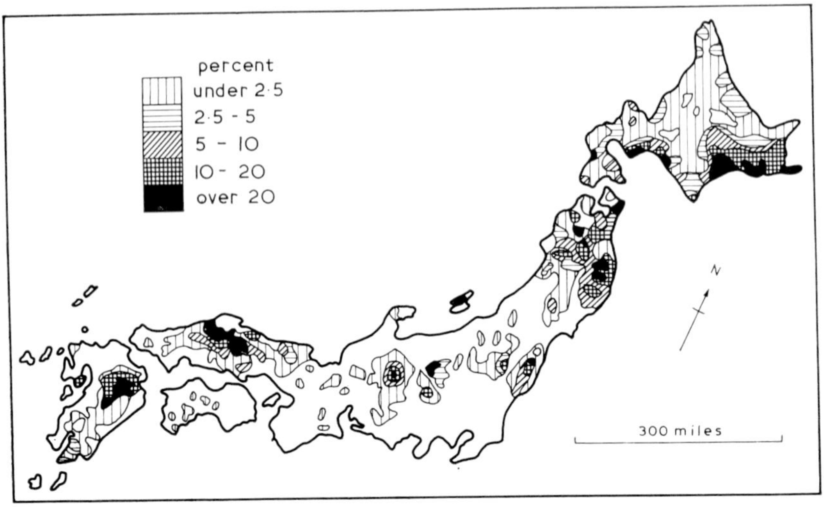

FIG. 66. The percentage of grazed land showing the importance of grazing in frontier and mountain areas (*after Yasuta*, 12).

importance. Stock formed 23% of the value of farm production in 1965 compared with 7% in 1935.

Cattle

Due to the growing demand from the cities *milk* production doubled between 1960 and 1966 (fig. 60), increasing faster than any other agricultural product except poultry and pigs. The 1950 Livestock Improvement and Increase Act was passed to give farmers government loans and grants to buy stock, but in spite of the very rapid increase in the number of cows only 8% of farmers keep dairy cows. Research has been undertaken to improve the techniques of pasture growing, fodder raising and the economical feeding of dairy cows. Manure and pastures with clover have improved the soil. Stock has been improved by breeding better bulls and through artificial insemination, so that milk yields are now second only to the Netherlands and butter fat yields have risen. Holsteins are popular in Japan because of their high milk yield and they account for 95% of Japanese dairy cattle.

Nearly a quarter of Japan's dairy cows are reared in Hokkaido (fig. 67), which is the most important producing area where 25% of farmers own cattle. Because markets are so distant most of the milk is processed into cheese and powdered milk; the Morninaga, Snow Brand and Meiji Companies largely control the processing of milk products. The Kanto Plain and bordering mountain prefectures produce fresh milk for the cities with another centre in Hyogo on the Inland Sea to supply the Hanshin cities. In spite of stock and pasture improvements, the high cost of fodder and the relative inefficiency of production and processing make the price of dairy produce in Japan 50% above the cost of imports.

Japanese Brown cattle (fig. 68) provide both *beef* and work animals. Beef production has developed where cattle are needed as work animals, and in western Japan and southern Kyushu and Chugoku, where there is more fodder for them.

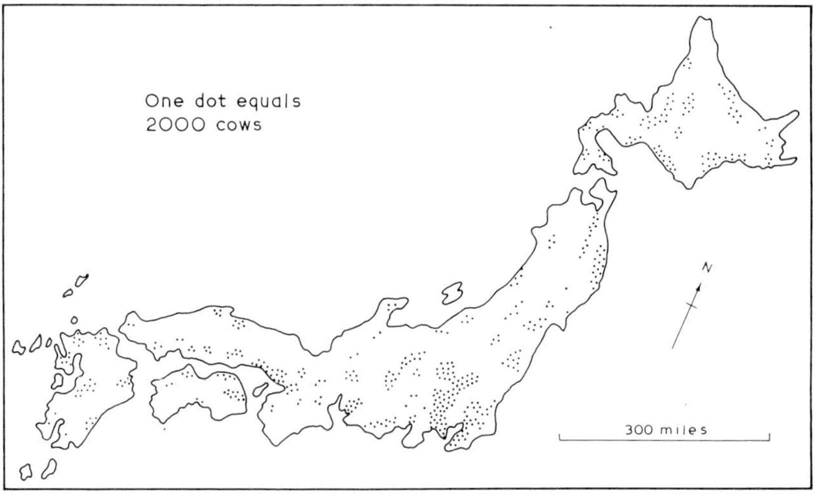

FIG. 67. The distribution of dairy cows showing the importance of dairy farming in Hokkaido and Tohoku where fodder crops are grown and there is grazing land, on the Kanto Plain, near Keihin cities where upland fodder crops are used and near Hanshin cities (91).

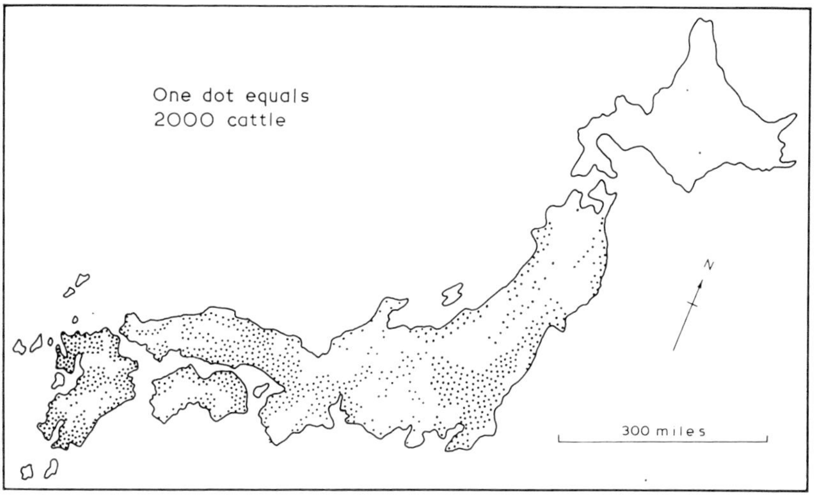

FIG. 68. The distribution of draft and beef cattle (91).

Kobe is renowned for its beef and the tradition of beef production in Hyogo is based on the careful feeding and massage given to the special animals which produce the highest quality beef in Japan.

Pigs

Pig production increased nearly threefold between 1960 and 1967, even more than dairy production. Most pigs are reared in the Kanto area where they can be fed on local upland fodder crops and sold in Tokyo. Hokkaido and Kagoshima, with supplies of cereals and sweet or white potatoes, are also important producers. Pig meat is now more important than beef in Japan, but it is a risky product liable to gluts as production can fluctuate greatly.

Chickens

The number of chickens kept has increased nearly three times between 1960 and 1967. They are mainly reared in the industrial zone from Tokyo to Kita-kyushu. *Sheep* production is of little importance. Corridales are reared in cooler Hokkaido and Tohoku, where many farms have one or two and use the wool to make cloth during the long winter but their number is declining.

The government encouraged the production of meat and dairy produce by introducing price support in 1961, but animal products with such high costs of production are continually threatened by the freeing of imports, which would compete with home products.

SILK

Most of Japan's raw silk is produced by feeding silkworms on the leaves of mulberry bushes (pls. 22 & 25) grown on the upland fields on the diluvial terraces

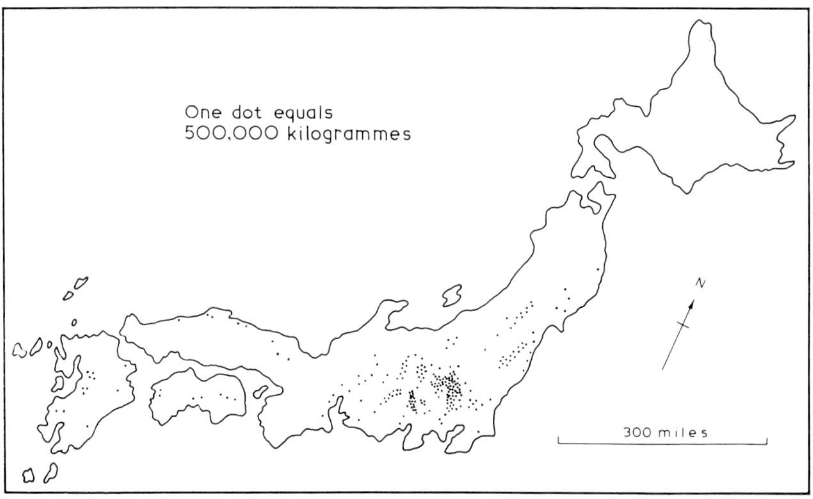

FIG. 69. The distribution of cocoon production which is concentrated on the diluvial terraces of Tosan and east Kanto (91).

in the mountains of east Kanto (220) and Tosan (fig. 69). Gumma, Nagano, Saitama and Yamanashi produce over half of Japan's silk. The rest is produced in nearby prefectures and in smaller quantities in most mountain areas except Hokkaido. Silk became important in Japan during the latter part of the nineteenth century when world demand for silk was great and disease reduced French and Italian silk production. The Japanese silk industry expanded to meet the need. The mild winter and long summer, enabling three or four batches of worms to be reared between May and October, is well suited to silkworms. Mulberry growing makes profitable use of poor upland soils. The worms are hatched in co-operative nurseries and the larvae, sold to the farm at ten days old, are fed by the farmers for twenty to thirty days until they spin cocoons. From early May to the end of September many Japanese homes are taken over by silkworms and their munching can be heard through the house by day and night. Farmers who produce cocoons on a large scale often have an upper floor in their house specially for worms. The returns are not high considering the great amount of labour required for picking the leaves, but it supplements the income from rice and provides useful cash in the summer before the main harvest. By 1921 a third of Japan's farm households were rearing worms, silk was the main cash crop in Japan and silk goods accounted for 39% of Japan's exports. Peak production was reached in 1930 but silk is a luxury, and was hit hard by the World Depression, and, since 1938, nylon and other synthetic materials have become serious competitors, especially as their production costs have been reduced and they have become much cheaper than silk. Before the war the area of mulberries was already declining and during the war, when supplies of imported food were cut off, many farmers grubbed up their mulberry bushes to grow much-needed cereals. By 1945 the mulberry area was only a third of the pre-war acreage. With recent prosperity there has been a growing sale for silk resulting in a slow increase in the area of mulberries up to 1959 but with the labour shortage since then it has declined. The mulberry area was a third of pre-war in 1965 and silk production a half because of the rise in yields. Only one in ten farms reared worms. Home demand has grown so much that raw silk has been imported since 1964 and export of silk fabrics has fallen.

TEA

Tea is the most popular drink in Japan and 11 lb per head is used each year compared with 8 lb in Britain. Tea is an important commercial crop and Japan ranks as fourth world producer after India, Ceylon and China. About half the tea crop is grown in Shizuoka (fig. 70) on the well-drained soils of wide diluvial terraces and plateaux, where the warm wet summers make the shoots grow rapidly and the winter with a January average temperature of 4°C is not too long and cold. Uji, near Kyoto, where tea was first grown in Japan in the ninth century, is still the home of the best-quality teas, including the green powdered tea drunk at tea ceremonies. The soil, and careful plucking and processing, make Uji tea the most highly prized. Tea is also grown on the diluvial terraces of the Kanto Plain in Tokai and in south Kyushu.

One of the main tea-growing centres in Shizuoka is the Makinohara Plateau above Kanaya (pl. 1) on the Oi River, where tea bushes looking like green rounded hedges cover the hillsides. The young plants are cultivated for five years before they are ready to be cropped. Japanese tea, except for that of the very highest quality, is cut with shears. It is cut four times a year between May and September and sent to small factories to be processed into green tea, which is prevented from fermenting and turning black by steaming it very soon after it has been cut. There are many very small green-tea factories which work for about two months during the summer steaming the tea, breaking up the leaves, rolling them, then drying them and breaking them again. Black-tea factories are larger and draw

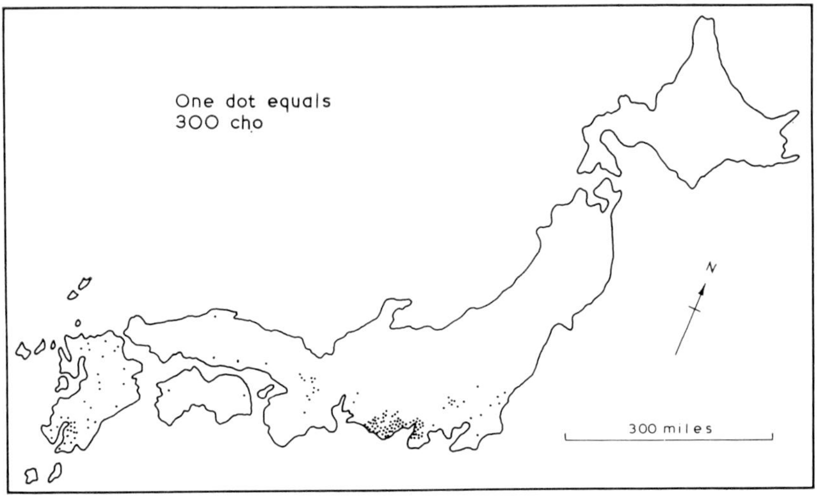

FIG. 70. The distribution of tea production which is concentrated on the upland fields in Shizuoka with some production on upland fields on the Kanto plain, near Kyoto and in southern Kyushu (91).

from wider areas because processing is less urgent. As with other commercial crops most tea is not grown on specialized farms like those on the Makinohara Plateau but by farmers like Mr Morita in Kumamoto (p. 77), who grows a row of tea along the edge of one of his fields (pls. 22 and 25). Tea yields in Japan are the highest in the world because research has produced bushes well suited to local conditions upon which a great deal of fertilizer is used.

Since the war the demand for tea has risen with the rising standard of living, from about 8 lb to 11 lb per head per year despite the growing popularity of coffee in the cities. With the growing home market for Japanese tea, production has almost doubled the pre-war figure, but on the world market Indian, Chinese and African teas are strong competitors. Before the war a third of the production was exported, mainly to the United States, North Africa and Afghanistan, but now only 10% goes abroad.

SUGAR BEET

The government has subsidized the growing of sugar beet since it was introduced to Hokkaido in 1919, and protected it from the cheaper imported sugar in order to save foreign exchange. Production increased five times between 1955 and 1967 and it now occupies six times the area of sugar cane, which used to be widely grown round the Inland Sea. Cane is now only important in Kagoshima where it does well. With increased production Japan now only imports half of her sugar supply. Sugar beet is a valuable crop because it takes little from the soil and the tops and pulp can be used to provide fodder. Successful experiments were made during the fifties in growing it as a winter crop south of Tokyo. It fits in well with crops in south-western Japan, as it can be grown as a winter crop on upland fields between August and February. It is a difficult crop to introduce, as the factory must be built and the crop planted at the same time. Factories have now been opened in Chugoku, Shikoku and Kyushu to deal with the new areas of production, and production is coming closer to meeting demand.

Increasing Yields

An increased yield of almost all crops since the war has helped to raise farm incomes. Improved farming techniques, new farming methods, including weed and pest control, better seeds, more irrigation and the greater use of fertilizers have all contributed to this. Yields per acre are well above those in most countries. They are half as much again as those in Britain (fig. 84).

Since Meiji times the government has played a leading role in raising crop yields. Research stations have worked to get the greatest possible yield from the limited land available. They concentrated on rice. Before the war they developed new strains of rice which would extend the cultivated area, which reached its present temperature limits in the thirties. New strains have trebled yields since 1880 (fig. 61). Yields increased by a third between 1945 and 1955. This has been particularly important in increasing rice production as the rice area increased by only 5%. With the great increase in yields up to 1955 rice production nearly meet the needs even of the greatly expanded population whereas 16% had to be imported before the war. Since 1962 yields have declined slightly with the growing labour shortage and 7% of rice had to be imported in 1966. Japanese rice yields at 52 kilograms per hectare are now very much higher than those in other countries in Asia (fig. 71). They are three times the Indian yield (16 kilograms per hectare) and 60% above the Chinese (32 kilograms per hectare). Yields in the mainland monsoon area of southern and eastern Asia are low because most Asian farmers are too poor to buy fertilizer and the new high-yielding varieties of seed. Many are illiterate and uninformed so that new farming methods spread slowly. Recurrent drought also reduces yields.

Some countries, including Italy and Australia, where rice is only grown on land well suited to it, have higher yields than Japan (over 60 kilograms per hectare). Yields in Australia (66 kilograms per hectare) are about 25% above those in Japan. This is because in Japan the popularity of rice has caused it to be grown

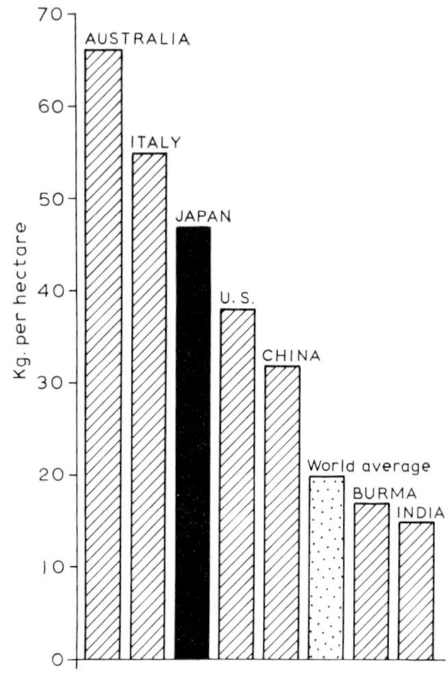

FIG. 71. Comparative rice yields 1966 (156).

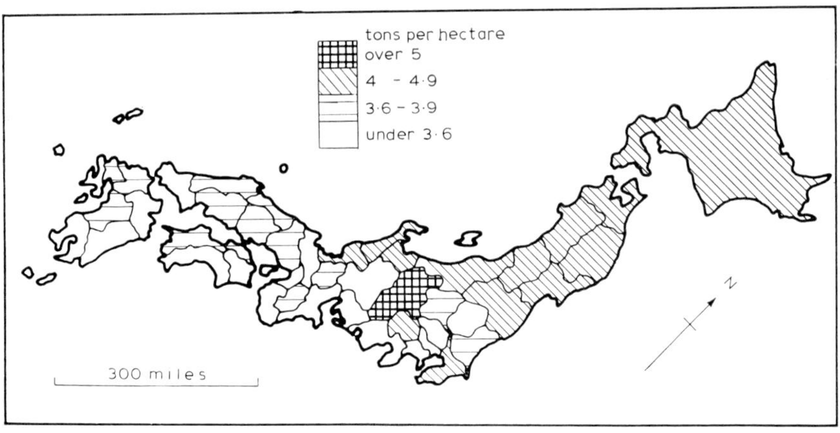

FIG. 72. Regional rice yields in 1961 showing the higher yields on the newer paddylands in cooler Nagano, Tohoku and Hokkaido and the lower yields in the south-west (117)

wherever possible, often on land which is poorly irrigated or liable to flood, in areas too cold to ripen the crop successfully every year and on soil which has a poor structure and has been exhausted by centuries of use. Ogasawara has estimated that 30% of rice in Japan is grown on land unsuited to it (145).

The highest rice yields in Japan are in Nagano in Tosan and on the west coast of Tohoku (fig. 72), where newly developed varieties of seed and new methods are used by progressive farmers who have produced record yields for the last few years. Yields are high because the heavy soil is well irrigated and no winter cereal crops are grown on the paddyfields to reduce the fertility of the soil. The soil has not been used here over many centuries as have many of the paddyfields in the Kinki. In Kyushu, Shikoku and western Honshu yields are lower and there has been little increase since the war, as the soils have been impoverished through long use. Insects flourish and diseases spread easily in the warm humid climate, and most of the research has gone into fast-maturing, cold-resistant varieties of rice that have extended rice growing in northern Japan. There have been some improvements in south-west Japan where typhoons bring wind and flood in mid-September when the rice is in the ear, damaging the heads and laying the plants. Today two crops are planted on a small proportion of the paddyfields in south Shikoku and south Kyushu to minimize damage and increase yields. An early crop of rapidly maturing seed is planted in March using plastic sheeting to protect the seed bed. It can be harvested in late July before the typhoon season and a second batch of seedlings, already growing in the nursery bed, are planted out immediately. These are not yet in head at the height of the typhoon season and so are little damaged and can be harvested in November. The yield from two crops is usually 60–70% above that from one crop and needs 30–40% more fertilizer. Where two crops are not possible short-stemmed varieties, less liable to laying, have been developed.

Since the war many schemes have improved yields on the paddyfields by controlling water supply but about 40% of paddyfields are short of irrigation water and nearly a quarter are poorly drained. Improvements have to be made in controlling floods, in drainage and in the regulated irrigation water. Summer floods have been controlled along the Kitakami in Tohoku by building dams. Draining paddyfields that were formerly waterlogged in winter has made it possible to grow more winter crops on the Nobi Plain in Aichi and along the Tone and Kiso river valleys, but much more could be done in Hokuriku and San In where three-quarters of the paddyfields are still waterlogged in winter, and along the Tone valley where the rice crop is still sometimes harvested by boat. In many villages irrigation and drainage have been reorganized to improve their efficiency (fig. 73).

Yields have risen with improved irrigation and are less liable to fluctuate from year to year. Around the Inland Sea, where drought is a hazard, irrigation facilities have been improved by the building of many new dams. The yields on dry upland fields have been raised by irrigating them from barrages on the large rivers. Much of the development since 1950 has been associated with multipurpose development schemes, controlling floods, providing irrigation water and producing electricity. Thus the Kitakami River development scheme will regulate the flow of the river which is notorious for its flooding, and supply irrigation water and electric power from the head of water at the dams. In Aichi a scheme, completed in 1960, irrigated 35,000 acres of upland from the Kiso River as well as supplying 130 million kilowatts of electricity and controlling flooding. The Sagami Plateau in Kanagawa was a military area because it was of little agricultural value until it was irrigated. On the Atsumi peninsula in Aichi 15,000 acres of

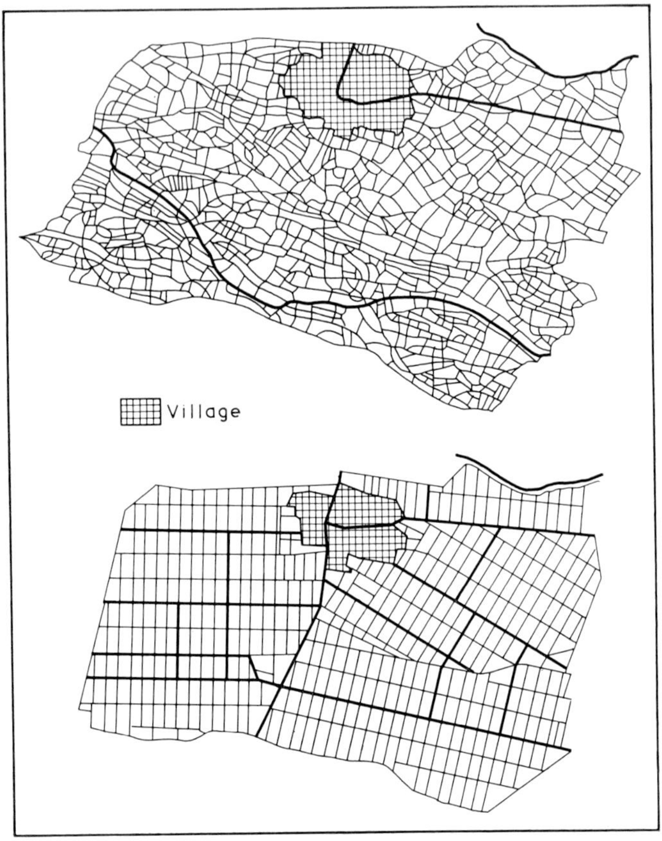

FIG. 73. Paddyland reorganization has increased the efficiency of irrigation and increased the cultivable area (152).

riceland and 10,000 acres of upland are being reclaimed and irrigated from the Toyo River.

Of the farmed area in Japan 38% (fig. 43) is *upland fields* (*hatake*) (figs. 11, 43, 44), where yields are far below paddyland yields and are increasing only slowly. Most of the upland area has poor, light, droughty, easily eroded diluvial or volcanic soil which give low yields and so low incomes, except where fruit and vegetables are grown. Wheat and barley and beans are among the most important upland crops and all these are low-income crops with a large world surplus. Since rice has always been the most important crop in Japan, research has been concentrated on this and little has been done to raise yields of poor upland soils until very recently. The yield from upland soils is being improved by deep ploughing to break up iron pan, by the addition of fertilizer, especially organic fertilizer which will improve the soil structure and so reduce the danger of erosion, and by introducing rotations of crops. Seeds for upland crops have also been improved. With the growing demand for livestock products more upland fields are being used for fodder crops and half the area is now cropped in winter. Winter cropping is possible much further north on upland than on paddyland. Some crops like clover cover the soil and so reduce erosion, as well as adding nitrogen and humus to improve the soil nutrients.

Japanese *soil* (p. 57) is generally not very fertile as it has been leached by the heavy summer rains, and continuous cropping with rice over hundreds of years has used up the soluble organic and mineral content and reduced the fertility of the soil, especially where two crops or more have been grown each year. In 1956 the White Paper on Agriculture and Forestry classified 27% of farmland as 'bad soil'. With few animals on Japanese farms there has been little manure available but humus from the forests, and human excrement (night-soil) has long been used. Recently there has been a very rapid increase in the use of artificial fertilizer (p. 61), so that now four times as much artificial as organic fertilizer is being used. Japan now uses more fertilizer per acre than any other country except the Netherlands, and the amount used is still increasing fast. The artificial fertilizers make the plants grow but do not always maintain the soil structure, and in some places *akiochi* soils are occurring in which rice will grow but not mature.

As scientific knowledge spreads farmers are improving soil by using more fertilizer, by adding small quantities of iron, manganese and borax to supply trace element deficiencies, by raising the organic content to improve the *akiochi* paddy-field soil, by neutralizing acid soils, feeding hungry leached volcanic and diluvial soils, mixing the subsoil with the leached surface layers by deep ploughing, marling peaty soils and controlling erosion. Rotation of crops would greatly help to improve soils. This is not often possible on paddyland but is being used increasingly on upland soils with the growing of green fodder crops to feed the larger number of animals.

The greater use of *insecticides* including BHC, parathion and mercuron, and of *weed killers*, has greatly increased yields. Weed killers have reduced the number of times that crops need weeding. Where once farmers went over their rice fields six times they now only need to do so twice. It is now the custom for all the farmers in a *buraku* to agree on a day to get together and spray or dust the rice crop with insecticides, often with power sprays or dusters, so that all the insects are exterminated together.

The more intensive use of land after the war with more double and treble cropping has increased yields. In 1932 the *land use rate* averaged 118% over all Japan but after the war, encouraged by high farm prices, it rose to 159% in 1955 (fig. 74). More recently farmers have been taking more outside jobs rather than making every effort to get as much as possible out of the land, and the land use rate fell to 123% in 1965. The land use rate has risen during this century because double cropping has been made possible by the development of new varieties of rice and other crops which will withstand the cold. Better drainage of paddyland in winter has increased the area of wheat and barley grown as a winter crop, and now about a third of the paddyland is cultivated in winter (fig. 43). With a growing market for vegetables many farmers near the cities grow several crops of vegetables, sometimes in plastic tunnels (pl. 32), instead of one crop of

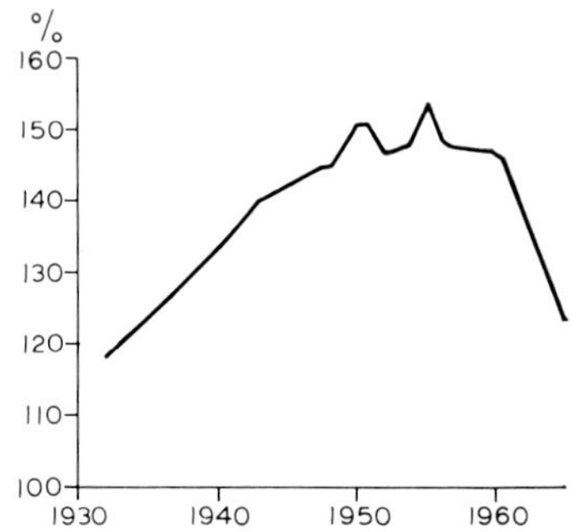

FIG. 74. The land use rate since 1930 (91).

winter wheat or barley, and intercultivate with vegetables between the rows of other crops, especially on upland fields in the south-west but also on paddyland, as Mr Morita does (p. 88). The use of more fertilizer helps by keeping up the fertility of the soil so that more than one crop can be grown each year. Double cropping is especially important in upland fields, half of which are cropped in the winter (fig. 43).

The intensity of land use in Japan varies from over 140% in most of Kyushu to under 110% in Hokkaido and western Tohoku (fig. 75). It is highest in Kyushu where it is easy to grow crops in the warm winter on paddyland and upland fields (figs. 75 & 76), and high in the Core Zone where farms are so small (pl. 49) that farmers are forced to farm intensively, growing several crops of vegetables and flowers for sale in the large urban centres. In this area only the poorly drained paddylands grow one crop. It is high too in the Kanto Plain where winter crops are grown on upland soils. Land use is least intensive north of about 37°N in Tohoku and Hokkaido and on the Japan Sea side of the mountains where it is too cold for a winter crop in the paddyfields. Farms are larger in the north so there is not the pressure for more than one crop. On the drier warmer upland soils two crops are grown much further north than in the paddyfields. Upland winter cultivation is reduced where mulberry, fruit or tea crops occupy the land all the year, and is higher near the cities where several crops of vegetables can profitably be grown.

Japan owes much of her increased yields to a well-developed *Agriculture Extension Service* (117) established as early as 1877, which brings information on new farming techniques from the experimental stations and universities to the farmer. Compared with other countries in Asia it is relatively easy to spread knowledge in Japan, where the population has a 98% literacy rate and a circulation of one newspaper to every two people, almost every home has a radio and 94% of rural and 98% of urban homes have television. The many agricultural high schools also help.

In the Agricultural Extension Service are over 13,000 advisers. These are

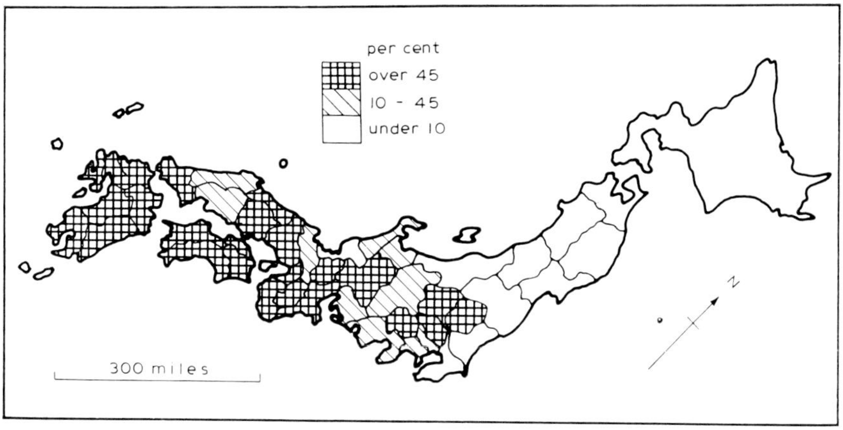

FIG. 75. Winter cropping of paddyland is possible south of 37° north except where paddyland is too wet ;1962 (156).

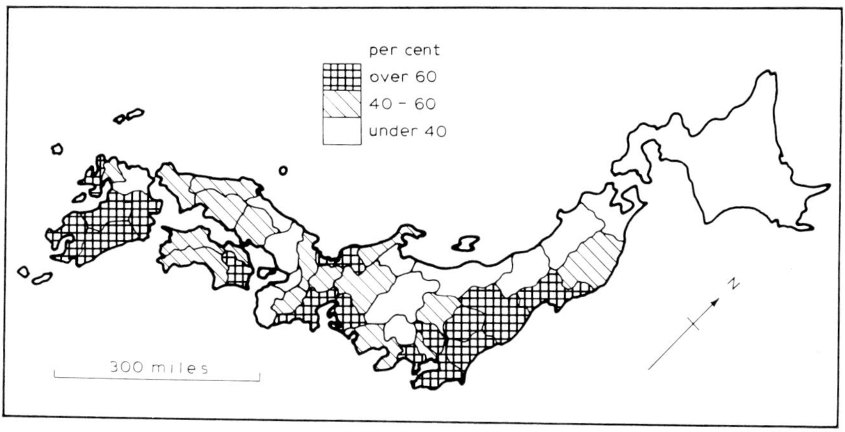

FIG. 76. Winter cropping of upland fields is possible everywhere except in the colder areas of western Tohoku and Hokkaido, 1962 (156)

general advisers and specialists in growing rice, other cereals and fruit and rearing stock, and women who advise farmers' wives on their home problems. Each adviser has an area with several hundred farms. He forms agricultural study clubs that meet regularly to discuss problems, and to read and discuss pamphlets produced by the Extension Service. The clubs also visit experimental stations, progressive farms, or demonstration plots where new methods of cultivation, new fertilizers or new machinery are being demonstrated. The Extension Service puts on radio and television programmes and arranges lectures, film shows, exhibitions, training courses and contests. The home advisers organize home improvement groups and discuss such things as ways of improving cooking stoves, cooking methods, diet and child care. For the young people between sixteen and twenty-three there is the 4-H Club which, like the British Young Farmers' Clubs, arranges discussions, projects and visits. Some of the members spend three to six months working on progressive farms in other prefectures to learn how things are done there.

As with most farming communities it is difficult to spread new ideas since all decisions on running the farm are made by the house head and by the time father retires and the son gains control of the farm he is often so set in his father's ways that it is difficult for him to change. In many *buraku* people who were landlords before land reform still hold a position of respect. A good *buraku* leader can do a lot to spread new ideas. In Minamidani, in Kyushu, Mr Tomita is a strong *buraku* leader. Before land reform in 1947, he had 15 acres of arable land, was the only farmer who owned his land and he is still revered as the local leader, so that any new methods he introduces are likely to be adopted by other farmers in the *buraku*.

The growth of the *co-operative movement* (117) has also helped prosperity. Farmers in Japan have always worked together. In Minamidani, in Kyushu, (p. 103) farmers work together to irrigate the paddyfields, spray the rice with insecticides and weed killers, to cultivate the rice and the tobacco nurseries and to transplant the rice. They also build houses and roads and have brought piped water to their houses. Because of this long tradition of Japanese farmers working as a team it has been easy for the co-operative movement to develop in Japan.

Co-operatives have been widespread since early in the century and since 1920 every Japanese village has had one. The Neshime general co-operative to which Mr Tomita belongs is typical of many. With 2,300 families in Neshime it has a membership of 2,200. Sixty people are employed in its four branches, which handle the rice, tobacco, sweet potatoes, livestock, barley, oranges, rape oil and vegetables that farmers have to sell. It has a shop stocked with farm supplies, provides banking facilities and loans, runs two starch factories, a rice mill and a tea-processing factory. It also provides an advisory service with a staff of seven.

In 1949 co-operatives were re-established in every town. They sell about half of all farm products, especially those bought by the government such as rice, wheat and sweet potatoes. They supply about 40% of all farm requirements, especially fertilizers, insecticides, weed killers and feedstuffs, and provide nearly half of all loans to farmers. There were 21,000 in 1966.

Many of the co-operatives process the farmers' crops. They mill wheat and rice, make noodles, process milk and tea, can fruit, and extract the oil from rape seed. They run advisory and welfare services, give medical insurance and often keep a library. Some of them, like the one at Obihiro (p. 117), own machinery which they hire out. This also has an artificial insemination service and by far the biggest general store in the village. Some have a room for functions like weddings and funerals and hire out wedding clothes. Some, like the one in Nagao, run a telephone service. General co-operatives are especially useful in Japan where farmers grow such a variety of crops on each farm.

For many of the crops that need special knowledge and great care in handling, like cocoons, animal products, fruit and vegetables, there are special co-operatives, for example there are special tobacco and wood co-operatives in Neshime. The handling of fruit through co-operatives varies very much from prefecture to prefecture. Most Aomori apples are packed and marketed by merchants because so much capital is needed to establish cold storage plants, and 70% of Shizuoka oranges are sold through co-operatives like the one run by the Hosodas in Hosoe (p. 125). A farmer may sometimes prefer to deal with a wholesaler who may be more efficient, as he has to attract custom, may have more specialized knowledge and provide better, more personal, service but he may not pay as much for the crop.

The number of *producer* co-operatives is increasing. In 1965 there were nearly five thousand like the egg hatchery near Tanaka and the silk worm breeding co-operatives in Tosan. They also rear pigs or hens or grow fruit. Each one has an average of 8·3 families owning it.

Land Rcform

One of the most important post-war changes in Japanese farming has been the land reform measures that reduced the amount of tenanted land in Japan from 46% in 1947 to 10% in 1948. A third of Japan's farmland was sold to tenants. Tenancy grew in Japan during the Meiji era when rice prices were low and many farmers were forced to sell their land to meet high taxes. The land was bought, in small areas, usually under 30 acres, by professional people and industrialists as a stable investment. There were no great landlords as in India, but by 1947 8% of landowners owned half the farmland in Japan. Many landlords lived in the towns and leased out the land at very high rents, often taking 50% of the crop.

Unrest grew among the tenants and the Japanese were already feeling their way towards land reform when SCAP (the Supreme Commander Allied Powers) issued an edict that this was to be done. A bill was framed by the Japanese government in 1946 providing that no farmer could own more than 2½ acres (10 acres in Hokkaido) or cultivate more than 7½ acres (30 acres in Hokkaido). The excess land was to be bought by the government, thus limiting the size of holdings to a very small area. Rents were limited to 25% of the value of crops. Payment was to be made in bonds redeemable over twenty-two years and the land was to be sold to tenants and distributed by local committees of landlords, tenant-landlords and tenants. Through land reform 5 million acres, or a third of Japan's farmland, changed hands. New owner farmers, with no rent to pay, have been able to spend money on machinery, improved irrigation and drainage and fertilizer as well as on consumer goods.

Post-war inflation reduced the value of the bonds and raised farm prices and so made it easier for farmers to pay off their debts very rapidly. For the landlord, the fall in the value of his bonds meant that he received very little for his land.

This reform in land holding, carried out mainly between 1947 and 1949, changed the *pattern* of farming very little. For the most part tenants took over the land they were already farming, so there was very little change in the size of farm units or the number of farm households. The redistribution of land has resulted in a levelling of incomes in each village, though in Japan there have never been the extremes of income that there are in many Asian communities between wealthy lord and half-starved peasant. In 1965 80% of farmers owned all the land they worked and only 7% of the land was tenanted compared with 51% in England and Wales in 1960.

In Tanaka (p. 77) before land reform the Moritas and Hayatas were landowners as were the Tomitas in Minamidani (p. 103). All the other farmers in the *burakus* were tenants paying up to half their crop to these two families in rent. These families, though now little richer than the other farmers, are still regarded as leaders in the *buraku* whose advice is often sought in the conduct of *buraku* affairs.

The ceilings on land holding instituted by the land reform laws set a limit on land holding that was as low as 2 acres in some prefectures until the law was modified in 1962 to allow larger, more efficient farms to develop. There is still a fear that landlordism might again develop in Japan and this hampers the increase in farm size needed for efficient mechanized farming.

Land Reclamation

Throughout history the Japanese have constantly worked to increase their farmland by reclaiming marshland, shallow lakes and coastal plains, and clearing forest and heathland. This was especially notable during the Tokugawa era when the cultivated area was greatly increased to half the present acreage (fig. 51). The

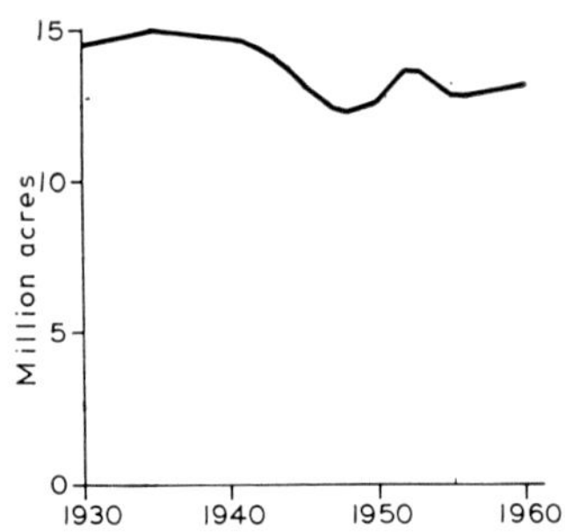

FIG. 77. Fluctuations in the cultivated area since 1930 (91).

Meiji government added another quarter, especially in Hokkaido. Between 1946 and 1965 another 2·8 million acres were added, especially poor upland in Hokkaido. In spite of this the 13 million acres cultivated in Japan in 1966 is little more than the $12\frac{1}{2}$ million cultivated in 1890 (fig. 77). Since 1945, in spite of the addition of 2·8 million acres, the equivalent of a fifth of the total cultivated acreage, the total amount of land cultivated has changed little, as the land in Hanshin and Keihin lost to cultivation through the spread of urban areas has been almost equal to the reclamation of new farmland. The area cultivated in 1966 was, at 12 million acres, equal to the area cultivated before the war. In the early years after 1945 there was a great drive to reclaim land to make Japan self-sufficient in food supply and to settle repatriates, but after the development of the better

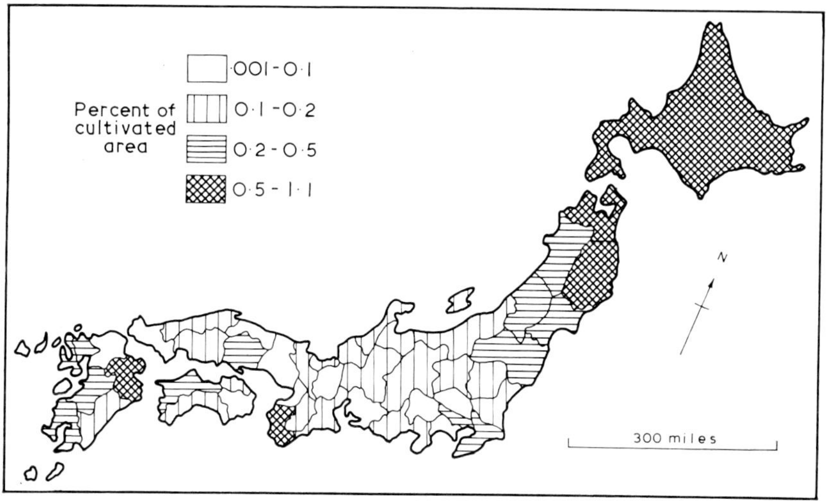

FIG. 78· The percentage added to the cultivated area by reclamation in 1960, showing the high proportion in Hokkaido and Tohoku and round Tokyo Bay and the Inland Sea (156).

areas and the rapid growth of industry, the reclamation of large areas of farmland would no longer pay. Between 1960 and 1965 little was reclaimed (only 80,000 acres). Most of the newly reclaimed land is upland (70,000 out of 80,000) in the less-developed areas with poor soil (fig. 78), half in Hokkaido and a quarter in Tohoku and most of the rest in Kyushu and on the coast near the industrial areas and in Kanto and Tosan. The greatest amount of potentially reclaimable land is in Hokkaido and Tohoku. This is mainly poor soil and does not compensate for the 125,000 acres of good paddyland lost to industry and housing near the cities (fig. 79). Between 1960 and 1965 upland reclamation (70,000 acres) was much greater than paddyland reclamation. Only 10,000 acres of paddyland were reclaimed during the period.

DRAINAGE

The *Koji Plain* in Okayama on the north shore of the Inland Sea illustrates the process of land reclamation on the seaward edge of coastal plains which has been going on since Yayoi times on most of Japan's coastline (120, 127, 220).

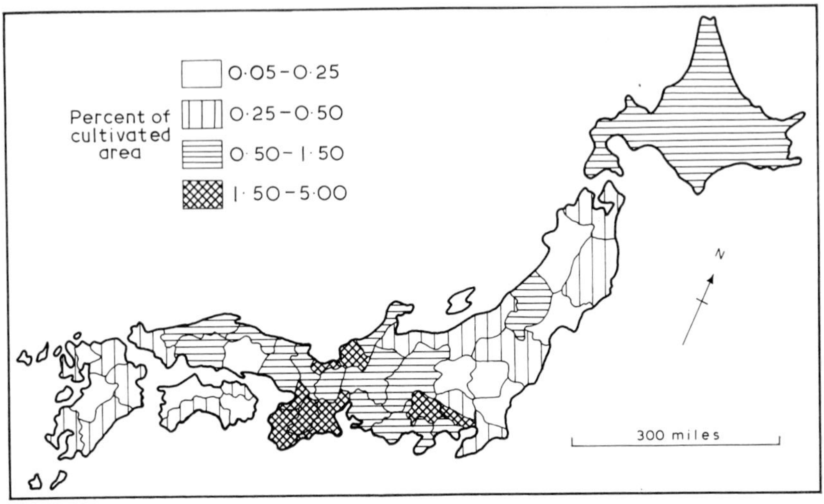

FIG. 79. The percentage of the cultivated area lost to other uses during 1960, showing the higher proportion lost in the industrial areas and in Hokkaido where poor farmland has ceased to be cultivated (156).

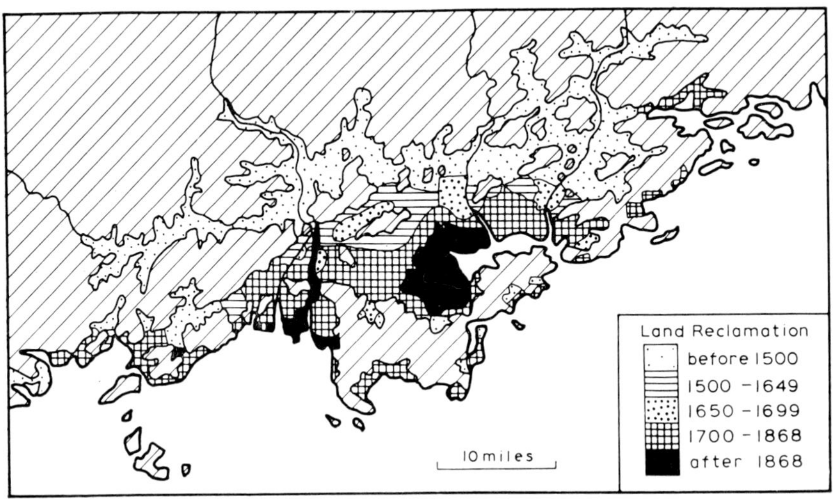

FIG. 80. Land reclamation in Okayama (120).

The Koji Plain (fig. 80) has been built out into Kojima Bay by sedimentation and the reclamation of polders. The Kibi Plateau lies to the north of the plain and shell mounds near its southern border mark the shoreline in Mesolithic times (fig. 9). At this time the Kojima granite area to the south of the present plain was an island in the Inland Sea. The first stage of development was during Jomon times when the sea retreated and rejuvenated rivers began to build new land southwards into the bay. This land now forms the Koji Plain. The shoreline of the Koji Plain about 1200 AD lay along a line from Saidaiji in the east through Okayama to Kibi and Kurashiki in the west; all these towns used to be tidal harbours along the coast. Being a flat, well-watered plain in the core area of Japan, it was settled early, using the *jori* system with agglomerated settlement often along the levées, and most of the land was being farmed before the sixteenth

PLATE 34. Okayama Bay reclamation looking north showing the reclaimed area (on fig. 81) between the coastal hills and the Kibi Plateau (220). In the foreground is the nucleated settlement area reclaimed during the eighteenth and nineteenth century and beyond are the polders reclaimed since 1868. Kojosan is on the left in the background.

century. After this easily reclaimable area had been developed the second stage of the reclamation of Kojima Bay began. During the last four centuries the area of the bay has been gradually reduced as the polders have been extended into it until now it is only a sixth of its original area. The irrigation and drainage pattern of the polders is not well organized as the blocks have been reclaimed piecemeal (fig. 81). During the seventeenth century, in the earliest development, the shallowest part of the bay in the west was drained and a land link formed between

Kojima Island and the mainland, thus dividing Kojima Bay from Achigata Bay to the west. The early development was carried out by large landholders who established agglomerated villages like those on the Koji Plain. In the later seventeenth and early eighteenth centuries large blocks of land were developed by local clans on the western and eastern extremities of the plain. These have the dispersed farm pattern characteristic of all later development. Disputes between the clans prevented further development until the early nineteenth century when the Bizen clan, using merchant capital, developed new polders in the south and west of the plain.

The third stage of development was begun after the Meiji Restoration in 1868 by the Fujita merchants from Osaka, and the last phase is now being completed by the government, who have built a dam across the mouth of the bay to make it into a fresh-water lake supplying irrigation and domestic water to the newly reclaimed polders. Before the dam was built the river and rain-water supply was not adequate to meet the needs of the increased number of farms. The dam has the added advantage of preventing salt water from seeping on to the farmlands.

On the newest polders farms are large and not very intensively farmed, but on older polders the farms are smaller and the farming more intensive. Since the war many new farms have been established on new land but the newest polders, near the remaining lake, have not yet been completely drained. The farms are large, about 5 acres, they concentrate on growing rice, and yields are low as yet because of the problem of ridding the soil of salt in an area with only 8 inches of rainfall.

Kojosan (fig. 52 no. 11) is representative of the polders reclaimed about 1870 during the third stage of development. The paddyfield landscape is scored into neat squares by deep canals and dotted with scattered houses. Between the thirteen households there are eleven different names which show that the settlement is recent. The great labour involved in irrigating and draining the relatively large 4-acre farms led to the introduction of irrigation pumps in 1924 and power cultivators in 1931. On these comparatively large farms machinery can be used economically and this is one of the most highly mechanized villages in Japan. In one of the *burakus*, Jurokumei, the seven farmers had ten power cultivators in 1960 and five of the farmers have had tractors for over twenty years.

Farms in Jurokumei are so large that there is little incentive to bother with winter crops of wheat and barley. Farmers grow a crop of rice in the summer, rear chickens as a sideline, and, despite low yields, are very prosperous. Mr Ishi, like five of the seven farmers, had a motor-bicycle, a television set and a washing machine in 1960.

Kitakobiraki buraku is in Obie town east of Kurashiki (220) and is on the polders that were reclaimed during the second stage of development 280 years ago. It has much better soil with a higher organic content than the Kojosan area and is the centre of the main *igusa*-growing area in Japan. *Igusa* is the rush used to cover the rice-straw *tatami* that are used in every Japanese home, and half the Japanese production is grown in Okayama. In Tokugawa times Obie was in an important cotton-growing area but *igusa* replaced it when home-grown cotton was replaced by cheaper imports.

Mr Fujiwara's farm of 5 acres is relatively large for the area and he is kept fully occupied on his land, growing rice in the summer and *igusa* and wheat in the winter. The paddyfield soil is rich and the heavy use of fertilizer, a dry climate, and long experience, brings high yields of the best quality *igusa* in Japan. Growing *igusa* demand a great deal of labour, some of it very unpleasant. It is planted out in December and January after breaking the ice on the flooded fields. The farmers in Kitakobiraki form two groups who share the planting, spray insecticides and weed killer and each co-operatively owns a huller. After planting the crop must be carefully irrigated and hand weeded. The length of the rush is very important and it must be left to grow until the last possible moment, so it is not harvested until July when the rice must be planted out. Six thousand workers are employed from prefectures round the Inland Sea, and work from 3 a.m. to dusk to complete the harvest. Each *igusa* plant has about 100 stems. These are coated with mud to hasten their drying and then spread out in the sun. When dry they are sorted into different lengths ready for sale. *Igusa* is a risky crop, subject to wide fluctuations in price, and depending to a large extent on costly outside labour. It holds up the planting of the rice crop and so tends to reduce rice yields, but it gives twice the profit of wheat. Some farmers are changing from *igusa* to sugar beet since a factory opened in 1960. It needs less labour and, with its subsidy, brings in a good return. These farmers, like those in Jurokumei, are prosperous and all but one have a power cultivator. Before land reform nearly 90% of the land here was owned by landlords who took most of the profits, but now higher yields and better methods put the extra money into the pockets of the farmers.

There are other large reclamation projects, notably Ariake Bay (220) in western Kyushu and Hachiro Lake in western Tohoku. The edges of *Ariake Bay* have been gradually drained since 1600. Several lines of dykes mark old shorelines on the Saga Plain. Now that reclamation is progressing faster than the silt is being deposited and deeper water is being drained it is difficult and expensive to make dykes strong enough to keep out the sea, especially in the typhoon season. The long-term aim is to build a dam and drain most of the bay, but this is an immense task as the bay is wide and deep (fig. 82).

Hachiro Lake in Akita Prefecture in Tohoku was under 15 feet deep and has been reclaimed since 1957. Nearly 5,000 new farms have been established and 7,000 old ones enlarged on about 140 square miles of land, leaving part of the lake to supply water.

The reclamation of peat bogs, notably in the *Ishikari Valley* in western Hokkaido, is also an important source of new land. In the Ishikari Valley the river is being straightened and controlled by thirteen concrete and earth dams and peat bogs are being drained so that 120,000 acres of new riceland will be created for 4,500 new farms. On the edge of the bog there is *heide* moor, where the peat has layers of mineral deposits in it but, in the centre near the river, the *hoch* moor is composed of organic matter. The shrinkage of the peat presents great problems in reclamation, as it dries out and the land surface may sink as much as 3 inches

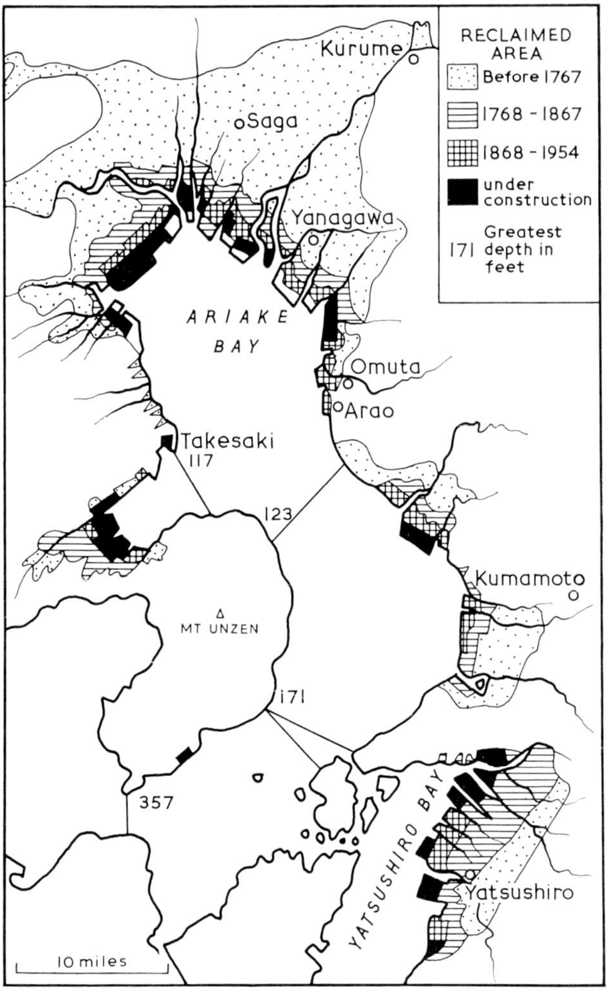

FIG. 82. Land reclamation in Ariake Bay (7).

a year until it is well below the level of the river. The shrinkage is being controlled by regulating the water table. Where the water table is lowered to only 6 inches or so below the surface, the land is pastured, and where it drops to 18 inches crops can be grown. Marl is added to improve the organic soil.

LAND CLEARING

In the *Konsen* development in eastern Hokkaido, as in the *Kamikita* development in Aomori and in Tokachi, land has been cleared of forest and *genya* to make upland fields. The ash-covered Konsen Plain is the most isolated pioneering area in Japan (fig. 52 no. 4). Some parts have been in process of development since 1915 and they have the least intensive farming in Japan. Eighty farmers at near subsistence level, breed and rear horses and cows, keeping only an average of four horses and three cows per farm. The animals are fed on natural pastures supplemented by oats and buckwheat, and potatoes are grown for food.

The new plan for Konsen development, that aims to develop 750,000 acres and settle 9,000 farmers, began in 1955 with the aid of the World Bank, which has helped almost all Japan's large-scale development projects. Here the government is doing much of the work of breaking in the land and developing services before bringing in the farmers. On the Nakashibetsu Pilot farm great tractors with ball and chain were used to sweep away the stunted trees, which were then pushed together by bulldozers. The land was then disced, the necessary superphosphate added and oats, rape and clover sown behind protective wind and fog breaks. Minimum buildings were put up and roads built. All this, which cost £5,000 per farm, was done before the farmers settled, to reduce the time taken for the farms to become profitable. The aim is for farmers to have twelve dairy cows, two horses, two sheep and five pigs and fifty chickens on each 50-acre farm with 25 acres of pasture, 15 acres for crops and 8 acres for forest grazing.

It may take ten years to build up a herd of twelve cows, as a farmer cannot afford to buy stock and can only add to his herd when a good heifer is born. By 1960 some farmers had two cows and others had been lucky and already had six. Farms need to be large to survive under these difficult conditions, but 50 acres though large compared with other Japanese farms, is small compared with such farms in other countries. In the early stages of the Kamikita development scheme in north-eastern Tohoku farmers had only 5 acres and three-quarters of them have failed. Even the 12½ acres on the newer farms is not enough. Fertility and yields on the light volcanic soil of the Konsen Plain are below those of the Tokachi Plain, partly because the farmers are not used to upland crops or to livestock. The poor soil structure and the intensely cold winter causes frost heaving which damages the pastures. Similar problems have been met in Tokachi development and, of the 5,000 farms settled since the war, only 2,000 are still cultivated.

Many of these development schemes provide farmers with a bare living and bring Japan nearer to self-sufficiency in food supply, but the great cost is not worth while when incomes are so low and the farmers could earn more by working in industry. It is cheaper to import food.

Mechanization

Farm mechanization has proceeded slowly since the war. Power cultivators have become more widely used since 1959 so that by 1966 one in three farmers owned one and four out of five farmers used them. Ninety per cent of them were under 10 horse power. By 1965 88% of the paddyland was ploughed by power cultivators. Only 20% of farmers still owned oxen (including beef cattle) and 5% owned horses. In 1960 power cultivators exceeded the number of horses and by 1966 exceeded the number of oxen.

Even this small amount of machinery has had a great effect on productivity and there is hope of greater progress if farms can be enlarged and machinery thus made more economical. Mechanization is not easy and is one of the greatest problems facing farming in Japan (117, 119). Without machinery a farmer can cultivate only a very small area and he can never earn a good income. Using animal power rice takes 280 days' work to produce a crop on 1 acre of land, with a small power cultivator 180 days and a large one 20. In Europe with industrialization during the eighteenth and nineteenth centuries farms became larger and one

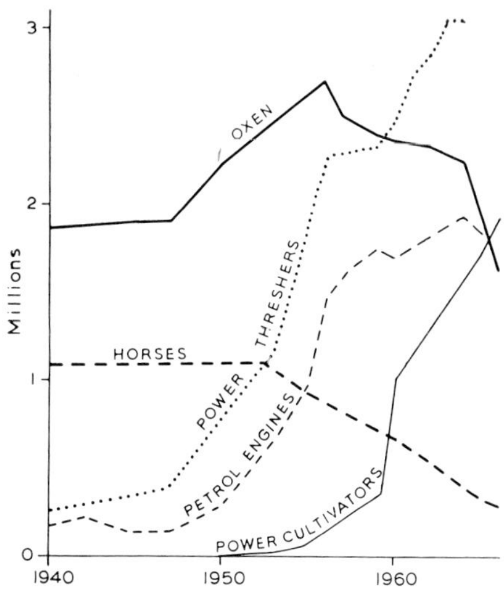

FIG. 83. Trends in farm machinery and work animals since 1940 (91, 117 & 119).

man with a machine cultivated a large area. In Japan farms have remained small, averaging only 2·7 acres, and there has been relatively little mechanization. By 1964 only one farmer in three *owned* a power cultivator and over a third of them used borrowed or co-operative cultivators, while a quarter still cultivated some of their land with animal power or by hand. The farmer's productivity, and so his income, remain low compared with those of western farmers and compared with highly mechanized industry. It is difficult to break into this vicious circle, for, without larger farms, machinery is not economical and without machinery, farmers cannot cultivate enough land to earn a high income to buy more land.

Before the war, and until 1955, research was concentrated on increasing yields to feed the fast-growing population, by improving fertilizers, methods and seeds, and yields are high in Japan (fig. 84). Since 1955 more attention has been paid to raising the productivity of farmers through mechanization, but still the productivity of farm labour in Japan is little more than a third of productivity in industry and the gap is widening. Production per worker is less than a tenth of that in Britain. Between 1960 and 1966 the productivity of labour in industry doubled and in agriculture increased by only 30%. In spite of increased production Japan's 9·7 million farmers who formed 19% of the work force earned only 12% of the national income in 1966.

Research carried out since 1956 by the Asia Foundation in Niiike *buraku* (133, 149) in Okayama Prefecture on the Inland Sea (page 94) has examined some of the problems of introducing machinery and analysed the social and economic effects of its introduction. In Niiike, as elsewhere in Japan, the most difficult

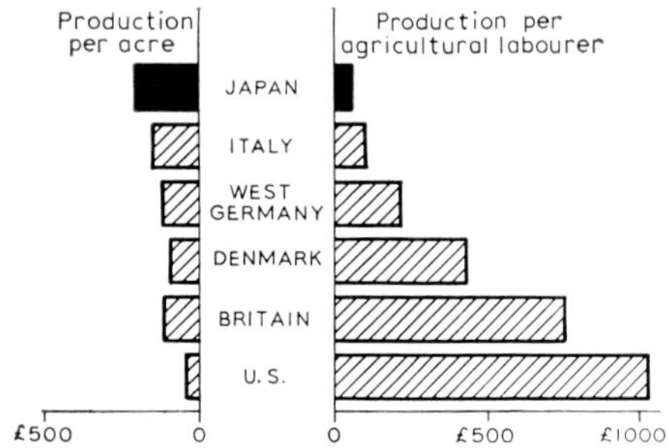

FIG. 84. Comparative production per acre and per worker in various countries in 1962.

problem in introducing machinery is the small size of the farms. In Niiike they average less than 2 acres, so that there is not enough work on one farm to make even the smallest hand tractor pay, as 200 hours of work a year is necessary for this.

Efforts are being made in Japan to solve this problem in many different ways. In some *burakus* one farmer with more land hires out his power cultivator. In others a group of several farmers – even as many as twenty in Hokiji *buraku* in Nara Prefecture – own a tractor. In 1965 8% of farmers owned power cultivators jointly, but responsibility for maintaining machines is a difficulty where a number of people are using them. In 1965 2% of farmers used co-operative owned tractors which did the work on contract. When the co-operative's operator uses the machine he can maintain it, but there is the problem of what he is to do in off-peak periods. Each of these solutions brings its own problems.

Since the law allowed larger farms in 1962 co-operative farms have increased. Farms have united to form more economic units. One farm in eastern Hokkaido near Nakashibetsu was started in 1958 by the grouping of four farms to make a combined acreage of 127 acres. The four family heads specialize in different sections of the work, one in field work, another in machinery, another does the book-keeping and the fourth runs the dairy. They already had thirty-four cows in 1960 and aimed to have fifty or sixty. With so much land they have been able to afford a full-sized tractor with a plough, drill, mower, hay rake and potato digger as well as milking machines and electric fencing. The problem comes when the income has to be shared out. It is difficult to agree upon the relative value of an hour's work in the dairy by the head of one of the families and an old man cutting wood for an hour. Rates have been carefully worked out giving a ratio of 130 in the dairy, 150 on the tractor, 110 in the kitchen and so on, but this is only acceptable by an understanding group working under a strong leader. By 1965 there were 380 such farms with an average of 5·3 families in each.

In Niiike (121) not only are farms small but fields are small too, averaging only

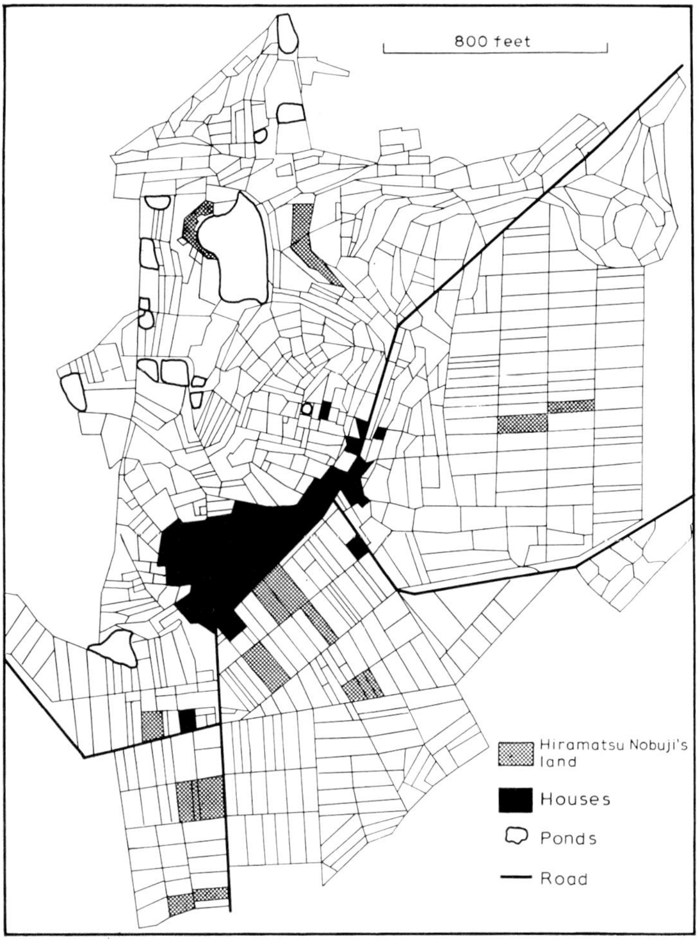

FIG. 85. Fragmentation of holdings in Niiike (120).

0·6 acres in 1958, and since each farmer's land is scattered through the *buraku*, it is difficult to operate machines (fig. 85). Mr Hiramatsu Noburi in Niiike, for instance, wastes time and energy in moving between his thirteen small plots. Many farmers in Japan have their land spread in a number of scattered plots. The average number of plots per farm in the 1960 Census of Agriculture was 5·2. Fragmentation has developed as plots of land have been bought, sold and leased when fortunes have varied, and because soil in different parts of the *buraku* is suited to different crops. In Niiike farmers like to have their land spread out to cover some that is better suited to early and some to later rice planting, some that is irrigated and some that is upland, since this spreads their work and also spreads the risk of drought or flood. There has been some consolidation recently but it is very difficult to ensure that everyone finishes with land of the same value he started with. Every farmer feels his plots have some particular advantages.

The problems of the small farm and field size have been partially overcome by making machinery smaller and better adapted to Japanese conditions. The early power cultivators were over 5 horse-power and were economic on farms of 35 acres or more, but the newer ones cultivate about $1\frac{3}{4}$ acres in a day and are suited to farms of 3 to 12 acres, but most Japanese farms are even smaller than this. Many of the latest power cultivators are more adaptable. They not only plough and break down the earth but can be used to make furrows between rows of wheat to help drainage, cultivate between rows of beans, sow seed, spread fertilizer and even spray insecticides and weed killer, or pump water. With this new flexibility one machine will do the work of several.

Some farm machinery was widely used in Japan before the war, including threshers, hullers which remove the husk from the rice after threshing, and water pumps. By 1940 all farms were using mechanical hullers, since hulling is not an easy job to do by hand. Threshing can be done easily with a pedal machine which rotates a spiked drum that knocks out the grain. The foot pedals can very easily be replaced by a motor and by 1955 three-quarters of farms were using mechanically driven machines. Effective small machines have not yet been invented to do the heaviest jobs of all, planting out rice seedlings and harvesting the crop. Only cultivation, irrigation, spraying, threshing, hulling and polishing have been effectively mechanized. It has been easier for farmers to buy machinery since the war as they are more prosperous and can make use of the government's low interest loans. In 1965 they were also using four times the number of farm trucks they had in 1960.

The increase in the amount of farm machinery has been counterbalanced by a fall in the number of working animals on the farm. The number of horses in Japan has fallen steadily since its peak in 1954 and this has been reflected in a fall in the acreage of oats. There are still many horses used in Hokkaido and Tohoku (fig. 86) where farms are large enough to make good use of a horse and it is useful in the snow. There are also many horses in southern Kyushu, where there are few power cultivators.

In the smaller farms of western Japan, small oxen which can be fed on a much poorer diet than a horse can do all the necessary work (fig. 68). Oxen cultivate the land, haul goods, and even where the farmer has a power cultivator he may still use an ox to cultivate between the rows where a power cultivator is too clumsy. The number of work cattle has not fallen as rapidly as the number of horses, as cattle are used on farms which are too small to buy a power cultivator, and because their calves can be sold to meet the growing demand for beef.

The use of machinery has spread very unevenly over Japan (fig. 87). There are most power cultivators per 100 farms on the Kanto Plain, where farms are relatively large and prosperous and upland fields lend themselves to the use of machinery. The large prosperous rice farms of Hokuriku need machines for

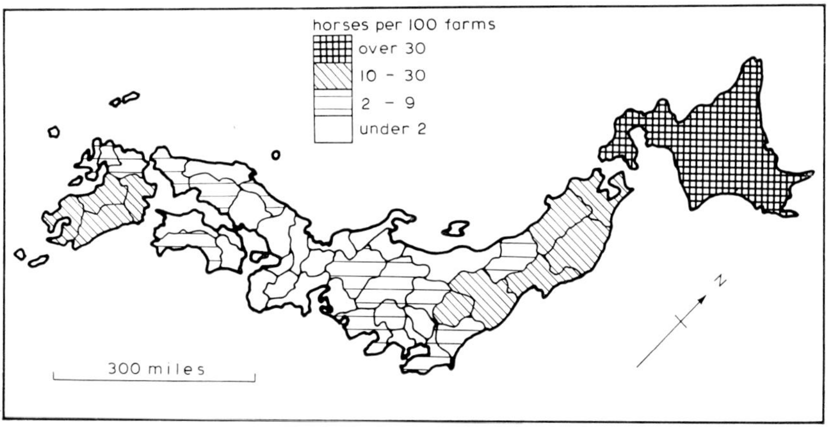

FIG. 86. The number of horses per hundred farms, 1962 (91). In 1965 there were fewer horses but a similar pattern.

cultivation because of their size and because the short growing season calls for speed. High yields and high incomes make it possible for the farmers to buy them. Okayama, where power cultivators originated in 1931, was still the leading

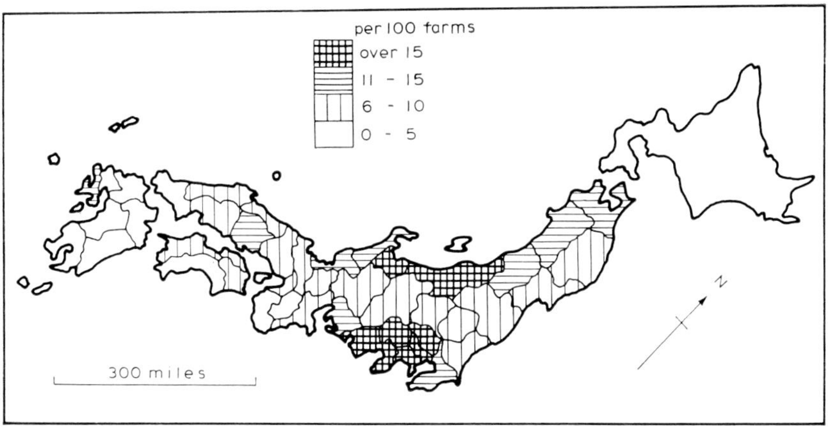

FIG. 87. The number of tractors per hundred farms, 1962 (91). The pattern remains similar with more tractors.

prefecture in 1958 but by 1962 had been passed by the Tokai–Kanto area and by Hokuriku. There are fewer power cultivators on the smaller farms of western Japan, especially in south Shikoku and southern Kyushu, where farms are small and incomes low.

If machinery is to be worth while it must raise farm incomes at least to cover capital and running costs. Cultivation by machine does not usually raise incomes by increasing yields, though deeper ploughing, to 10 inches instead of 4, as in the very heavy soils of Kojosan in Okayama, can raise yields by as much as 20%. The advantage of machine cultivation is that it enables work to be done more quickly and so allows one man to cultivate a larger area or frees time for other productive work.

Farmers are using the time they save to grow valuable crops which need a great deal of labour, such as vegetables and fruit, to rear cows, pigs or chicken, or take a job off the farm. They have more time for irrigation control, weeding and pest control. In Niiike the time freed by mechanization has been used by several farmers to reclaim and terrace upland fields on which they grow pears and peaches, which are crops that bring in a high income. One farmer now grows grapes under glass, others are keeping chickens or dairy cows, and some are planting more *igusa* than they had time for before. Since mechanization eight extra people have taken outside jobs, four full-time jobs and four winter jobs so that now only seven farms out of 24 have no outside income. Farmers have had time to improve *buraku* roads and, by developing the irrigation system, have made more land available for two crops a year and have raised rice yields by a third when in nearby *buraku* they are stable. Home industries have taken up some of the spare time. More people are weaving *tatami* covers and using their rice straw to make mats, bags and rope for sale. Niiike incomes have risen from below average for Okayama to above average.

Everyone is taking advantage of increased leisure. The old people can take a rest after perhaps fifty years of farm work. Farmers can spend more time reading farm magazines and newspapers and have more time to visit local research stations and progressive farms, see demonstrations and learn of new methods. Women have formed a club and have time to meet, discuss household and general topics and go on outings. The results of this can be seen in kitchen improvements in Niiike and the broader outlook of the women. Traditionally the older generation are very much in control of the farm, but in Niiike the young people, who understand the machinery, have a greater say in farming now, and are keen to experiment so that with mechanization new ideas and methods are being spread more rapidly.

In 1967 there were signs of a new situation in farming. The number of people in farming fell from 11·1 million in 1966 to 9·7 million in 1967. Production did not fall correspondingly so farm incomes rose. The acute shortage of labour to help on farms at busy times raised wages steeply. This may lead to more rapid mechanization and larger farms which will raise farm incomes and bring them closer to urban incomes. The average amount of land per farm only increased from 2·1 acres in 1955 to 2·7 acres in 1966. Since 1960 the number of farms with over 3·7 acres has increased and the number with below 3·7 acres had declined. A much more radical change than this is necessary. The Ministry of Agriculture estimates that only 10% of farms are viable units and that these produce 30% of farm production.

Government Policy

The government is trying to deal with the persistent problems of the small scale of agriculture, the lack of mechanization, the continued low productivity and the gap between urban and rural incomes by offering loans to help in the establishment of co-operative farms, to help with buying machinery and to extend marketing co-operatives. There is also the problem of the high cost of Japan's farm products, few of which can compete with cheaper imported goods. Imported rice, wheat, sugar, beans and dairy produce all cost 50% less than the home product. World farm prices have fallen as more scientific farming has produced growing surpluses including rice, wheat, dairy products and sugar since 1945 which poor countries can not afford to buy. The cost of production in Japan has increased so that the gap between the price of home and imported products has widened.

Japanese farming depends on a home market protected by tariffs and subsidies. Government policy protects the farmer from outside competition to maintain farm incomes and to produce as much of her own food needs as possible to avoid spending scarce foreign exchange she needs for raw materials on food. She imported 16% of her food supply in 1955 but this had risen to 23% by 1966. Seventy per cent of Japan's farm production is protected, with guaranteed prices for rice, meat and dairy produce and subsidies on wheat, barley, potatoes, rape, soya beans, silk and sugar, all of which could be imported more cheaply. Fruit, vegetables and beef are the main unprotected items.

Japan became a member of GATT (the General Agreement on Tariffs and Trade) in 1955 and has freed most imports from restrictions but farm products are difficult to free because without very high government support prices food imports would undercut the prices of farm produce and necessitate the reorientation of Japanese farming. Greater competition would force farmers to improve their efficiency, which would be a painful process but advantageous in the long run. Rice from other Asian countries and meat and dairy produce from Australia and New Zealand could increasingly be exchanged for industrial products.

At the moment Japanese policy, as in many European countries and the United States, is to feed the population on more expensive home-produced food for the good of the farmer and the foreign exchange balances. This was Britain's policy before the repeal of the Corn Laws. Since, her government has favoured a policy of importing cheap food to feed her industrial population so reducing the cost of the goods they produce. This cheap food policy has been modified by farm subsidies and guaranteed prices in Britain. There are arguments in favour of both free food imports and protected farming and the government's decision on these complex issues will determine the future of Japanese farming.

CHAPTER SEVEN

Rural Settlement

Japan's villages have been referred to constantly in Chapter 6. Tanaka *buraku* in the town of Shisui in Kumamoto Prefecture in Kyushu (pp. 77–89 and fig. 40) is typical of the many rural communities in Japan (75). Like the majority of hamlets it is closely nucleated and the group of families work together to control irrigation water, transplant rice seedlings and spray their crops with insecticides. This pattern is found in most of the lowland areas in Japan and much of the high land as well. Hamlets are often in the middle of the fields worked by the farmers or, where there is higher land, houses are often aligned along the edge of the plain or valley just above the paddyfields, as they are in the hamlets near Tanaka (fig. 41) and in Niiike (fig. 54, pl. 24). This linear pattern is very common in Japanese lowlands. Houses are often strung along the river levée as they are on the Nobi Plain or along the line of coastal dunes on the Japan Sea coast, or along a road on the Kanto Plain with the farmland in a strip behind each house (fig. 88).

Tanaka is a cluster of houses (fig. 40, pl. 16), seventeen in all, that lie on either side of the rough muddy track coming from Shisui town a mile away. As in many rural *buraku* not all the people in Tanaka are farmers. Only eight of the families, each of which has more than an acre of land, get most of their income from farming and two of these have other income as well. Four of the families have less than an acre of land and most of their income comes from work in the town. Five families have no land at all and do a variety of jobs, such as carpentry and tailoring, trading in eggs or animals, selling insurance in the neighbourhood of Tanaka or working in shops in Shisui, or in the Waifu printing works or the ice factory. Settlement density in rural Japan is often sufficient to support a town that is close enough for people who live in a farming *buraku* to commute daily. Before the war, when there was less opportunity to find work off the farm, people could only do extra jobs in their homes, such as making mats and shoes from rice straw. Now that towns and industries have grown many more people commute to nearby towns to work.

One of the most widespread nucleated settlement patterns is the *jori* system (fig. 89) (73, 82, 83). This was based on the *handen* system of the Taika Land Reform of 645. All the riceland controlled by the Yamato rulers in the Core Zone from the Kinki to north Kyushu was organized under the *jori* system from the time of the reform until the tenth century, and in many places the custom continued after this period. In the Nara Plain the pattern of the *jori* system has

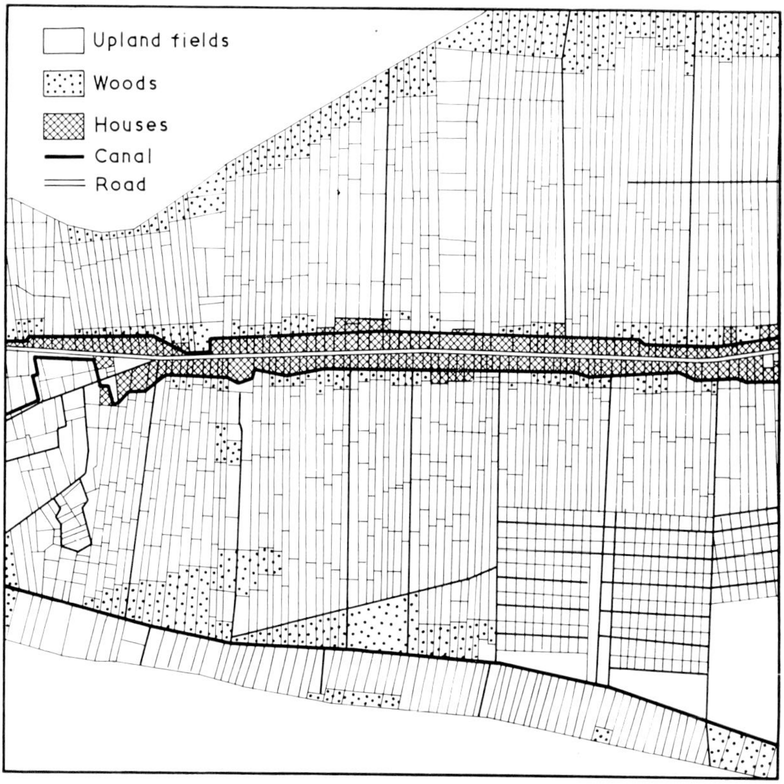

FIG. 88. Linear settlement on the Kanto Plain showing the strip of land originally cultivated by each farmer with woodland at the end of the strip (*after Yazima*).

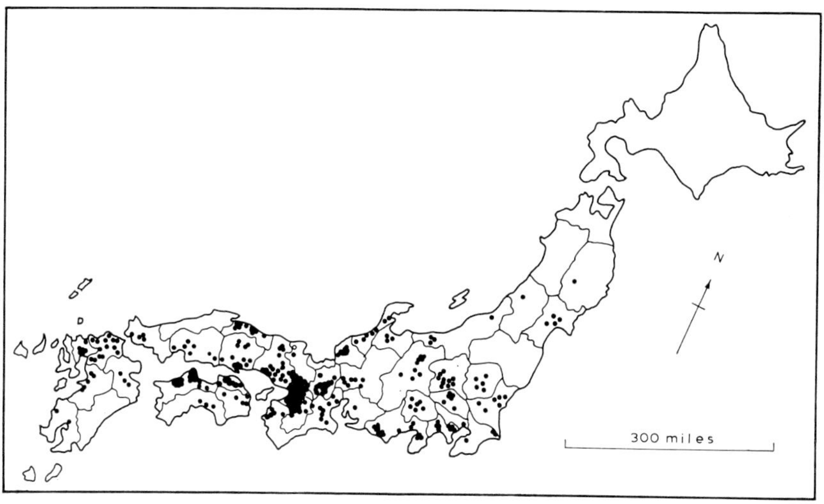

FIG. 89. The distribution of relics of the *jori* system in paddyland areas especially in the Yamato heartland and around the Inland Sea but found from north Kyushu to central Tohoku (*after Fuikaya*, 8).

been almost perfectly preserved (pl. 2, fig. 8, pls. 6 & 36). The whole plain was divided into a system of square blocks on the Chinese system. The blocks were related to a central north–south road, the *Naka Gaido* or middle avenue, and an east–west road, the *Yoko Oji* or great cross street. Each block or '*ri*' was 36 *cho*, sub-divided into 36 squares each of 1 *cho* (2½ acres), which was just the right size for one family. Each *ri* provided for about thirty-five families with one square for the houses, often with a moat round it in the Nara area where some squares were used for ponds. The edge of the squares formed the lines for irrigation channels and tracks. The fields belonging to any one household were scattered and were redistributed every few years, so that as the size of families changed the amount of land they had was altered. Boys were given a quarter of an acre at the age of six and girls about a seventh of an acre. As it is today in Niiike (fig. 85) the farmers lived together in one part of the block and went out to their scattered fields. The size of the squares was related to the area needed to feed a family of six people, so that where the land was poorer, especially on less productive upland areas, a *ri* was often twice as large as in the Nara Plain. This settlement pattern resulted in a very regular grid landscape usually oriented north–south, except where this did not fit the landforms. Even the houses were laid out on a grid inside the moat. There was a fairly even spacing of villages every kilometre with larger castle towns and pilgrimage centres along the main roads. The *jori* system extended mainly from the north Kyushu to Tosan and Kanto and was especially important in the Kinki and around the Inland Sea (fig. 89). There are some relics of it in the Kanto area and even as far north as Akita in western Tohoku, but in many places it has been obliterated by the reorganization of rice fields. Even after the Yamato regime ended in the tenth century most of the newly established villages and hamlets were nucleated or agglomerated in the lowland areas (fig. 90).

Dispersed settlements with isolated farmsteads are found mainly in mountain areas, especially in Tosan and Tohoku where with upland farming there is less need for co-operation and where the area was often settled by younger sons who built a house and farmed one continuous piece of land round it. On newly developed land in Hokkaido and the newly drained polders in Old Japan farms have been planned as one unit, with each farm set in its own land.

Scattered settlement is very common in the upland areas, especially in eastern Tohoku and strikingly on the Japan Sea coast in Toyama Prefecture on great alluvial fans which have been developed for rice farming. There is no very conclusive explanation of this pattern but it has been suggested that here the reason for separation may be the great danger of fire to a nucleated village when the warm winds blow down from the mountains in the spring, or that the land was gradually cleared in Tokugawa times by individual farmers who built a house in the land they cleared to be near the riceland that needed a great deal of labour.

Scattered settlement is characteristic of all the areas developed during the nineteenth and twentieth centuries in Hokkaido, notably on the Tokachi Plain, both where upland and paddyland farming is carried on, and in the many polders elsewhere in Japan formed by draining river deltas and shallow bays. Here the area has been planned and laid out as one unit and each farmer works one piece of land near his farmhouse. In Okayama there is a striking contrast between the old nucleated villages on the edge of the polders and the new farms evenly spaced

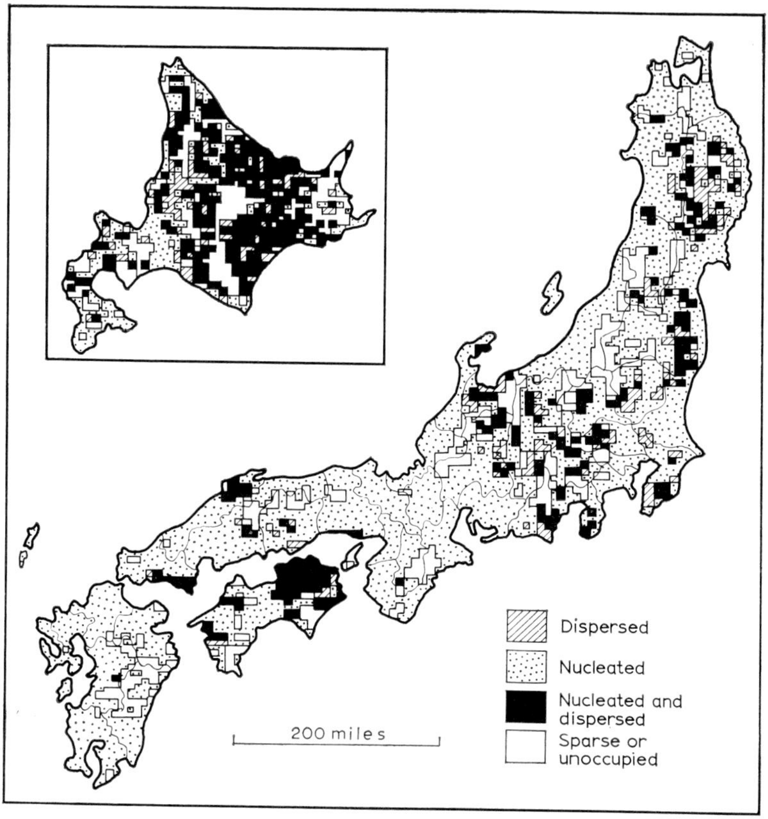

FIG. 90. The distribution of settlement types based on a study of 1 : 10,000 map sheets by Takeo Tanioka.

along the main tracks (fig. 81, pl. 34). The farmhouses are scattered not only on the land drained since the war but also on the land drained as far back as 1700.

The Sanuki Plain in north-eastern Shikoku has an unusual settlement pattern as it is a paddyland area with scattered houses (fig. 53, pl. 23). There the *jori* grid pattern rules the landscape but the farmhouses are scattered with a plot of land adjacent to each home.

From these examples we can see that nucleated or aligned settlement is generally characteristic of the old-established ricelands and so it is found especially in the Core Zone, and scattered settlement is more often found on the newly developed land where a farmer's fields are more continuous and have never been redistributed, and on land which is not irrigated, where co-operation is not so necessary.

In rural areas as well as the small hamlets there are many villages and towns which serve the surrounding hamlets: Hosoe (p. 125) is one of these. Bordering the main street (pl. 38) are shops with sliding glass doors. Each specializes in selling different goods – vegetables, raw or dried fish, ironmongery, clothes, *saké*, beer or soya sauce. Many shops make the *geta*, cushions, kimono, *tatami*, cakes or bean paste they sell. There are schools, larger shrines, a town office, several co-operatives, a pinball saloon, cafés, banks and a cinema. People can travel easily from here to Hamamatsu by bus or train.

CHAPTER EIGHT

The Growth of Population

In 1860 30 million Japanese subsisted in a largely agricultural economy but by 1968 100 million, more than treble the number (fig. 91), flourished in an industrial economy with a higher standard of living and an expectation of seventy-one years of healthy life, more than double that of 1860. Since 1945 the population has increased by a quarter, from 72 to 100 million.

The Japanese population (52, 61) has grown slowly from Mesolithic times as

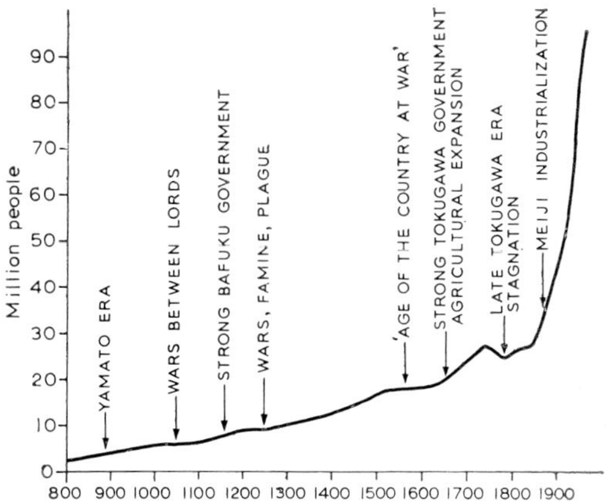

FIG. 91. Population growth since AD 800 showing its rapid growth since the mid-nineteenth century (61 & 85).

new land has been cultivated, increasing in peaceful periods as new land could be colonized and stagnating in more difficult periods until the explosive growth came that accompanied industrialization after the establishment of the Meiji government in 1868. During the stable ninth and tenth centuries the country was peaceful, farmers extended the area of cultivation northwards and into the borders of the mountains and at the same time they improved the yield from their land. The increased food supply could support more people. During the Feudal Period the Malthusian controls of famine, pestilence, fire and war operated to keep the population in check until the country was again strongly united under the early Tokugawa shoguns in the seventeenth century, when the cultivated area doubled and yields rose once more.

By the middle of the Tokugawa era in the eighteenth century 30 million Japanese had cultivated most of the plains in the warmer south-west and were gradually colonizing the marshy, shallow bays and lagoons in the north (fig. 51).

A period with droughts and cool summers caused widespread famine. 'Life was difficult for the peasant, land was scarce, production was limited and levies were high. Poverty was omnipotent, malnutrition common and starvation a recurrent threat' (61). This was a difficult time for all classes: the farmers had poor harvests, the samurai with their fixed incomes were in difficulties because prices were continually rising, and the merchants and artisans had to find the money to meet high taxes. In the farming economy with limited cultivable land these circumstances made it essential to control family size, and abortion and infanticide became a common practice in all classes during the later half of the Tokugawa era. 'It is a very terrible fact that in a village consisting of ten houses, every year over two babies are killed'. Ro Tozan in 1754 described the custom of limiting the size of the family in twentieth-century terms as probably 'A product of luxury' but for many it would seem to have been necessary in seeking survival rather than a device for living luxuriously.

During this era industry was growing and the Tokugawa shogunate realized the need for labour in new industries and in farming, where machinery had not reduced the need for labour as it had in Europe. With a high death rate and a high rate of infant mortality they feared that infanticide and abortion would cause a shortage of labour for cultivation and the decline of tax revenues and passed laws making infanticide punishable by death, forbidding the advertisement of abortion and granting family allowances. In spite of this the population remained at 30 million until increased prosperity came with industrialization, especially after the beginning of the Meiji era in 1868.

Industrialization and growing prosperity made it possible for people to feed larger families and the Japanese birth rate rose from 25 per thousand in 1878 to 34 in 1910, bringing an explosive period of growth between 1870 and 1914. In spite of an increase of 20 million people the standard of living rose. The main factor behind the great expansion in population in Japan in the late nineteenth and early twentieth centuries was a rising birth rate (fig. 92) encouraged by a rising standard of living and the suppression of infanticide. Unlike Japan, in many other countries it was the fall in the death rate which led to population growth. In England and Wales a fall in the death rate in the first seventy years of the nineteenth century led to a similar population explosion. A better food supply and the control of disease reduced death rates which raised the expectation of life and so rapidly increased the population (56, 59, 60) in Britain.

In Japan the rapid increase of population continued when birth and death rates fell after 1915 as they had in England in 1870, fifty years before. The twenties and thirties were a period of population growth in which death rates continued to fall and so did birth rate in spite of the military government's demand for an expanding population. As in Hitler's Germany the Japanese government wanted a large population both as cannon fodder for the service of the country and to add to the glorious Japanese race, descended by Shinto tradition from the sun goddess. 'If we give heed to the glorious history of the Japanese race, the one thing of which we can never have enough is the number of supreme people belonging to the imperial nation' (60). They encouraged births to achieve this but changed to a policy of birth control after about 1918.

World War II temporarily halted the steady increase in population; 6 million returned from the colonies after the war whereas about 4 million soldiers were lost, but a post-war baby boom between 1946 and 1948 lifted the birth rate tempor-

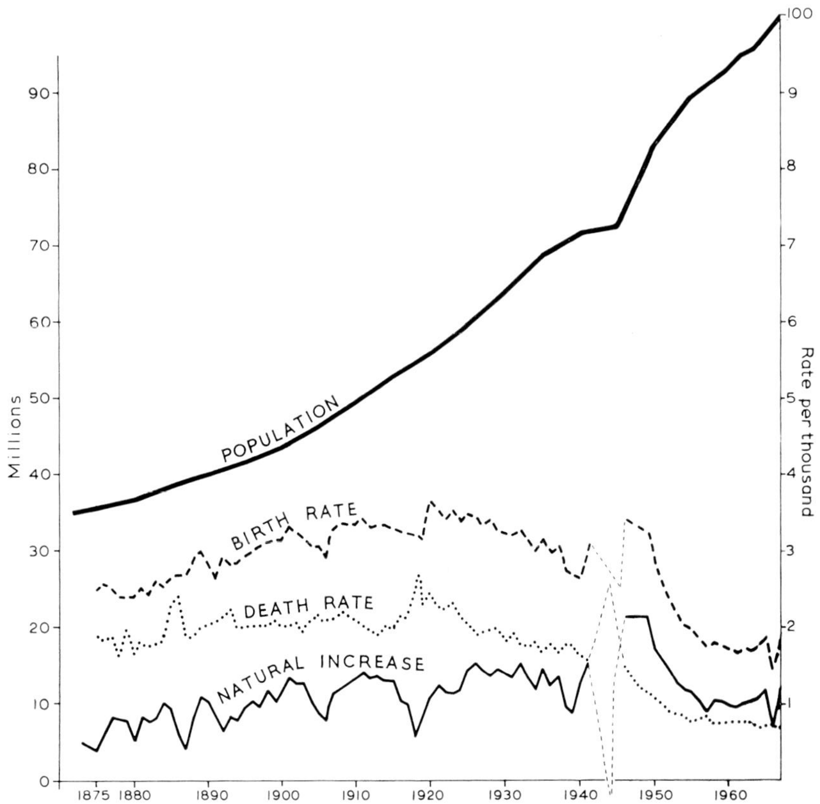

FIG. 92. Trends in birth, death and natural increase rates and in the total population since 1875 (61 & 88).

arily almost to 1920 levels. By 1949 the pre-war downward trend was resumed at an even greater rate and, as in England, it looked as though the falling birth rate would stop the Japanese population from growing or even cause it to decline, as the rate of growth fell to 0·8% per year in 1959 compared with 1·4% in the thirties. Birth rates fell from 29 in 1940 to 19 in the sixties, compared with 18 in England and Wales. The control of family size is nothing new in Japan. Abortion and infanticide were common practices in the nineteenth century in spite of generally accepted Buddhist principles. With more general education, a rising standard of living and the legalization of abortion in 1948, after the Eugenic Protection Law, urban birth rates were reduced by birth control and abortion.

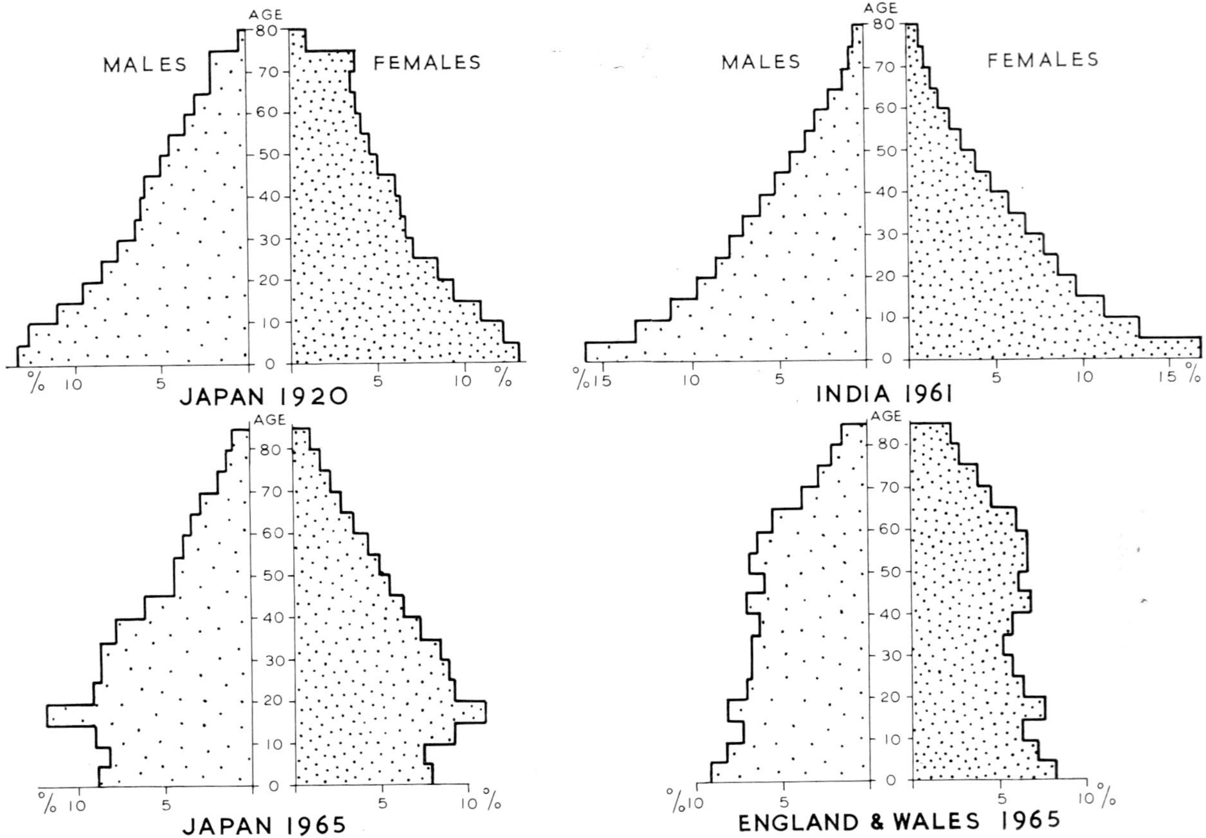

FIG. 93. Population pyramids showing how the Japanese population structure has changed from one similar to India to one more nearly like that in England and Wales (*Census figures*).

In the late fifties the same pattern followed in rural areas. Legal abortions rapidly became an important factor. They increased from 209 for every thousand live births in 1950 to a peak of 676 per thousand in 1956 and fell to 625 in 1963.

With reduced birth and death rates the population structure in Japan has changed (fig. 93). In 1920 it was like that in present-day India and in nineteenth-century Britain. The population pyramid had a broad base showing the high birth rate, and narrowed sharply showing that about 16% of children died before they were one year old and the large proportion of people who died before reaching maturity. Now it is very similar to the pattern of highly developed countries. The base is narrow because of the lower birth rate and the pyramid narrows less rapidly towards the apex as people now live longer; only 2% die before they are one year old and the expectation of life in Japan is 71 as it is in England and Wales, and well above India's 45. There is a high proportion of people of working age and a growing proportion of elderly people to support. Japan is the only country in Asia which has been able to reduce birth and death rates to such low levels, and this is an indication of her advanced stage of economic development.

Government policy since 1947 has been to limit population growth by setting up birth control clinics and legalizing abortion, fearing that limited capital resources could not provide jobs for a fast-growing population, but economic expansion has been so rapid that there has been a shortage of school leavers entering industry since 1959, in spite of the fact that this age group in the early sixties is an especially large one dating from the post-war baby boom. This labour shortage has raised wages especially since 1965 and is encouraging firms to use labour more productively. The rate of growth has been stable at about 1% a year since 1955 so the population has increased by about a million each year. The very low birth rate in 1966 reflected the difficult economic situation in 1965 but the higher birth rate in 1967 partly compensated for this. This is a clear indication of the high degree of control.

CHAPTER NINE

The Industrialization of Japan

The Rise of Industry

Japan is the only industrial country outside Europe, USSR and North America. Her industrial development has taken place in spite of geographical obstacles rather than because of geographical assets. Japan has few natural resources, little cultivable land and is densely populated. She lacks the foundations for industry and has to import half the coking coal, most of the iron ore and scrap steel, and almost all the oil, raw wool and cotton she needs.

During the last thirty years of the nineteenth century Japan was socially, economically and politically transformed. In 1868 she was a feudal country mainly of subsistence farmers (figs. 94 & 31). Her roads were frequented by nobles riding in palanquins or on horseback with their retainers on foot, and traders carrying goods on their backs (pls. 35 & 36). Her small amount of industry was carried on in homes or small factories without steam power.

Now she is a modern democratic state with a good communications network and a fully fledged industrial and commercial organization. She is with Britain the fourth largest manufacturing country in the world after the United States, USSR and Western Germany. She leads the world in the production of ships, cameras and transistor radios, is second only to the United States in electrical machinery, synthetic fibres, television sets and textiles, and is third in the production of steel, vehicles, cement and plastics. Her economy has grown rapidly during the last ten years at an average pace of 10% per annum between 1953 and 1966, faster than in any other country; her industrial production quadrupled in the decade up to 1966, her exports quintupled and she added ten years to the average expectation of life and 2·7 inches to the average height of her 11-year-old children. Her prosperity is indicated by the fact that in 1968 96% of homes in Japan had television, 85% had washing machines and some 78% refrigerators compared with 82%, 45% and 30% in the UK. She has between Tokyo and Osaka the fastest train service in the world. Her high quality cameras, tape recorders, radios, ships, clothes and cars are selling in the great industrial countries of the west.

To appreciate how this development has been brought about in spite of a lack of raw materials, it is necessary to examine not only her resources but also her political situation, social evolution, economic background and philosophical outlook.

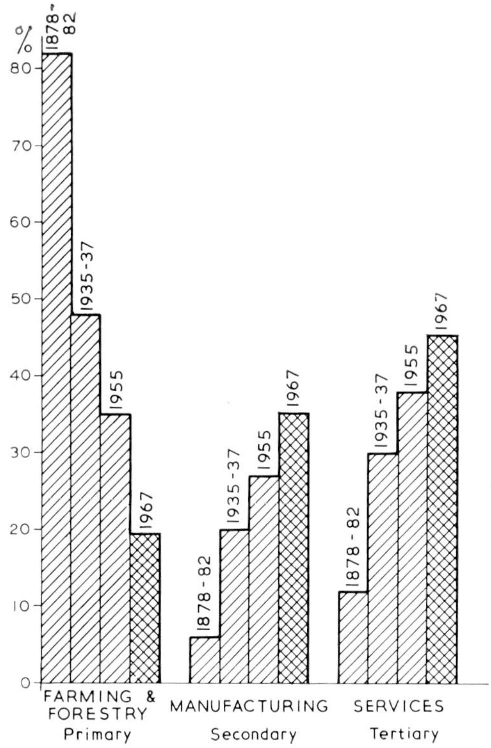

FIG. 94. The changing distribution of the labour force between farming and forestry (primary) industry, manufacturing (secondary) industry and services (tertiary industry) since 1878–82 (85 & 91).

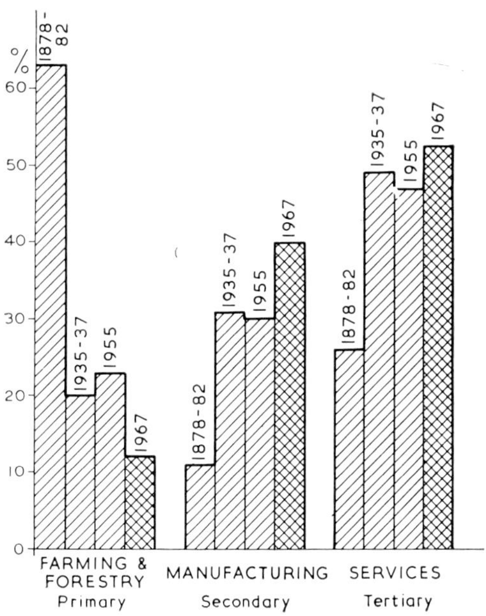

FIG. 95. The changing distribution of the origin of national income since 1878–82 (88 & 91).

PLATE 35. One of Hiroshige's woodblock prints of Fuji and the Tokaido made in the early nineteenth century. It shows clearly the simple means of travel on foot and horseback used until less than a hundred years ago.

Her development can best be explained in four stages. During the early part of the Meiji era from 1868 to 1880 agriculture was developed to provide capital for industrial expansion and an improved food supply for the growing population. 1880–1931 covers the first phase of industrialization, the period when the simpler types of large-scale industry were founded and developed, at first textiles and later iron and steel. It was also the age of colonial expansion and so of new sources

PLATE 36. The old and the new exist together in Japan. Japan's new roads cut across the farmlands and are as modern as any in the world. This new complex intersection with its tolls and service area is on the Nagoya Expressway between Osaka and Tokyo; here it runs parallel to the Nagara River west of Nagoya.

of raw materials and larger markets. From 1914 to 1931 industrial expansion was so rapid that for the first time industrial production became more important than agricultural production. The third period, 1932–51, was significant as the second phase of industrialization with the growing efficiency of production. This was accompanied, during the thirties, by the increasing control of industry by a military governing group. The period 1937 to 1951 began with the enormous growth of industry leading up to and during World War II followed by its exhaustion and destruction, so that by 1945 44% of factories had been destroyed and production was a quarter of that before the war. Following this was the economic malaise of the years of acute shortage from 1945 to 1948. The period since 1951 and the Korean War has been one of rapid recovery, followed, since 1955, by the expansion of third stage capital intensive industries including the motor-vehicle industry, shipbuilding, oil refining, petrochemicals, synthetic fibres, resin and the plastics industry. In this stage Japan has emerged as one of the world's leading industrial countries.

THE FOUNDATIONS OF INDUSTRIAL DEVELOPMENT 1868–1880

The first steps in modern economic development were possible when the country was united under the very strong and far-sighted centralized Meiji government, which aimed at 'the enrichment and strength of the nation' through military and economic development. At this time the government was supported by a people whose loyalty had its roots in a nationalist religion and philosophy. As in the period of Chinese influence during the sixth to ninth centuries, so with westernization in the nineteenth century, new ideas were introduced from abroad and adapted to Japan's needs. The 'barbarian' was accepted for his usefulness. Radical changes in the structure of society and the economy followed.

Great importance was attached to armed strength and so German military advisers and British naval advisers were called in. Military might needed a foundation in industrial strength; an iron and steel industry was required to make armaments and to provide the machinery for the development of other industries. The government bought machinery from abroad and brought in advisers to set up model factories which others would copy. Almost every industry in Japan today had its beginnings in those established by the Meiji government.

Nineteenth-century industrial growth depended on agricultural advance, because the capital for early industrial development had to be collected from the farmers. The progress of underdeveloped countries today is hampered until they can break the vicious circle of low yields, poor health, apathy, and so poor farming and again low yields. The Japanese made progress by far-sighted planning. Farm yields were improved with better seeds and greater use of night-soil and other fertilizers, so that not only did farming provide the capital vital for industrial development, but also the surplus of food for the people working in the newly established industries. The government established experimental stations to improve seeds and develop better methods, and an Agricultural Extension Bureau and many schools and colleges to spread the new ideas throughout the farm community. They gave subsidies to encourage farmers to apply the new methods and to help them to develop their farmlands. Larger farmers with 5 or 6 acres of land gave demonstrations to their less prosperous neighbours. Farmers had an incentive to increase their yields to meet the tax demands of 30% to 40% of their crops and to ensure that there would be enough food left to feed their families. Thus by education and taxation farmers were encouraged to use more irrigation and better seeds, to improve weeding practices and use more fertilizer, especially night-soil. This enabled them to raise rice yields by 80%

between 1880 and 1920, and by extending the area farmed by 35% to produce enough rice and other food crops to feed the growing number of industrial workers and town dwellers, and at the same time to produce, through taxes, the capital needed by the government to establish industries.

During this period farmers were under great pressure both from high taxation and competition from foreign cotton and sugar. To pay the high taxes some were forced to sell their lands and to become tenants, whose landlords often claimed half their crops as rent. At the same time the competition of imported food and raw materials forced farmers to change the crops they grew. Home-grown sugar and cotton, that had been grown round the Inland Sea, were replaced by cheaper imported supplies while, in their place, more mulberries, fruit and vegetables were grown.

The Meiji government swept away the limiting stratification of feudal society. The samurai were discharged and given government bonds to replace their stipends. Many of them invested these in industry, so providing a valuable source of capital. As educated people capable of organizing others they were available to fill managerial posts in the new industrial society. Industrial labour came from among the farmers' daughters and the younger sons who did not inherit the land.

Recognizing the need for literacy to speed the dissemination of technical knowledge, the government made education compulsory in 1872, only two years after England took her first steps in that direction. The early spread of education has been one of the most important factors in the development of industry and farming. Even under the Tokugawas 30% of the population were literate. By 1885 65% of boys and 31% of girls were literate and it is estimated that, by 1900, 95% of the Japanese were literate. With a literate population new ideas and techniques in farming and industry spread more rapidly.

The government developed the public utilities needed for industrialization. They built the first railway from Tokyo to Yokohama in 1872 with the aid of British advisers. Others soon followed and they improved the roads. They built the ships for a navy and merchant marine in their new shipyards. In 1871 they established the post office with a telephone and telegraph service.

The government led the industrial development. They modernized the old factories set up by the shogun and lords. They built textile mills before 1890, and later, iron and steel works, engineering plants and shipbuilding yards, especially in north Kyushu and in the Osaka and Tokyo areas. The model factories they built led the way in mechanizing the old cotton, silk, iron, paper, glass, cement, ceramic and many other industries. Model coal and copper mines were also opened. In 1877 the government sponsored a great exhibition in Tokyo to spread the knowledge of new farming and industrial methods. The tradition of frugality helped to keep down consumer demand, and freed new capital for use in the basic, producer-goods industries, whose metals and machinery could be used to build other industries. Developments in USSR have followed a similar pattern during this century.

The government sold the new factories cheaply and many passed to ex-samurai families, who gradually gained more and more influence as they built up trade, industry and banking concerns, and became the great financial groups or *zaibatsu*, of which Mitsui, Mitsubishi, Sumitomo and Yasuda were the largest.

A steady flow of capital was essential for the continuance of this rapid industrialization. Little came from abroad but at home, although at first it came from farm taxes and samurai bonds, soon industry made a vital contribution from its profits. As they paid little to their workers, who were used to living frugally, most of the profits could be ploughed back into industry and the rate of capital formation was very high. Even those with low incomes were thrifty and small savings were tapped by a network of savings banks in which small individual deposits from a large number of depositors yielded a worthwhile total.

Trade was controlled by the government, who ensured that the scarce foreign currency resources from the sale of silk, tea, copper and craft products were used to buy the raw materials and machinery most necessary for the growth of the basic industries. Almost all the new industries depended on imported raw materials. Japan had her own supplies of coal and wood for fuel and silk for the growing textile industry, but needed to import more iron and cotton and industrial machinery. As early as 1869 the government established the Commercial Bureau to inspect exports and to improve their standard.

Thus the Meiji government, with the enthusiastic support of a loyal, patriotic, frugal and increasingly literate people, laid the foundations of industrialization with compulsory education, the establishment of industries, the development of public utilities and the organization of trade. Upon these foundations industry and trade was developed by private enterprise, led by the *zaibatsu* who came to control a large proportion of it. All this was accomplished by a strong central government that was determined to strengthen the military and economic power of Japan in spite of a shortage of essential raw materials.

THE FIRST PHASE OF INDUSTRIALIZATION 1880–1931

After the establishment of many new industries in Meiji times the period from 1880 to 1931 was one of political stability and of expansion of industry in scope and in scale. The Sino-Japanese war of 1894–5 provided an impetus to industrial development, while the unexpected success of the Japanese encouraged them to even greater patriotic fervour and brought the country to the notice of the great powers as a new force to be reckoned with in the Far East. She extended her frontiers (fig. 96), using her new military power, to build up an empire in the east. She gained control of Formosa in 1895. In 1905 she defeated Russia and acquired Southern Sakhalin and in 1910 moved into Korea. This brought her growing power to the notice of the West. World War I, in which she sided with the Allies, gave her control of the former German colonies in the Mariana, Caroline and Marshall Islands. Her power extended further in the thirties when she annexed Manchuria in 1931. At the peak of her power during World War II her control stretched from New Guinea to Manchuria.

The textile industry, producing mainly cotton and silk goods, expanded faster than any other, and two-thirds of factory workers were making textiles in 1900. It grew rapidly, using existing skills and simple new techniques, and the fact that it could use home-produced silk and needed relatively little capital helped speedy development, although the industry soon depended almost entirely

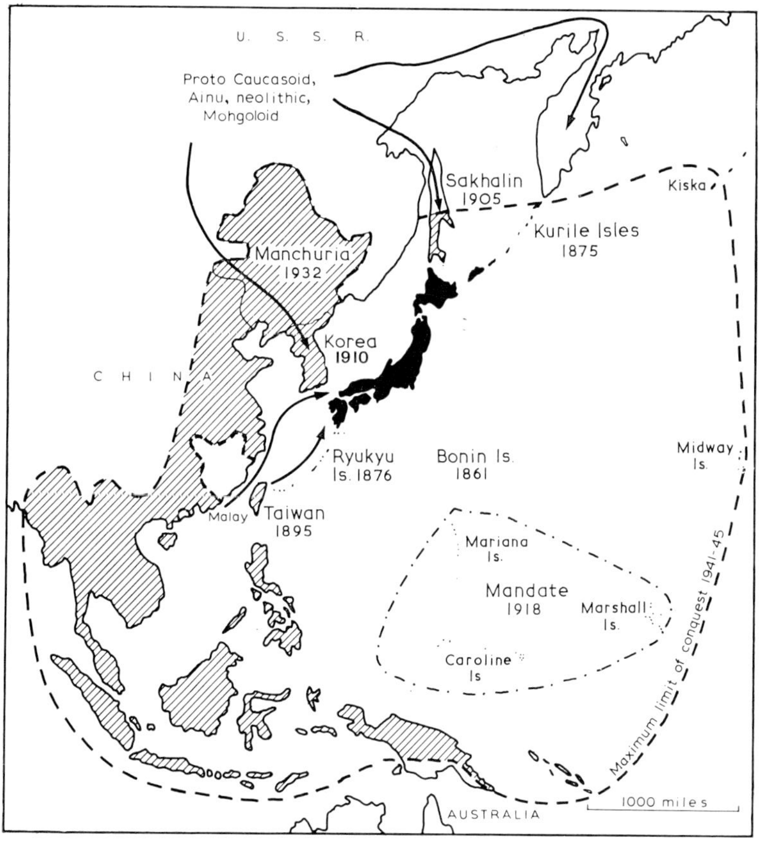

FIG. 96. The peopling of Japan and the growth of the Japanese Empire.

on imported raw cotton. Despite rather inefficient production, the low wages in Japan made her able to undersell the Lancashire industry.

The government continued to establish new factories in the basic industries, notably the Yawata iron and steel works, established in north Kyushu in 1901 to make use of local coal though most of the iron ore had to be imported. The Mitsubishi shipbuilding yards were subsidized to build up naval and marine power. Foreign firms, as well as sending advisers, also began to establish some plants themselves, especially in the Osaka and Tokyo areas. The Dunlop, Ford and General Motors Companies all established plants during this period and foreign merchants played a small though important role in organizing trade.

The power of the large-scale industrialists grew and by the turn of the century the pattern of modern industry was set. Large-scale factories in an industrial zone from Tokyo to north Kyushu were producing iron and steel, heavy machinery, ships, cement, paper, glass, beer, fertilizer and pottery, all of which needed considerable capital and new techniques, and were labour-intensive. North Kyushu was the main centre of iron smelting and Osaka grew as a textile centre with many other small- and large-scale industries. At the same time small family workshops, often organized by merchants, continued to develop, especially in the new industrial Core Zone, in industries where large-scale machinery was not essential. The merchant saved the cost of building a factory and used valuable labour resources by organizing the production in homes. Small engineering goods such as bicycle parts and silk and cotton clothing were made in and near Osaka, pottery in Seto and Arita and craft products in domestic workshops in Kyoto and many other towns. This duality of large- and small-scale industry, usually making different types of goods, but at times closely interdependent, is still characteristic of Japanese industry today.

With the growth of industry Japan's pattern of trade changed. By the turn of the century manufactured goods were beginning to be exported and textiles, especially silk and cotton, made up more than half the total. The government subsidized exports to meet the growing need for imported raw materials, including cotton and iron ore which with silk were the mainstays of the new industry, and the industrial machines needed for further development.

The period from 1914 to 1931 was one of expansion and the value of industrial production overtook farm production in Japan. Though farming yields had continued to improve and more land was being irrigated, food production failed to keep up with the growing population and Japan had to import a third of all her food supplies, including 20% of the rice she needed. World War I stimulated industrial development, since European supplies of machinery, ships, textiles, chemicals and ceramics were cut off from Asiatic markets, and Japan had just reached a position where her industry could be expanded to meet the demand. After the war most of these new markets in Asia were retained. The Depression of 1930 to 1931 caused a business recession in Japan but thanks to her monetary policies and the rationalization of her methods of industrial production, she came out of it with productivity increased and costs and prices reduced, especially in the iron and steel, engineering, shipbuilding and textile industries.

During this period many of the *zaibatsu* amalgamated to form larger, more powerful groups which became a strong political force. The government retained the iron and steel works and shipbuilding yards which were of military importance, but sold most of the remaining factories they had established. This was the heyday of the textile industry and, though silk production was hit by the slump, the cotton industry and the rayon industry, using home-produced wood pulp, developed rapidly.

During the twenties and thirties Japan extended her control over large areas of the neighbouring Asia. To Korea she added Manchuria. Her expansionist policy was founded on economic need for food and raw materials and ambition for political power. Her new colonies supplied her cheaply with food which her limited farmland could not adequately provide for the fast-growing population, and raw materials not available in Japan but much needed for her growing industries. Formosa supplied sugar and rice, Korea rice, and Manchuria the coal and iron ore so necessary to Japanese industry, but China was her main source of raw materials and her main market. They also provided growing markets for textiles, machinery and other industrial products, much as the British colonies had done during her period of industrialization a century before. Trade with these new markets expanded rapidly. The Greater East Asia Co-Prosperity Sphere of the years leading up to 1941 and World War II was intended to provide other raw materials and larger markets. Malaya could provide rubber and tin, India iron, Burma and Thailand rice and the Dutch East Indies oil and rubber, and all were potential markets for industrial products in return.

The colonies were also regarded as possible outlets for the rapidly growing population. Before World War II there was a world-wide feeling that a country could only be politically secure if it could feed its population (49–58). During the twenties and thirties Japan's food deficit was growing as the population expanded much more rapidly than the area cultivated and the crop yields, and there was increasing pressure for emigration to relieve the pressure of population on Japan's limited land area. Emigration, however, never reached very significant proportions. There were grandiose plans for the Manchurian Colonization Company to settle 5 million people in Manchuria, but the Japanese were loath to leave Japan especially for cold, wheat-growing Manchuria, which was not well suited to houses with paper screens, and their taste for rice. Other countries were unwilling to accept them. Up to 1938, only three-quarters of a million Japanese had migrated, most of them to Hawaii, mainland United States and Brazil. This was very few compared with the 18 million emigrants from Britain between 1846 and 1932. Today there are only one million Japanese abroad, half of them in Brazil and a few less in the United States including 206,000 in Hawaii.

THE SECOND PHASE OF INDUSTRIALIZATION 1932–1951

During the thirties the industrial population of Japan, feeling the effects of the Depression, became disgruntled with the *zaibatsu* as a political force and this enabled a ruthless military group who admired the authoritarian, totalitarian governments of the West to rise to power. The new government's 'guns not butter' policy of militarization influenced industrial development and effected increasingly rapid growth in scale and variety of production of the iron and steel, chemical and engineering industries. The authoritarian government increased its power over industry through the formation of cartels and guilds for co-operative marketing, a transition that was comparatively easy since most industry was already organized into the large units of the *zaibatsu*.

During the thirties the composition of Japanese export trade was gradually changed. Textiles became less dominant as the rate of growth in the metal, engineering and chemical industries overtook that in textiles. Textiles made up 59% of exports in 1930 but fell to 38% by 1936, though more textiles were being exported. During the same period metals and machinery rose from 16% to 28% and chemicals from 8% to 11%. Japan came to rely increasingly on imported iron ore and steel scrap. Shipbuilding, engineering and precision instrument industries were all based on imported iron ore and steel scrap, but before the defeat in 1945, about 44% of the plant and machinery had been lost through air raids and much of the rest was in such an overworked state that industrial production in that year was only 30% of the pre-war level. After the war Japan was occupied by the Allied powers. The policy of the Supreme Commander was to punish Japanese war criminals, to reform Japan into a democratic country incapable of waging war and to rid her of the idea that she was destined to lead the whole of Asia. The powerful *zaibatsu* were prime targets and they were partially dismantled. During the unstable period between 1945 and 1947 there was little foreign exchange to spend on raw materials and little desire among the demoralized Japanese to restart industries. At this time over half of Japan's imports were of food, to meet the shortages that caused wildly inflated prices from which only the farmers and black market operators prospered.

The year 1947 saw the beginning of the Cold War and SCAP, having already paid out $3,386 million in aid mainly from the American taxpayer, realized that Japan was a very expensive liability since without industry and exports she had no source of foreign exchange with which to buy the food she needed. So in 1949 SCAP instituted a recovery policy to make Japan a bulwark against Communism in eastern Asia, with aid for the redevelopment of the iron, coal, petroleum refining and cotton textile industries. It was not until the Korean War in 1951 brought orders for $46 million worth of goods from the USA, and until Japan became a base for UN forces that Japanese industrial production began to climb back to pre-war levels.

INDUSTRIAL CHARACTER IN THE THIRD PHASE OF INDUSTRIALIZATION, SINCE 1951

Since 1951 Japan has entered a third phase of industrialization. By 1955 production was back to its wartime peak, by 1960 it doubled and between 1960 and 1966 it doubled again (fig. 97). She became with Britain the world's fourth most important industrial and trading nation, after USA, USSR and West Germany. Her prosperity grew so that by 1966 her income *per capita* was equal to that in Italy, double that in Portugal and ten times that in India. Her lead over the underdeveloped countries is growing but she has still only a half of the income *per capita* of Britain and a quarter of USA (fig. 98). Manufacturing income is now four times as great as farming income, and industry employed 35% of the total work force in 1967 compared with 19% in farming. The balance of Japanese industry has changed away from labour-intensive industries with a low requirement for capital, including textiles and the many small goods made in workshops (fig. 99). These can now be made by many underdeveloped countries using much labour, little capital and paying relatively low wages.

Since 1945, though textile production has risen it was only 10% by value of the

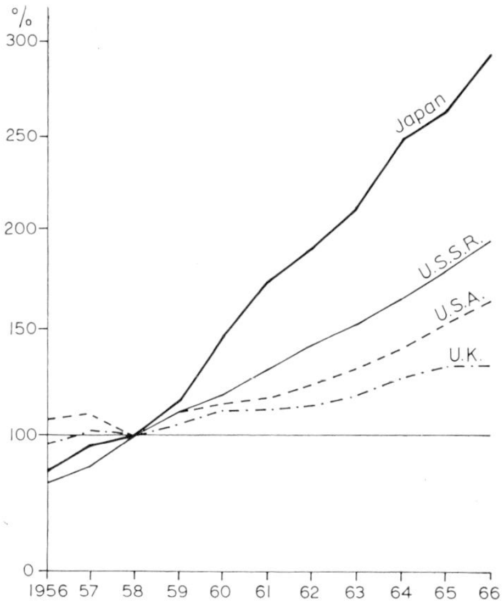

FIG. 97. Comparative growth of industrial production since 1958 (90).

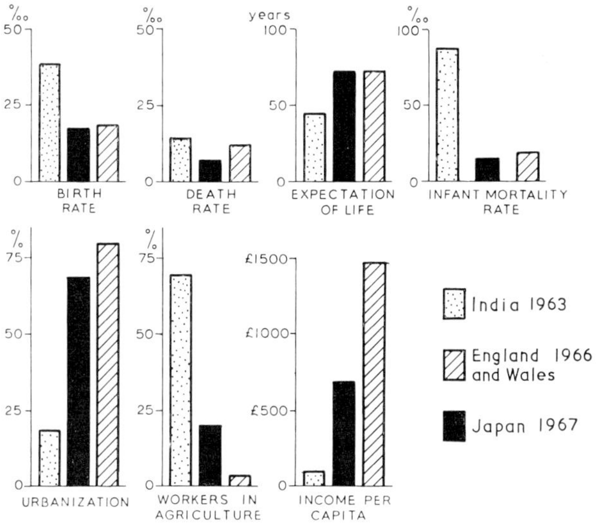

FIG. 98. Some indicators of the stage of economic development in India, Japan, and England and Wales (90, 91 & 99).

total production in 1962 compared with 19% in 1935. The leading place has been taken by the engineering industry, which now makes 36%, including ships, electronic and electrical equipment and motor-vehicles. Textiles were well

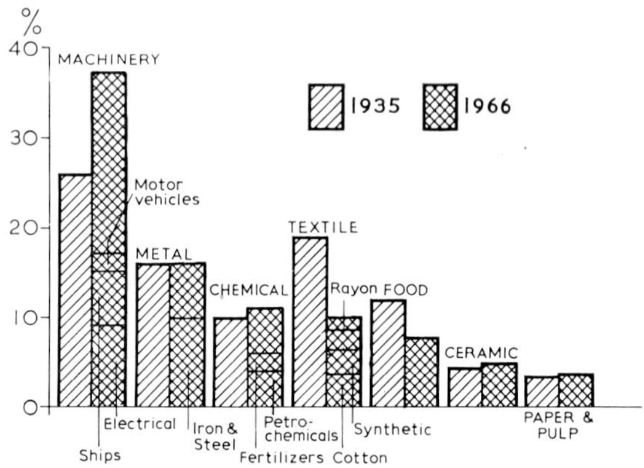

FIG. 99. The relative importance of industries in 1935 and 1966 by value added (90).

suited to the first phase of industrialization as little expensive capital equipment was needed, skills were quickly acquired and wages were low. But now that wages are higher in Japan many less developed countries like India and China, where labour is still cheap, are in their turn encouraging a textile industry which, often helped by subsidies and protection, can undercut Japanese prices.

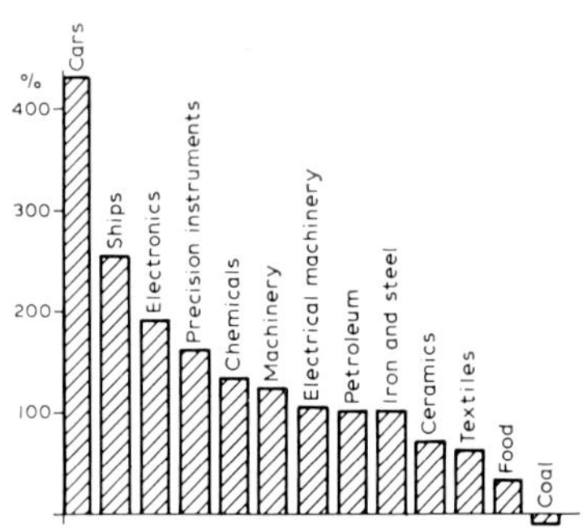

FIG. 100. The relative growth of various industries between 1960 and 1966 by value added (90).

Since 1951 and especially since 1955 industries involving advanced technology and large amounts of capital have expanded (fig. 100). The government has encouraged the development of key industries such as iron and steel, electrical goods and transport, petroleum refining, petro-chemicals, synthetic fibres, resin and motor-vehicle equipment, by direct subsidies and loans through the bank and the large industrial groups.

Only highly developed countries, mainly those of western Europe and North America, have the capital and the technical knowledge and skill required for setting up such industries as these. Japan, who has so recently entered this field, has already reached such a state of industrial maturity that even in these modern industries she is among the leaders, being second only to USA in synthetic textiles and having already the third largest motor-vehicle industry. She has led the world in shipbuilding tonnage since 1956, is a leading producer of steel, radios, electrical goods, precision instruments, transport equipment, plastics and textiles, and is able to compete with the highly industrialized countries of Europe and North America in the marketing of engineering, textile and chemical products. Japan's rate of growth of 10% per year between 1955 and 1966 exceeded that of every other country. Production increased 4 times during that period. Production in the USSR, Japan's nearest rival in rate of growth, only doubled and in the United Kingdom and the United States it lagged far behind with increases of 33 and 67%. During this period United Kingdom exports increased by only 34% while Japan's grew by 260%. Real incomes in industry increased by 29% in Japan between 1960 and 1966 (fig. 97).

Industrial growth has provided increasing supplies of industrial products at home, both of machinery for the further development of industry and of consumer goods to meet the rise in incomes, especially those in industry.

Today instead of spending most of their income on rice to eke out a bare existence as many Indians do, the Japanese can afford more luxurious foods such as fish, dairy produce, fruit and vegetables and sometimes meat, and still have money to spare for television sets, washing machines, cameras and motor-cycles, imported foods, skiing holidays and golf. This increased prosperity has taken the Japanese economy steadily away from those of its neighbours in Asia and, since progress is more rapid in Japan than in most industrial nations, she is catching up with the standard of living of the most prosperous western countries, though she has still a long way to go. Japan had only 1 car to 36 people in 1966 compared with 1 to 6 in Britain (fig. 98) and 1 to 3 in the United States.

Japanese industry relies heavily on export markets and 29% of industrial products are marketed abroad. This means that industrial development in Japan since the war has depended more and more on world prosperity and expanding world markets.

THE LARGE INDUSTRIAL GROUPS

Great industrial groups play a leading part in Japan's industry. Many of them originated with the great *zaibatsu* which were broken up by SCAP after the war but have re-formed without the family control as new combines in which banks control much of Japan's industry, transport and trade. Each group has its own particular character but they all have a similar grouping of associated companies round a bank with trading firms and factories. There is competition between the groups but they are closely interrelated and often co-operate in planning developments as they have done in the petro-chemical industry. This grouping in industry makes it easy for the government to keep in close contact with industrial activities. Mitsubishi, Sumitomo, Mitsui, Fuji, Daichi and Sanwa are six of the ten larger groups

Mitsubishi was founded as a shipping company by the Iwasaki family in 1870. It expanded to manufacturing the raw materials it imported, opening coal mines to produce coal for its industry and metal mines to supply other raw materials. In 1963 it had twenty-one manufacturing companies with 103 factories, plants and mines all over Japan. The iron ore she imports can be processed by one of her iron and steel companies in Tokyo, made into a cracking tower by a company in Kawasaki to be used for a petro-chemical plant at Yokkaichi, which uses the oil she imports to make synthetic fibres which are woven into cloth in Nagoya, stored in her warehouses there and exported by her trading company in her own ships made at a company yard in Nagasaki, Yokohama, Kawasaki, Tokyo or Hiroshima.

The *Sumitomo* group grew from a different beginning and has a similar variety of associated industry but with a different bias. It grew from the foundation of the Besshi copper mine by a samurai in Shikoku. A smelter was built on the island of Niihama on the north coast of Shikoku and a factory making copper wires was set up to use the copper produced. Coal mines were opened in Kyushu to provide the necessary fuel; a chemical works was built to use the by-products of smelting the ore. Local forests were used to supply wood for a pulp and paper industry and later on a rayon industry. Hydroelectric and thermal power stations were constructed in Kyushu to meet the demands of the smelting, chemical, pulp and paper, rayon and other industries, all in northern Kyushu. Sumitomo activities have expanded, like other *zaibatsu*, to include 5% of Japan's trade, banking, insurance and a variety of industry and to employ 200,000 people. The company is still Japan's largest producer of chemicals. She has a great new petro-chemical complex at Yokkaichi which is one of Japan's largest, and plants producing fertilizer, rayon, glass, and rubber. Mining is still one of her leading activities. She is the fourth largest producer of coal with mines in Kyushu and Hokkaido, and produces copper, silver, gold and nickel. The iron and steel and aluminium she smelts are made in other of her factories into a wide variety of engineering goods, including aeroplanes, pipes, electrical goods and precision instruments. Her present interests are still biased towards the metals and chemicals with which she began.

The *Mitsui* group dealt with a third of all Japan's trade in 1966, and prides herself on dealing with everything from bridges to buttons and cars to canned foods. She includes such large and famous companies as the Mitsui Steamship Company, Toyo Rayon, Asahi Breweries and Mitsui Petro-chemicals.

During the sixties the large groups have acted increasingly as consultants in building mines, dams, power plants and factories abroad and have established many joint companies. Mitsui, for example, has built pork and poultry processing plants, spinning and wire rope factories in Taiwan; adhesives, spinning and cement factories in Singapore, salt fields in Western Australia, a fertilizer plant in Brazil and a spinning plant in Portugal.

Reasons for Japan's Economic Growth

It is impossible to explain in terms of geographical assets the fact that Japan alone among all the nations of Asia and the underdeveloped world has been able to break through the barrier to industrialization. Her resources of raw materials and power are very limited and she depends on imports for 30% of her coal, 97% of her iron ore and steel scrap and 99% of the oil, which is her main source of energy. Land too is short, though this is perhaps an advantage in that it has forced her to industrialize to feed her growing population. Only labour has been plentiful.

In attempting to explain her growth it is very difficult not to over-generalize, but some points stand out. If one looks at the early stages of industrialization one sees that attitudes were all important. The government was backed by a united loyal people who had great pride in their culture and who were determined to gain a place in the modern world. They were as advanced and cultured as were the people of western Europe at the time of their Industrial Revolution. To every Japanese it is very important not to be done down and thought poorly of and so to lose face. This pride has engendered a revolutionary zeal which can stimulate individuals and through them the body politic to make great sacrifices for success. Japanese philosophy puts the good of the nation above any individual desires so that people work for national progress. In what British factory would the workers sing this before starting work?

For the building of a new Japan
Let's put our strength and mind together,
Doing our best to promote production,
Sending our goods to the people of the world,
Endlessly and continuously,
Like water gushing from a fountain.
Grow, industry, grow, grow, grow!
Harmony and sincerity!
Matsushita Electricity! (96)

This puts national attitudes in a nutshell. The same co-operative, progressive enthusiasm is shown at all levels of society and in the close collaboration that exists in all planning. The great industrial groups are co-operative in putting into action government plans. Japan is not a planned economy in the Russian sense and industrialists would deny that there is any overall planning, but government departments are constantly putting out plans, for example, on the development of new industries and their location (fig. 107). These are not put into effect by order but rather through the close, subtle relationships between the government, the central bank and the industrial groups who either own or control much of Japan's large-scale industry. Pride is important in the relationship between the industrial groups, for if one establishes a petro-chemical complex the others must have a bigger and better one to gain prestige. National and factory statistics constantly refer to their place in world and national production.

There has been remarkably little foreign capital used in industrial development. Until 1967 foreign companies were limited to a holding of 15% in any company. In 1968 18% of capital was foreign, 66% of it American especially in petrol refining, chemicals and engineering.

Japanese attitudes are partly explained by the philosophical tradition of national unity and loyalty, but education has also played a big part. The Meiji government gave this high priority when they made education compulsory in 1872, so that by 1900 over 90% of the population was literate. Today there is great emphasis on education and especially on technical education. As many as 45% of Japanese boys stay at school after the end of compulsory education at fifteen, compared with 30% in Britain. At eighteen 24% stay for further education, compared with Britain's 18%. Factories are very keen on training their workers, so that educationally the Japanese worker is more highly educated than his British counterpart. Children and adults are anxious to learn, as any visitor to Japan will rapidly find when he is cross-questioned by children and adults alike. Well-developed communications help to disseminate ideas. Even the most remote farmer has television, 45 million newspapers are circulated each day and there are hundreds of technical magazines which are avidly read.

The traditional thrift of the Japanese has helped development, as people are apt to live frugally and save and can easily invest their savings by buying securities in an office in their local shopping centre. Industrial profits are high and a very large proportion of them are ploughed back into further investment, so that industrial investment is a third above that in UK. Each year since 1960 33% of the national income has been invested, which is well above Britain's 11%. Japan, like Western Germany, has had the great advantage since the war of spending only 1·5% of her national income, compared with Britain's 6·5% on defence, so much more of her financial resources have been available for industrial development.

Japan has gained from the newness of her industry. Most of her industrial equipment is new; much of it, like that of Western Germany, she was forced to replace after wartime destruction. This means that production is more efficient. For example her cotton factories are more up-to-date than those in Lancashire.

The government has played a leading role in the growth of Japanese industry since 1868. The Meiji government laid an integrated plan for industrial growth; first they developed farming and later established new types of industry. Since 1945 the government's part in industrial development has been more indirect. It has planned the direction industry should take and guided development in that direction by discussions with the large groups and, through more positive action has created high trade barriers to protect the new motor-vehicle, petrochemical and other engineering industries until they were large enough to become profitable. Key industries have been encouraged to develop and industries have been encouraged to decentralize by cheap loans and exemption from taxes.

Since 1951 Japanese goods have become increasingly competitive in foreign markets. The efficiency of her industry has increased and so goods have become cheaper and of better quality. Larger, more efficient plants have been established with all the advantages of new equipment. Small plants have been integrated, modernized and rationalized in the engineering, shipbuilding, motor-vehicle, iron and steel and chemical industries. The reorganization of shipbuilding yards has greatly increased the speed and efficiency of building ships, thus helping to sell them abroad. The need to import raw materials and fuel has led her to develop mines abroad to insure supplies and stimulated a search for economies in their use in the iron and steel and chemical industries. For example, the amount of coke used in smelting a ton of iron ore in Japanese blast furnaces has been cut by nearly a half since 1951, so that it is now the lowest in the world. There was a strong incentive to economize in fuel and raw materials which are costly, because most of them must be brought from distant countries – for example, coal and iron ore from Australia and iron ore from India and Malaysia. There was less incentive to economize on labour which was still relatively cheap (two-thirds British cost and one-third USA). until the labour shortage since 1959, aggravated by the low wartime birth rate. Since 1961 labour has become increasingly in short supply and so more expensive. This is forcing industry to use labour more efficiently.

The standard of products has been improved through research and technical agreements. It is in high quality goods that Japan is most competitive. Industrialists are constantly on the watch for new ideas. Agreements for technical assistance have been made in the electrical, machinery and chemical industries especially with American companies. Matsushita Electrical Company have agreements with Philips in the Netherlands, and ICI sold Japan rights in the terylene process. The government's voluntary inspection system applies to about half the goods exported, including machinery, textiles, pottery and cameras and foods, and this has helped to improve the quality of the goods produced. Thus the expansion of Japan's industry has been helped by the improved quality of goods, reduction in the cost of production, increasing world prosperity and growing markets.

In spite of progress in establishing new, efficient, profitable industries, Japan's industry is still hampered by the large number of small, much less efficient workshops which still employ a third of the labour force. In these capital is lacking, labour often lacks skill and productivity and wages low. Half Japan's labour force is still employed as 'temporary' labour at low rates of pay or in low productivity jobs with low wages in small workshops, at home as unpaid family labour, in shops or on farms. With the shortage of young labour in the sixties there has been a growing transfer of this labour to more productive employment. The number of people in farming and small-scale industry is declining and the efficiency of small-scale production increasing. Some of the problems involved in this are discussed in the next chapter.

Thus industrialization has been possible in Japan in spite of the lack of resources because of the enthusiasm, determination and hard work of a plentiful, cheap (at least until recently), and increasingly productive labour force, and Japanese industry has moved rapidly through three stages of development; from being a purely farm economy she first developed industry requiring relatively little capital and simple technology – at first the textile industry and then ceramics, simpler engineering, including bicycles, and sewing machines, leather and rubber goods, all of which thrived in the early stage of industrialization but are now meeting growing competition from countries now starting to industrialize. These industries are becoming less important in total industrial production. Then followed the more highly capitalized and more complex shipbuilding, electrical engineering, iron and steel and coal-based chemical industries for which Japan retains an advantage. These industries are growing ones. Recently she has entered the third phase with industries with complex technology requiring great capital resources. These new industries including the motor-vehicle and petro-chemical industries have only just become large and efficient enough to be able to compete with similar industry in highly developed countries. These are the industries which only Japan, in all Asia, is developing and where her advantage will grow in the present phase.

All these industries like Britain's, but unlike the USA, are dependent on imported raw material and the sale of manufactured goods abroad.

Industrial Structure

Japan's industrial structure is markedly different from that of western nations. Alongside vast new petro-chemical plants, shipyards, and automated factories

Factory size 1964		*% of factories*	*% value of production*	*% of labour*
Domestic workshops	under 9	75	6	16
Workshops	10–29	11	10	17
Factories	30–299	9	33	35
Large factories	300–999	0·5	21	14
Very large factories	1,000 +	0·1	30	17

	1955	1964	1955	1964	1955	1964
under 300	99·6	99·4	56	48	73	68
300 +	0·4	0·6	44	52	27	32

		value added		*wages*				**productivity*	*Britain sales*	*Britain wage*
		1958	*1965*	*1958*	*1965*	men	women	*1960*	*1958*	*1949*
Domestic workshops	under 10	19	26	38	—			24	75	—
Workshops	10–49	31	44	44	75	31	16	34	74	83
	50–99	41	49	50	78	22	16	42	74	84
Factories	100–499	59	64	61	81	33	16	57	82	86
Large factories	500–999	75	84	75	84	24	20	80	86	89
Very large factories	1,000 +	100	100	100	100	39	18	100	100	100

*thousand yen per month

TABLE 3 The distribution of labour in factories of various sizes, wages and productivity as a proportion of those in factories with over 1,000 workers (88, 91, 98).

assembling television sets she retains many less capitalized small workshops. There is a striking dichotomy between workshops employing up to fifty people earning only 75% of the wages in very large factories and using simple techniques that lead to a third of the productivity and yet employ a third of the labour force, and vast automated works established by large firms with an army of youthful workers using the latest equipment which ensures high productivity and high wages. These two extremes are in many cases interdependent, the large works sub-contract component making to small workshops. In 1964 75% of the factories in Japan had less than ten operatives and these made up 16% of the industrial labour force. No less than 86% of factories had fewer than thirty workers.

SMALL-SCALE INDUSTRY

Small-scale industry is organized in workshops by one family which sometimes employs one or two farm girls often from Tohoku and Kyushu, where there is

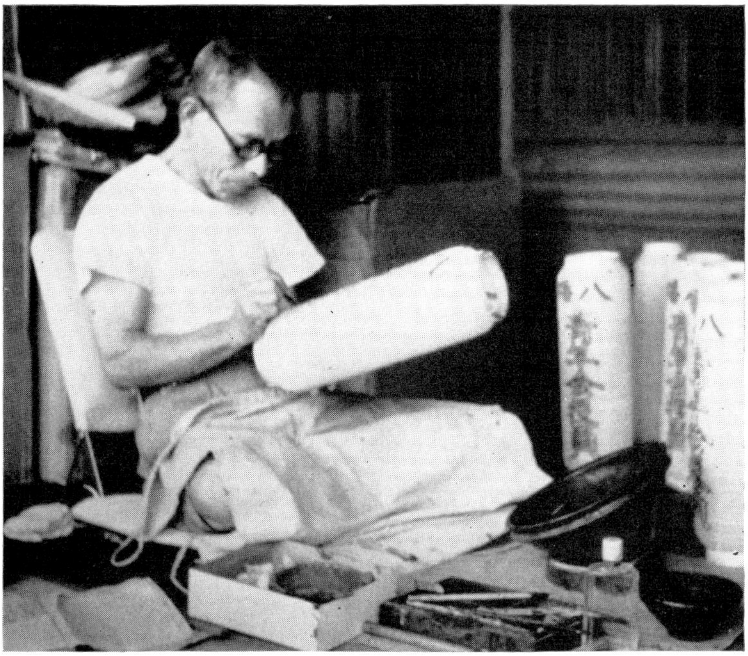

PLATE 37. Lanterns are still made in home workshops and are a relic of the pre-modern era. Such crafts are no longer very important but they have influenced the way modern industry is organized.

little work to be had away from the farms. These girls join the family when they leave school at sixteen and stay until they marry at about twenty-three, and so much are they a part of the family that the employers arrange marriages for them.

The workshop often manufactures goods for a merchant at piecework rates, much as the jewellery and cutlery industries do in Britain, or makes goods for local use. Small-scale industry is particularly important in three main types of industry: in the old craft industries making lanterns (pl. 37), fans, dolls, lacquer-

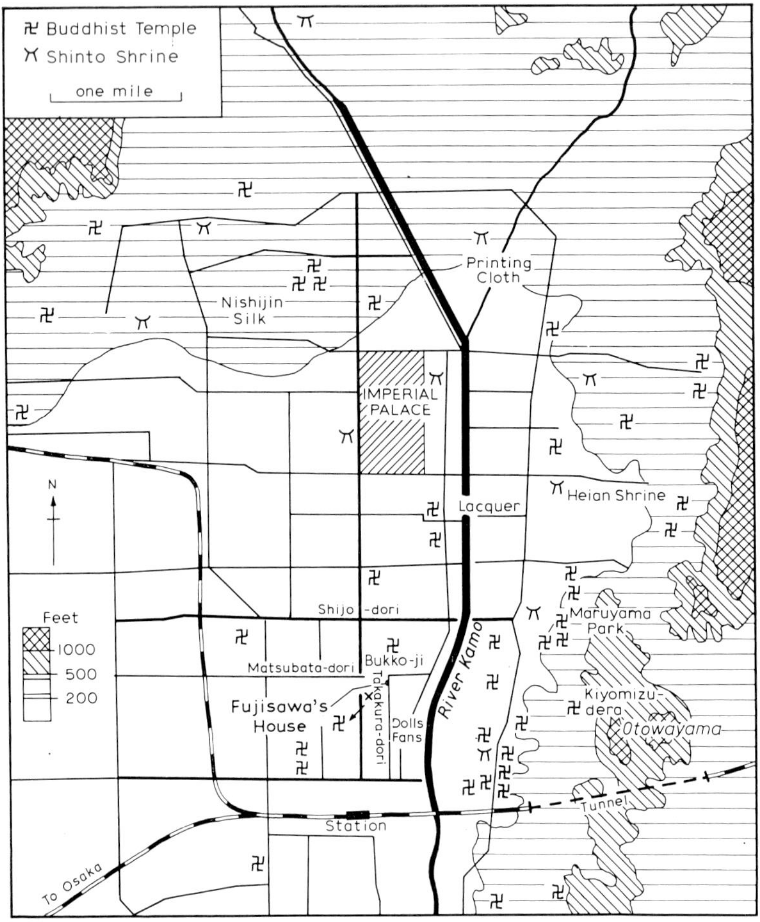

FIG. 101. Kyoto showing its position in the north-east corner of the tectonic basin, the square layout of the city on the ancient Chinese pattern, the many shrines and temples and the traditional industries.

ware and brocades, where special skill is needed; in the industries in every small town that make bread, cakes, cushions and kimono for local use; and also in recently developed industries making parts of cameras, television and radio sets and sewing machines.

Many of the ancient *craft industries of Kyoto* (fig. 101) making lacquerware fans, cloisonné, wood-block prints, dolls and fine silk brocades, are organized on a small scale by merchants. The merchants plan production and arrange marketing. They supply the materials to be worked to independent workers who work at home at piecework rates. Very typical of this is the fan making organized by Mr Fujisawa in Takakura-dori. In his office he receives orders for fans, buys in the paper, wood, paint and glue for making them, and inspects and packs the finished goods. Many people in family workshops in nearby homes work for him, each being responsible for a different process in the making of the fan. In one workshop the family and helpers cut the paper, then they take it, strapped on to a bicycle, to a second house where the basic pattern is printed on to it. In a third

PLATE 38. Hosoe High Street has many small shops and workshops. It is usually crowded with bicycles, cars, trucks and buses (fig. 64) (220).

the detail of the pattern is added and in other homes the paper is folded, the frame is made and the fan is assembled. Altogether a dozen or more workshops may help to make one fan. Many more take part in making a doll where body, head, clothes and properties must all be made separately and assembled.

The woollen industry around Ichinomiya in Aichi Prefecture has a complex organization based on this putting out or sub-contracting system. Usually the merchant designs the cloth to be made and large spinning firms contract to spin it for him. The yarn is then dyed in large workshops, woven to the merchant's design in smaller establishments and finished in large workshops before being sold by the merchant. Thus spinning uses the advantages of large-scale production, whereas in the Ichinomiya area, as in Kyoto, most of the weaving is done in small workshops with one or two looms, where the family work perhaps with the help of a girl. In Kyoto 85% of the silk-weaving workshops have less than five looms, the rest employ only ten to twenty people.

Hosoe town (pl. 38) in Shizuoka Prefecture lies near the north-east shore of Lake Hamada. It is a small town of 13,000 people and is typical of many small towns in its wide variety of small-scale industries. Many of the families in Hosoe have a very small piece of land which barely grows enough rice to feed the family, and they derive their main income either from running a shop or workshop in their homes, or from the work they do in one of the larger workshops in the town,

PLATE 39. The *tatami* maker sews woven rush matting on to a base of pressed rice straw in every village.

none of which employs more than thirty people. Along the main street almost every house has either a small shop or a workshop, or often the two combined. In the alleys behind the main street too there is a buzz of activity. There is the *tatami* maker (pl. 39) crushing the rice straw in his press and stitching on the woven reed cover, the *shoji* maker producing the wooden screens which form the walls of Hosoe homes. Another family makes wooden *geta*, others tailor suits or sew kimono, quilts and cushions; some shell and bag peanuts, some make fish sausages, bake bread or cakes or make any of the many goods needed by the people of Hosoe. Most of the workshops sell direct to their customers. The larger workshops, where ten to twenty people work, make *saké*, mill rice, weave cloth and mill timber. All these workshops use small machinery, such as electric drills and saws to make the wood into *geta* and *shoji*, they grill fish sausages on a moving belt and use electric-powered looms for weaving.

In villages in and near the Hanshin city region, where Osaka is the centre of the manufacture of a variety of *small goods*, there is a great deal of merchant-organized industry making small goods. This type of domestic system is well suited to making goods where there is no advantage in mass production because a large variety is needed and the demand is continually changing, as small workshops are more flexible than mechanized factories. Thus in Hokiji *buraku*, in the Nara Basin, one family makes glass beads for Christmas decorations in their workshop. The merchant provides the glass, they melt and mould the long red-hot tubes into a row of beads. They then pour the dye inside, cut the beads apart and put them on a string. One family moulds goggles for underwater fishing while another grinds the glass to fit them. Others nearby make mosquito netting and hosiery. Furniture, clothes and toys are often made in this way, and there is a chain of families in one *buraku* or street each specializing in a different stage of processing, passing on the work from one to another. In Sumida ward in Tokyo a whole street specializes in shirt or furniture making, as they do in the east end of London.

Many domestic workshops are *sub-contractors* for large industrial firms making such things as radio and television sets, cameras, electrical goods, cars and motorcycles. They make the parts that are designed by the large firms and assembled on a conveyor-belt system in large modern factories, so that small-scale old-style workshops and large-scale modern factories are interdependent.

From these examples it is apparent that while small-scale industry is important in making goods where little capital is needed, it often exists where great skill is required, as in the craft industries, and also because mechanization and large-scale production are difficult because of the variety, individuality and change in the patterns of the product. It has the drawbacks of costly raw materials and shortage of labour and capital, labour that is often old, poor sales organization often with overproduction and fierce competition all contributing to low productivity and low wages and so a high labour turnover. Instability results both from this and often from dependence on the firm sub-contracting the work for sales and sometimes for capital. It has the advantage of making use of the cheap, older, often part-time, rural labour and does away with the need for large capital investment in setting up a factory.

LARGE-SCALE INDUSTRY

Large-scale industry with factories employing over 300 people in 1964 made up less than 1% of the total number of factories but they employed 32% of the industrial labour force and made 52% by value of the goods produced (table 3). Large factories have been established in industries where it is much cheaper to produce on a large scale, for example in the iron and steel industry, in shipbuilding, in the manufacture of chemicals, transport equipment, electrical goods and in oil refining, and motor-vehicle manufacture. In these industries a great deal of capital is required to establish a plant.

A large factory like the Matsushita Electrical factory (pl. 40), which makes television sets in Osaka, employing 2,000 people and using the most up-to-date methods, looks very much like any modern factory in Europe or America but there are significant differences. Japanese large-scale industry combines the techniques of modern industry with the social relationships of her not so distant

PLATE 40. Young girls assembling television sets at Matsushita Denki in Osaka using the techniques of modern large-scale mass production with conveyor belts and electronic testers.

feudal past. The firm is a united community providing not only work but housing, medical services, leisure activities and education facilities, so that the worker can live his whole life within the community. The firm is like a family which workers usually join when they leave school and stay with for the whole of their working lives. They become part of the firm and, as in a family, workers and employers take on obligations to one another. The workers accept a duty of lifelong service to the firm and in return the employers are paternalistic, looking after the workers and continuing to pay them even when in a period of depression there is no work for them to do, and looking after them in their retirement.

Workers and management are interdependent, co-operating together in production and, as in family relationships, the idea of service is important. The individual works for the community, not for himself; individualism in Japan is tantamount to egotism. Something of the same relationship exists between the firm and the state, for here too there is a strong sense that the nation must come first. It is difficult for us to believe that when there has been a shortage of jobs employers have felt it their duty to take on a larger number of workers than they need (163). The emphasis is on mutual obligation not individual rights.

A corollary of this paternalistic attitude and the idea of service is the way that wages are based on family size, age and qualifications rather than on the value of the work the employee does for the firm. Wages are not high by British standards, though earnings are higher than in small-scale industry, but to the wages in large factories at least 20% must be added for fringe benefits. Large factories provide very cheap subsidized meals, free travel, working clothes, free or cheap residential accommodation, holiday homes and facilities for sport, and evening classes for continuing education in many subjects, ranging from flower arrangement to technical subjects. All this helps to increase the strong feeling of community in the firm. Work is a way of life rather than an exchange of labour for wages.

Large groups are important in Japanese industry. Some like Mitsui and Sumitomo date from the Tokugawa era, others like Mitsubishi from the Meiji era, when the government established factories and sold them to leading ex-samurai families. The large merchant and banking companies gradually spread their holdings to all large-scale industry. SCAP broke up the *zaïbatsu* after the war but the groups have re-formed in weaker structure by interchanging shares between companies and interlocking directorships and are still a strong force in leading Japanese industrial development, especially through their banks, which are very important in financing industry, as 70% of company capital is borrowed in Japan compared with 50% in Britain and 30% in the US.

The scale of industrial concerns in Japan is increasing in the sixties. Large firms like Yawata in iron and steel, Toyota and Nissan in the car industry, Hitachi and Matsushita in electrical goods and Toshiba in electric power have expanded. There have been many mergers notably in the iron and steel, cars, shipbuilding, sugar and paper industries and more are mooted. Some of these mergers have followed the old *zaïbatsu* grouping. In many industries a few companies already control a large proportion of production. In 1967 Nissan and Toyota produced 58% of Japan's cars; Honda 73% of motor cycles, Kirin 51% of beer; Fuji and Yawata half the pig iron. Two firms produced 69% of her nylon and three firms 54% of ships. Mitsui and Mitsubishi handled 68% of her imports and 60% of her exports.

Wages are low in Japanese industry partly because productivity is relatively low. US wages are six times as high and British double. They are about equal to French wages. Weak trades union organization has not made pressure for higher wages easy. A high percentage (40%) of the labour force (19 millions) are women earning about half male wages. Industrial workers are young as employees in large factories come straight from school and, as many factories are new, their workers are still very young, and earning only half an older man's salary. In the Matsushita Electric factory the average age is nineteen and many are girls, and there will be a problem for these factories as wages will rise as age rises (the average age in industry rose from thirty-one in 1952 to thirty-five in 1966) and when the retirement age is raised above the unusually low fifty-five that it is at present.

Productivity in terms of output per employee is rising faster than in any other country but it was only half of West Germany and a fifth of US productivity in 1966 because firms aim to minimize the amount of capital used since interest rates are high, often 11%, whereas labour is relatively cheap.

Real wages have risen by 10% a year with the shortage of labour since 1959 and productivity by 12½% a year. They vary from one industry to another. In iron and steel, engineering and chemicals wages are high, because modern equipment requires skilled workers with a high level of technological ability and productivity is high. In textiles, clothing and food industries, where there is less mechanization and more unskilled female labour, wages are lower.

Many firms employ what they call 'temporary' or day-wage labour. These are people who are not fully accepted as part of the firm. They are often older people or farmers who work for a low wage during the winter, especially in the electrical, iron and steel and shipbuilding industries, and sometimes they make up as much as half of the firm's labour force. With mechanization in farming more people are working all the year in factories and the amount of temporary labour from this source is declining.

Trade unions are not a strong force in helping to raise wages among industrial labour. In 1966 they included only 35% of the labour force among their numbers, compared with 45% in the UK in 1965. This is partly because many industrial workers are self-employed or work within the family, and partly because the family feeling and attitude to service does not fit in with the idea of workers versus employers that trade unions imply. Trade unions have developed especially in more impersonal large factories in the iron and steel, electrical engineering and chemical industries and in mining and transport. They are almost all 'enterprise' unions, that is, they include all the workers in one factory, so they are small and, averaging only 200 members, have little bargaining power because they are not united with other unions and have very small financial resources.

There is a great difference in wages between workshops employing under thirty people and the larger factories (table 3). In 1958 the average workshop wage was 44% of that in factories with over 1,000 employees. The wage gap grew until 1959 when a shortage of school leavers arose because of the industrial expansion and the growth of further education. There was no shortage of older people. The labour shortage hit smaller firms who have had to raise wages to attract labour, so that wages in smaller firms have risen faster than those in larger ones and in 1965 were up to 75% of those in large factories.

In workshops people often work long hours and earn little for it though the statutory limit is an eight-hour day and the average is a 48-hour week compared with 47 in United Kingdom and 40 in USA. With little machinery and inefficient organization each worker produces little and therefore can earn little. In 1964 although 68% of the workers were in factories with less than 300 workers they only produced 48% of the goods, while factories with over 300 workers with only 32% of the workers produced 52% of the goods and so could earn more. The labour shortage since 1959 has forced small producers to raise wages to attract labour, and has forced them to rationalize and mechanize their workshops so that workers can produce more to cover their increased wages. Since 1948 the Smaller Enterprise Agency in the Ministry of International Trade and Industry has been advising small proprietors on ways of improving their methods. They have given special attention to textiles, ceramics, engineering and small goods in which they are helping to raise both productivity and the quality of the products, and to arrange co-operative marketing.

Changes are taking place in Japanese industry. Rising wages are bringing increased mechanization. Her labour is well educated and still cheaper than that in the highly industrialized nations but is more costly than that in the rest of Asia, Africa and South America. The scale of industry is growing but needs to increase even more so that the iron and steel, chemical, motor-vehicle and other engineering industries can benefit from the most advanced mass production methods. New iron and steel, chemical, and engineering combines meet this need. New problems are arising as the new industries age and meet the problem of obsolescence. The increasing age of workers is leading to higher wages and a less flexible labour force. Pressure is increasing movement in the traditionally immobile labour force.

Location of industry

About 74% of Japan's industrial production is manufactured in the main industrial belt (fig. 102) stretching along the Pacific coast from the Kanto Plain in the east, through the Inland Sea to the Japan Sea coast in north Kyushu in the west. Of Japan's industrial labour force who are in factories, with four or more employees, 80% work here, and most of Japan's large-scale heavy industry depending on imported raw materials and fuel is concentrated here.

The industry is concentrated in four main centres: Keihin on Tokyo Bay on the Kanto Plain, Nagoya near Ise Bay at the seaward end of the Nobi Plain, Hanshin on Osaka Bay on the Settsu Plain, and north Kyushu.

The largest industrial centre is Keihin on the Kanto Plain (fig. 103), which includes the great cities of Tokyo and Yokohama, and produced 31% of Japan's industrial goods in 1965. Kei-Hanshin on the Settsu Plain, that includes Osaka and Kobe (fig. 104, pl. 41) and stretches north to Kyoto, produced 22%. Chukyo on the Nobi Plain, that includes the city of Nagoya, is smaller than the two greatest centres and produced 11% of the goods. Smaller still is the Kanmon

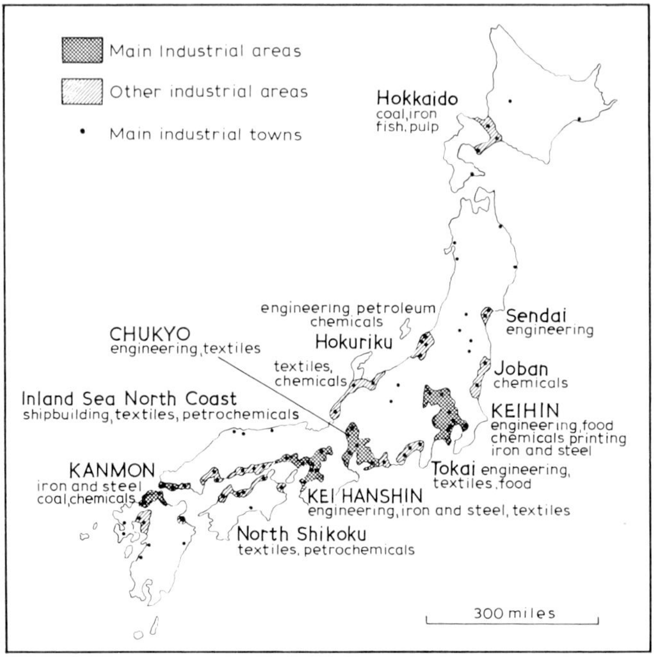

FIG. 102. The main industrial areas (190).

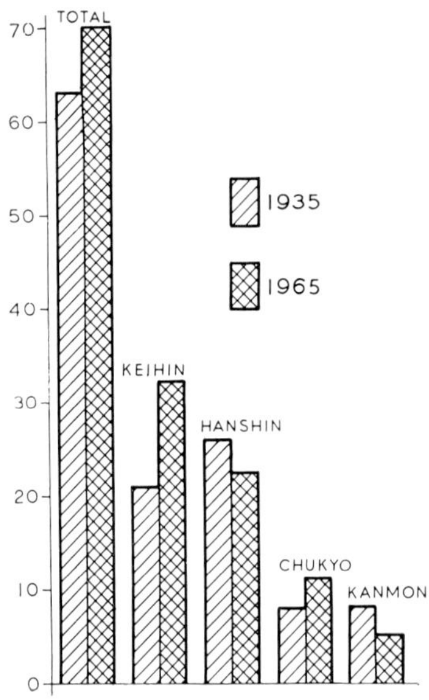

FIG. 103. The percentage of industrial production in the prefectures in the four main centres of industry by value added in factories with over 5 employees in 1935 and 1965 (182).

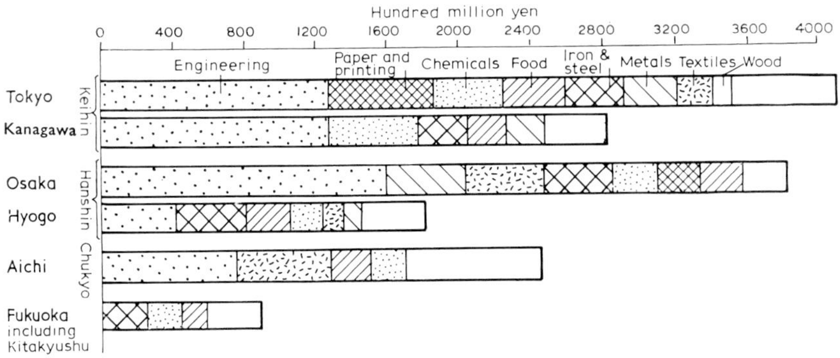

FIG. 104. The main industries in six leading industrial prefectures, 1964 (91).

industrial area which produced 5% of the goods. It stretches from Kitakyushu, which includes the five towns of north-east Kyushu, across the mile-wide Shimo-moseki Strait to the western tip of Honshu.

The main industrial centres are on Tokyo, Ise and Osaka bays, which arc tectonic basins which provide sheltered though shallow harbours. Each is backed by a densely populated plain, with a large river. These conditions provide the harbour space, water and labour needed for industry. North Kyushu also has sheltered harbours and Dokai Bay is also tectonic, but industry here has grown mainly because of the proximity of coal supplies from the Chikuho field. The drowned Inland Sea area which is the ancient heart of Japan provides many small sheltered plains where small ports have developed, protected by Shikoku Island from the south-east monsoon and by Chugoku from the north-west winds in the winter. In 1965 of the main industries 85% of iron and steel; 68% of the engineering, 50% of the chemical industry and 61% of the textile industry was concentrated in the four largest industrial port centres because these industries depend on imported iron ore, coking coal, fibres and crude oil arriving in large bulk carriers and tankers, and many of their products are exported. Each of these areas has the necessary transport and commercial services. Industry has grown up there because of the densely populated plains and sheltered harbours and because this was the pre-industrial population centre where there were many ports, castle and post towns, linked by the Tokaido and San Yo highways.

Although each industrial region has important engineering, iron and steel, chemical, metal and food industries, there is some regional specialization (fig. 104).

Hanshin is the oldest industrial and commercial centre in Japan as Osaka was the port for the ancient capitals in the Kinki. Engineering, especially heavy engineering, including shipbuilding and locomotive manufacture, is the largest industry in Hanshin, but industry is very varied and iron and steel, chemicals and the small goods industries are also important. Osaka has very large, heavy industrial plants, shipyards, huge factories making railway equipment, chemical plants and oil refineries alongside small-scale industries making such things as

PLATE 41. This view of Osaka looking west along the coast illustrates the character of much of Japan's industrial development. Much new industry is on reclaimed land on the edge of the old industrial areas. This provides good access, even for seagoing vessels, to industrial sites along numerous canals. There is little flat land between the mountains and the sea. Industry is close packed with shipyards in the foreground, iron and steel works with chemical works on the opposite bank and other engineering and metal industries behind them. In the shallow sea offshore on the left more land is being reclaimed for new factories. The general layout of Osaka can be seen in fig. 145.

thermos flasks, bicycles and toys, and domestic workshops making fountain-pen parts, beads, handbags and parts of cameras. Its industry is characteristic of the second phase of industrialization with heavy industry, textiles and small-scale industry. It is the old centre of the textile industry which developed here when this was the centre of cotton growing in Japan, and it is still an important textile-producing area although it has now been surpassed in production by Chukyo, which is the leading textile centre.

Keihin is the largest industrial area, including Tokyo, Yokohama, Kawasaki and Chiba, and took over Hanshin's dominant position during the war when the government helped to establish many factories there. It has the advantage for industry of being Japan's largest centre of population and therefore a reservoir of labour and her largest market. Its more recently established activities include the more complex industries developed during the third phase of industrialization, including engineering, especially light engineering, which makes up a third of total production. The chemical industry with petro-chemicals and iron and steel are also very important, but textiles are less important than in the older centres further west. The paper, printing, food and furniture industries were the large market.

Chukyo is the leading textile centre using wool, rayon and synthetic fibres as well as cotton. The transport equipment industry makes motor vehicles and aeroplanes, and the chemical industry and ceramics are also especially important there.

Kanmon's development lags behind the other large centres with only 5% of industrial production. It differs from the other three regions as industry is based on local coal supplies rather than market and port facilities. The range of industry is more limited. Iron and steel making, which needs a great deal of coal, is important at Yawata and Tobata, and the chemical industry using coal as a raw material is also important. Industry has not been developing as fast in Kyushu as in other industrial areas, as coal has given place to imported oil as the leading fuel in Japan and as there are no large ports and great centres of population here. It lacks large areas of flat land and a large labour supply, and industry has been limited to small isolated plains. It now has a much smaller share of industry than before the war.

Within the industrial belt there are many smaller industrial centres, especially around the *Inland Sea* where 8–9% of Japan's goods are produced, in small ports. Iron is smelted and steel made at Himeji, petro-chemicals are made at Otake-Iwakuni, ships at Kure, machinery at Hiroshima, textiles at Okayama, and chemicals in north Shikoku (pp. 282 and 294). There are smaller centres in *Tokai* where hydroelectric power is used in engineering and textile, pulp and paper works, to make 4% of Japan's goods. In some places industries have been built in rural areas to make use of rural labour supplies, as has the rubber factory at Tsuda, and the factory among the paddyfields in Nara Prefecture (pl. 42).

Many smaller industrial centres make light industrial goods including textiles, wood products and paper, process food and make agricultural implements in small factories and workshops. These industries are not dependent on larger quantities of imported fuel and raw materials and do not need port facilities, so they are sited in small towns.

Only 26% of Japan's industrial production comes from outside the main *industrial belt*. In this area industry is concentrated mainly in the larger towns. In 1965 Hokkaido, Tohoku, Shikoku and Kyushu together manufactured only 12% of Japan's industrial products. In the more important centres outside the industrial belt the industries are mainly lighter ones processing local dairy products, sugar beet, rice and wheat. Iron and steel and chemical works are based on local coal at Joban and Muroran and on oil supplies in Niigata and Akita. The chemicals, textiles and engineering based on hydroelectric power supplies in Hokuriku are important. Iron and steel works at Muroran use local coal and the Fuji Iron and Steel Company at Kamaishi uses local ore (pl. 42).

Among the most important industrial centres outside the industrial zone are Hokuriku, the towns on the Japan Sea coast of Tohoku, Sendai and scattered industrial towns in Kyushu and Hokkaido (see Chapter 14).

In contrast with the large-scale industry there is some industry in many *buraku* in Japan, as farmers use their spare time to supplement their income making

PLATE 42. The tyre factory in the background is in Tsuda in eastern Shikoku. It uses rural labour and has the advantage of easy access to Kobe which is the centre of the rubber industry. The village is a good example of a linear village lying along the road. The farmhouse in the foreground is typical of many in Shikoku. The edge of the hills behind marks a fault line.

things out of their rice straw. They weave straw mats, pads and sacks, make straw shoes, bags and hats. With the growing demand for industrial labour these inefficient home industries are declining. Every small town has industries which supply local household needs. In Hosoe near Hamamatsu in Tokai (p. 191) rice is milled, *saké* made, bread, cakes, fish, sausages and bean paste preparations are cooked, kimono, cushions, eiderdowns, *tatami* and *shoji* are manufactured.

Many small towns, especially near the larger industrial centres, have other more *specialized domestic industry* making a variety of textiles, clothes, and small goods for sale in a wider market. Some have their own special traditional craft, especially near the old Core Zone. Gifu is famous for its parasols, Kagawa for fans, Ishikawa for lacquer. Even before Tokugawa times craft industries had developed in the Kinki near Kyoto, and spread south to nearby Wakayama on the Inland Sea, and north to Fukui on the Japan Sea coast. After 1600 castle

PLATE 43. The Fuji Iron and Steel Company works at Kamaishi on the ria coast of Iwate on the dissected edge of the Kitakami Plateau, was established as early as 1857 to use local iron ore and is still one of the main producers of steel. Now Fuji employs 6,500 workers smelting ore and making steel which they use to produce steel shapes, rails and wire. The picture shows the beautiful but inhospitable nature of the hilly landscape which makes it necessary to use every bit of flat land in the narrow valley, which is a silted-up ria. The area at the mouth of the river has been reclaimed for industry. Large bulk carriers unload ore and coal and other minerals at the wharves beside the stock piles and take away the steel products. The harbour shelters small fishing boats. Raw materials pass across the river to the blast furnaces and gas-fired open-hearth furnaces with five tall chimneys on the right and on to the rolling mills behind. The incised river valley is crowded with houses.

towns grew and craft industries were established to serve the many nobles and samurai who lived there.

Deep water port and commercial facilities act strongly to increase the concentration of Japanese industry in the four great centres, which are becoming increasingly congested but land costs are high, labour is costly, water and housing are short and the transport system is overburdened. In spite of this industry grew faster between 1955 and 1965 in the most industrial prefectures, especially in Keihin and Chukyo. In 1959–60 47% of investment was concentrated in the four leading industrial areas and 68% in the ten leading prefectures. Average incomes are closely related to the distribution of industry. They are highest in the three largest industrial centres. Tokyo's were double the average in 1959 and still 26%

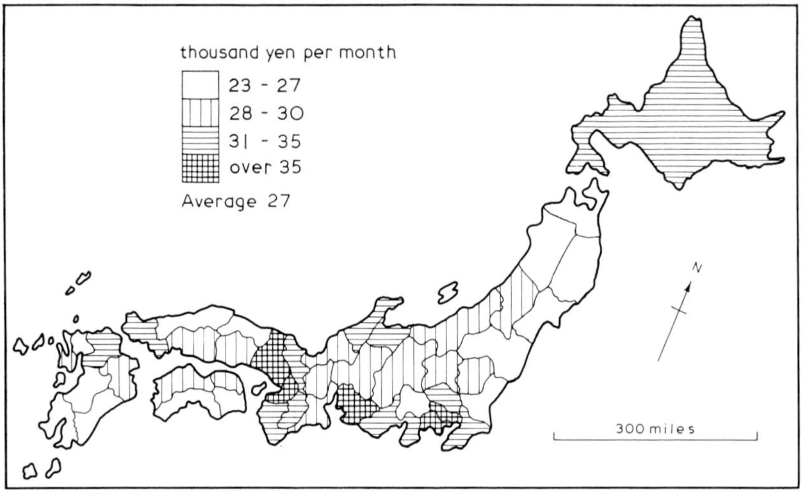

FIG. 105. Regional variations in income per household in 1959 (91). The pattern is still similar but with less difference between industrial and rural areas.

above average in 1964. Incomes are above average in the whole industrial zone, in the secondary industrial areas in Hokuriku and also Hokkaido, where farm incomes are high and lower in the more backward Frontier Zone though the difference is decreasing.

The shortage of suitable land for industry in the main coastal areas has led to the large-scale land reclamation illustrated in plates 42, 45 and 48. In Chiba Prefecture land is being reclaimed on the shores of Tokyo Bay (fig. 158) as it is on the coasts of Osaka, Ise and Sagami bays, and around the Inland Sea at such places as Hiroshima, Mizushima and Okayama. An oil refinery and petrochemical complex have been built on reclaimed land at Kawasaki and Chiba, and others at Yokkaichi, Otake–Iwakuni (pl. 48), there are shipbuilding yards, iron and steel works in Chiba, iron and steel and chemicals in Nagoya and others at Osaka and Sakai. The 1960 ten-year plan aimed at half new industry being established on reclaimed land. Fortunately for this purpose the bays in the main industrial areas are shallow. Deep channels can be dredged for ships and the material used for building up the land. Most of the newly reclaimed land is in the industrial areas. Ten thousand acres of land was approved as reclaimable for

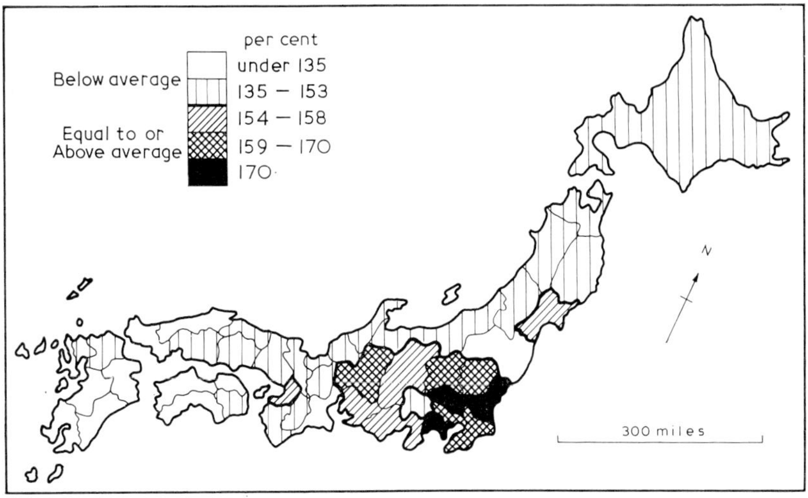

FIG. 106. Growth of industrial employment between 1955 and 1960 (91).

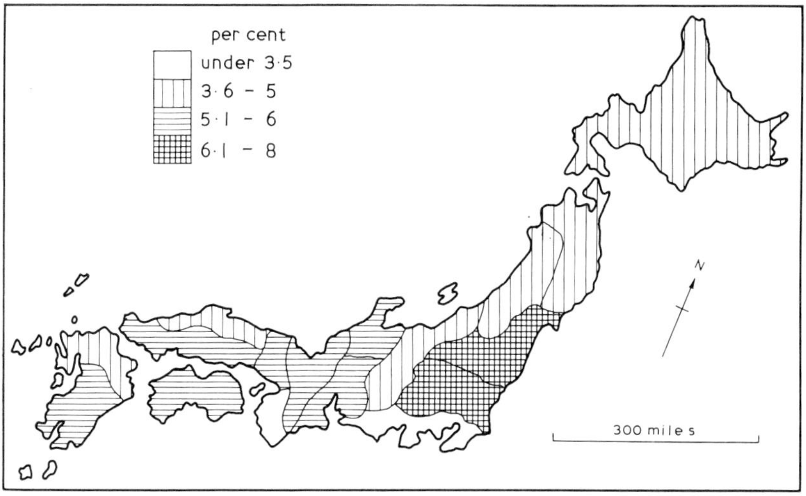

FIG. 107. Projected industrial development per annum, 1959 to 1970 (*Data on Regional Development Japan Institute of Location Economy*, 1962).

industry during 1954–60. Of this 77% was in the industrial belt with 32% in Keihin, 35% in Hanshin, 6% in north Kyushu and 4% in Chukyo.

There is a gradual north-eastward trend in the location of Japanese industry.

This is illustrated by fig. 103, which shows the greatest increase in the proportion of industry in Keihin, a small increase in Chukyo and a decline in the total percentage in Hanshin and especially in north Kyushu. This trend is reflected in fig. 106, which shows the fastest growth of industry to be in the area stretching from Chukyo to Keihin and especially at the Keihin end. Recommendations by the Economic Planning Agency for the growth between 1958 and 1970 continue this pattern in that most growth is shown even further north-east in south-east Tohoku, and inland Kanto (fig. 107). There are also areas of faster growth recommended in Chukyo, in the Fukui–Ishikawa–Toyama area, around the Inland Sea and in an area at present growing little in south Kyushu. Some of these areas are already developing, notably Yokkaichi on Ise Bay, Mizushima in Okayama and Iwakuni in Yamaguchi on the Inland Sea, and Miyazaki. It remains to be seen how far these recommendations are met, but government influence is usually effective in Japan. Government policy supports the dispersal of new industry and the development of centres outside the main industrial areas is being encouraged by tax rebates and the provision of roads, water and other services. Some new industry is being established in other places including Toyama, Tohoku, where the Sendai–Shiogama area is growing, Nobeoka in south-east Kyushu where electro-chemical and electro-metallurgical industry has been established and Tsurusaki where steel and chemicals are produced. In spite of these government efforts to disperse industry there is a continuous flow of people from the more isolated backward parts of Japan, notably Tohoku and southern Kyushu, to the most rapidly developing industrial centres (fig. 131).

Power

With the rapid expansion of Japan's industry her need for power is doubling every five years and her coal, hydroelectric power and small oil resources are quite

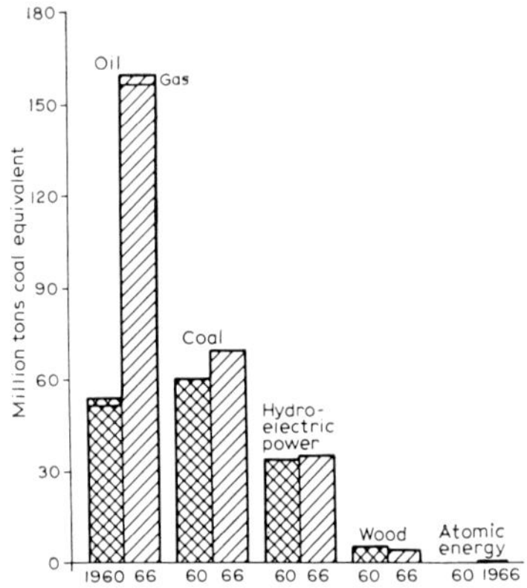

FIG. 108. Energy consumption in Japan 1960 and 1966 (90).

unable to meet the growing needs of industry. She is relying increasingly on imported oil (fig. 108), which has been her main source of power since 1961 and supplies half her needs. Oil is cheaper and easier to use than poor-quality home-produced coal, but the need to import it makes her energy supply costly. In 1966 her first atomic power station was completed and this holds possibilities for the future in a country which in 1967 depended on imports for 74% of her fuel supplies. In 1967 oil and gas supplied 66% of her fuel needs, coal 24%, hydroelectric power 9%, wood 1%, and atomic energy began to make a contribution with barely 0·1%.

COAL

Coal supplied 24% of Japan's power needs in 1967. Before the war it was very much more important, but it has been challenged first by hydroelectric power and more recently by imported oil which is cheaper and has become much more important than coal.

Japan produced 70% of the coal she used in 1966, but it was of poor quality, costly to mine and mainly unsuitable for coking. These factors make it expensive compared with the coal she imports and compared with oil, and have resulted in

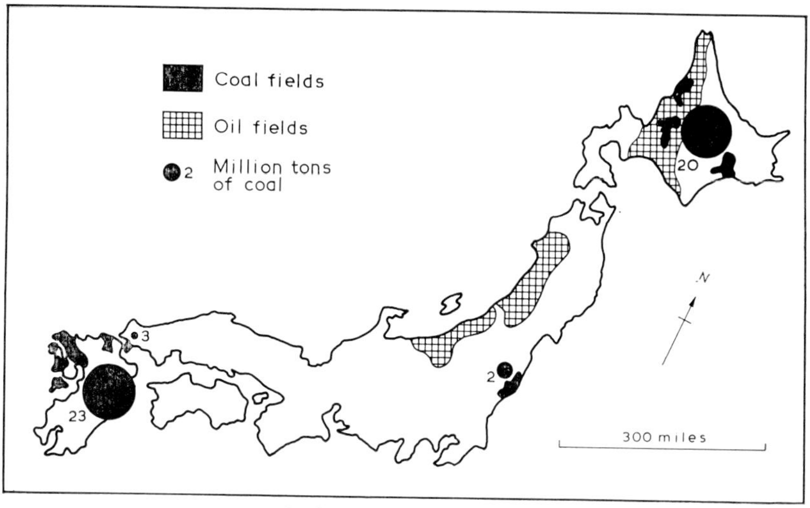

FIG. 109. Coal and oil production in 1962 (91).

a contraction and reorganization of the industry during the sixties. At its post-war peak production was 55 million tons in 1961, but this fell to 48 million tons in 1967.

About 80% of Japan's coal measures are in relatively young Tertiary rocks (fig. 109) yielding poor bituminous and sub-bituminous grades with a low carbon content, so that only 25% of her production is suitable for coking. This makes it necessary for her to import half her coking coal requirements and 30% of her total coal supplies. Japanese coal is costly to produce as the seams, especially in Kyushu, are thin, contorted and faulted into many small coal basins. Moreover the many underground springs and dangers from gas and earthquakes make them difficult and costly to work. A great deal of capital is needed for their modernization. Under these conditions the output of coal per man shift is only 1·5 tons, which is little below the 1·85 tons in Britain but only a quarter of that in USA. Rising wages, through the pressure of the trade unions, are also increasing the cost of Japan's coal. All this means that American coal of better quality costs less to buy in Japan than the home product, in spite of the cost of transport via Panama.

Two main coalfields produced 89% of Japan's coal between them in 1965. North Kyushu and Hokkaido both produced 44%. There are also small fields in south-east Tohoku at Joban and the Ube coalfield in western Chugoku. The Hokkaido fields have the greatest reserves and production here developed later and is increasing while North Kyushu is declining. Most Japanese fields have the advantage of being on or near the coast, facilitating and keeping down the cost of transport.

The north Kyushu field, extending across north Kyushu and into western Chugoku, produces 44% of Japan's coal. It has been separated by tectonic movement into many coal-producing basins, the most important of which, the Chikuho Basin on the north-east coast near Kitakyushu, extends under the sea as do many of the others. The second is the Miike field in north-west Kyushu, and the third is the Sasebo field. Kyushu coal is very poor and is particularly difficult to work. It has been exploited longer than the Hokkaido fields, many of the better seams have already been worked out and its production fell from 27 million tons in 1962 to 21 million in 1965. During the war, when there was great pressure on coal supplies, some of these were wastefully mined for the sake of speedy production. The Kyushu coalfield has the great advantage of easy access to the sea, by which it is shipped to the main industrial centres where most of it is used. In North Kyushu, on the Chikuho field, industries developed using large quantities of coal as fuel or as raw material, including iron smelting and steel making, which use large quantities of coal as fuel, and the chemical industry which uses coal as a raw material.

The Hokkaido coalfield lies along the eastern edge of the Ishikari lowland with Yubari as one of the main mining towns. The thicker, less distorted seams of the Hokkaido coalfields lend themselves to modern large-scale mining methods. Many of the seams are 2 to 3 feet thick, which makes large-scale mechanization easier and production more efficient. In 1965 they produced 43 tons per miner per month, compared with 31·6 tons in Kyushu. Hokkaido mines produce the highest-quality coal in Japan, including half the coking coal, as well as bituminous and sub-bituminous coal and lignite. Production doubled between 1955 and 1965 from 11 to 22 million tons to equal Kyushu, but distance from the industrial centres and from the sea is a big disadvantage. It is 600 miles to Tokyo and the main Ishikari fields are 35 miles from the coast. The coal is shipped through Muroran and Otaru, and a large steel works has been established at Muroran using iron ore back-loaded by the returning ships. The coal is used mainly on the Pacific coast as far south as Nagoya and on the Japan Sea coast to Niigata (12). *The Joban field* is much less important, although it has the advantage of being closer to Tokyo. It extends under the sea and mainly produces lignite. Chemical plants have been built to use the coal on the spot.

The *Ube field* in Chugoku is very small and an extension of the north Kyushu field supplying western Japan with coal.

In spite of rising production per worker Japanese coal is still more expensive than American and oil is also cheaper. After supporting the use of home-produced coal rather than import oil to conserve foreign exchange the government has realized this policy is misguided. In spite of bitter strikes the industry has undergone major contraction and reorganization to adjust to falling demands for coal. Government policy, like that in Britain, is to increase efficiency by subsidizing the rationalization and modernization of pits, improving training and closing the least efficient mines. As in Britain they aim to maintain production at 50 million tons and to increase coal consumption by electric power stations. Since 1959 two thirds of Japan's mines have been closed and the number of employees has fallen from 256,000 to 104,000. Production in 1959 was 47 million tons, in 1967 45 million tons, so that productivity per worker has more than doubled. The remaining mines have been made more efficient, with government loans for reorganization and development. The government is encouraging the development of new industries in mining areas to absorb the surplus labour so created.

Before the war most of Japan's coal came from China, but since 1965 most of her coal has come from Australia which in 1967 sent her 42% of her imports. The USA sent her 37%. USSR, China and Canada also sent coal to Japan. To ensure supplies Japanese companies have invested in joint coal mining projects as Mitsui has at Mount Moura in Queensland and Sumitomo has in Canada.

OIL

Though oil and natural gas now supply two thirds of Japan's fuel needs she is a very minor producer of oil, and in spite of doubling her pre-war production she produces only 1% of her own needs. Her resources are limited and there seems little likelihood of new discoveries. In her growing economy the demand for oil for industrial fuel, as a raw material in the chemical industry, and for transport has increased her oil consumption nine times in the last decade. In 1967 oil accounted for 66% of her fuel requirements compared with 5% in 1940 (fig. 108).

Japan's oilfields extend from the Japan Sea coast at Hokuriku and Tohoku (fig. 109) to the Ishikari–Yufutsu lowland in Hokkaido. The Honshu area produces 99% of the total, in Akita, Yamagata and Niigata Prefectures. Most of the drilling is done by one large company which was under government control until 1950. Natural gas produced in Niigata, Akita and Chiba has been increasingly important in the last ten years and its thermal value is now double oil production. A pipeline from Niigata takes some of it direct to Tokyo.

Most of Japan's oil imports before the war came from California but now the Middle East is the main supplier, with some from Indonesia and the USA. The Arabian Oil Company of Japan has very successful concessions in the Persian Gulf which promise to make Japan one of the largest producers in this area.

Japan has had oil from the North Sumatra Company since 1961 and is also developing oil resources elsewhere in Indonesia in N.E. New Guinea and Western Canada. Almost all the oil imports are now of crude oil, as many refineries have been established (fig. 110). Her refinery capacity quintupled between 1960 and 1966 and is now third, next to the United States and the Soviet Union. Most of the refineries are on the Pacific coast near the main industrial centres, many of them on newly reclaimed land. Some are near the supplies of home-produced oil in western Tohoku and were severely damaged by earthquakes in 1965.

ELECTRICITY

Electricity is becoming increasingly important in Japan. Production in 1966 was double 1960. Before the war hydroelectricity formed 85% of Japan's electricity, but sites for development are limited and by 1966 thermal electric power using oil and coal had increased and formed 64% of her electric power in 1966. Most of the hydroelectric development is concentrated in central Honshu (fig. 111), where rainfall is high and the mountains are highest and the rivers longest. In

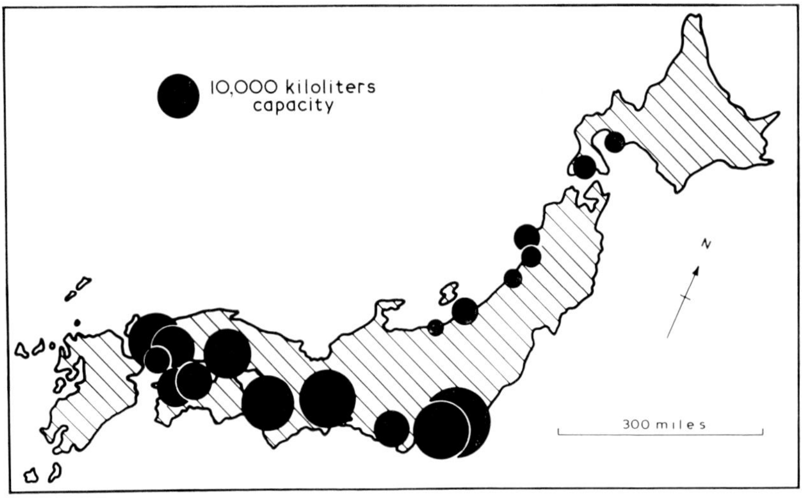

FIG. 110. Oil refinery capacity (12).

central Honshu the Tone, Tenryu and Kiso that flow into the Pacific are all very important producers, and the Agano and Shinano that flow into the Japan Sea are especially useful. Their regime is less variable than Pacific coast rivers, as they are fed by snow melt in the spring and by rain in the summer. Most of the smaller rivers on both sides are also used. Hydroelectricity is also important in Kyushu and western Tohoku where gradients are steep, but there is little in Hokkaido and Chugoku where the mountains are lower. In western and northern Japan thermal power is more important.

Hydroelectric power is well placed for use in the great industrial areas of

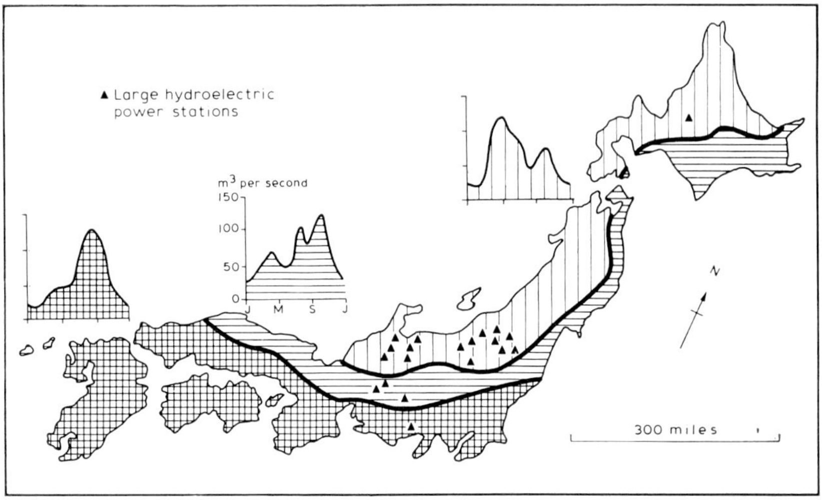

FIG. 111. Hydroelectric power supply, showing three regions with contrasting river regimes (8).

Keihin, Chukyo and Hanshin, and in Hokuriku on the Japan Sea coast. In spite of the advantages of Japan's high rainfall and the steep gradients of the mountains, Japan's physiography and climate are not altogether suited to hydroelectric development. The river basins are small so that the volume of the short, swift streams is not great, run-off is rapid from the steep slopes and the markedly variable and seasonal rainfall means that the stream flow fluctuates very widely between summer floods and winter drought and from year to year. In winter there is little precipitation except on the Japan Sea coast and in the mountains much of it is in the form of snow and the upper reaches of many of the rivers are frozen. It is difficult to provide storage, for, although there are many narrow valleys (pl. 44), their sides are often formed of faulted rocks or volcanic rocks which do not provide solid impervious foundations for dams. Most of the hydroelectric plants are small and aligned along the rivers, being powered by the run of the stream so that their production fluctuates. They produce a great deal of electricity during the summer but need to be supplemented by thermal power in the winter. Capital must be invested in both thermal and hydroelectric plants, neither of which are in full use all the year round. Hydroelectric power is often a standby supply to relieve peak loads. This makes electricity costly.

Since the war there have been developments in connection with multipurpose irrigation and drainage schemes like those in the Kitakami, Tenryu and Ishikari valleys, and some for power only, but it has become increasingly difficult to find sites to develop, as the most easily developed rivers have already been harnessed although it is estimated that only 40% of Japan's potential hydroelectric power has been developed. With these limitations on hydroelectric power the production of oil-fired thermal electricity has become increasingly important and supplied 73% of electricity production in 1967, compared with only 16% in 1941.

PLATE 44. The Kurobe dam on the river Kurobe is on the northern edge of the Japan Alps in Toyama. It was relatively easy to dam the narrow V-shaped valley but the amount of water available is not very large. The mountain scenery is typical of much of the Japan Alps with narrow ravined ridges clothed in forest (220).

Most of the thermal power stations have been established on waterside sites near the main industrial centres to which coal or fuel oil can easily be brought.

Increasingly costly hydroelectric development, expensive coal supplies and the need to import most of her oil make atomic power important to Japan's future development. Japan opened the Tokai atomic power station in Ibaragi Prefecture north of Tokyo in 1966, one is being built at Tsuruga north of Osaka, three will be completed near Tokyo by 1970, and others are scheduled.

Iron and Steel

Japan's steel production doubled between 1961 and 1967. Her steel industry is growing faster than that of any other nation. With the building of many large new integrated iron and steel works she became the world's third largest steel producer, exceeding Western Germany in 1963 in spite of having to import 97% of her iron ore and 70% of her coking coal. She produced 13% of world steel in 1967 and exported 20% of her production. Her industry has expanded to meet the needs of her fast-growing engineering industry, producing heavy and consumer goods for home and foreign markets. Steel production reached 62 million tons in 1967 compared with 25 million in Britain. This was eight times her war-time peak (fig. 112) and half the US production.

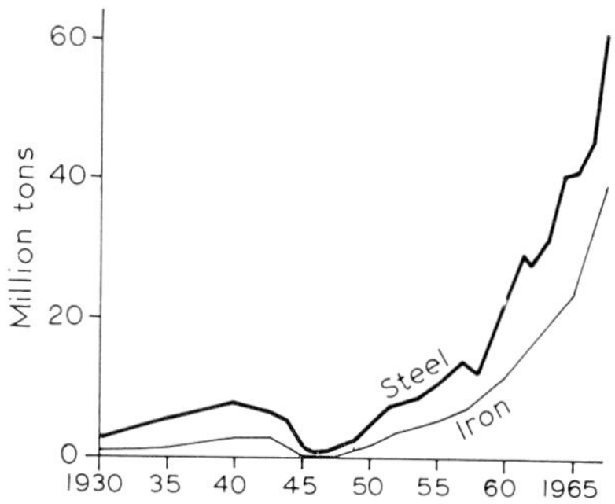

FIG. 112. The growth of iron and steel production since 1930 (88).

Even before the development of modern industry in Japan iron and steel was made by the local lords and the shogun to make the weapons for their private armies. Modern production dates from 1901 when the government built the first modern iron works near the small fishing village of Yawata on Dokai Bay in north-eastern Kyushu, on the edge of the Shimonoseki Strait between Kyushu and Honshu (fig. 118), siting it near Japan's largest coalfield, with ore supplies from China. The Yawata company produced a quarter of Japan's pig iron and 19% of her steel in 1967. The industry grew steadily until the thirties, when it expanded rapidly under the control of the military government. The war led to further great demands on the industry, but much of the plant was destroyed during the last years of the war or earmarked for reparations, so that in 1946 under SCAP the production of steel was negligible. The iron and steel industry recovered more quickly than most industries after the war for, like the coal industry, it had priority of development as a basic industry. The government helped by making loans available and assisted in modernization, but progress was slow and it was not until 1953 that steel production was back to its wartime peak. Since then it has increased ninefold.

The iron and steel industry is based almost entirely on imported iron ore and steel scrap. Only 3% of Japan's iron ore is produced at home and these are low-grade ores from many small inefficient mines, mainly in Hokkaido and north Honshu. The largest is the Kamaishi mine in eastern Tohoku, which has ore of 59% ferrous content. Iron sand deposits are also used and iron pyrite sinter which is a by-product of sulphuric acid plants.

In 1967 30% of the imported ore came from South America with 14% from Chile and 12% from Peru. India sent 19%, Australia 15%, South East Asia 12%

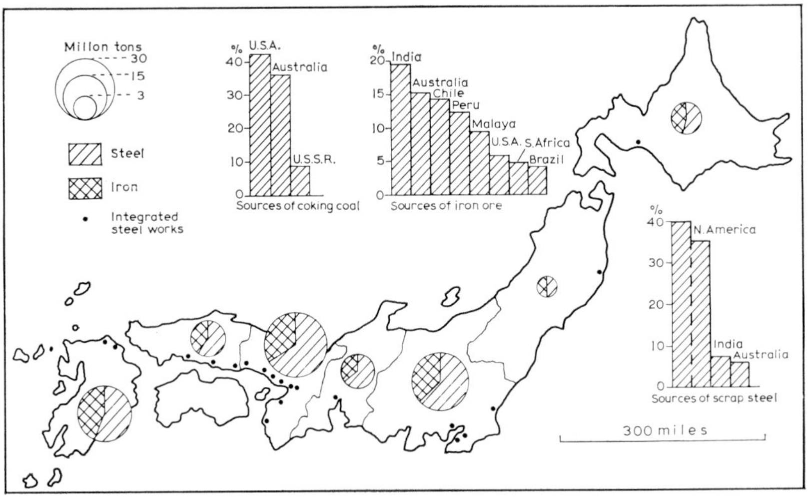

FIG. 113. The location of the iron and steel industry in 1967 (180).

including 9% from Malaya (fig. 113), and 9% from North America. Three-quarters of the imported steel scrap came from the United States and coking coal from USA, Australia, the USSR and Canada. The large quantity of imported steel scrap makes Japan's steel production a third greater than her pig iron products.

Imported iron ore and coal are so expensive that in 1962 her raw materials for steel making cost $40 per ton, compared with $37 in the United States and Western Germany. This is partly because Japan imports only top-grade, rich iron ore. To compete in the world's markets to which she exports 20% of her products she has needed to economize radically in the use of raw materials and to increase the efficiency of her production.

Three five-year rationalization plans starting in 1951, 1956 and 1961 have increased efficiency with technical improvements and huge new integrated plants. The amount of ore used to produce a ton of pig iron was reduced between 1951 and 1967 by 25% and of coke by 50%. In 1965 Japan used 507 kilograms of ore per metric ton compared with US 676, which is less than that in any other country with the possible exception of the USSR. Pressure control and the injection of oxygen and heavy oil into the blast furnaces speeds up the smelting process and reduces the amount of fuel required, and large oxygen steel converters are rapidly replacing open-hearth furnaces for steel making. They produced 65% of Japan's steel in 1967. Her productivity per man hour doubled between 1960 and 1967, so that production per worker in 1966 was 187 tons in Japan, 167 in USA and 113 in UK. Her steel plants also are more efficient because blast furnaces, steel converters and rolling mills are new and integrated so that the molten iron goes in ladle cars from the open-hearth furnace to the steel converters. Then it is poured and solidified into ingots which are then 'soaked' and rolled to avoid costly reheating.

The Japanese steel industry produces not only heavy rails and plates but with computer control produces high quality special steels for use in her fast-growing engineering and vehicle industries. This has been possible because of improved techniques in high-grade steel production and is necessary to make the most profitable use of relatively costly steel. Even so Japan's steel production is still predominantly heavy goods, so that in 1966 30% was steel shapes and bars, 28% thick and medium plates, and 23% sheets. Much of it was used to make heavy machinery, ships and locomotives.

Integration in the iron and steel industry has led to the dominance of five great firms, Shin Nippon Sietetsu (Yawata-Fuji),* Nippon Steel, Kawasaki, Sumitomo and Kobe Steel, which between them produce two-thirds of Japan's steel. Fuji, Yawata and Kawasaki produced 61% of Japan's pig iron in 1967. Such large firms have been able to build extensive modern plants, to do research and introduce technical improvements from abroad and to form an export association that controls production, prices and the quality of products. They have invested money in the development of ore supplies in Malaya, Brazil, the Philippines, Pakistan, Rhodesia, India and Swaziland, and made agreements with Australia and America to ensure their future supplies. All this has reduced her costs of production, which now compare favourably with US and UK. Her new integrated works have the advantage of all the newest techniques and some of the largest furnaces in the world. Increased efficiency makes it possible for Japan to export 20% of her steel which, with iron, is her largest single export.

YAWATA, AN EXAMPLE

Yawata is Japan's largest iron and steel company. Established by the government in 1901, in 1967 it produced a quarter of Japan's pig iron and 19% of her steel, employing 50,000 people in six large works at Yawata, Tobata and Hikari in north Kyushu, Nagoya, Sakai, south of Osaka, and Chiba, east of Tokyo. The company smelted iron ore and made 10 million tons of pig iron. They made 8 million tons of steel in 1967 in very large open-hearth furnaces, new huge oxygen converters and electric converters for special steels. The steel passed on to her

* Yawata and Fuji merged in 1969 to form Shin Nippon Sietetsu (New Japan Iron and Steel) which is second only to US Steel and larger than the British Steel Corporation.

three hot and nine cold strip mills for rolling and then billets and sheet passed to subsidiary companies to be made into shapes, tubes, rails, tins and many other products.

The Yawata Company uses home supplies of coal for a third of her needs but little of her ore comes from home producers. She needs to import oil and limestone from abroad. She has joint iron mines in India and Australia and long-term

PLATE 45. Looking west across the new Yawata steel works at Tobata to Dokai Bay. The view includes much of Kitakyushu (fig. 149). The new works are still being constructed and more land is being reclaimed. There is very little flat land in the area so that seaward development has been necessary. Raw materials are unloaded at the wharves on the left near the stock piles. Furnaces are being built to the right and behind this are the rolling mills. To the left of the stock piles is the Nittetsu chemical works, which uses many of the by-products of iron and steel making. Oxygen is made for use in the modern furnaces (219 & 220).

contracts with companies in India, Australia, Africa, on the west coast of North and South America to ensure her future supplies of high-grade ore, and contracts in the United States, Australia and Canada for coking coal. The iron ore she imports is high grade, much of it with a ferrous content of over 65%.

Each of her six iron and steel works has its own specialities. Yawata is the oldest centre, which is being modernized with the building of new larger furnaces. It produces structural and sheet steel. Tobata (pl. 45) is a new plant developed since 1956 and specializes in sheet steel. Like many of Japan's new large-scale industries it has 1,433 acres of land, 445 acres of which have been reclaimed from the sea. New wharves will accommodate 70,000-ton bulk carriers, though most ore comes in 15,000- to 40,000-ton carriers at the moment. It is a fully integrated works with very large equipment laid out so that the ore goes straight from the three blast furnaces to the two huge oxygen converters and on to the four cold strip and two hot strip mills. The blast furnaces are the largest in Japan and use the most up-to-date techniques of heavy oil firing and oxygen injection. This large-scale production and new techniques have reduced the cost of Japan's steel. The main products of the works are stainless steel, which is rolled in the cold mills and sold as sheet. Other Yawata Company works are at Hikari, where special alloy steels are the speciality, and at Nagoya, where sheet steel is made for use in the motor industry. There is a huge new integrated works at Sakai just south of Osaka making heavy steel plate and shapes for Osaka's heavy engineering industry, and especially for shipbuilding. The new integrated plant in Chiba serves Japan's leading engineering centre, producing sheet steel for the motor-vehicle and electrical goods industries in Keihin.

LOCATION

About 85% of Japan's steel is produced within the main manufacturing belt (fig. 102). The earliest modern iron and steel works at Yawata in north Kyushu were based on home supplies of coal from the nearby Chikuho field and Chinese iron ore and limestone. Before the war, with ore and coal from China, north Kyushu produced nearly half Japan's steel but this fell to only 18% in 1967. Some of the other producing centres are located near iron ore and coal, notably Muroran, which produces 6% of Japan's iron and steel and uses coal from the Ishkari coalfield and iron from north Tohoku, and Kamaishi, using local ore and producing 3%. All these centres rely mainly on imported ore. Since the war it is the iron and steel centres on tidewater sites in the main industrial areas which have grown most rapidly; their harbour facilities enable iron ore, steel scrap and coal to be imported. Production can be used by local industry and scrap from the local factories can be returned for reprocessing. In Hanshin, which produced 32% of Japan's steel in 1967, plants along the coast from Sakai in the south to Kobe in the west are used to supply heavy engineering firms with steel plate for ships, rails, bars for locomotives (fig. 145). In Keihin (25%) and Chukyo (9%), sheet and lighter steel products are made for the engineering industry, including motor vehicles, and consumer goods, including refrigerators and washing machines.

Other Minerals

Coal represents half Japan's mineral products by value. She produces small quantities of a wide variety of other minerals (fig. 114), but most of those she needs must be imported. She produces most of her own requirements of copper, zinc and lead ores, sulphur and silver, and has small quantities of many other minerals, including tin, gold, manganese, tungsten, chromium, molybdenum and vanadium ore, but has little or no rock salt, bauxite, nickel, cobalt or oil. Her deposits are poor and her mines are small and inefficient, often producing small quantities of several minerals, so that her production is costly. She is developing overseas sources of ore, including tin in Thailand. In spite of high costs improved methods are making it possible to expand her production of copper, zinc,

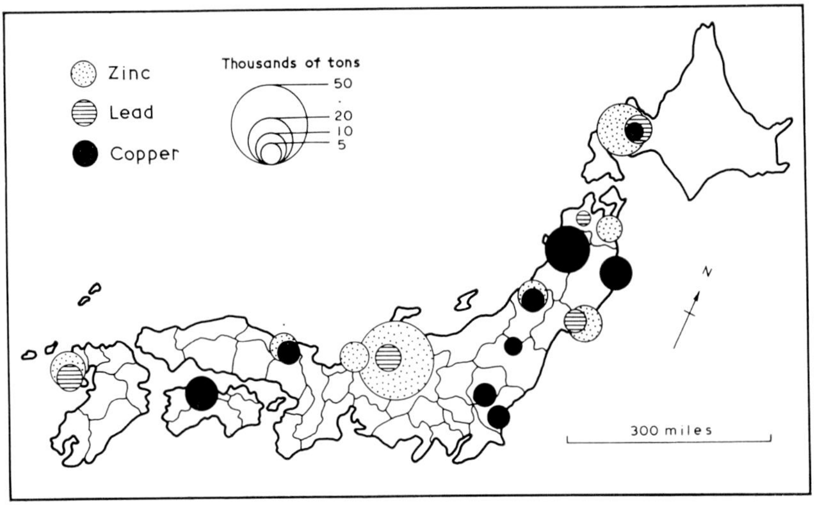

FIG. 114. The main non-ferrous metal mining centres (91).

aluminium and lead. Copper is Japan's most important metallic mineral. There are almost a hundred small mines in Tohoku and Shikoku. Lead and zinc are often found with copper and are also important.

Engineering

Since the war the production of machinery has grown faster than any other industry, especially ships, motor vehicles and electrical machinery, and is now Japan's largest industry, accounting for 41% of her production by value in 1967 compared with only 18% in 1955 (fig. 99) and 34% of her exports. Production doubled between 1960 and 1966. The three most important products are electrical goods, which make up 9% of the total, ships 6% and motor vehicles 2%. Products are very varied and the organization and location of the industry ranges from large shipyards in Hanshin and factories like the Toyota car works in Aichi, to small rural domestic workshops where screws are turned on a hand lathe.

Much of the engineering industry is concentrated in Keihin, which has 34% of the industry, including two thirds of the precision instrument production, a third of the general engineering and nearly half the electrical engineering. Hanshin produces 21% of Japan's machinery and Chukyo with 11% specializes in vehicles. The remaining quarter of the industry is scattered in many smaller centres (fig. 115).

Before the war engineering already made up 26% of industrial production for, as the Japanese army expanded during the thirties, the industry grew to supply its needs. During the China war technical quality improved greatly and production expanded, so that it was three times as great in 1940 as in 1937. After

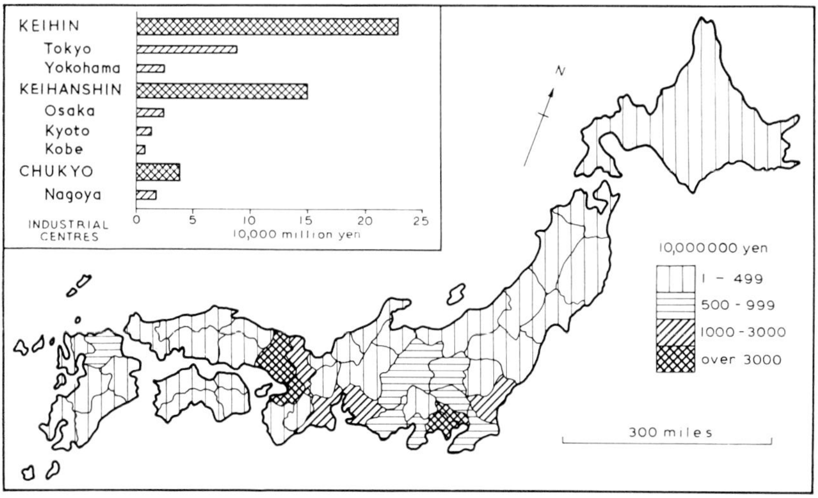

FIG. 115. The distribution of the electrical machinery industry 1962 (91).

almost complete destruction in the last few months of the Pacific war the industry was only slowly rehabilitated, but as soon as redevelopment started after 1949 it went ahead faster than in any other industry and markets grew both abroad and, with increasing prosperity, at home. Two branches of the industry have expanded most rapidly. With growing prosperity the demand for electrical goods for use in the home has created a *denki* (electrical) boom, and electrical machinery production doubled between 1960 and 1966, especially the production of radios, television sets, washing machines, refrigerators and communication equipment. The transport section has increased its output, especially of small trucks, cars and motor-bicycles, and more recently, with new railway development, of railway rolling stock. There has also been an increase in shipbuilding and cameras are a recent and very important addition.

SHIPBUILDING

Since 1956 Japan has been the leading world producer of ships. In 1967 she produced 48% of the world's total tonnage of new shipping, mainly tankers and bulk carriers; this was six times that of the United Kingdom and Western Germany and in 1967 was four times her 1960 production. In the engineering industry ships take third place after iron and steel and electrical goods (fig. 99). They are a major export item. Shipbuilding is concentrated in the main industrial zone, where sixteen yards produce ships of over 20,000 tons (fig. 116). Most of them are in the great trading area of Hanshin and in ports around the Inland Sea where there are good sheltered harbours; others are in good harbours at Nagasaki and Sasebo in north-west Kyushu and at Kawasaki near Yokohama. They use local steel supplies in Keihin and Hanshin.

The first modern shipyards were opened by the government at Kawasaki

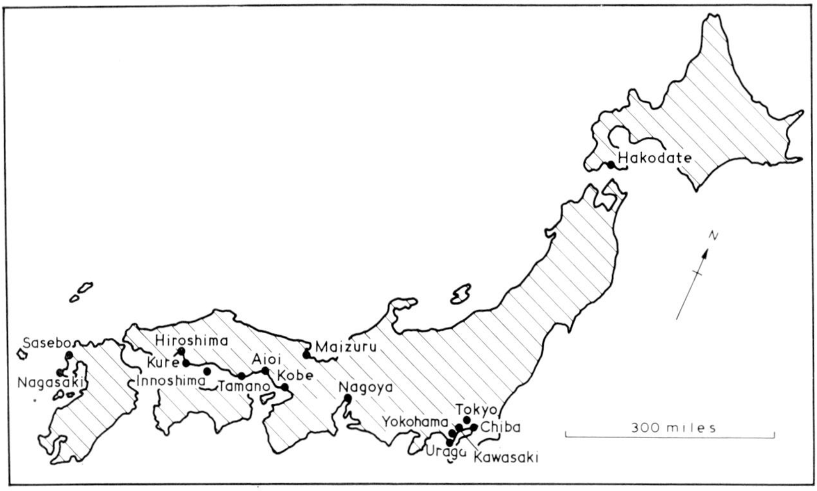

FIG. 116. The sixteen yards building ships of over 20,000 tons in 1967 (235).

outside Yokohama in 1878 and were later taken over by the Mitsubishi *zaibatsu*, who expanded with the encouragement of a government subsidy to build ships for the navy and for trade. Many companies established shipyards during the thirties and they were little damaged by the war.

Three companies built 54% of Japan's shipbuilding tonnage in 1967 – Mitsubishi 24%, Ishikawajima-Harima 17% and Hitachi 13%. The large yards use large building docks suitable for building huge tankers up to 300,000 tons rather than slipways and often make engines and fittings as well as ships. Japanese shipbuilding has expanded since 1949 with the help of loans from the Japan Development Bank. The Korean War and the Suez crisis both helped to increase the demand for Japanese ships. It has not been easy for her to compete in world markets as her steel costs are high and her labour costs rising. This has forced her to become efficient and her relatively cheap labour, efficient speedy production and technical progress have brought success. Since 1950 yards have been using the electric block welding system by which ships are made in sections and then assembled (pl. 46). This speeds production, cuts

PLATE 46. Oil tankers are the most important product of Japan's shipbuilding industry and a major export. These ships are being made at the Hitachi Shipbuilding and Engineering Company shipyard at Inoshima, a small port on the Inland Sea. The men below the ship give an idea of size. Modern prefabrication techniques are used; sections are assembled in huge workshops and lifted by giant cranes on to the slipway.

labour by over a third and saves 15% on costly materials. This together with the large capacity of her yards and *enterprise* unions which reduce the disputes that delay British shipbuilding make it possible for her to build ships in three or four months that would take six or seven months in Britain. With speed, relatively low labour costs, attractive credit terms and the capacity in large building docks to build the world's largest ships, attract many orders. In 1966 she built 48% of the world's tonnage and exported 60% of her production, especially of large tankers.

RAILWAY ROLLING STOCK

The making of railway rolling stock, like shipbuilding, needs large quantities of costly steel and makes it difficult for Japan's producers to compete with other countries. Recently her techniques of production have rapidly advanced. There has been rapid growth to meet the needs of the home railway development programmes and the output of the industry shows an overall increase. There is a considerable export of rolling stock and economies in the use of raw materials and improved techniques are increasing these.

MACHINE TOOLS

The machine tool industry, including the manufacture of lathes, and drilling and grinding machines, still lags behind foreign producers in costs and standards. The gap is closing but production costs are high and Japan can sell little abroad. The industry grew until 1963 but has stagnated since so that Japan imports more than she exports, which indicates the immature state of this industry which serves too small a market for such specialist production.

INDUSTRIAL MACHINERY

She also needs to import industrial machinery, including civil engineering and construction equipment, mining, textile and chemical machinery. The great public works programme for building roads, harbours, railways, power stations, multipurpose schemes and land reclamation projects has caused the production of *constructional machinery* to treble between 1962 and 1966.

MOTOR VEHICLES

The motor vehicle industry has expanded greatly since 1962 when production became on a large enough scale to take advantage of the economies of mass production. In 1966 Japan passed Britain to become the third largest producer after the USA and West Germany, producing 3·2 million vehicles including 1·8 million trucks and 1·4 million cars in 1967. The industry was late to develop as it is a stage three industry with complicated technology needing technical agreements like the one between BMC and Toyota and large firms and a large market. The industry was protected by import restrictions while it developed. These were partly liberalized in 1965 and further liberalized in 1968.

As production has increased the price of cars has been reduced so that they have been able to compete in world markets since 1963. In 1967 20% of cars and half the trucks were exported. Many small cars are sold in the USA and increasingly in Europe and small trucks have a good market in South East Asia. The home market has expanded with growing prosperity but as recently as 1960 90% of cars were sold to companies or government offices. Only now is the private car market growing. The number of motor vehicles on Japanese roads rose sharply from 3·6 million in 1962 to 8·5 million in 1966. The motor vehicle industry is still biased on the side of trucks which still formed over half the total in 1966 though the number of cars is fast catching up as home and overseas markets expand.

The wave of mergers in Japanese industry during the sixties has been very significant in the motor vehicle industry where there is much to be gained from large scale units. By 1967 companies had formed into two main groups making 60% of trucks and 78% of cars. One around Toyota produced 35% of trucks and 46% of cars and the other around Nissan produced 25% and 35%. Mitsubishi was the only other large producer with 10% of trucks and 8% of cars. The industry is concentrated in Chukyo and Keihin with the Toyota works which dates from 1933 in Motomachi in Aichi and the Nissan works in Keihin.

With a large home market, less need for large-scale production and a great deal of research, Japan's *motor cycle* industry has been the largest in the world

PLATE 47. A final assembly line at the Toyota works at Motomachi in Aichi, which produces nearly half of Japan's cars, using modern assembly-line techniques.

since 1960. In 1967 2·5 million bicycles were made which was 40% of world production and 38% were exported. Together Honda (57%), Susuki (20%), and Yamaha (18%) produce 95% of the total. They go to the less developed countries of Asia and South America and the more highly developed countries of Europe and North America. Like the motor vehicle industry production is concentrated in Chukyo and Tokyo.

As early as 1930 Japan came to lead the *bicycle* industry but production is static at 3·9 million in 1967, half of them exported, especially to the USA. Parts made in domestic workshops are assembled in small factories but other countries can now under cut Japanese prices in this relatively simple industry. *Agricultural machinery* is made for both the home and Asian markets. The production of power cultivators increased greatly during the late fifties but has levelled off. *Aircraft* exports are just beginning and are likely to be important in the future.

ELECTRICAL INDUSTRY

The electrical industry, that has developed faster than any other since the war, is the fourth largest electrical industry in the world, and is second only to the iron and steel industry in size (fig. 99). The *denki* (electrical) boom in the fifties resulted from the rising standard of living, as people have money to buy fires, rice boilers, fans, irons, radio and television sets, washing machines, refrigerators, record players and tape recorders. Home sales have slowed since 1959 as so many people have already bought electrical goods. In 1968 96% of homes had television, 85% washing machines and 78% refrigerators. Exports are growing and production doubled between 1960 and 1966. Exports are flourishing in radios, micro television, tape recorders, communications equipment and fans which can compete in price and quality with foreign products. Japan's radio production is exceeded only by that of the US. Radios, especially transistors, make up three-quarters of the production but other household and communications equipment is important. The industry is efficient and has technical agreements with many foreign firms, especially American and Dutch. It uses cheaper, dexterous female labour in making such things as transistors and can serve the growing protected home market, a growing export market for radios, tape recorders and television sets.

The industry is concentrated in Keihin (fig. 115) and Hanshin. Half the value of production comes from new factories with over a thousand workers. The heavier equipment, including generators, is mainly made by the six large companies, including Hitachi, Mitsubishi and Fuji, but there are many small factories and workshops making parts as they do for the Matsushita Electrical factory (p. 194).

LIGHT ENGINEERING INDUSTRY

A large variety of light engineering goods are produced in Japan many of which such as sewing machines, cameras and binoculars, are finding a growing market in the highly developed countries of North America, Europe and Australasia, as well as at home. The parts are made in workshops where wages are lower and they are assembled in small factories. Standards are variable, though the best products are of very high quality.

Japan is the largest producer of *cameras*. Production has been static at about 4 million since 1960. The home market has been saturated but exports doubled between 1960 and 1966, and 2 million cameras were exported in 1966 mainly to the USA and Europe. Cine-cameras, telescopes, binoculars and microscopes are all of increasing importance.

Japan now produces 40% of the world's *sewing machines*. Like many other light industries it centres on Nagoya, where parts are made in workshops and assembled on a moving belt in a factory. With the adoption of western dress many Japanese now own sewing machines, but two-thirds of the production goes abroad, the United States being the largest customer.

Another fast growing industry is the making of *business machines*. The export of typewriters, computers, copying machines, dictating machines and tape recorders is growing. Since 1960 *clocks and watches* have been mass produced by four large firms. Production (32 million in 1967) was double 1960 and exports are expanding fast.

The Chemical Industry

The chemical industry is one of Japan's leading industries, producing 11% of manufacturing production in 1967 (fig. 99). Since the petro-chemical industry started to develop in 1955 the industry has been changing from one concentrated on the production of fertilizers, paints, dyes and drugs, using coal as a base, which only requires a relatively small amount of capital and is simple technologically, to one based on oil making plastics, synthetic fibres and resins, and

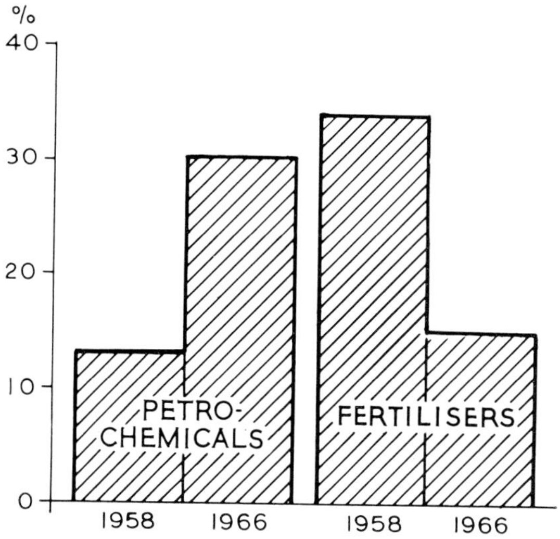

FIG. 117. The changing balance of the chemical industry between 1958 and 1966 by value (182).

needing a very large amount of capital and a high degree of technology (fig. 117). The chemical industry was important in Japan even in the second phase of industrial development before the war, but the development of the petro-chemical industry which increased ten times between 1960 and 1966 has been the main factor in the doubling of the total production of the industry during this period (fig. 100). It forms 30% of total production.

The pre-1955 chemical industry depended on coal as its main raw material and was associated with the Chikuho field in north Kyushu, with most of the producing factories within the north Kyushu industrial area (fig. 118). Coke making by the great iron and steel works there produces many valuable by-products that form the main basis for this part of the chemical industry. From these by-products, fertilizers, plastics and resins, including bakelite, synthetic polymers for textile fibres – especially nylon – dyes, drugs, insecticides, cos-

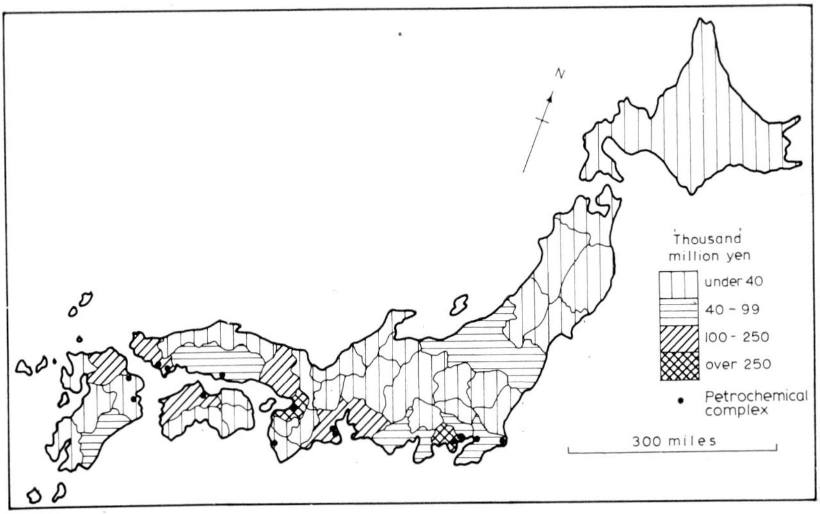

FIG. 118. The distribution of the chemical industry in 1964 (91) and petro-chemical complexes complete and under construction in 1967 (*Oriental Economist*, Jan. 1968).

metics and paints are made. Recently oxygen-making plants have been established adjacent to the iron and steel works to provide oxygen for the new high-speed smelting of iron and steel, for example at Tobata (pl. 45) the Nittetsu factory is next to the new Yawata plant. In other areas too great iron and steel and chemical industrial combines are growing to make similar use of coking by-products, notably in the new Chiba coast industrial area and on the coast in Sakai, south of Osaka, where there are huge new iron and steel plants. Others are at Muroran near the Hokkaido coalfield and at Joban on the Joban coalfield.

A second type of chemical industry is the *electro-chemical* industry based on hydroelectric power (fig. 111). This industry is especially important on the coast of Hokuriku in Niigata and Toyama Prefectures, in the Chukyo industrial area, both close to the mountains of central Japan, and in Shikoku, where the Sumitomo Company has developed chemical plants using hydroelectric power and by-products from the smelting of copper and other non-ferrous metals. Another centre is at Nobeoka in south-west Kyushu.

The new *petro-chemical* industry has grown since the inception of the First Period Plan in 1955. Under this plan, the large groups, who were the only industrialists who could afford to buy the costly plant necessary, agreed on the establishment of four great petro-chemical complexes each with an oil refinery, a naphtha cracking plant and an electric power station using oil as fuel. A Mitsui plant was built at Iwakuni at the western end of the Inland Sea near Hiroshima (pl. 48), a Sumitomo plant at Niihama near their chemical works in northern

PLATE 48. The Iwakuni–Otake petro-chemical complex west of Hiroshima on reclaimed land on the shore of the Inland Sea uses imported petroleum to make petro-chemicals, which are the raw materials for many associated textile and plastics industries.

Shikoku, a Mitsubishi plant at Yokkaichi, on Ise Bay, and a Nippon petro-chemical plant at Kawasaki. Five additional huge plants were completed by 1966 and two more will be ready by 1969. All these plants are situated on land reclaimed from the sea. The adjacent sea is dredged for infilling, so making it deep enough to accommodate oil tankers. Several others are in Keihin, Chukyo and on the Inland Sea.

Among the most important products of the petro-chemical industry are synthetic fibres, including terylene, acrilan and many others. These are used both alone and mixed with natural fibres. They are especially important to Japanese industry as she has no large home sources of natural fibres. Many varieties of plastics and resins are produced, including melamine, polythene, polystyrene, polyethylene, and new ones are constantly being invented. Other products include synthetic rubber, which formed 54% of the rubber used in Japan in 1966, and detergents. All these products result from cracking oil. The method of cracking can be adjusted to produce the proportions of the petroleum products required by the market. Petro-chemical products are replacing wood, metal and glass for many household and industrial purposes, including containers, piping, sheeting, tableware and toys, all of which have a fast-growing world demand. Associated with these new cracking plants, and often on the same site, new factories are being built to make these consumer goods.

These new plants have all been located on tidewater sites where land has been reclaimed and the water made deep enough for 150,000-ton tankers. They are mainly in the industrial zone in or near the great industrial areas of Keihin, Hanshin and Chukyo, and around the Inland Sea. On the Inland Sea they are very closely related to the older chemical industry at Niihama and to the rayon industry. Others are the focus of new industrial centres at Mizushima in Okayama and Mishima in Tokai. Overall the chemical industry is concentrated in the main centres of industry.

The size and technical efficiency of this new industry is now up to that in the advanced western nations. It was protected by high tariffs while its efficiency and size increased and has been greatly assisted by many technical agreements with foreign companies, for example the terylene-making process was bought from ICI. The price of petro-chemical products has fallen sharply. It was only 53% of the 1960 price in 1967. The chemical industry plays an important part in exports especially of chemicals to South East Asia and the Communist Block and increasingly of synthetic fabrics and other petro-chemical products.

The Textile Industry

The textile industry played a dominant role in the industrialization of Japan. Since World War II textiles have been superseded in importance by the engineering, chemical and iron and steel industries, but textiles, especially cotton, rayon and synthetic fibres, are still, with metals, Japan's second largest export, forming 18% of the total. Japan's cotton yarn production is double Britain's

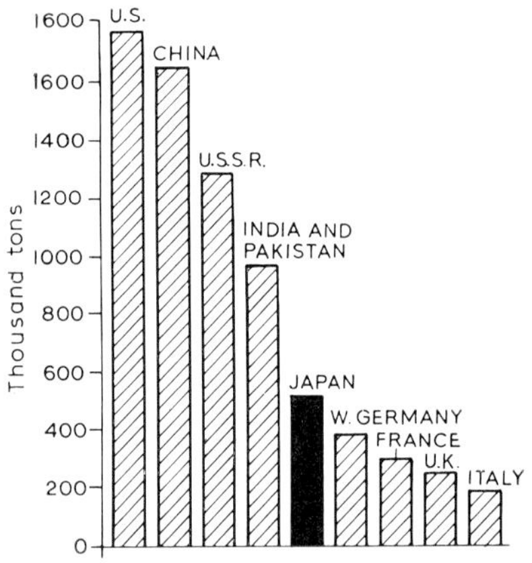

FIG. 119. The main world cotton yarn producers 1961 (*United Nations Statistical Year Book*).

(fig. 119) but only a third of USA and China. The industry is concentrated in the Nobi Plain, where a third of Japan's textiles are produced. Hanshin is also important. Much of the industry, especially weaving, is scattered in rural areas.

The modern textile industry is founded on the small-scale industry which existed before the Meiji era, using cotton and silk grown in Japan. Silk was manufactured in the towns and villages of the Kinki, especially in Kyoto, in nearby Fukui, and in Tosan where the silkworms were reared. Cotton was manufactured in the Osaka area using cotton grown in the nearby hot dry Inland Sea area. To meet the demand for warmth during the cold winter quilted material was produced.

In 1867 the Lord of Satsuma in South Kyushu bought British machinery to establish the first modern factory, and in 1878 the Meiji government established a model factory with the advice of British experts. It was an industry well suited to the early days of industrialization as it could make use of skills already available, the modern techniques were relatively simple, factories needed relatively little capital and could use local power supplies. Employing young farm women, who were paid very low wages, in three shifts a day, their products could undercut world prices so that after 1890 textiles became an important export. The textile industry grew rapidly until World War II, and in 1966, with the growing importance of synthetics production, is double pre-war. The engineering, iron and steel and chemical industries have grown very much more rapidly than the textile industry, which has encountered competition from countries with lower labour costs and their own raw materials, so that the textile industry has lost its dominant position in Japanese industry. In 1934 Japan was the leading world producer of cotton cloth, and textiles formed 34% of Japan's total industrial production, but in 1967 this had fallen to 9%. Textiles fell from 76% of her exports in 1925 to 60% in 1934–6, and then to only 16% in 1967 (figs. 99 & 155).

During three periods of textile development the type of textiles produced has changed (fig. 120). In the first period up to the thirties silk and cotton were the main textiles produced, with a small quantity of woollen goods after the establishment of a woollen industry in the late nineteenth century using imported wool, primarily for clothing the army. Until the mid-thirties cotton accounted for half the total textile production and silk a third. In the second era, during the thirties, the rayon industry, which had been growing in importance during the twenties, followed by cotton and chemical fibres, became more important than silk. Japan's cheap rayon staple production, using home-grown wood pulp, led the world just before World War II. Silk production was hit by the 1931 Depression, by the war, and by the competition of cheaper nylon, and has not regained its pre-war place. In the third era, since 1950, synthetic yarns including nylon and terylene have become almost as important as cotton. They formed 32% of all textile production in 1967 while cotton formed 28% and rayon 20%. They had the initial advantage of using home-produced coal and relatively cheap hydroelectricity, though more recent technology requires the use of imported oil. Japan is now second in synthetic textile production to the USA. Silk production is only a third of pre-war production, a mere 1% of her total textile production, and wool, though a growing part of the industry, forms only 8% of the total.

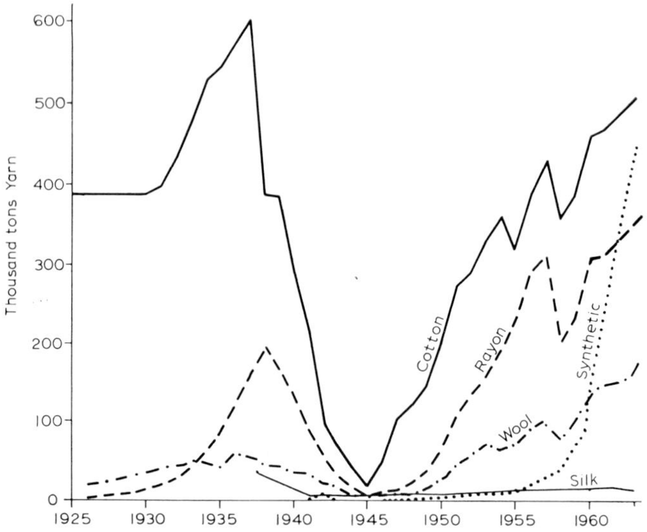

FIG. 120. Trends in yarn production since 1925 (88, 182, 200).

Since the war the rising standard of living has increased the home sales of textiles, especially of woollen materials as more people are wearing western dress, and half Japan's textiles are sold at home. It has been increasingly difficult for Japan to sell textiles abroad as there has been a world surplus of cotton, wool

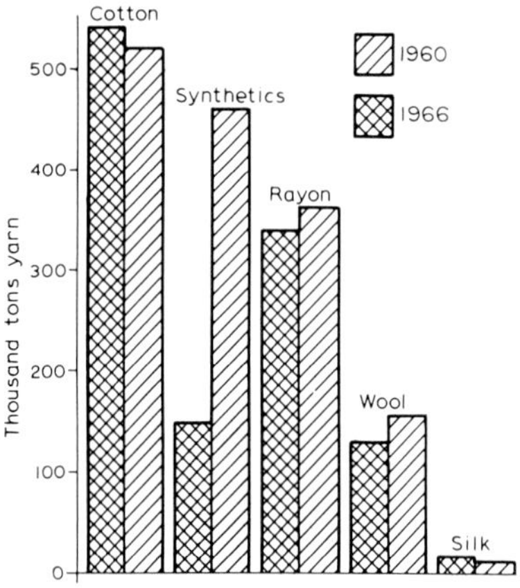

FIG. 121. The relative importance of various textiles 1953 and 1966 (182).

and rayon cloth and many markets have been closed to Japan by tariffs protecting newly developed industries.

Japan finds it difficult to compete with poorer countries, as her higher wages and costly imported raw materials make her cloth more expensive than that of India and China. Cheap Indian and Chinese cloth is underselling her in Africa and Asia. These markets have been replaced by sales of high-quality goods to the highly developed countries of North America and Europe, and in Australia and New Zealand where she can sell fine cottons and materials made of synthetic yarns and clothes. Since 1956 the main textile exporters have co-operated to limit exports to the United States, Canada and Europe through the Japan Textile

PLATE 49. Spinning in the Toyo factory in Osaka. Toyo is one of the 'big ten' companies.

Export Association, because they fear that if they export too much their products may be excluded completely. With young, relatively cheap and skilled female labour operating first-class equipment (pl. 49) Japan can make high-quality goods better than China or India. Her fabrics are cheaper than those of Britain and the United States, in spite of the transport costs of raw material, as wages are lower. They were 20% of United Kingdom wages in 1961 but have risen sharply since then. The new continuous automatic spinning process has changed the look of new spinning mills from the one above.

Productivity is rising as large-scale production becomes more important and the industry becomes more efficient. The productivity of the larger firms has doubled the pre-war figure but is still well below that of the United States. In 1962 it took 3 man days to spin a standard bale of cotton yarn in the United States, compared with 3·9 in Japan and 6·3 in Britain.

THE COTTON INDUSTRY

The cotton industry lost its dominant position in the textile industry in Japan to synthetic yarn in 1967 when it produced 28% of the total and 16% of the textile exports. Production of cotton cloth has been static and exports falling since 1960, but in 1960 Japan was still the leading exporter of cotton goods with 30% of the world total. Half of the raw cotton comes from North America (in 1966, Mexico 28% and United States 26%) and most of the rest from India, Pakistan, Brazil and the United Arab Republic. Though production has been growing again since the war the production of yarn in 1966 was only 75% of pre-war. The cost of labour is rising as it is in Lancashire and women are being attracted by industries that pay better.

Before the Meiji era cotton was grown in Japan, but since then cheaper supplies have been imported. The cotton industry has developed in the areas where cotton was grown. These areas are mainly round the Inland Sea, on the Nobi and Kanto Plains and in Toyama in Hokuriku on the Japan Sea coast. All these areas both spin and weave although all the raw cotton is now imported. Most of the spinning is done in factories in the larger towns in Chukyo and Hanshin and on the north coast of the Inland Sea and in Toyama. There is some spinning in north Kyushu and Keihin. Weaving is increasingly being associated with the spinning mills, but there is still much done in small factories and in workshops in towns and villages. Production focuses on Osaka and Nagoya and there are factories in Nagoya and in the countryside to the north and west, and at the eastern end of the Inland Sea (92). There are less important centres all round the Inland Sea and on the Kanto Plain.

The cotton industry is carried on both in small-scale workshops and large-scale factories. Most firms do one of the processes, for though large-scale spinners and merchants organize the industry they do not own the weaving, dyeing and finishing plants, so there is relatively little vertical integration in the textile industry. Large factories are especially important in spinning, where the Big Ten companies spin almost two-thirds of the cotton yarn. They also weave one-third of the cloth, which is almost entirely for export. The proportion they weave is rising as integration within the industry increases. Small workshops are more important for weaving (p. 191). Three-quarters of the weaving firms have less than 300 workers. These make specialized goods like velveteen and gingham, often for sale at home, and make knitted underwear and hosiery on contract to merchant spinners.

THE SILK INDUSTRY

Silk formed 30% of Japan's exports during the twenties but it has declined since 1930 and today, although Japan is the leading world producer of silk, her production is static and only half pre-war. Silk forms only 1% of Japan's yarn production (fig. 121), and because of increased home demand she has imported raw silk since 1964 and exports are declining.

Most silk reeling is done in the areas where the cocoons are produced (figs. 69

& 122), one the western edge of the Kanto Plain in Saitama and Yamanashi Prefecture, on the northern border of the Nobi Plain in Gifu Prefecture and in scattered mountain valleys of Tosan in Nagano and Guma. Some is done near the markets where it is sold. Weaving is widespread in many small workshops, especially on the Japan Sea coast in Fukui and Ishikawa Prefectures and in Kyoto, which have a long tradition of fine silk production, in the spinning area in west Kanto, and to a lesser extent in Gifu and Tosan and in the isolated

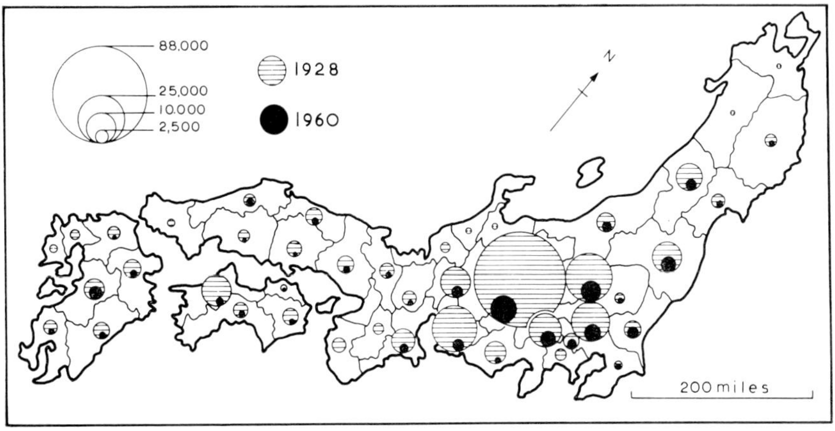

FIG. 122. The distribution of silk reeling capacity 1928 and 1960 (*after R. Hough*)

valleys of south Tohoku. There is very high-quality production in and around Kyoto, where for many centuries it was made for the emperor's court.

THE WOOLLEN INDUSTRY

The more recently established woollen industry is growing steadily. It has been based from its beginning on imported wool from Australia which has come especially through Osaka, Nagoya and less through Yokohama to towns and villages in their hinterlands where it is spun and woven. The demand for woollen cloth is growing with the wearing of western dress. The woollen industry forms 10% of total cloth production, production is rising steadily despite new competition from polyacrylic fibres and exports are growing.

CHEMICAL FIBRES

Japan is the world's largest producer of *rayon* staple and the second largest producer of rayon filament. The industry is over-equipped and stagnant because of market resistance and the competition of synthetic fibres, but rayon still forms nearly a quarter of all the textiles produced. Production is concentrated in western Japan especially around the Inland Sea, where local and imported supplies of timber can be used.

Synthetic fibres are the only rapidly growing part of the textile industry.

Production quadrupled between 1960 and 1967 and since 1955 synthetic fibres have been produced by new petro-chemical complexes; synthetic yarn formed 32% of textile production in 1967 and exports are growing. Factories are large and modern and the industry is located (fig. 123) at such places as Matsuyama and Mizushima on the Inland Sea, in south-eastern Tohoku in Fukushima Prefecture and in Hokuriku in Toyama and Ishikawa Prefectures where supplies of petro-chemicals are accessible and it is associated with rayon producers. Nylon formed 32% of synthetic yarn produced in 1966, polyester with its good mixing qualities 26% and acryl, which is rather like wool, 22%.

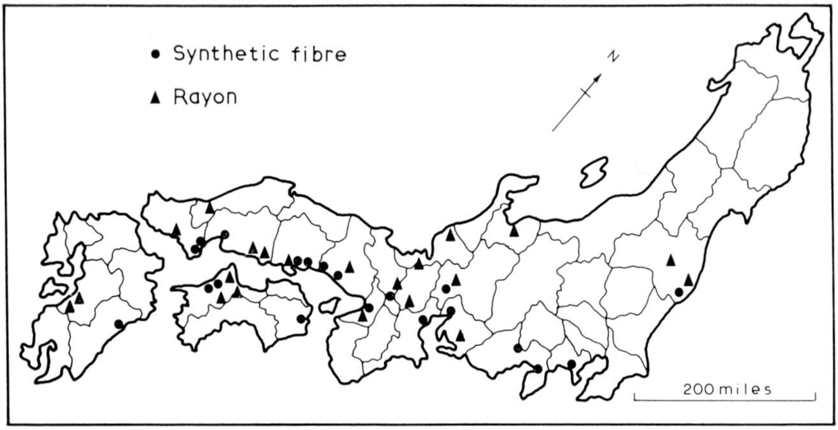

FIG. 123. The distribution of the synthetic fibre and rayon industries (210).

The future of Japan's textile industry lies in synthetic textiles or in a mixture of synthetic and natural fibres, rather than in cotton and rayon in which she has lost her relative advantage. Wool production is growing but is still small and silk is now of little importance. Clothing has become a very important export, especially to USA.

Food Industries

Food processing is one of the most important industries in Japan as it is in all urbanized industrial countries. There are large factories in the cities where such products as wheat are imported or brought from the country to be processed. In rural areas many small factories process tea, can fruit, mill flour, polish rice, make *saké* (rice wine) and soya sauce or extract starch, near the farms where they are grown. Much of the rice, flour and *saké* are consumed in the area on which they are produced. Some products like milk and sugar are processed in large factories in rural areas. Sugar beet is refined in large modern factories in Hokkaido and Kyushu and around the Inland Sea, where the pulp can be sold back to the farmer to use as fodder. Similarly cream is made into butter, milk is dried, condensed or evaporated in factories in Hokkaido, north-east Tohoku and central Honshu where the milk is produced. The Meiji, Morinaga and Snow Brand firms have almost complete control of milk processing. The canning industry, started for the army, is growing now that the housewife has more to spend. Fish canned in the ports makes up half of all the canned goods, and fruit and vegetables are of growing importance. Japanese beer production doubled between 1960 and 1967. It is brewed in large plants, mainly by the Asahi, Sapporo and Kirin companies.

Small Goods

There is an infinite variety of smaller products, including toys, leather goods, pins, cutlery and musical instruments, which are of growing importance in Japanese industry. Many of these are produced cheaply in small workshops for the home market and increasingly for export. In Osaka merchants organize the production of leather goods, toys, hollow ware and matches, in both urban and rural homes and in the Tokyo area, where these and many other things are made. Some areas further afield have their own specialities, for example Tsubame in Niigata specializes in cooking utensils and cutlery, Seki in Gifu Prefecture in cutlery, and Toyama in needles. The habit of gift giving on all occasions makes a big home market for gifts and many of the small attractive articles are sold all over the world.

Ceramics

Ceramics is one of the important minor industries in Japan, and Japan is the leading exporter. The industry is carried on both in workshops and large-scale factories. Master craftsmen make costly Japanese-style pots in Kyoto, families make Japanese and western-style goods and large modern factories produce western-style tableware, tiles and sanitary ware. Suitable clay is widespread; Chukyo, Hanshin and Keihin are all leading production centres and Fukuoka is also important. There are many small centres like Seto near Nagoya and Arita in north-west Kyushu, where a craft industry based on family tradition has expanded into a workshop and factory industry to produce larger quantities of goods. Workshops have been set up in Arita, where a family employs a few people to make special orders for hotels. There too larger factories crowd into the valley, and the Koransha, Fukagawa, Iwao and Kakiemon factories make Japanese-style tea-cups and bowls and western-style tea and dinner services. Arita is not far from Nagasaki, which was an important port for trade with the Dutch in Tokugawa times, and the influence of blue Korean and Dutch pottery on the local products is very striking. Seto near Nagoya is another important centre, where even as long ago as 1893 there were 434 master craftsmen and 3,000 workers working in small domestic workshops. Today they make both Japanese-style goods and western-style figurines for sale abroad. Merchants organize the industry and workshops specialize in cups, saucers, plates or any of the other varied wares. In Chukyo many western-style articles are started in workshops in the nearby small towns and brought into Nagoya for finishing, so that they are standardized.

In contrast with the domestic industry Nagoya is the centre of a large-scale western-style pottery industry, making china for export. The Noritake works in Nagoya is much like a large British factory and much of its western tableware is exported to America, and it can also be bought in Britain. Most of the tiles, the ceramics needed for the electrical industry and the sanitary ware are produced in large factories in the Nagoya and Osaka areas. Recently the Japanese Design Centre has helped to improve the quality and design of the western-style products and now over half Japan's ceramic production, mainly tableware, mosaic tiles and ornaments, is exported. Sales of the less valuable bulky goods are limited to nearby countries because of the high cost of transport. Such things as mosaic tiles are sold in Britain. Half Japan's exports are now sold in USA and much of the rest goes to Asian countries and to Australia. Asian countries are now developing their own industries and this market for cheaper goods will probably decline while western markets for more costly goods are growing. Two large firms produce 89% of Japan's glass. The industry is growing with the building boom.

Rubber

Rubber forms the basis of another small but important industry, and Japan is now the second largest world producer of rubber articles, especially tyres and footwear. Dunlop established the first tyre factory in Osaka in 1909 and now Goodyear, Goodrich and Bridgestone all have large factories, especially in Hanshin around the eastern end of the Inland Sea, where half the industry is centred, and also in Keihin and north Kyushu, where they both use imported Malaysian rubber and home-produced synthetic rubber which has been produced in Japan in the last few years, and already, by 1966, formed 54% of the total used. Small rubber goods like shoes, rubber hoses, belts and rubbered cloth are made in many small factories like the one at Tsuda (pl. 43). The finished goods are exported especially to south-east Asia. The rubber industry is technically simple and one of the industries of the earlier stage of industrialization which is likely to suffer increasingly from competition from newly industrialized countries with low labour costs. The demand for tyres is growing.

The Fishing Industry

The waters around Japan are one of the world's three most important fishing grounds and Japan was the leading fishing nation until 1959 when Peru, with a large amount of UNESCO aid, surpassed her. Her catch forms about 13% of world production, and includes a wide variety of fish such as salmon, herring, cod, tuna, shellfish and whales. Pearls are also an important product (fig. 124).

Because of political and economic difficulties the catch has been static since 1962 though in 1967, at 8 million tons, it was double the 4 million tons before the war. Fish has always had an important place in the Japanese diet, as the population is concentrated near her long coastline and since relatively few animals have been reared. In spite of the recent increase in animal rearing, fish production still provides half of the animal protein in the Japanese diet. Fish is eaten at most meals and in many forms: raw, dried or salted, as a paste, as a sausage, or as the basis for a soup. With growing home demand and static production fish prices rose by 40% between 1960 and 1966. Fish has been imported from China and Korea since 1960 but 10% of the catch, by value, is sold abroad. The more expensive products include pearls, tinned and smoked salmon, frozen and tinned crab and lobster, and whale oil. Japan's best markets

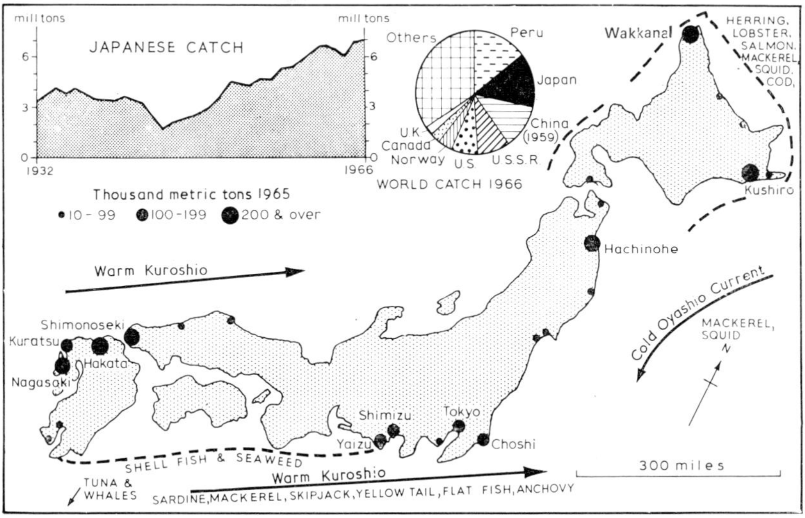

FIG. 124. The main fishing ports (162), trends in fishing and Japan's world position.

for these are in North America and Europe. China and south-east Asia buy cheaper dried and salted fish. Fish forms 4%, by value, of Japan's exports but it is a very minor industry compared with engineering and chemicals. It employed only 1% of the work force in 1967 which was 15% below 1960.

Japan has long been important as a fishing nation by virtue of her position at the meeting of the cold Oyashio current from the Arctic and the warm Kuroshio current from the tropical waters to the south. As in the two great fishing areas north of about 45°N latitude in the Atlantic Ocean, around Britain and Newfoundland, there are conditions which are ideal for plankton which provide food for a great variety of fish. There are salmon, herring, cod, crab and whales in the colder waters to the north of Japan, and tuna, skipjack, bonito, mackerel, sardines and shellfish in the warmer waters to the south.

Like many other industries in Japan the fishing industry is carried on both on a small-scale family level and also as a large-scale highly organized industry. There are about 200,000 fishing concerns in Japan, but about 96% of these are small family units with boats of less than 10 tons and operate in coastal waters which are very much over-fished. They caught 37% of the catch in 1965. Of all the boats only 45% are powered. Catches are low and most of the fishing families also work small farms near the shore. Many small-scale fishermen work from the shore from small unpowered boats, using fixed nets, rod and line or purse seine nets.

At the other end of the scale are the companies that own fleets of ships from 100–2,000 tons and carry on deep sea fishing. Though these form only 4% of the total number of enterprises in Japan they accounted for 67% of the total tonnage and brought in 52% of the value of the total catch in 1965.

FISHING PORTS

Of the 2,000 fishing ports in Japan four have been chosen to show the variety within the fishing industry. *Tsuda* in Shikoku (pl. 43) represents the simplest

PLATE 50. Tomo, an attractive little port on the Inland Sea; it is typical of many of Japan's small fishing ports. A small peninsula has been lengthened to provide shelter for small family boats which fish only within the Inland Sea. The rounded granite hillsides, clothed in pines, fall steeply to the sea and leave little room for farming (220).

and smallest. Here there is no real harbour and small rowing boats and a few small boats with outboard motors are pulled up on the shingle beach. The boats are taken out early in the morning and work in pairs with a purse seine between them. By breakfast time they bring in a small catch of sardines, prawns, octopus and shellfish. When the catch has been taken to the co-operative the boats are cleaned and the nets mended and each family goes to work on its land.

Tomo on the coast of Okayama (pl. 50) is like many of the small fishing ports in Japan. Although there are small boats like those in Tsuda there is a harbour and most of the 200 boats in it are small, powered trawlers of between 2 and 8 tons. With a crew of two or three they go out all day into the Inland Sea. Early in the morning the tiny fleet chugs out of the harbour (pl. 3) to fish in the calm waters. They return at about 4 p.m. with a catch of mackerel, octopus, squid and shellfish. These are sorted and taken to be auctioned by dealers in the co-operative market. The fishermen's wives supplement the family income by

PLATE 51. Small 'catcher' boats catch salmon and sea trout in nets and bring them back to be canned on board the factory ship. This 'catcher' boat is setting off again after delivering her catch.

farming, or making boxes, baskets or nets, and the fishermen work on the land on stormy days and in the off season.

Unlike these smaller ports a catch of over 100,000 tons a year is landed at *Hachinohe* in north-east Tohoku. Most of the 2,000 boats here are between 15 and 60 tons and need a crew of about ten. Hachinohe fishermen specialize in catching squid and mackerel in offshore waters. They catch the mackerel by line and by trawl and the squid by attracting the fish with lights set to shine over a net fixed from the side of the boat. There is a large market on the quay where the fish are sold. The catch is large enough to supply processing plants which freeze, smoke, dry, can or salt the fish. Many of these fish are sent to China and south-east Asia.

The largest fishing ports in Japan have facilities for both the smaller boats and the large company-owned ships. The largest, each of which lands over 100,000 tons of fish a year are grouped in Hokkaido, Tokai-Kanto and West Kyushu.

L

Boats from Kushiro, which is one of six large fishing ports in Hokkaido, fish in the North Pacific for mackerel, salmon, cod, herring, squid and lobsters. Many company boats use the harbour. There are 20,000-ton mother ships each with a fleet of ten to thirty catcher boats, some of about 100 tons with a crew of seventeen, and others which are small and go out on board the mother ship (pl. 51). These fleets go out to catch salmon, crab or lobster for two to three months in the North Pacific. The catcher ships take each day's catch to the mother ship, where it is canned or frozen for export. The salmon ships have a busy day. They set their nets from 10 p.m. to 12 midnight, rest midnight to 3 a.m., haul in the nets 3 a.m. to 10 a.m., take the catch to the mother ship 10 a.m. to 4 p.m., and return to fish from 4 p.m. to 9 p.m.

FISHING AREAS AND TYPES OF FISHING

There are four main areas in Japan concerned with fishing. Hokkaido leads with six large and many small fishing ports which land over a quarter of the total catch. As in eastern Tohoku, where there are four large ports, much of the catch comprises fish from the cold coastal and offshore waters of the North Pacific and Sea of Okhotsk, and includes salmon, herring, crab, lobster, cod, whales, squid and mackerel. A third concentration of fishing ports includes Nagasaki and Shimonoseki and is in northern Kyushu and western Honshu, where a quarter of the total catch is landed mainly from the warmer waters south of Japan, including tuna, bonito, skipjack, mackerel and whales from the Antarctic. There are four important ports in Tokai-Kanto on the Pacific coast of central Honshu, where fish are also landed from warmer waters and shellfish and seaweed are especially important. Antarctic and North Pacific whales bring in 6% of the value of the catch. The catch in 1965 could be divided into high seas, 27% by value, offshore 25%, coastal 24%, shallow sea culture 14%, inland 4% and whales 6%.

Small fishermen in Japan fish from small boats in inshore waters, but the growing number of larger company boats fish further from the coast and increasingly in all the oceans of the world. Japanese boats fish in the North Pacific, in the South Pacific off Equador and north-east of Australia, in the Atlantic in equatorial waters off Brazil and West Africa, in the Indian Ocean and in the Antarctic. In 1965 Japan had seven factory ships catching whales in the Antarctic, each with ten catcher boats. Many of the newly developed fishing grounds are in equatorial waters where tuna and bonito were caught and canned by 90 factory ships in 1965. There are Japanese processing plants in countries abroad including Canada, South America, India and Malaya.

Fish culture is increasing in importance. The production of many high-value marine products is deliberately fostered, including pearls and crabs, octopus, yellow tail and prawns in sea water and carp, trout and eel in fresh water. Fish culture is carried on in small ponds and irrigated fields in many parts of Japan, notably in Tokai, Ibaragi, Nara and Arita, and the Inland Sea is being restocked with young fish. There are many trout and salmon hatcheries.

Pearls are of growing importance as an export to the United States. Rafts are placed in the calm waters of bays on the warm Pacific coast of Japan from Nagasaki in the west to Matsushima (pl. 7) in Tohoku. A tiny piece of shell is placed inside the oyster to cause irritation and encourage it to produce a pearl. The oysters are hung in bags in the water under the rafts for two to three years. *Seaweed* is another important product. Gathered from shallow water on the Pacific coast west of Tokyo, it is dried in sheets and is a favourite delicacy on the Japanese menu.

CHANGES

The pattern of the Japanese fishing industry has been changing since the war. As small fishermen find more productive employment, the number of small fishing boats has declined. The increasing number of large boats, especially those over 200 tons, has raised the total fishing tonnage and the catch to nearly double the pre-war catch. The efficiency of the fishing industry has increased now that all but the very smallest boats have engines, and there are now many boats with radar apparatus to find the fish and more efficient nets with which to catch them. Co-operatives have been set up to help fishermen to buy equipment more cheaply and to provide marketing facilities. The government encourages higher productivity by making loans available for installing power units and buying improved equipment. Larger boats are able to fish all the oceans of the world and the proportion of fish from distant waters has risen. Fish culture, though only 14% of the value, is increasing and the government has set up experimental stations to study techniques of rearing fish. In spite of these improvements the Japanese fishing family still has a lower income than the farmer, since the majority of family boats operate in crowded coastal and offshore waters which have been over-fished for generations.

Incomes are higher for those who have larger boats, but they have their own difficulties. Many of the fishing grounds accessible to the larger Japanese craft before the war are now closed to her since all her neighbours have excluded Japanese ships from a wider area round their coasts. The USSR has excluded Japanese boats from the Sea of Okhotsk, which is a valuable salmon-fishing area, Canada has set a limit to Japan at 175°E, Korea has set the 'Rhee Line' in some places as much as 90 miles from its coast. China set new coastal limits in 1955 and Australia has claimed the whole of the continental shelf area off her coast where Japanese pearl fishermen have worked in the past. Over-fishing in the North Pacific made a Japan-Soviet Fishing Convention to conserve the fish a necessity. The convention limits the tonnage of salmon that may be caught each year and the original quota has been reduced. The use of larger boats and factory ships in more distant waters has only partly counteracted these restrictions and catches have been static since 1962. The 1964 Five Year Fisheries Plan is developing co-operatives and fish culture and improving fishing techniques.

The Tourist Industry

Japan has many attractions for the tourist. The landscape itself is beautiful. There are rocky, forested mountains, rushing streams and narrow valleys. The blue sea is dotted with islands and bordered by rugged bays with green pines. The volcanoes are graceful and awe-inspiring, with snow-clad peaks and clear crater lakes, roaring geysers and bubbling mud pools. Every season has its attractions with cherry blossom in the spring, fields of golden rice in the summer, the red and burnished gold of the trees in the autumn and the snow in the winter. The Japanese have a deep appreciation of simple, beautiful things. Wooden shrines and temples have graceful curving roofs, towering pagodas and painted sliding doors which reveal the graceful living of feudal times. Shrines and temples have gardens designed to reproduce in miniature the natural beauty of water, rock and trees found in the Japanese landscape. Every tree and rock is placed to produce a perfect view. Every individual branch and stone is trained or chosen to be in itself of great beauty. One perfect flower is appreciated rather than a herbaceous border.

Craft products have a subtle sophistication. Simple stoneware, subtly coloured silk, decorated fans, fine dolls, lacquerware, woodblock prints, all have their own beauty. Japanese food is an acquired taste. Most people appreciate *sukiyaki*, which is a mixture of finely cut beef, vegetables and soya sauce cooked over charcoal on the table and served with raw egg. They also enjoy *tempura*, which is prawns fried in batter, but the great variety of raw fish, including tuna, squid, octopus and many seaweeds, are not perhaps so easily appreciated.

Festivals are still great occasions in Japan, especially when there is dancing in the rice fields and at the shrines. At the Bon festival after the rice harvest in the autumn the spirits of the family ancestors are conducted with many candles from the cemetery to join the family at home for the evening. At local festivals wars are waged between groups of local youths, and in Kyoto high decorated floats pass in procession through the streets in July at the Gion Festival. New Year is the chief festival of the year, preceded by special cooking of rice cakes and hard work to make sure that all the old year's letters are written and jobs done, and the house clean to welcome the New Year. New Year's day is everyone's official birthday. People dress in their best silk kimonos and go with offerings to the shrines. It is a great time for visiting when they welcome all their relations and friends with tea, *saké* and rice cakes.

As well as the natural and historical things of beauty and interest there is much that is new to interest the visitor. Fine new buildings, huge department stores, modern bridges, the overhead railway to Haneda airport from Tokyo, shipyards towering above tiny islands in the Inland Sea and great petro-chemical plants, are all impressive. The crowded cities with their jostling crowds; the busy rural landscape with its tiny fields and fantastic terracing; the crowded smoky industrial landscape of Kitakyushu are all interesting. Not all the Japanese landscape is beautiful. It is said that the Japanese appreciate beauty but do not see ugliness, and this is certainly true of the untidy chaos of some of the industrial areas and the monotony of much of the urban landscape.

All these things make Japan an interesting and beautiful country for the tourist to visit. The number of tourists visiting Japan doubled between 1960 and 1967 when nearly half of a million visited Japan, especially from North America but increasingly from Europe. The Olympic Games in Tokyo in 1964 did much to bring Japan on to the television screen. The Japanese built new roads, railways and new hotels for visitors to the Olympic Games.

There are many Japanese and western-style hotels in Japan. Japanese hotels provide a *tatami* room where meals are eaten and where one sleeps on a comfortable mattress spread on the floor. The Japanese-style bath is something of an experience. One needs to learn that the correct procedure is to wash before getting into the deep, extremely hot water and not to let soap contaminate the bath which must be left for the next person. Larger hotels have big communal baths with water over 2 feet deep, one for women and another for men. Many western-style hotels have been built for foreign and Japanese businessmen and tourists, especially in the big cities and in the most popular tourist areas. There are many in the Kinki, where tourists visit the ancient cultural treasures of Kyoto and Nara. Kyoto has nearly a thousand hotels. Other favourite tourist centres are the spa towns of the Fuji Hakone area within easy reach of Tokyo, the three famous seaside beauty spots: Amanohashidate, a beautiful pine-clad spit on the coast north of Kyoto, Matsushima (pl. 7) and the beautiful shrines on Miyajima in the Inland Sea. The Inland Sea is a particularly popular area. All over Japan there are spas, and in the mountains there are skiing resorts to which the Japanese go on holiday.

The Japanese holiday crowd is unlike our own. People generally go on holiday in groups. Women's organizations, factories and schools all organize group holidays. One sees groups of men, women or of schoolgirls or schoolboys in their uniforms, only occasionally families and sometimes couples on their honeymoon. The tourist industry is growing fast, with the increasing prosperity of the Japanese and of the foreign tourist. Of the 477,000 tourists in 1967 about half were American.

Conclusion

In Japan raw materials, power and capital are all expensive, but labour is still relatively cheap compared with western countries so that industries requiring a great deal of labour – such as the engineering industry, clothing and ceramics – can compete fairly easily with western costs of production, but the iron and steel and chemical industries which need costly imported raw materials need to be extremely efficient to compete with foreign products in the world market. Their products have recently reached the very high quality needed to sell in the highly developed countries of the world which offer the main markets for industrial products.

CHAPTER TEN

Transport

The transport of fast-growing quantities of freight and an increasing number of commuting industrial workers and holidaymakers is a major problem in Japan. Population and industry have outstripped the development of railways, roads, and sea and airports. Ports, mainly on shallow delta sites, are too shallow and small to cater for the ever-increasing size of ships and the growing import and export trade, as well as the very important domestic trade which distributes the raw materials needed for industry, brings food to the cities and collects industrial produce for export, bringing it to the few large ports that can cope with foreign trade. Railways are mainly single-track and heavily overloaded, especially in the industrial zone. They carry the highest number of passengers per mile in the world. Roads are in an even worse state. They were not built for huge modern lorries and buses. No less than 60% of main roads are too narrow even for lorries to pass each other, and two-thirds of the main roads are only surfaced with gravel. Much building is going on to improve transport facilities. Main roads are being surfaced, expressways and new railways built and harbours dredged, but the poor facilities are still hampering industry.

Japan's mountainous physiography, which isolates the many centres of population, makes it costly and difficult to build roads and railways. Her island nature provides many coastal plains with access to the sea which seem, at first sight, to be a great advantage, but unfortunately the tidewater beside these delta plains is shallow. So that, although there are thousands of ports in Japan, only a very few have facilities for ocean-going ships of over 10,000 tons. Coastal traffic is carried on by small, inefficient ships. Recent developments in the iron and steel and petro-chemical industries have necessitated the dredging of deep-water channels to cater for cargo boats and large tankers alongside newly reclaimed industrial sites; for example, at Yokkaichi, in Tokyo Bay and at sites on the Inland Sea coast.

Roads

With steep mountains often coming down to the sea, wide flood plains and broad braided streams which turn into raging torrents in the summer, roads and railways are costly to construct and to maintain. Both the long bridges across the rivers and embankments across valley floors (pl. 13) are liable to be washed away by sudden floods. The roads have steep gradients to negotiate and the railways wind and tunnel to pass from one small valley or plain to the next. Travel until the last hundred years was mainly on horseback or on foot, as wheeled traffic was not easy when so many rivers had to be crossed by ferry. There were post towns every few miles to provide facilities for travellers, and towns developed also at ferry crossings (pl. 1).

Many modern main roads (fig. 125) and railways are based on the road system organized after the Taika Reform in 645 that developed into the system of post

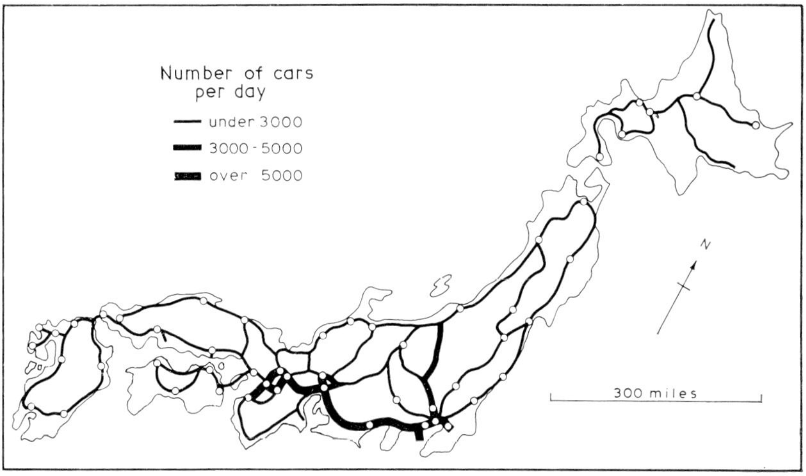

FIG. 125. The pattern of road traffic in 1960 (*Nippon no Chiri*, vol. 8).

roads built by the Tokugawa government to unite the country. The Tokaido linking Kyoto to Yedo was the most important road, and others linked northern and western Japan to the capital. Most of the roads run through the most densely populated parts near the coasts, where they must cross the wide lower courses of the rivers by long bridges, which must be strongly built against the summer monsoon floods. Even now there are few roads across the mountains linking the Pacific and Japan Sea coasts.

The modern road network lags far behind railway development in Japan (fig. 126). As in many less-developed countries the government has preferred to spend money on less costly railways, which carry freight to market, and bring in a direct financial return. In 1961 roads carried only 27% of passenger traffic and 30% of all goods traffic carried by land but by 1967 this had risen to 38% and 57% (fig. 128). Most of Japan's roads are narrow; 60% are under 22 feet – that is too narrow for two lines of traffic. They are often difficult to widen because of the steepness of the mountainside or the width of the embankment on which they perch. Only 29% were asphalted in 1966. The amount of road traffic has increased rapidly since the war. The number of vehicles in 1968 was four times 1960 and the many lorries and buses are much wider and heavier than the roads were intended to carry. A great deal of money is being spent in developing trunk roads (pl. 36). Parts of the four-lane Meishin Expressway from Tokyo to Nagoya and Kobe that will serve the Tokyo–Kobe industrial zone are open and are the first motorways in Japan (fig. 127).

As in Britain the roads in and near the cities are becoming congested. By-passes are needed as industry develops and there are more goods to be transported and more commuters. With greater prosperity people can afford to go on

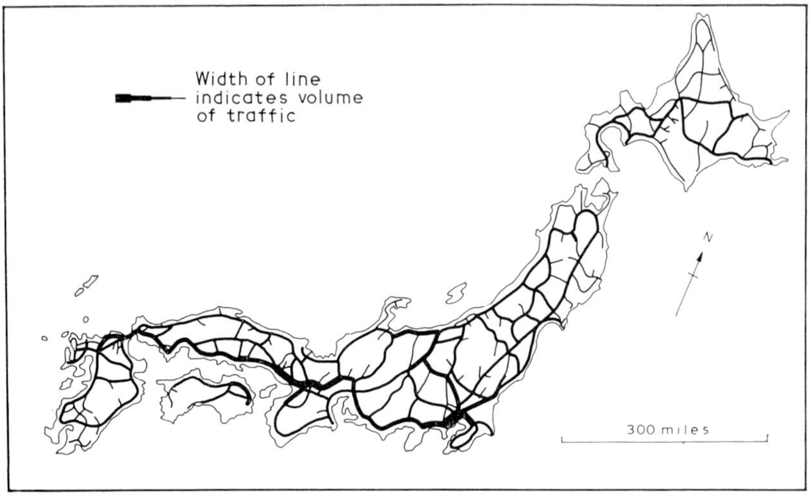

FIG. 126. The pattern of rail traffic, 1960 (*after R. Isida*).

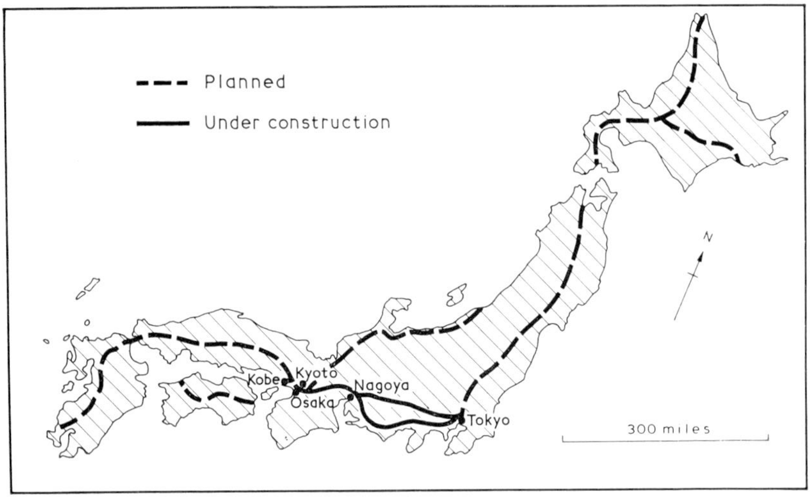

FIG. 127. Expressways (197).

holiday and the number of coaches on the road in cherry-blossom time and at other festivals is growing. The city roads are busy with trucks, taxis, buses and trams, scooters and bicycles. There are a growing number of private cars as more people are able to afford a car but the number of cars on the roads increased four times between 1960 and 1966 and trucks doubled. There was 1 car to 68 people in Japan in 1963 but this rose to 1 : 36 by 1966 compared with 1 to 6

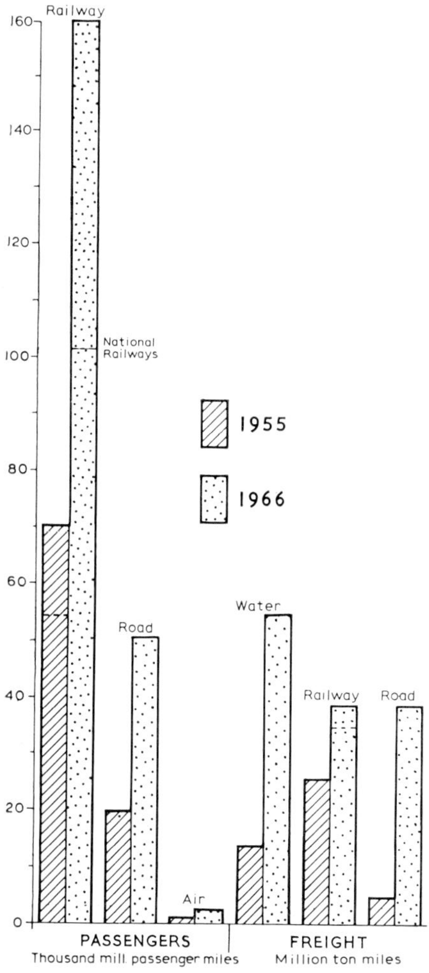

FIG. 128. The relative importance of various means of transport in 1955 and 1966 (91).

in Britain and 1 to 3 in the United States. The total number of motor vehicles was 8·5 million in 1966 compared with 2·4 million in 1961. City rush-hour traffic is already a nightmare and high-level roads (pl. 54) have been built through the centre of Tokyo to alleviate this problem.

Railways

Japan's first railway was built from Yokohama to Tokyo in 1872 with the assistance of British advisers, and extended to Osaka in 1887. The narrow 3 foot 6 inch gauge was adopted because of the difficulties of the terrain. The main lines follow the old coastal road pattern very closely with links at right angles across the mountains. The government realized the importance of railways in economic development and constructed a remarkably close network, which in 1967 carried 43% of the goods, especially coal which was 20% of the total tonnage, timber (7%), cement (6%), ores and oil. Railways carry 60% of the passenger traffic. The government owns four-fifths of the railways. Those in private hands mainly carry commuters and tourists. Unfortunately 82% of JNR lines are still single-track though 21% are electrified (fig. 126).

The railways are run with outstanding efficiency. Such is the punctuality of the trains that if the commuter's train is late by more than a few minutes he will be issued with a statement to show his employer. The new four-foot-gauge Tokyo to Osaka line, opened in 1964, has trains travelling at 130 miles an hour, the fastest in the world. Electric trains do the 310 miles journey in three hours and have trebled the capacity on the Tokaido route. The length of track has increased by only 29% since pre-war days, but the freight carried has grown by 230% and passengers by 550%, so that now Japan's railways have the highest density of passenger traffic per mile in the world. In the lethal crush in the Tokyo rush hour, or in a crowded train heading out of Tokyo at the weekend, this is not hard to believe. Unlike Britain, Japan has plans for further development of lines. The laying of double-track and electrification of main lines and dieselization of local lines and more rolling stock will speed up trains so that more can use the same lines. One can already travel from Hiroshima via Tokyo to Sendai or Niigata by electric train, and the busiest Tokai and San Yo lines are also electrified. In the cities more underground lines are being built to cater for ever-growing commuter demands. The 23-mile Seikan railway tunnel will link Hokkaido to mainland Japan by 1975.

Sea

Sea transport has always been important in Japan, because most people live very close to the sea and the forested mountains and wide river beds have always made land transport difficult. The Japanese have always been seafarers, getting fish from the sea and going as far afield as the Indian Ocean early in the fourteenth century. During the Tokugawa era the government forbade the building of boats of more than 50 tons to prevent contact with the outside world, so that in 1853 Japan had no ocean-going merchant fleet. The Meiji government built ships and after 1874 subsidized the Mitsubishi family to organize trade.

Japan's industry depends on foreign trade for the import of raw materials and the export of manufactured products. She has developed her own large fleet of ships to carry goods and has the world's fifth largest merchant marine, carrying 7% of world international trade including about half of her own foreign trade. Her own shipbuilding industry concentrates especially on building tankers and freighters for her own and foreign merchant marines. Most of her ships were sunk during the war, but she has now built up a fleet of double the size with new, fast, modern ships, 70% of them less than ten years old. Only Liberia, whose flag is used as one of convenience, UK, US and Norway have larger fleets.

Japan's foreign trade is highly concentrated in her two great ports Kobe and Yokohama, which handle 60% of her export trade and 35% of her imports. These ports were created as outports on the nearest deep water to serve Osaka and Tokyo respectively, which are situated on deltas and so have only shallow harbours. Osaka and Tokyo with Nagoya form a second group of ports handling more than 8% of Japan's trade each. A third group comprises Yokkaichi, Kawasaki and the combined ports of Kitakyushu, each with 4%. There are details of many of these ports in the chapters on the cities and regions.

Japan's physiography gives sea transport great advantages over land transport, as most of her population centres are near the coast. There are a thousand small ports. Of her domestic trade 40% is carried by sea compared with 30% by road and 30% by rail. The tonnage of her domestic trade is equal to that of her foreign trade. Coal forms 43% of the total volume of her domestic trade and wood, cement, ores and oil are also important. Coal is transported from north Kyushu to many ports along the Inland Sea and to Hanshin ports. Hokkaido coal is transported especially to the ports of Keihin and Chukyo. Imported fuel and raw materials are often trans-shipped at the main ports on to smaller ships which can take it to the many hundreds of small ports throughout Japan. Industrial products are collected to be shipped from the large ports and rice comes from areas where there is a surplus.

With the opening up of new industrial areas on land reclaimed from the sea, new deep-water harbours are being built so that supplies of oil and other raw materials and fuel can come direct from foreign countries in large ocean-going ships. By using larger ships and avoiding the need for trans-shipment the cost of transport is being reduced. This is reducing the cost of Japan's imported raw materials, which bear high transport charges. The pattern of Japan's trade is being influenced by the development of these new harbours and by new container ports. The 1965 Social and Economic Development Plan proposes much needed harbour developments which should relieve congestion, cater for a growing trade in larger ships much of it carried in containers or needing bulk handling facilities. At the end of 1967 port development came under central government control.

Air

Air transport can overcome some of the physical problems of transport in Japan. Domestic flights link the main cities, but it is difficult to find enough flat land for airports. Tokyo airport has had to be built on reclaimed land in Tokyo Bay. Air traffic has grown more rapidly than any other since the war. Between 1960 and 1965 passenger and freight traffic increased three times. Japan Airlines, which carried 17% of the traffic into and out of Japan in 1960, has a high international reputation. Domestic air traffic is increasing rapidly.

CHAPTER ELEVEN

The Population Pattern

Japan with an average density of 271 per square kilometre in 1967 is now one of the most densely populated countries in the world. Only three countries have a higher density – the Netherlands 366, Belgium 310 and Korea 288. Most of the population is crowded into pockets of high density. The 'densely inhabited districts' (DID), defined by the Census in 1960, take up only 1% of the area of Japan, but had as much as 49% of the population in 1965, with an

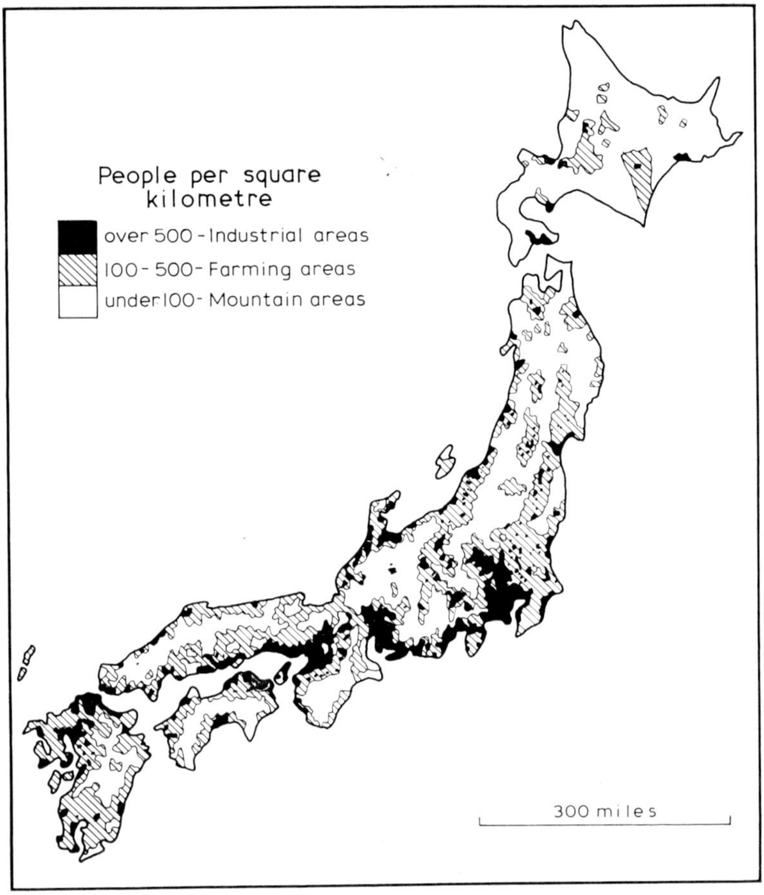

FIG. 129. The distribution of population (2).

average density of 10,600 per square kilometre (fig. 129). The pockets occur in the many scattered coastal plains and in a few interior basins where there is a town centre surrounded by an area with a high rural density. The basins are separated by large, almost deserted, and increasingly depopulated, mountain areas. The flat densely peopled plains give way abruptly to steep inhospitable forested mountainsides. Japan's four main population centres have developed on large plains in the industrial zone, which stretches from the Kanto Plain in the east to north Kyushu in the west. The three largest centres have developed on the Kanto, Nobi and Settsu plains, where Tokyo, Ise and Osaka bays provide sheltered harbours. Industry and housing compete with the farming for some of the best agricultural land. In north Kyushu there is a smaller centre near Japan's oldest coalfield.

Population regions

Japan can be divided into three population zones, the mountains, the farmlands and the densely inhabited districts. *The mountain area*, as defined for this purpose, comprises 58% of Japan but has a very small percentage of the population. The poor soil, rugged relief and difficult climate only provide a living for the forester, the poor farmer, or, where there are hot springs or skiing, the hotelier. The mountains of Japan are far less important for farming than the corresponding mountain areas of Europe. Pastoral farming has never been important in Japan, for the natural pastures are poor, and when land is cleared of forest the soil is easily eroded by the heavy rainfall and the land is often colonized by *genya*, with unnutritious bamboo grasses. Although there has been more pastoral farming in the past in the mountains of Tohoku, Chubu and Chigoku, there is no widespread tradition of pastoral farming. Since the beginning of this century the population of almost all the mountain areas in Japan has declined, and this process is proceeding as the cities become more prosperous and work there becomes increasingly attractive. Thus there is a steady flow of people from country prefectures to the cities (fig. 131).

The farmland area includes the valleys, plains and basins and the lower slopes of the mountains (figs. 11 & 129). Within this zone the density of population varies very widely, from 500 per square kilometre near the Inland Sea in the historic core area with its warm sheltered lowlands and sunny summers, where farms are very small, intensive farming is practised and yields are high; to colder Hokkaido with under 100 per square kilometre, where the relatively new farms are large and less intensively worked (fig. 130). Densities are higher west of Tokyo, where it is warm enough for winter crops to be grown on the paddyfields and farmers can live on a smaller acreage and farms average less than 2½ acres. The density is especially high near the industrial centres, where labour-intensive market-garden crops are grown and there are many part-time farmers.

The highest rural population densities lie around the eastern end of the Inland Sea in north-eastern Shikoku, Osaka, Nara and Hyogo Prefectures. Much of the area was settled as early as Yamato times, so that the farms have been minutely sub-divided, but farmers contrive to make a living by multiple cropping. Sometimes they produce four or more crops a year from the same ground, and this is one of the most intensive and productive market-gardening areas in the world. There are many factories in the towns and cities of the area, and the city and townsfolk provide a constant market for the vegetable and fruit crops that the farmers grow. Farmers' families commonly help with the farm work, and many members of the rural communities travel daily to work in office or factory in the easily accessible towns and cities by bus and fast electric train services. Life in

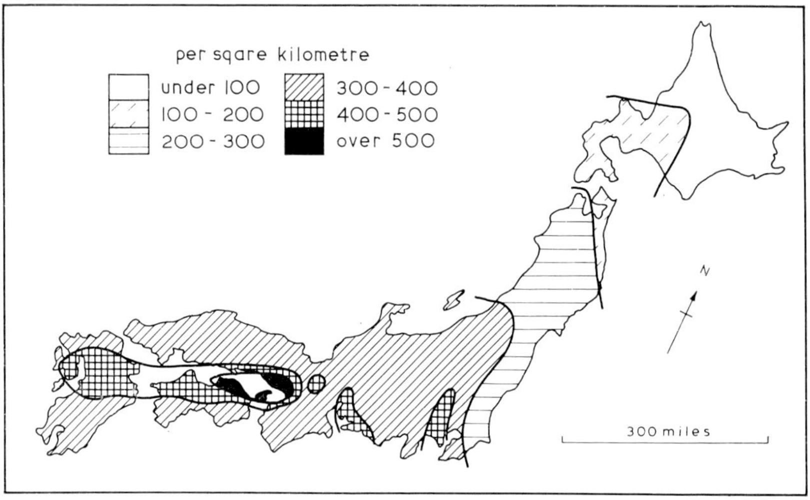

FIG. 130. Rural population density zones (*after S. Inoue*).

town and country is becoming closely knit and interdependent, as in the factory-farm communities of the Belgian Plain. Many factories have been established in these rural areas, near to industrial cities, to take advantage of the plentiful rural labour without losing the benefit of contact with commercial centres, easy transport and convenient markets (pls. 32 & 43).

Beyond these areas rural densities drop both towards the south-west and the north. They drop less quickly in the west, where farming is more intensive because it is possible to grow two or more crops a year on the rice fields, but north of 37°N the growing season is much shorter and only one crop a year is possible and farms are rather larger averaging over $2\frac{1}{2}$ acres. The 350 per square kilometre rural density isoline corresponds approximately with the limit of two crops a year. Farming is much less intensive in the north, as well as being more risky, and in highland areas less advanced technically. There is little industry to employ seasonal or part-time labour surpluses. Hokkaido, except for its southern peninsula, has a rural population density far below the rest of Japan. The farming has been developed only during this century and is on a relatively large scale, using machinery.

The densely inhabited districts are the most densely populated. These are mainly in the industrial belt stretching between north Kyushu in the west and Tokyo in the east. This belt is dominated by the four main city regions of north Kyushu, Hanshin (including Osaka and Kobe), Chukyo and Keihin (the Tokyo–Yokohama area). The area has a population density of over 500 per square kilometre and it included 49% of the population in 1965. The industrial centres have developed on large plains in the part of Japan with the most favourable climate, with easy communications by land and sea and with the best ports. Keihin and Hanshin are the most important areas, but there are other regional centres with large populations like Sendai in Tohoku and Kumamoto in Kyushu. Most of these are old castle towns on coastal plains which used to be the centre of a lord's land.

The Changing Regional Population Distribution

The changing regional population distribution in Japan is a product of internal migration and of regional variations in natural increase. The general flow of migration is away from rural areas (fig. 131), especially from western Tohoku and the more isolated areas of Kyushu, Shikoku and San In, and towards the three main urban centres in the industrial core zone. Only ten prefectures, all in the main industrial belt, had an increase in population by migration in 1966–7. In the quinquennium up to 1965 the population of Tokyo, Kanagawa and Osaka grew by over 20% and Chiba, Saitama, Aichi and Hyogo by 10%. Fukuoka, in spite of its industry, had a net loss of 1%. The number of workers engaged mainly in farming has remained stable at about 14 million during the century up to 1958, though it fell to 9·7 million in 1967 (fig. 32). The surplus of younger sons and daughters has migrated to the cities. Most of the migrants were under nineteen and this youthful section of the population of marriageable age has helped to increase the urban population. Until the sixties natural increase (fig. 132) was greatest in the more isolated and backward areas of Japan, that is, in eastern Tohoku, southern Kyushu or what can be called the northern and southern 'frontier' areas of Japan (see p. 93) as birth rates there were above the national average but birth rates fell there in the sixties and became the lowest in Japan. Natural increase is relatively high in Hokkaido and in the main urban centres as young migrants' families increase the population.

Japan's population is increasing most in the three industrial centres (fig. 133), Keihin, Hanshin, Chukyo. The flow of inward migrants add greatly to the natural increase. The Tokyo Prefecture population increased by 20·5% between 1955 and 1960, 14·6% by migration and only 5·9% by natural increase, but natural increase has been higher in the sixties.

It is in the eastern end of the industrial zone that population has grown most, between 1955 and 1967 with an increase of 43% in the population of Tokyo, 73% in Yokohama, 35% in Nagoya and only 26% in Osaka and 21% in Kobe. Internal migration has played an important part in the development of the industrial areas of Japan.

The origin of the migrants to the four main industrial areas, recorded for 1960 (fig. 131), gives some indication of the pattern of movement of population. People moved mainly to the nearest centre. They came to Tokyo from all over Japan but mainly from Kanto northwards, especially from the nearby prefectures of Kanagawa, Chiba and Saitama, within the industrial area, and Shizuoka, where people are sufficiently in contact with the cities to realize the benefits of

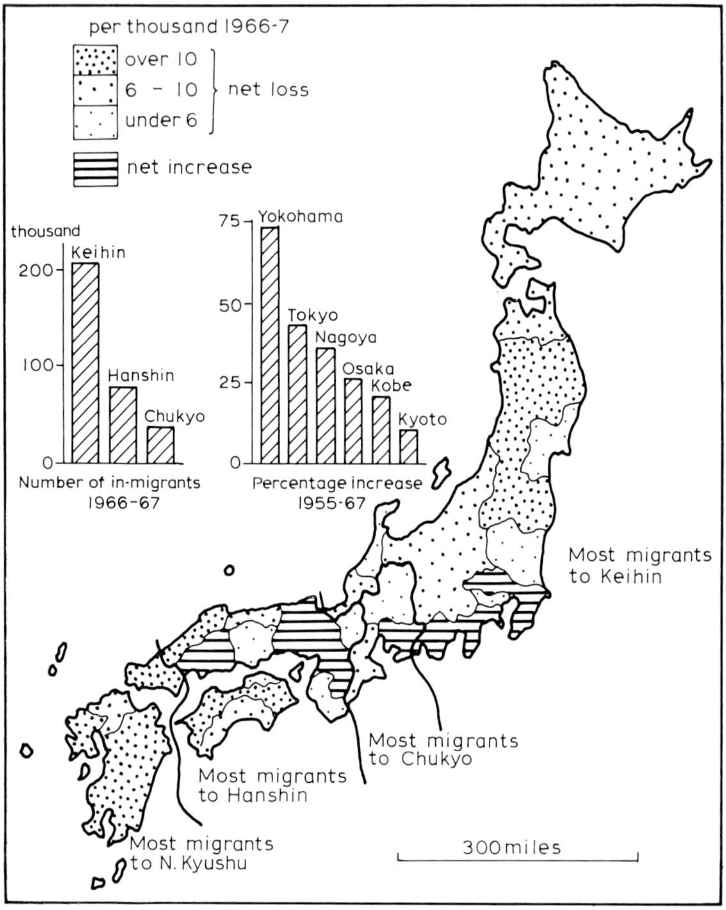

FIG. 131. Net migration 1966–7. (Japanese Government: Bureau of Statistics, Population Estimates Series). The source area for each of the main industrial centres is based on the 1960 census as this information was not included in the 1965 census (59).

moving there. Until 1960 northern Tohoku has supplied fewer migrants, despite the lower incomes of most of the prefectures in this area (fig. 105) and the high rate of natural increase (fig. 132), as the people were less in contact with urban areas. Since 1960 there have been more migrants.

Most of the migrants came to the Hanshin area from the Kinki, Chugoku and

Shikoku. To Chukyo most of the migrants came from the three nearby prefectures of Aichi, Mie and Gifu, and to the Kitakyushu industrial area from the whole of Kyushu and nearby Yamaguchi to the east. The 1966 figures show that

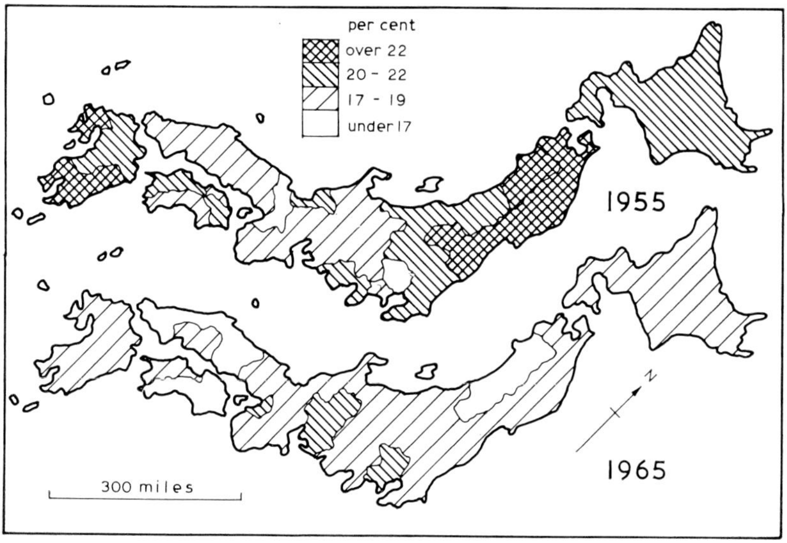

FIG. 132. Birth Rates in 1955 and 1965 (91) show the complete change of pattern caused by the spread of birth control to the more isolated areas by 1965 and by the migration, mainly of young people, to the industrial areas bringing relatively high birth rates in 1965 to industrial areas in contrast to low birth rates there in 1955 and even as late as 1960.

most of the migrants came from the poorer prefectures in Kyushu, Shikoku, San In and Tohoku (fig. 105).

Hokkaido's population is also increasing (fig. 132), as there is a fairly high birth rate in the relatively youthful population. The population in Hokkaido has

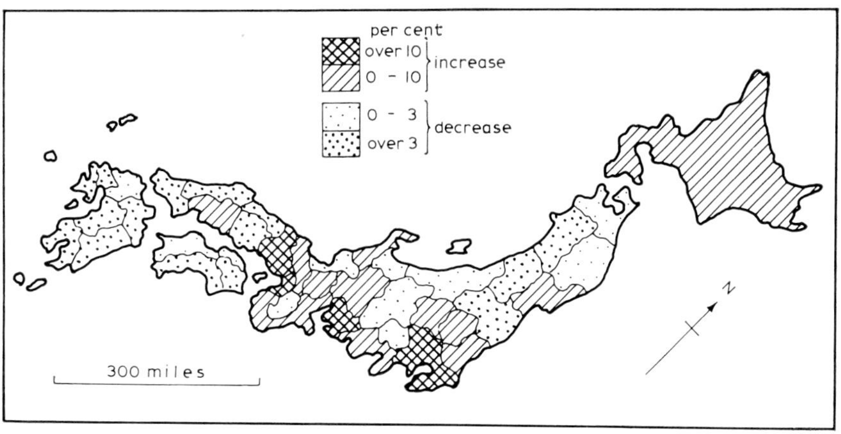

FIG. 133. Population change between 1960 and 1965 (59).

increased also with the further development of agriculture and very varied industries, including iron and steel, fishing and chemicals.

Most of the mountainous areas of Japan and especially in Tosan, western Tohoku, Shikoku, San In and south Kyushu there were high birth rates in the fifties but the population in these areas declined as many people left these relatively unproductive areas where there were low incomes for the more prosperous cities. By 1965 so many young people had left the areas that the birth rates among the ageing population was the lowest in Japan. Migration to the cities continued so that the population in all these areas continued to decline.

Throughout the history of Japan the centre of population has been moving eastwards as land was colonized from south-western Japan (fig. 29). In Yamato times the emperor moved by sea from south-east Kyushu to the Kinki. Then the centre of power moved east to the Kanto area, first to Kamakura and then in 1601 to Yedo, 'the Eastern Capital', which is modern Tokyo. They only reached north beyond the southern peninsula of Hokkaido in the late nineteenth century. As they spread they settled first on the more attractive plains where they could fish, hunt and farm, subsequently spreading into the more difficult mountain terrain inland (fig. 52). Industrial development has also spread eastwards from the Kyoto–Osaka region to Tokyo (fig. 106). Both population and industry are continuing to move east, as most of the farmland still to be developed is in Hokkaido and Tohoku and industry is developing faster in the Keihin area than anywhere else in Japan (fig. 78).

The rural–urban movement is even more important and the urban belt has increased in relative significance because of its advantages for industrialization with good ports, a suitable climate, transport facilities, good labour supply and large city markets. The mountain areas have lost population because the climate and terrain are not suitable for prosperous farming or industry. The increasing concentration of population in the industrial belt is causing problems of congestion. The government policy in the 1960 Ten Year Plan is to decentralize new industry by offering special facilities outside the main industrial centres. It has had some success in attracting industry away from these centres, and in 1959–60 32% new industry was established outside the ten leading prefectures.

In spite of population pressure few Japanese have gone abroad. Only one million people are now living in foreign countries, half of these in Brazil and most of the rest in Hawaii, the Philippines and the United States.

CHAPTER TWELVE

The Cities

Today the largest Japanese city centres have been internationalized. The main street of Hiroshima (pl. 52) is typical. Its modern rectangular buildings, fine shops and busy streets, but for the signs, might be at first glance anywhere in the world. The residential streets retain the traditional character even in Hiroshima, with terraced wooden houses with little space between them. Only the few live in high

PLATE 52. Hiroshima main street has been rebuilt since the atomic bomb with little Japanese character. Half Japan's city houses were destroyed during the war. There is a high proportion of trucks in Japanese streets as fewer people can afford cars.

blocks of flats and western-style homes, though the number is increasing with growing prosperity (pl. 13). Most homes in the city have two storeys with one or two rooms downstairs and the same upstairs, all, as in the country, used for sleeping. There is a tiny kitchen with refrigerator, washing machine, rice boiler and calor gas stove, but no bathroom, as many town dwellers use the local bath house.

The rooms are small, as there is little furniture to take up space. Housing densities are extremely high, as houses are in continuous terraces on the edge of the narrow roads and almost back on to their neighbours behind (pl. 57). Many towns have an area of better houses, often on the higher land of a diluvial terrace or on a hill slope. Here the houses lie behind high fences or hedges with a small patch of garden in front set out with stones and shrubs. Many of the larger houses have a western-style room and there is a fast increasing number of western-style houses and flats. Many of these have a Japanese *tatami* room.

The Evolution, Function and Location of Towns

Cities in Japan have grown rapidly with the growth of population since the beginning of the Meiji era. There has been a steady flow of people from rural areas where there is very little work for younger sons and daughters on their parents' farms. High city wages have attracted people from country areas, especially young people, most of them under nineteen. All Japan's increase in population has been absorbed by migration to the towns, leaving the number employed in farming at 9·7 million in 1967 (fig. 32), 4 million less than in 1868. Only in Hokkaido and parts of Tohoku and other more isolated areas has the rural population increased. Birth rates in the cities are high as the large influx of young people has helped to swell urban populations with their families.

Urban development in Japan had very early beginnings. Even in Yayoi times agriculture was sufficiently productive for farms to support specialist potters and metal workers, who exchanged their products for rice grown by the farmer class, in small market towns. The clans of south-western Japan had a capital (Heijokyo) at Nara in AD 710. Many emperors established a new city when they came to power so that the capital moved to a new site within the Kinki. By AD 800 Kyoto had a population of half a million and was one of the greatest cities of the time. The early capitals housed the emperor and his court, the administrators and military forces, as well as the many craftsmen who made wooden, lacquerware, pottery and other craft goods for the nobles and for temples and shrines, in much the same way as is done in Kyoto today. Kaempfer in his *History of Japan* described the Kyoto of the seventeenth century as 'a city of nobles, artisans and craftsmen. There is scarcely a house in this large capital where there is not something made or sold. Here they refine copper, coin money, print books, weave the richest stuffs with gold and silver flowers. The best and most brilliant dyes, the most artful carving, all sorts of musical instruments, pictures, japanned cabinets, all sorts of goods wrought in iron, gold and other metals . . .' But for the addition of modern large-scale industry in the suburbs of Kyoto his description could be used equally of both eighth- and twentieth-century Kyoto.

Many administrative and market centres and ports had already become towns in Feudal Japan, but widespread urban expansion only began in Japan about 1600 under the Tokugawa Shogunate with the development of regional control by local lords. During this period Tokyo was the military centre with the Shogun and samurai, Osaka the merchant city and Kyoto, the cultural centre. Many *castle towns* were established between 1580 and 1610. The merchant homes and artisans' workshops were built round a fortified wood and plaster castle with high stone walls and a moat, like those in Tokyo and Osaka today (pl. 53). The roads of the city were laid out in a complex network to make attack more difficult in contrast with the regular grid of the older towns like Kyoto laid out on the Chinese pattern. Half the population of these castle towns were samurai ready to serve the lord in time of need, and the rest were merchants and artisans. Many castle towns were at the centres of fertile plain areas and these form the basis for 34 out of today's 46 prefectural capitals. There have been few new centres formed in the twentieth century except in Hokkaido.

PLATE 53. This street-corner guide to shops and houses is very necessary where streets have no names. The Japanese need to be expert map readers.

Under the Tokugawa regime the central government required all the lords to spend every other year in *Yedo* (modern Tokyo) and to leave their families behind there as hostages when they went to their domains. With the growing importance of the capital as an administrative centre and with the establishments of the lords, Yedo grew from a tiny fishing village in the sixteenth century to a city of a million inhabitants by 1700. From the late seventeenth to the early nineteenth centuries it was probably the largest city in the world. Its growth was only possible because farm yields were high enough for the Tokugawa Shogunate to be able to raise enough taxes from the farmers to support the nobility and the samurai as unproductive members of society, though this was a great strain on the economy. It was not until the Industrial Revolution in Europe that people flooded into the towns and cities grew that surpassed Yedo in size until her own industrialization in the last 100 years again made her a leading city in the world, with 13 million inhabitants in greater Tokyo.

Trading developed as the country became more strongly united under the Tokugawa Shogunate and *market towns* and *ports* grew up. Market towns grew often as the focal centre of a plain to collect and exchange farm and craft products. People travelled more along the routes, especially those radiating from Tokyo. *Post* towns grew up where people could get food and a night's shelter (fig. 134). The towns along the Tokaido route from Yedo to Kyoto grew as the route became busier. Lords and their retinues used this route and supplies were brought from Osaka, which was the main trading centre. The towns comprised usually only two lines of buildings along the edge of the road. Each town was a day's journey of about 8 miles from the next, the distance depending on the terrain.

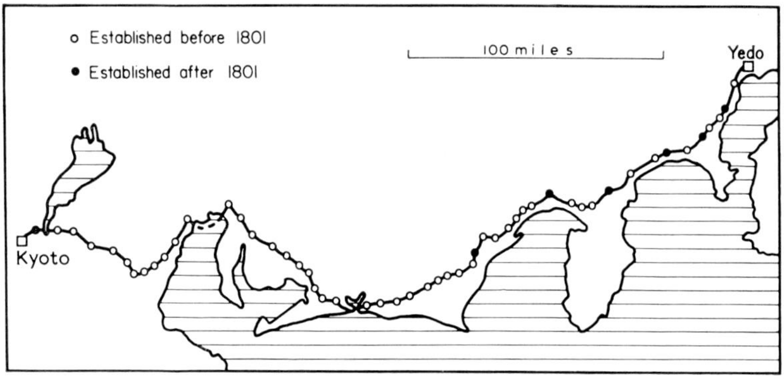

FIG. 134. Post towns on the Tokaido (74).

During this time centres of pilgrimage became more accessible and towns grew up to accommodate pilgrims at the gate of the shrine, like Kotohira in Shikoku and Ise near the ancient Ise shrine in Mie.

Towns grew steadily as market centres with small industries making textiles, *saké*, pottery and metal goods during the Tokugawa era, but their main development came rapidly with industrialization after 1868. Most modern *industrial centres* developed from the old towns like Osaka and Nagoya, but some new mining and industrial towns, like Muroran in Hokkaido and Hitachi in Ibaragi, were established. The Tokugawa Shoguns had only allowed trade with the Chinese and the Dutch through Nagasaki. Domestic trade flourished by land and sea, but ports for large ocean-going ships were developed only after 1853. More recently with growing prosperity *spas* and other resorts have grown. With more money and easier travel holidays became possible and towns like Beppu in Kyushu, Arima near Osaka, Noboribetsu in Hokkaido and many smaller places now flourish where hot springs have special qualities. Skiing resorts have been established in the mountains. The old castle towns still form the basis of many of the modern market and industrial towns, but the function of Japanese towns has changed from one of defence to one of commerce and industry, as it has in countries of the west.

Japanese towns (fig. 135) are concentrated on the peripheral plains throughout Japan, but especially in the Core Zone. Many of them lie on or near the coast and

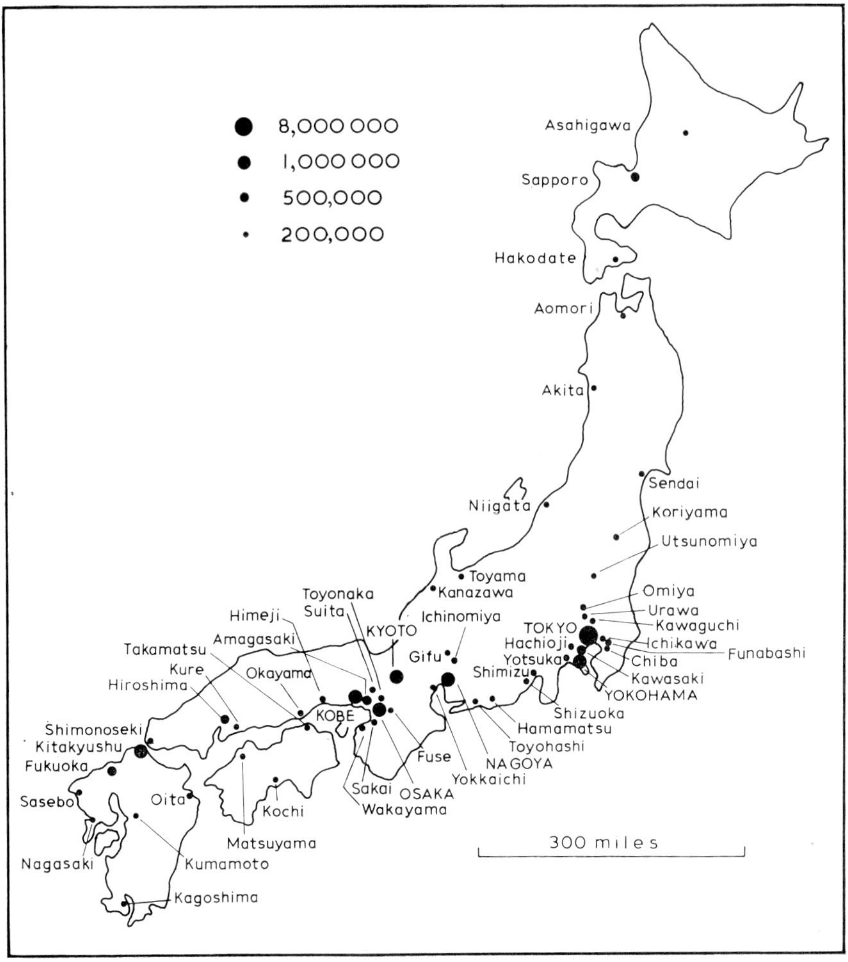

FIG. 135. Towns of over 200,000 in 1965 (59).

some lie in inland basins. The largest, 'the big six', all with populations of over a million, are on the Pacific coast, where except for Kyoto, each city extends to the sea and has port facilities. Tokyo and Yokohama together with their satellites form the Keihin conurbation, Osaka, Kobe, the Hanshin conurbation and Nagoya is the centre of the Chukyo region. Kitakyushu, the group of five towns in north Kyushu, reached a million in the mid-1960's and so makes a seventh millionaire city.

Administrative Units

Like the administrative areas of Britain those of Japan do not coincide with geographical units. The smallest unit is the *buraku* or hamlet. It is a nucleated or agglomerated group of ten to one hundred houses. Although it is not a recognized administrative unit it is often used as a unit in local records and as a social and economic group for co-operative work, such as spraying crops and building tracks and irrigation ditches. Sometimes there are even smaller units with four or five families as a sub-unit of the *buraku* which share threshing machines, hullers or cultivators. In the city there are similar neighbourhood groups which meet to run local affairs. A *tonari gumi* usually has five to ten houses, a *chonaikai* or ward is larger and arranges for the collection of rubbish, fire watching and the training of the fire brigade, poor relief, the organization and upkeep of the shrine and the arrangements for festivals and the employment of watchmen.

The *mura* or village may be a larger group of houses with a shopping centre and farmhouses with farmland round about, but often it is composed of a number of scattered *buraku* with one larger one that serves as the administrative centre but

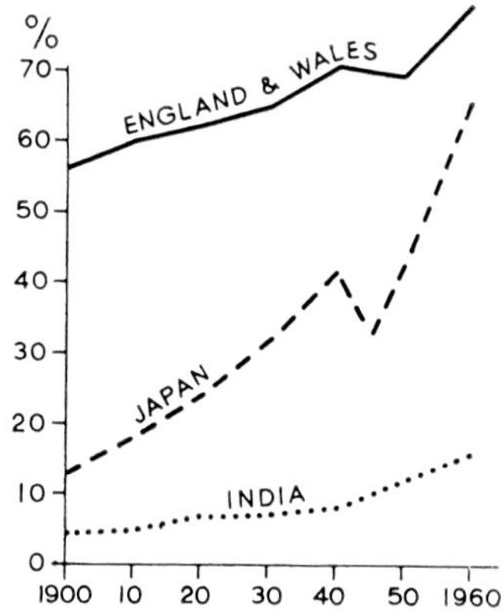

FIG. 136. Urbanization trends since 1900 in Japan, India and England and Wales (administrative units with over 20,000).

has no well-developed shopping centre. In rural areas several *mura* are grouped to form one 'town' or *machi*, which is not a geographical unit but an administrative area. Where there is a larger centre it is called a city or *shi*. In 1953 many of the smaller administrative units were amalgamated to form 'cities' of over 30,000 people. That this is an administrative and not a geographical unit is illustrated by the fact that there are 142 'cities' with more than half their working population engaged on the land, which might be described as 'farming cities'. The equivalent of a British county is a *Ken* or prefecture. Tokyo, Osaka and Kyoto are independent prefectures and are called *to* or *fu*.

It is necessary when considering the relative size and importance of *urban units* to bear the above definitions in mind and especially to note that many smaller units were amalgamated in 1953, and because of this statistics before and after 1953 are not strictly comparable.

Today urban life dominates the Japanese scene, and 68% (fig. 136) of people lived in towns of over 20,000 in 1965 compared with only 13% in 1900 and 38% in 1950. This is by far the highest urban percentage in Asia. India still had only 16% in 1960. Japan is closer to England and Wales, which had 80% of the population living in towns of over 20,000 in 1961.

The Millionaire Cities

A striking characteristic of Japan's towns is the dominance of the 'big six' cities, with over a million inhabitants (fig. 137). Tokyo has 9 million people, Osaka 3,

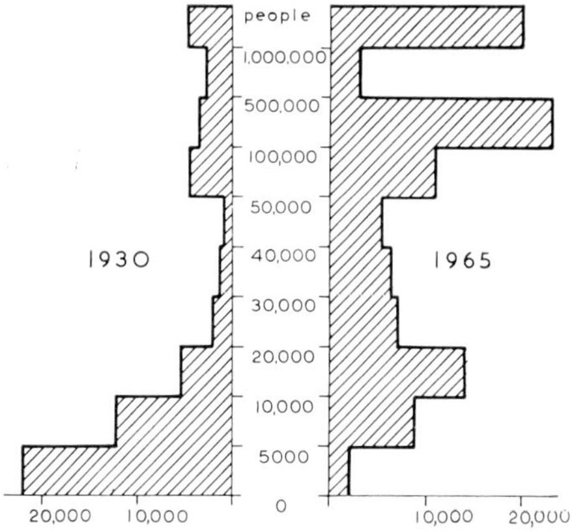

FIG. 137. Population in towns of various sizes in 1930 and 1965 (59).

Nagoya 2, Yokohama nearly 2 million, Kyoto 1½ million and Kobe 1 million; Kitakyushu, which has just reached a million, makes a seventh. Thus 19% of the urban population lives in the 'big six' alone, compared with 10% in 1920. The four great industrial regions together have over 47 million people, nearly half of the total population. Keihin has 21 million, Kei-Hanshin 14, Chukyo 6 and north Kyushu 6 million.

TOKYO

The Tokyo Metropolitan Government area housed 12 million people in 1967, which is over 12% of Japan's population (fig. 138). Nine million live in the Tokyo ward area, which is the centre of a conurbation of 18 million people. It is the largest Japanese city and three times the size of Osaka its nearest rival, but it is typical of most of Japan's 'big six' cities in its castle foundation, bay-side site with an alluvial plain and diluvial terraces, modern central buildings and largely wooden houses (figs. 139 & 140). It is centred round the Imperial Palace built on the site of a twelfth-century castle perched on the eastern edge of the ash-covered diluvial Yamanote (Upper Town) Upland which is a diluvial terrace rising to over 60 feet above sea level and overlooking the Shitamachi (Lower Town) on the alluvial plain in the Sumida and Arakawa valley to the east. The upland area now forms the main residential area of Tokyo. The lowland has been drained for the commercial and industrial quarters of Tokyo, and the mouth of the Tone River has been diverted to the sea further north to prevent it flooding the city.

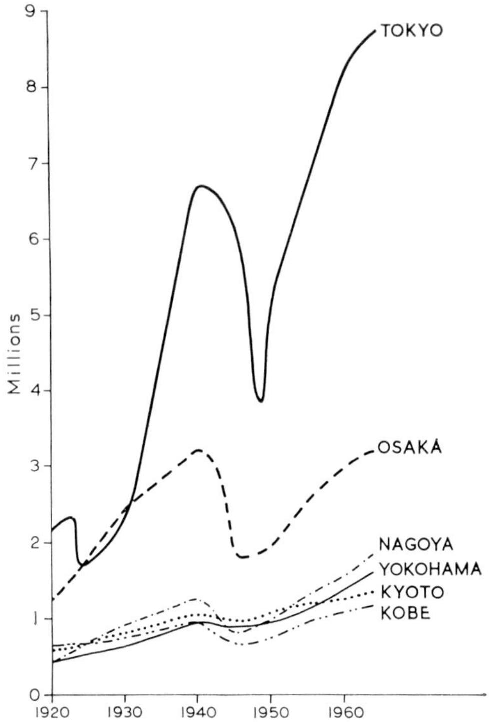

FIG. 138. The growth of the 'big six' cities since 1920. The figures between 1940 and 1945 are estimates (59 and 88).

PLATE 54. Modern Tokyo looking east. The skyline has changed much more rapidly than that of London. The castle, the old city centre, is in the park on the left (fig. 140). Between the castle grounds and the railway is the Maronouchi, the business centre of the city with some old blocks of offices built by English architects in 1892 and other pre- and post-war blocks. Over the railway and the high-level road is the Ginza, the main shopping street, and between this and the river Sumida is the wholesaling area. Beyond the river there is much industrial development (220).

Yedo became the 'Eastern Capital' of the Tokugawa Shoguns in 1601, when it had only a hundred or so houses, but by 1700 it had a million inhabitants and later in the century, with $1\frac{1}{2}$ million, it was the largest city in the world. It is the political, industrial, commercial and cultural centre of Japan, having superseded Kyoto as the educational and cultural centre and Osaka as the industrial and commercial centre. It is the main transport centre and has the largest labour supply and the greatest market. With the growth of industry since Meiji times

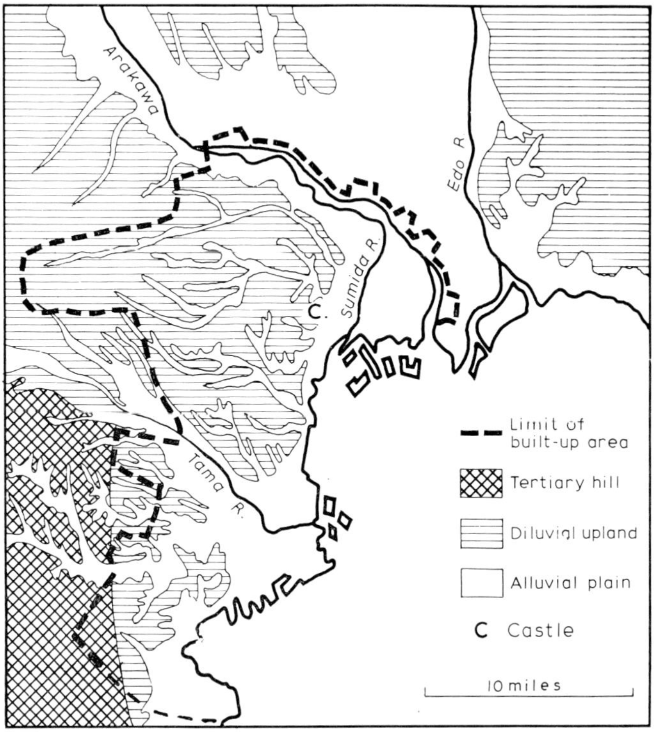

FIG. 139. The site of Tokyo, Kawasaki and Yokohama (81).

Tokyo has expanded even faster and, by some reckonings, is again the largest city in the world. It is still growing rapidly and there is much redevelopment in progress in the central areas.

Tokyo has well-marked functional zones. On the lowland between the castle and the Sumida River is the modern commercial Marunouchi area with its towering, international-style concrete and glass office blocks, housing the headquarters of banks and trading firms conveniently placed, with the central station just to the east of it. Further east runs the Ginza, the main shopping street of Tokyo, lined with fine modern department stores which compare favourably with any in Britain. Their wide selection of western and Japanese goods are well displayed in air-conditioned comfort, with lifts, escalators and soft music. The streets are thronged with prosperous men and women in smart western dress, schoolboys and girls in their navy-blue uniforms and a sprinkling of women in kimonos. Coffee-bars with Brahms and Tchaikovsky in the background vie for custom with Japanese and foreign restaurants. Theatres, nightclubs, amusement centres and pinball parlours all flourish under their neon signs. The streets are busy with lorries, trucks, trams, buses, modern coaches, scooters, bicycles and

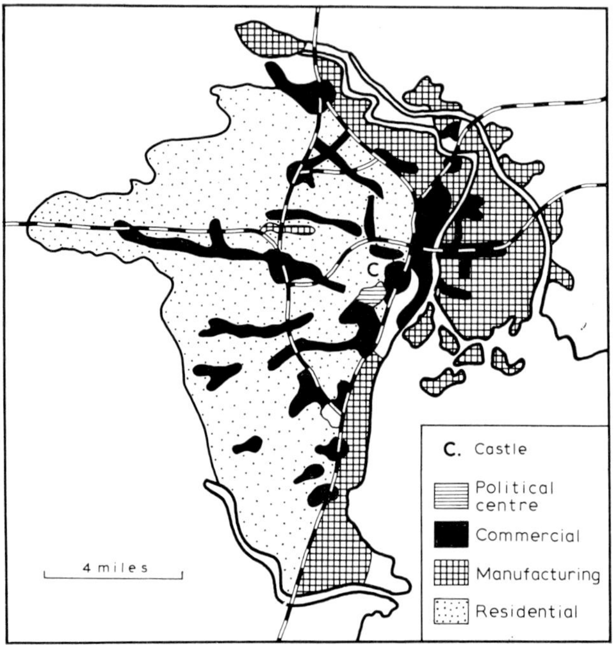

FIG. 140. Functional zones in Tokyo (81).

cars, with great congestion at rush hours. This international part of Tokyo was planned on a grid pattern and one might be in any big city in the world. Underground and elevated electric trains and buses go to all parts of the city, and trains and the high-level road bring in people from the surrounding countryside and take Tokyo people to the nearby hills and lakes on holiday excursions.

North of the castle lie several universities, many of them occupying the sites of old lords' homes. East of this area lie Nihonbashi and Asakusa, the main wholesaling areas of Tokyo. South-west is Kasumigaseki, the administrative centre of Tokyo with the Diet, government offices and the Supreme Court.

Surrounding the modern international Tokyo, which includes the Marunouchi, Ginza and Kasumigaseki, is a maze of narrow alleys lined by two-storey wooden houses. Narrow shopping streets with small shops serve the daily needs of the local people, and bath houses function as community centres. To the west of the castle, on the Yamanote Upland, bounded to the north by the Sumida River and the south by the Tama River, spread the main residential areas of Tokyo with long fingers of development following the railway lines into the countryside. The vista of low, brown, crowded, monotonous houses (pl. 57) is occasionally broken by blocks of tall modern flats. Most of Tokyo has been rebuilt twice during this century, once after the fires of the great earthquake in 1923 and again after the fires of World War II, especially the incendiary raid of 9th March 1945 which cost 100,000 lives, nearly twice as many as the notorious Hiroshima atom bomb (65,000). In the modern city houses have changed little and only the blocks of

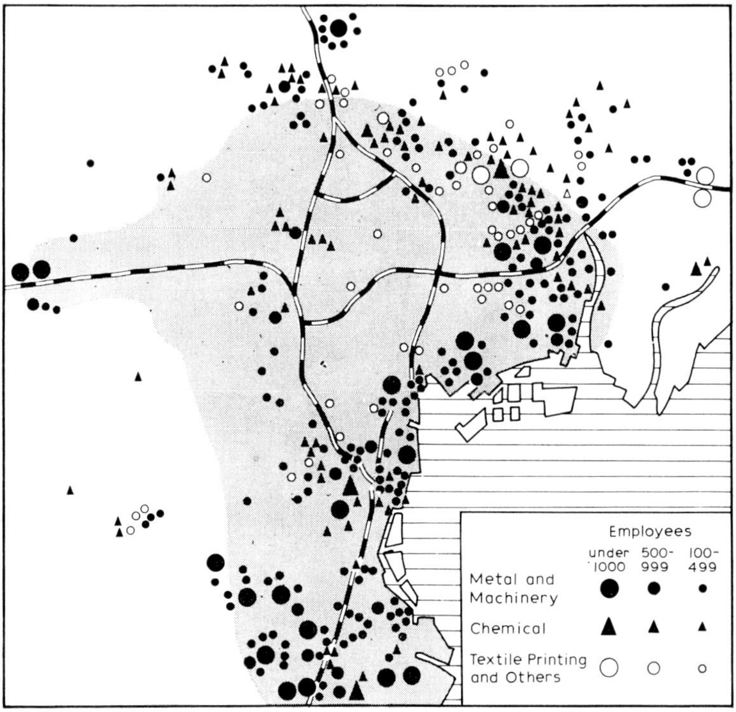

FIG. 141. Tokyo's industries (81).

flats and the western-style houses of the rich stand out from the rather monotonous wooden houses.

The industries of Tokyo are mainly modern consumer industries making metal engineering and chemical goods. Production is carried on in workshops, factories and huge modern plants. The main industrial area (fig. 141) lies along the Sumida and Arakawa valley to the east, where there are older smaller factories in the western part producing chemicals, metal goods and machinery, and larger factories further east. Along the coast where new land is being reclaimed, and there is easy access to the sea, there are many large-scale iron and steel plants (fig. 159). From Chiba, 20 miles to the east, industrial development spreads almost continuously in a great curve to the steel works of Kawasaki and on to Yokohama, 20 miles to the south. Along the valleys in the Yamanote Upland light industries have developed making such goods as electronic and precision instruments, food products, books and other printed goods. In the more residential area of western Tokyo there are many scattered light industries. Apart from the coastal industries firms are medium or small in size, and there are many family workshops who sub-contract to do 'out-work' in engineering and textiles, so that the whole of one street or one district may contribute a part or do one process in making the final product.

The great prosperity of Tokyo, where incomes are 26% above the national average, is attracting more and more people to the city. There is a great shortage of housing and the separation of the main industrial and residential areas aggravates commuter congestion. In the industrial area around the Sumida River there is a growing danger from flooding and subsidence in some areas that are below sea level.

Tokyo was the main port for the Keihin area until modern times, when in the Meiji era large foreign vessels had to be accommodated. Built on the Sumida and Arakawa delta, silting is rapid and the port shallow so that it caters mainly for home trade, which is three times her foreign trade. The main goods handled are imported coal, cement and food. Yokohama has been built as an outport on deeper water to meet the needs of larger ships. Up to 1950 Tokyo harbour was dredged only to accommodate ships of up to 10,000 tons. The only access to the sea is by a channel 29 feet deep and 450 feet wide. Yet she handled 8% of Japan's trade with 28 million tons in 1965. The trade is mainly domestic, as she can only handle small ships. By 1970 Tokyo plans to reclaim 22 square kilometres of new land to build a new port and factory facilities. Dredging will provide wharfage for 20,000-ton ships, and so will nearly double her trade to 48 million tons by catering for more foreign trade.

The growing urban sprawl across valuable farmland moved the government to establish the 'Capital Region' (fig. 142) in 1956 with a radius of 60 miles from the centre of Tokyo. Within this they planned an inner urban zone surrounded by a green belt 6 miles wide and an outer suburban area with thirty industrial satellite towns beyond this. With the continued pressure for housing development little has been done to implement this plan, and Tokyo continues to grow with little planning, with increasing traffic problems on overloaded roads and railways and overcrowded housing. Houses are low and densely packed with few gardens and limited open spaces. Many are along narrow alleys not built for road traffic. Roads make up a remarkably small percentage of Tokyo's total area. In 1963 only 11% compared with 23% in London, 24% in Paris and 35% in New York.

Tokyo and Osaka were larger than the other 'big six' cities during the whole of the Meiji period. Tokyo led from mid-seventeenth century after it became the Tokugawa capital. The 1923 earthquake killed 100,000 people and many who lost their homes built new ones outside the city area (fig. 138). Many new suburbs developed and Tokyo expanded rapidly, until by the beginning of the war it had nearly 7 million inhabitants. Like all Japan's cities except Kyoto, Tokyo's population rose in the early years but fell greatly during the later part of the war period due to voluntary and official evacuation. A third of all city housing was destroyed, largely by fire, and casualties were heavy. Afterwards there was little

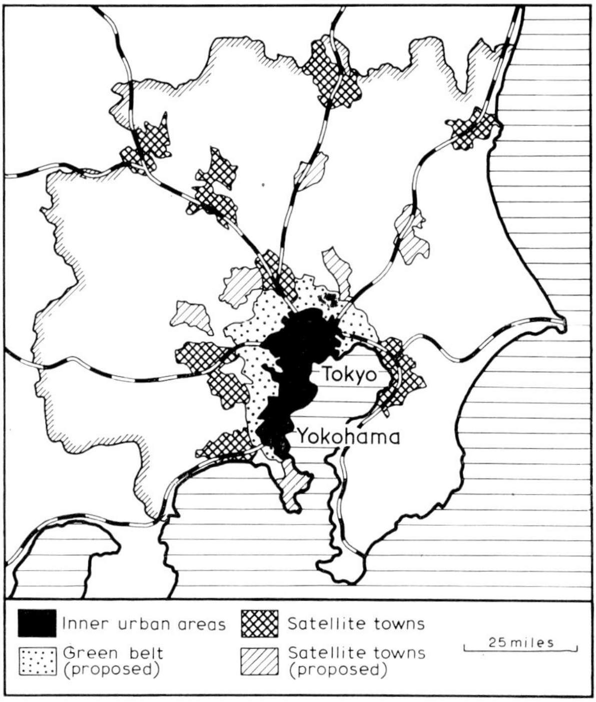

FIG. 142. The capital region showing the Tokyo conurbation and its satellites (81)

employment until the early fifties, when industry gained new life. City population figures are somewhat misleading, as after wartime devastation many people moved to new suburbs which were contiguous with the city but not included within the administrative area. This makes city figures after the war appear lower than they actually were. By 1955 Tokyo, like the rest of the 'big six' except Osaka, had regained its pre-war population of 7 million; since then it has increased rapidly. Migrants have flooded into Tokyo giving rise to acute problems of housing, transport and public services.

YOKOHAMA

Yokohama (fig. 143) (220), the fourth largest city with 1·9 million people, is the main port for northern Japan as well as for Keihin. It has grown to serve the industrial area, and acts as the outport for Tokyo on deeper water 20 miles to the south to handle large ships of up to 50,000 tons which cannot use Tokyo's shallow harbour. In spite of its depth most ships unload by lighter, as the wharves are so congested. It is built on the deltas of three small rivers which have been added to by further coastal reclamation and whose streams form useful canals. The rivers are too small to bring down much silt so that the sheltered bay remains deep. Long breakwaters protect the wharves. The city is divided into three by two diluvial terraces which are only now being built on. Until the earthquake in 1923 Yokohama was the leading port. Kobe then led until 1966 when Yokohama regained her lead because there has been more industrial development in her hinterland since the war.

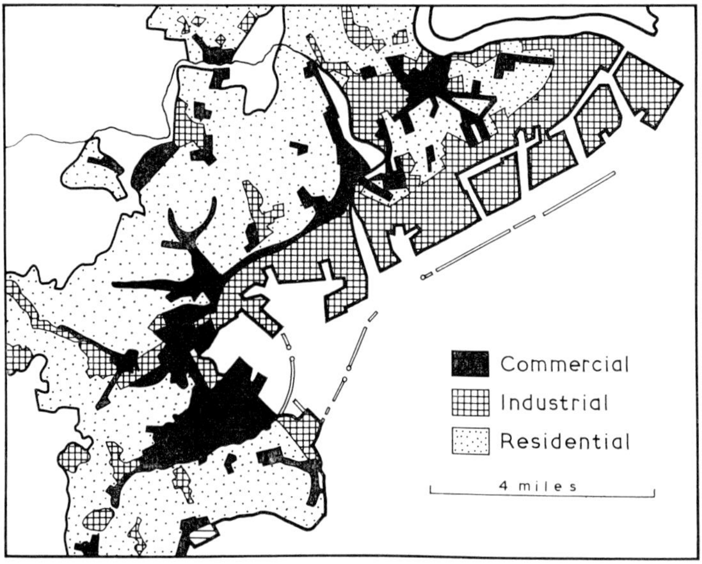

FIG. 143. Functional zones in Yokohama (*Kanagawa Prefectural Office*).

She handles 21% of Japan's foreign and an equal tonnage of domestic trade and is a busy industrial town but with a limited area of lowland available for development. Much heavy industry is dependent on imported iron ore and pig iron, coal and oil. Iron and steel, shipbuilding, vehicle assembly, petroleum refining and chemicals are all important. The Keihin Sea Canal serves the industrial coast of Kawasaki, where the great iron and steel works making transport equipment and chemical plants produce more than those of Yokohama.

Yokohama, like many other seaboard towns, has developed a banded pattern. There are residential areas on diluvial terraces above the coastal strip, the commercial centre lies at the foot of the hills, older industries lie on older reclaimed polders and are served by canals which lead to the sea through newly drained polders with new industries.

Since 1953 a new tidewater industrial area has emerged from Tokyo Bay in

Chiba along 30 miles of coast east of Tokyo (fig. 159). It provides valuable new sites for thermal power stations, chemical works, integrated steel works, oil refineries and petro-chemical complexes, shipbuilding, metal and machinery plants. New channels are being dredged to serve its wharves. This vast new area will equal that further round the bay. It is not surprising with such developments that Keihin between 1955 and 1965 census acquired 62% of Japan's total increase in population.

OSAKA

Osaka is a city of over 3 million people. It is the banking and trading centre of Japan and the centre of the Hanshin industrial area, which has 11 million

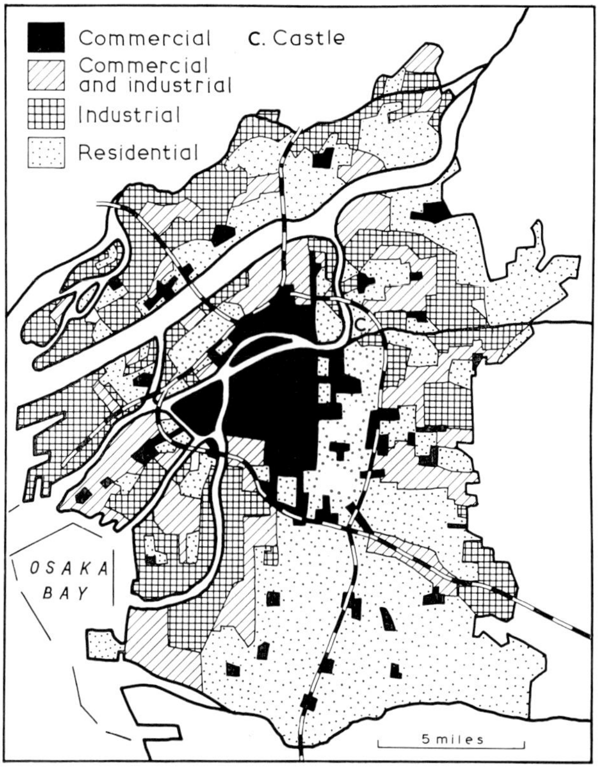

FIG. 144. Functional zones in Osaka (*Nippon no Chiri*, vol. 5).

people and is the second largest industrial area in Japan. It is the second largest city in Japan but only a third the size of Tokyo, though it is a much older city. It was the port and commercial and industrial centre for Kyoto and Nara, the ancient capitals. During the fourth century it was itself the capital. Hanshin retained its leading place in Japanese industry until World War II, when it

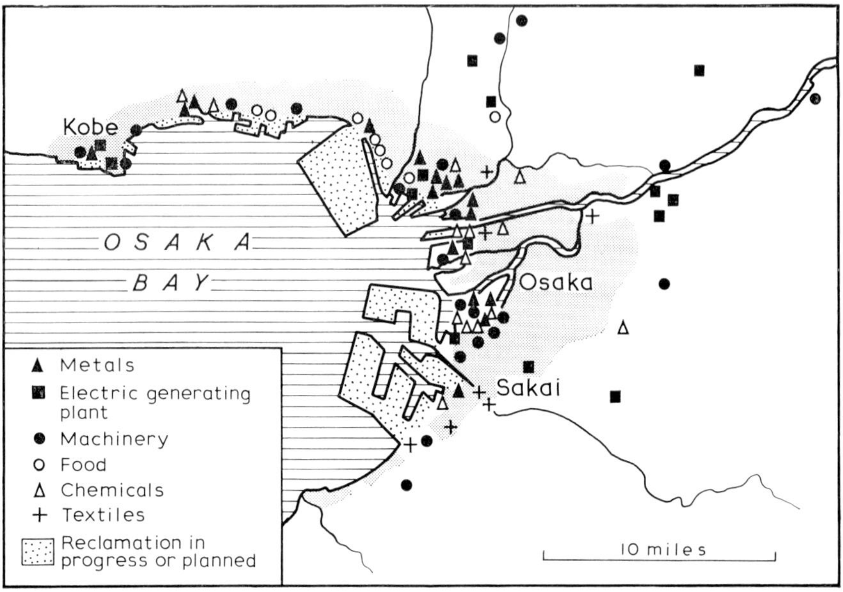

FIG. 145. Osaka's industry (*Nippon no Chiri*, vol. 5).

PLATE 55. Osaka castle on a misty spring morning. Its stone walls and moat are old but the wood and plaster keep has been rebuilt many times.

PLATE 56. The centre of Osaka is even more cut by rivers and canals than most other Japanese cities. It lies on the Yodo delta with many distributaries running through the city. With constant silting the water is very shallow and not very useful for modern traffic (220).

became second to Keihin, which since then has grown much more rapidly than Hanshin. Hanshin still has 20% of Japan's industry. It is the leading centre for older labour-intensive and heavy machinery industry, including metals and textiles, chemicals and heavy engineering, but has not acquired as many of the new electrical engineering and petro-chemical industries.

The city lies on the Settsu Plain on the delta of the Yodo River. It is the centre of Hanshin and lies at the heart of an urban area stretching round the eastern end of the Inland Sea from Kobe in the west through Nishinomiya and Amagasaki, to Sakai, Izumi-Sano and Wakayama, an outlier, in the south (figs. 144 & 145).

Its castle lies on a diluvial bluff 4 miles inland, north-east of the fine modern commercial centre (pl. 55), which spreads along one of the many distributaries of the Yodo which have been joined by the canals which make Osaka accessible to boats. Both canals and roads are dominated in the centre area by a grid pattern. The main distributaries run through Osaka to the heavily silted coastal area to the west, where dredging has deepened an artificial harbour so that it can accommodate ships of 20,000 tons with a 27-foot draught. Congestion causes most ships to unload by lighter, and few ships of over 10,000 tons use the port. New dredging is being done so that ships needing 38 feet will have access to new industrial areas, and a scheme to build a new breakwater enclosing Kobe and Osaka is contemplated. Osaka harbour, like Tokyo harbour, was adequate for domestic trade which still forms three-quarters of Osaka's trade, but after 1868 the port of Kobe developed 16 miles to the west, along the bay, for larger ships supplanting Osaka which now only handles 11% of Japan's foreign trade, little more than that of Tokyo.

Industry (fig. 145) has developed along the coast in a continuous belt from Kobe to Izumi-Sano. Many modern factories have been built along the banks of the Yodo to the north, and reclamation is being carried on in the Yodo delta to accommodate heavy iron and steel and chemical industries. The best residential area overlooks the city from a low north to south diluvial bluff to the east. The castle is sited on the north-western edge of this just north-east of the commercial centre of the city.

KOBE

Kobe, which (fig. 146, pls. 41 & 58) was Japan's leading port until 1966, serves not only Hanshin but the whole of south-west Japan including the great industrial area round the Inland Sea. It handles 21% of her foreign and an equal amount of domestic trade. It has grown up since 1868 as an outport for Osaka 16 miles further west to handle most of Hanshin's foreign trade. It stretches for over 10 miles along a narrow coastal plain barely a mile wide and bordered by much reclaimed land between granite mountains and a relatively deep sea. As in Yokohama industry depends on imported fuel and raw materials. Iron and steel making, shipbuilding and many large-scale heavy industries are located on tidewater sites on reclaimed land. They include the great Kawasaki and Mitsubishi yards, which make use of deep water to build very large ships. Rubber, machinery

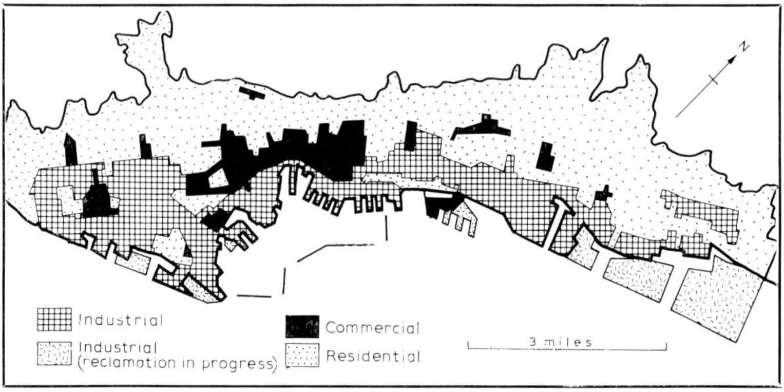

FIG. 146. Functional zones of Kobe (*Kobe Municipal Offices*).

and chemical manufacturing are important. Even this, the largest port, could not be said to have a good natural harbour as it needs dredging, to 30 feet deep, and has to be protected by long breakwaters like those at Yokohama.

NAGOYA

Nagoya, Yokohama, Kyoto, Kobe and Kitakyushu all have populations between 1 and 2 million. Nagoya (fig. 147) is the largest with a population of

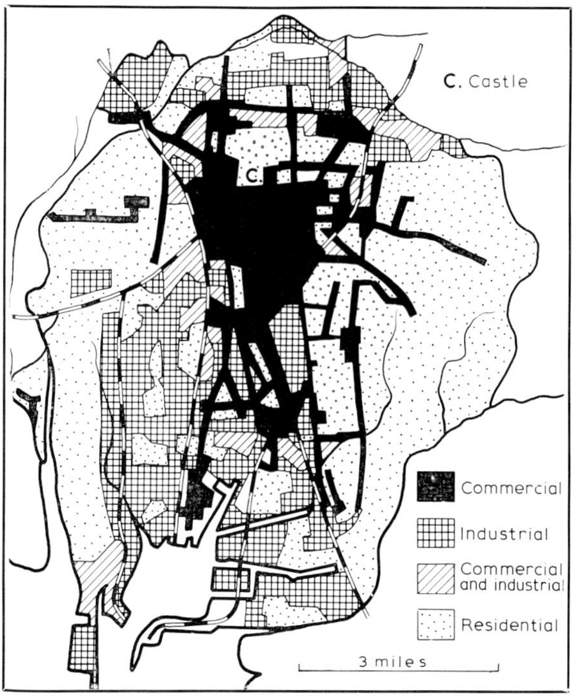

FIG. 147. Functional zones in Nagoya (8).

two million. Two-thirds the size of Osaka, it is the third largest city in Japan. It is an industrial rather than a commercial city and its hinterland is limited by those of Osaka and Tokyo. It is the centre of the Nobi Plain and forms a conurbation of 5 million people. It has grown on a low diluvial terrace 5 miles from the sea and only 40 feet high, out of danger from flooding by the Kiso and Nagara rivers. It grew in importance as one of the main centres on the Tokaido route from Kyoto and Osaka to Tokyo, but has been hampered by being cut from the sea by a low marshy area and by the shallow depth of its harbour. This has recently been dredged to 38 feet, and a new breakwater built to protect it from tidal waters. The town has grown with a strong grid pattern from the castle in the north towards the sea, but urban development is still mainly away from the sea. Its industry includes textiles and ceramics which have been surpassed by motor vehicles and aircraft factories and other engineering products, electro-chemicals, and synthetic fibres, making use of hydroelectric power. Yokkaichi has developed as an outport. Pre-war textile and ceramic industries are being overshadowed by engineering and petro-chemicals.

KYOTO

Kyoto (pl. 57, figs. 7, 101 & 148) has a very different character, setting and history from the other large cities of Japan. As the capital seat of the emperor for eleven centuries until 1869, it drew people to the court and was the political, cultural, educational and religious centre of Japan. Craft industries developed (p. 190) to serve the court with silk brocade, china, and their many other luxuries. Laid out on the Chinese grid pattern with many temples and fine gardens, it has remained a quiet city with no great modern commercial centre. It is isolated in its tectonic basin from the bustle of coastal cities to the south and is still a religious, educational and cultural centre. The tourist industry is very important in Kyoto and there are nearly a thousand hotels that catered for 10 million tourists in 1960. Modern textile and engineering industries have grown up on the outskirts to the west and south, making industry Kyoto's largest employer but little affecting the atmosphere of the old city. Kyoto is growing more slowly than any of the other large cities, as it lacks the seaboard position and commercial facilities of the other cities.

On facing page

FIG. 148. Functional zones in Kyoto (*Takeo Taneoka*).

PLATE 57. Kyoto's crowded wooden houses are typical of Japanese towns. In Kyoto the grid street pattern stands out clearly. It is the many shrines, temples and gardens in and around Kyoto and the crafts that make Kyoto a mecca for the tourist. This view shows one of the small typically Japanese shopping streets on the right leading down to one of the main temples and to the station. Beyond the railway rise the chimneys of the industrial area and the edge of the tectonic basin. Kyoto retains its Japanese character with few modern commercial buildings (figs. 101 & 148) (220).

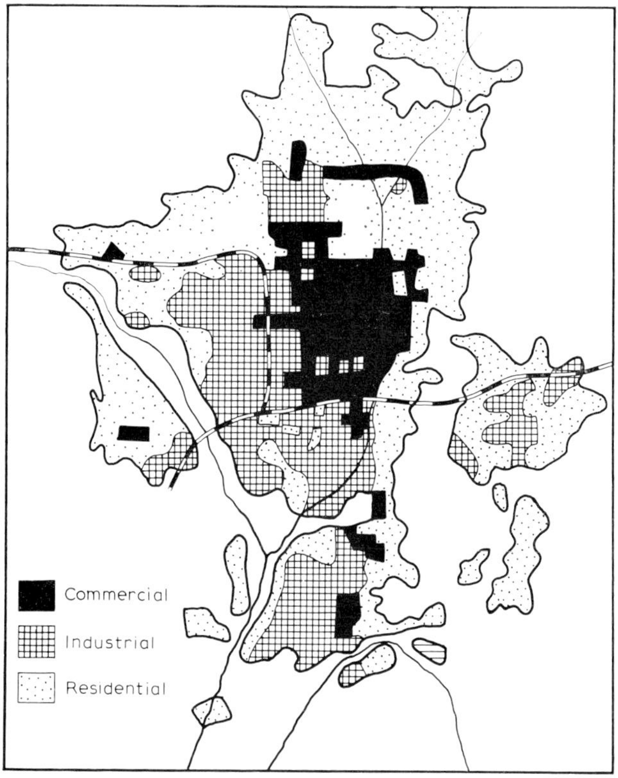
Commercial
Industrial
Residential

PLATE 58. In the Port of Kobe, many quays have been built out into the Inland Sea to provide wharfeage for the largest ships, which use their own tackle to unload goods on to the wharf lined with warehouses. Many tugs are used to manoeuvre ships in the limited space. The port is protected by breakwaters (right background) from strong south-east winds. On the left is the edge of the commercial area of the port and behind is part of the industrial area (220).

KITAKYUSHU

Kitakyushu (220) (pl. 45, fig. 149) differs from Japan's other urban centres in being composed of five centres, Wakamatsu, Yawata, Tobata, Kokura and Moji, which coalesced in 1963 to form an urban area extending over 20 miles along the coast. The whole community includes a million people. All five centres lie on tiny plains only a mile wide almost divided from each other by mountainous terrain, and each has a different character. Wakamatsu, Tobata (machinery) and Yawata (steel) lie in the west on Dokai Bay, and to the east of them are Kokura (chemicals and textiles) and Moji (port), which are almost continuous with Shomonoseki across the strait less than 2 miles away in Honshu. Kokura is an ancient castle town but the area has developed mainly since 1868, and especially since the foundation by the government of the great iron and steel works at Yawata in 1901, with industry on the plains and houses on the hills. Industry developed using the local supplies of coal from the Chikuho field, which are used in the iron and steel industry and in the manufacturing of chemicals in a convenient position for trade with China, Manchuria and Korea and North America and for the distribution of goods by rail and sea all over Japan. The area has never become as important as other industrial areas as it lacks flat land and a good harbour, for Dokai Bay, though sheltered, is very shallow. With a declining dependence on coal and on trade with China, Japan's industry has grown on the larger Kanto, Settsu and Nobi plains, where there is a large labour force, a large market and good trade facilities.

In 1965 Japan had seven millionaire cities, five cities in the 500,000 to 1 million group – Kawasaki, Sapporo, Fukuoka, Hiroshima and Amagasaki and as many

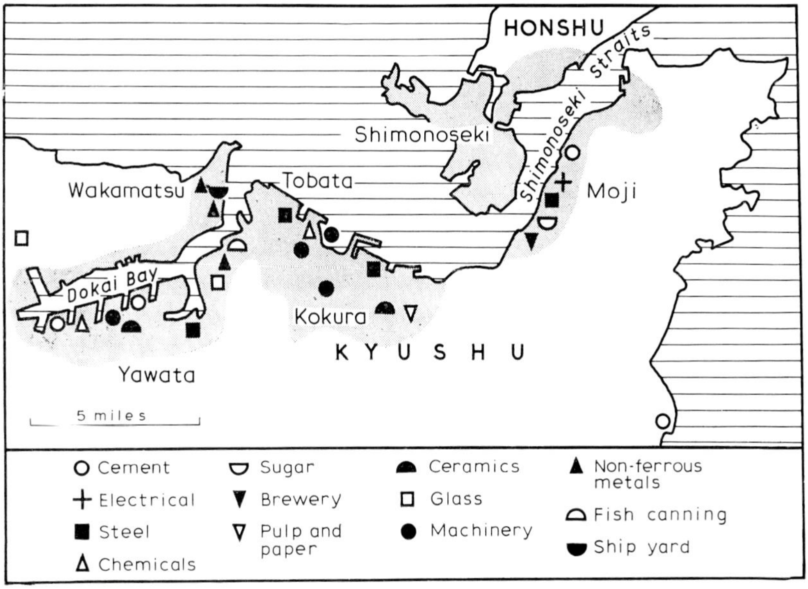

FIG. 149. Kitakyushu industries.

as 119 in the 100,000 to 500,000 group. Many of these are regional centres, which were founded as castle towns. Others are now industrial towns, often near the big cities.

Provincial Cities

Separate clans peopled Japan's many isolated plains in the past. During the Feudal and Tokugawa era the community on each plain was governed by an often powerful lord. He built a castle and gathered round him samurai and the artisans who made the goods needed by the people.

These castles form the nucleus of most of today's prefecture capitals and many of the other provincial cities. Outside the industrial zone they maintain their ancient character with old shrines and temples. Most industrial cities were originally castle towns, but in them the original character has often been overlaid by modern development.

Okayama. Okayama (220) near the north coast of the Inland Sea is typical of Japan's provincial cities. It is one of the old castle towns, the seat of a lord in

Tokugawa times, and developed as a small town on the San Yo railway line with an outport at Uno on the Inland Sea. The old narrow streets were planned in a complex network to make attack difficult. Around this spread the close network of narrow alleys lined with rows of two-storey wooden houses of grey unpainted wood. Most Japanese towns, like Okayama, are unattractive with their drab grey houses in endless rows looking closed to the passer-by, despite the fact that they line so closely the narrow roads which have no pavements. Since the war the monotonous skyline has been broken by the new shop and office blocks rising along the main street, that have replaced the wooden buildings which burnt so easily during the war. About a quarter of Japan's city houses were destroyed during the war, as they were built of wood and so closely packed that fire spread easily. Behind the new modern façade along the high street little has changed. Each *chonaikai* or ward is a close-knit community both physically and socially. Streets are narrow, often unsealed and so complex that maps are often provided on street corners. The Japanese are expert map readers of necessity, for there are few street names even in Tokyo (fig. 39).

The character of Okayama, like many other cities, is changing. New industries are being established on reclaimed land to the south of the city and deep water is being provided to serve these. Modern shop and office blocks are being built in the city and it is taking on a new character much more like that of the big cities.

In addition to the provincial centres there is another group of market, fishing and small industrial towns which have 10,000–20,000 people. The apparent rapid growth of these towns and the decline of the towns of under 10,000 since 1950 is largely due to the amalgamation of many small towns in 1953. In spite of this the fact that in 1920 nearly 70% of the population were in towns of under 10,000, but in 1955 10% lived in them, is significant and shows how, with industrialization, larger centres have grown, leaving the smaller ones behind.

CHAPTER THIRTEEN

The Pattern of Trade

Growth

Even before the war Japan had an important position in world trade. Now she is the fifth largest trading nation after the United States, United Kingdom, Western Germany and France (fig. 151), and has the fifth largest merchant fleet. Japan,

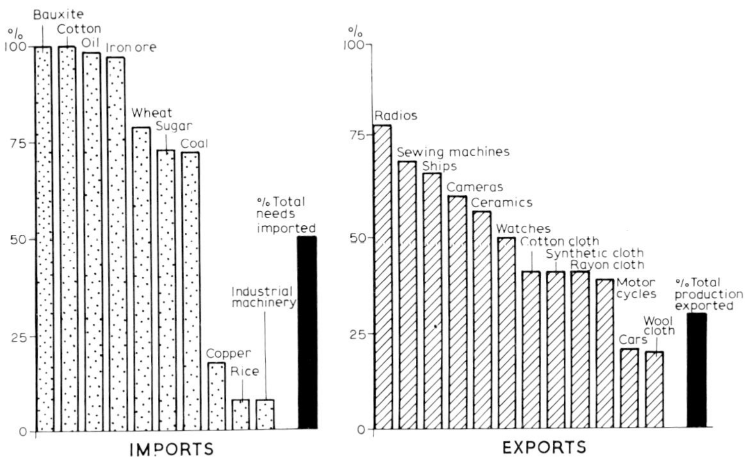

FIG. 150. Japan's dependence on trade in 1966 (91).

like Britain, has become an important trader of necessity. She has very few of the raw materials necessary for industry and she needs to import all the cotton, wool and bauxite that she uses, and almost all the petroleum and iron ore and much of the coking coal (fig. 150). She also imports over 70% of the wheat, sugar and soya beans she uses. In order to pay for these she relies on her export trade. Her home market has expanded with post war prosperity. Over half the radios, sewing machines, ships, cameras, ceramics and watches she produces are exported and a substantial proportion of her synthetic cotton and rayon cloth, and a growing proportion of cars. As in Britain, exports are very important in the economy; 29% of her manufactures were exported in 1966 and 14% of her national income came from exports, compared with 18% in 1960 in the United Kingdom and much above the 5% of the more self-sufficient United States.

World War II was a great setback for Japan's export trade. In 1952 she only had 1·5% of world trade compared with 5% before the war. Her exports revived slowly and only returned to pre-war level in 1958, but by 1966 they had trebled (fig. 150). World trade had increased too, so that in 1966 she had 5% of world trade as she had before the war, and was exporting £4,000 million of goods in 1966. This is equivalent to £40 a head of the population.

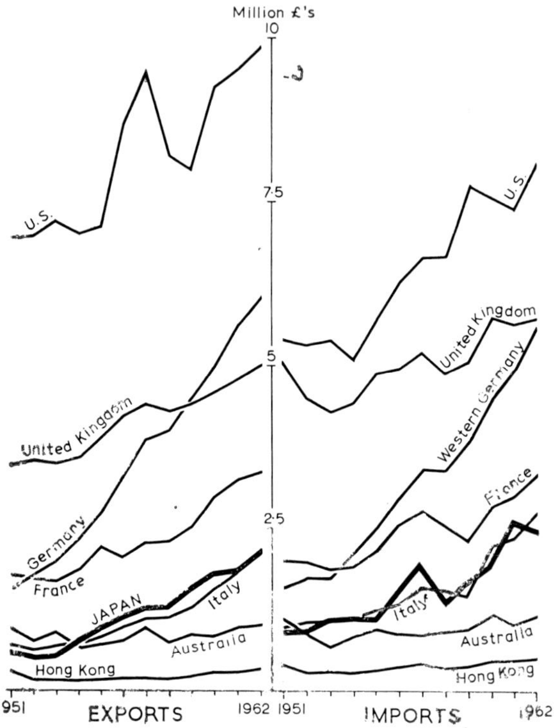

FIG. 151. Japan's position as a trading nation since 1951 (90).

Japan's exports have gradually changed as her industry has developed during the last century. In the eighties she was exporting little but farm produce such as raw silk, tea and rice, and small quantities of pottery. As early as the nineties she had begun to export industrial products such as silk, copper and coal; by the turn of the century cotton and silk had become more important and by World War I silk accounted for over half her exports. Textiles continued to be the mainstay of her export trade, forming two-thirds of the total in 1929, but with the Depression of the early thirties the market for silk declined and engineering production began to grow in importance so that today it dominates Japanese industry.

Since 1945 the emphasis in Japan's trade has changed from textiles to machinery (fig. 152). Before the Pacific war textiles formed 52% of her total exports, but the competition of textiles produced in less developed countries with cheaper labour, like India, reduced them to 18% by 1966. During the same period the engineering industry developed rapidly and now accounts for 37% of the total export trade, ships, radios and motor vehicles being very important. The export of metals and chemicals has grown too and these form an increased per-

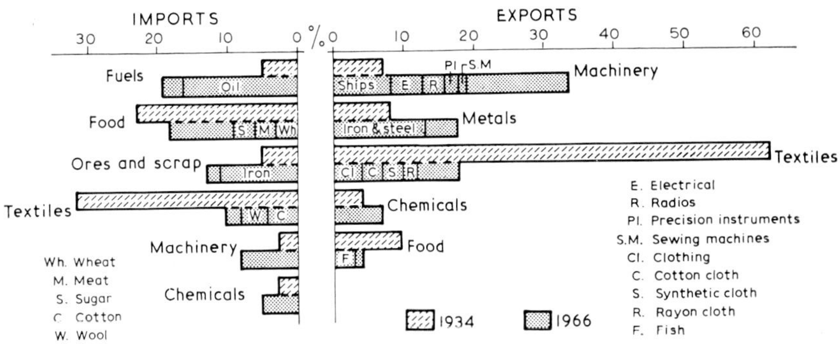

FIG. 152. Main imports and exports in 1934–6 and 1966 (177).

centage of exports. Japan is now the world's largest exporter of ships, sewing machines, ceramics, transistor radios and plywood. Steel, cotton, rayon, clothing, optical instruments and fish, fertilizers and motor vehicles are also important.

Japan's trade is developing faster with the highly developed countries of Europe, America and Australasia (fig. 153) than with the poorer countries of Asia. Before the war Asia was the market for two-thirds of her exports and the source of over half her imports, but since the war her business with China, who took 43% of Japan's goods in 1936, has been almost closed to Japan and her newly developed engineering industry has found markets in the highly developed nations rather than in Asia. These are taking a growing proportion of Japanese goods, 54% in 1966, compared with 24% in 1956. The United States took a third of Japan's exports and supplied a third of her imports in 1966.

Imports

As in Britain raw materials are Japan's most important import, making up 60% of the total. The most important are natural fibres (especially cotton and wool), iron ore, steel scrap, fuels (especially oil, which is the largest single import item), coal, timber and rubber. The import of raw materials is increasing to meet the needs of the rapidly developing engineering and chemical industries. Japan is producing more goods with high value added by manufacture to make the best use of expensive raw materials and cheaper labour, for which Japan is still in a comparatively advantageous position. Foods form a large group of imports and trebled between 1960 and 1966, rising from 12% of imports in 1960 to 22% in 1966, as home demand has grown for meat and other expensive foods. She is almost self-sufficient in rice but needs to import 79% of her wheat, 72% of her sugar, 90% of the soya beans and an increasing amount of meat, coffee and cocoa.

Before the China war in 1937 10% of her imports came from China, who sent most of her imported coal and soya beans and nearly half her iron. China was also her most important market, taking 43% of her exports, especially textiles including nearly half her cotton goods, as well as engineering products, iron and steel and fish. Since the war Japan has had to find new, more distant, sources of raw materials and markets. She has been very concerned at losing her nearest source of supply for raw materials, but has increasingly realized that whatever the political situation China could no longer provide her with the vast quantity

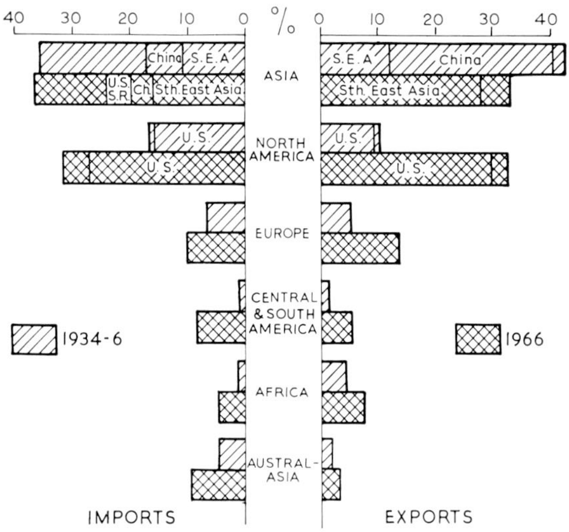

FIG. 153. Source of imports and destination of exports in 1934–6 and 1966 (177).

of high-quality raw materials she now needs and, like other Asian countries, China could not buy the high-quality goods Japan now produces. With recent trade agreements Japan has imported foods and iron ore from China but Chinese trade is insignificant and it is clear that economic as well as political considerations prevent its expansion (fig. 152).

China's pre-war position in Japanese trade, both as a source of raw materials and a market, has been taken on by the USA, which now supplies 28% of Japan's imports. She sends most of Japan's imported cotton and food, especially wheat, in which she is joined by Canada, and soya beans. She sends most of Japan's imported synthetic rubber, coking coal and specialized machinery, more than half her imported steel scrap, and chemicals and also petroleum (fig. 154). Australia is the second largest and growing source of imports and sends wool, coal, iron, wheat, sugar and steel scrap. From Asia come iron ore from India and Malaya, rubber from Malaya, oil from the Middle East and hardwoods from the Philippines. Latin America sends Cuban sugar, Brazilian coffee and Mexican cotton. Canada sends softwoods and Europe supplies specialized machinery.

Japan became a full member of the General Agreement on Tariffs and Trade (GATT) in 1955, hoping that by removing import duties she would be able to buy the raw materials for her industry more cheaply and that the concessions she gave to imports would make other countries readier to accept her exports and not keep them out by protective tariffs. By 1960 it was felt that Japanese industry was strong enough to stand the increased competition that would force her industries to become more efficient and so to improve their competitive position in world

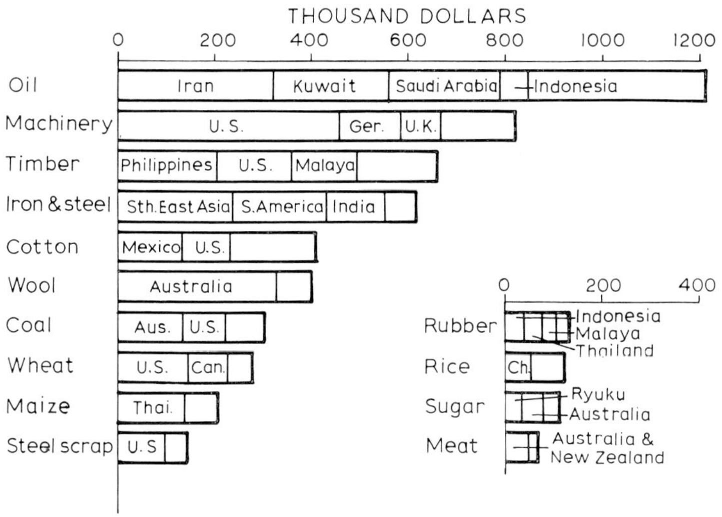

FIG. 154. Sources of main raw materials in 1966 (177).

markets. The greatest problem was competition in farm products, as the production cost of almost all of these except mandarin oranges is well above the world average. New industries have become competitive, notably, the production of motor vehicles and petro-chemicals.

The first stage in trade liberalization took place in 1959, and by 1961 many of Japan's raw material imports had been freed from import duty, notably cotton, wool, iron ore, non-ferrous metals and wood pulp. Some industrial machinery necessary to Japan's development was also freed together with such manufactured goods as cameras, binoculars, radios and bicycles, none of which could compete with the cheaper Japanese products. By this move 62% of Japan's imports were liberalized and, by 1964, 93% of goods were freed, including iron and steel, chemicals and textiles. Some of these are less able to face outside competition.

Producers, who had been working to improve the efficiency of their production, met the first real impact of free competition in 1964. The iron and steel industry has been increasingly efficient with huge new plants, and forms the basis of the engineering industry which has such an important place in her industrial structure. The machine-tool industry is still relatively new and not yet efficient enough to compete in world markets, as they are backward technically and production is on a smaller scale than in other countries because of the small home market. Cotton manufacturers find it difficult to face the competition of cheaper Chinese and Indian goods except in the medium- and high-quality ranges. Japan's coal is poor and costly and cannot compete with foreign products. Less efficient mines are being closed and others modernized, but the industry will need to continue to be protected.

Farming is the greatest problem. Maize for fodder, and hides have already been freed, as these are little produced in Japan. The freeing of soya beans has reduced the amount grown. Rice and wheat both cost 50% more in Japan than on the world market. Rice comprises 41% of Japan's farm income, so they merit consideration. As Japanese soil is poor rice and wheat yields are below those in countries which sell rice and wheat. Both dairy products and sugar cost half as much again to produce in Japan. Cheese prices are double those of Australia and Denmark. Dairy farming is a new venture and, though milk yields are high, fodder is expensive and farmers keep only a few cows. A great deal is added to the cost of butter by inefficient marketing and processing. Both dairy products and sugar beet are important to supplement the farmers' income. It is a matter of policy to decide whether it is better for the industrial workers to have cheap food and so be able to accept lower wages and keep down the price of industrial products and therefore of exports at the expense of ruining a large number of Japanese farmers; or whether it is better to continue to protect and subsidize the farmers so that Japan can continue to produce 77% of the food she needs, but at high prices. In this case she must export more manufactured products to pay for these imports of food. The government must choose between the cheap food policy that Britain adopted with the repeal of the Corn Laws, now modified by subsidies, and the policy of other western European countries of protecting the relatively inefficient farmer so maintaining a peasant population. Japan's present policy is not unusual. Many GATT countries, notably the United States and Western Germany, have freed industrial products as Japan has but continue to protect farming.

Exports

Markets for Japanese goods are growing in all parts of the world. They fall into two types. In the more highly developed industrial countries she can sell industrial goods that need a lot of skilled labour, like ships, radios, silk, clothes, plywood, toys, cameras and sewing machines. Many of these are made in her small workshops where wages are low and little outlay of capital is needed. They benefit from wages well below those in the highly developed countries. Japanese wages were only a sixth of American wages and half of United Kingdom wages in 1966. On the other hand in the less developed countries there is little demand for these costly consumer goods, and here the market is for goods produced cheaply in large highly mechanized or technologically advanced factories, which the poorer countries have neither the capital to build nor the technical skill to operate. It is to these countries that she sells cars, fertilizer, railway rolling stock, rayon, textile machinery, iron and steel, aluminium, chemicals, heavy machinery.

A third of Japan's exports are marketed in the United States (fig. 155); a quarter of these are textiles (especially silk, cotton and clothes), machinery (especially radios, sewing machines, cameras, binoculars and cars), wood products, toys, pottery and fish, Europe and Australia import a similar range of goods. Because of her proximity, her ability to supply raw materials and food and her

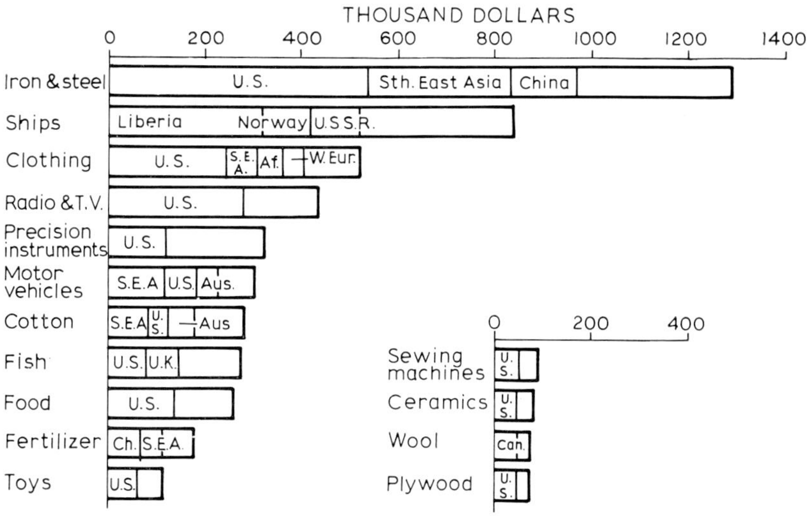

FIG. 155. Destination of main exports in 1966 (91).

need for cheap manufactured goods, Australia's trade with Japan is growing rapidly. Britain's main import is still tinned and smoked fish, but each year an ever-increasing number of cameras, binoculars, toys and electrical goods, cars and motor-cycles, are being imported. The future of Japan's trade with Europe will be affected by policy of the Common Market and the European Free Trade Area organization.

Underdeveloped countries take half of Japan's exports, especially south-east Asia (which takes a quarter) and Korea. Both have the advantage of being relatively close to Japan. Recent agreements with Brazil and Argentina are increasing trade. Ships registered in Liberia made up half the trade with Africa, and ships are also sold for registration in Panama.

Japan is, however, finding it difficult to increase her exports to the underdeveloped countries, and the percentage of her exports going to them has fallen from 76% in 1954 to 46% in 1966. This is mainly because these countries are finding it difficult to import, since they cannot export enough to secure the foreign exchange they require to buy the goods they need. There is a world surplus of the primary products they produce, such as rice, cotton, wheat, maize, sugar, so that prices are low. Many Asian and African countries are trying to become self-sufficient in manufactured goods, protecting their home market with tariff walls; others have courted financial disaster in political adventures.

In south-east Asia China is a growing competitor, not only in textiles but also in ceramics, cement, fertilizers, machinery and metal goods. In selling capital goods, plant and machinery to Asia Japan has to face strong competition from other industrial countries some of whom have, like Britain, the Netherlands and France, old colonial ties. Japan has the unintended advantage of having had to send goods to many of the countries in south-east Asia as war reparations. Having become used to her textile machinery, outboard motors, and so forth, they tend to order replacements and spare parts from the same source. In the long term she is expanding her markets by giving aid and technical assistance to develop farming and small-scale industry in many underdeveloped countries so that they can develop their productive capacity, and have more to sell and so more money to buy her goods. She has also invested capital in such projects as iron mining in India and Malaya, oil in the Middle East and copper mines in the Philippines, which helps both their productive capacity and her supply of raw materials.

To sum up, Japan has had difficulty in expanding her exports, as her costs of production for many goods have been relatively high. Raw materials and fuel are costly, as they must be imported from distant countries. Capital costs are high, as interest rates are often 11%; Japan's bank rate is 7%, compared with Britain's which is usually around 5%. Wages are well above those elsewhere in Asia and are rising. Production is not as efficient as in other industrialized countries, so that productivity is comparatively low, though this is rising fast and manufacturers are cutting their costs and prices as they become more efficient producers.

A further difficulty is the increasing economic nationalism which has given rise to tariff restrictions against Japanese goods in many countries. The underdeveloped countries are protecting their newly established industries and the industrial countries fear the competition of Japanese goods, which are cheaper than their own because of Japan's relatively low wages. In many countries there is prejudice against Japanese goods because of their old reputation for shoddiness and as poor quality imitations. Improved techniques of production and export inspection have helped to raise standards. There is still prejudice against Japan in Asia, America and Australia, resulting from their unhappy contact with the Japanese during the war.

In spite of these obstacles Japan trebled her exports between 1955 and 1966. Her relatively cheap, skilled, hard-working labour in small workshops and large factories is making goods with increasing efficiency. She is using her advantage of cheap labour in producing labour-intensive goods for industrial countries, and she is using her advantage in producing capital-intensive goods for the less developed countries. The government has contributed to the development by organizing trade fairs and trade centres and by giving technical assistance and tax incentives. The great pre-war *zaibatsu* which organized three-quarters of Japan's trade have reorganized into modern concerns, each with an interest in both trade and industry. Mitsubishi, Mitsui and Sumitomo and many other large companies import the raw materials, make the goods and export the finished products and are in an excellent position to develop large integrated combines, sending representatives abroad to find out which goods are needed. Market research, advertisement, and improving after-sales service are all helping to increase her trade.

Ports

Japan's long coastline provides few deep sheltered harbours within easy reach of industrial areas. The main ports are on Tokyo, Osaka and Ise bays (fig. 156),

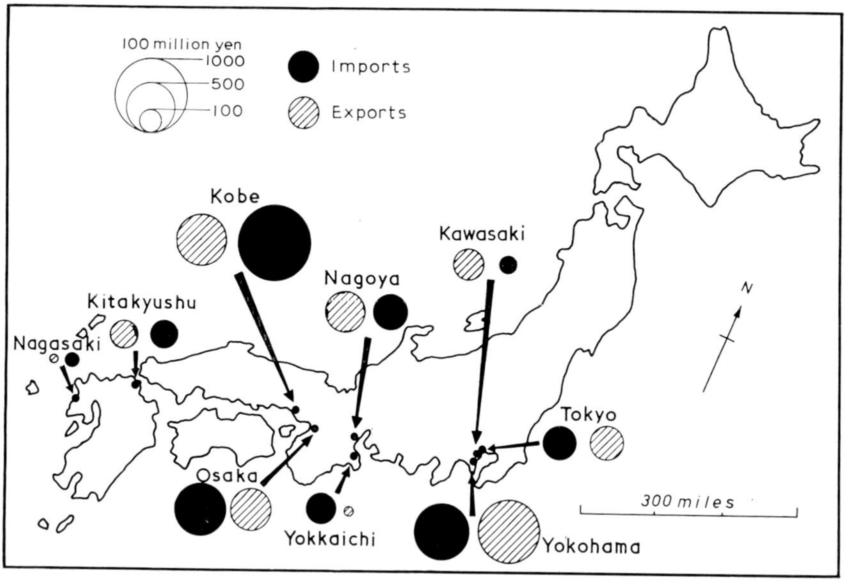

FIG. 156. Main ports and their trade in 1966 (91).

which are sheltered faulted bays with an adjacent plain with space for industrial development. Each industrial area is centred round a river which has built a delta out into the bay. Silt is constantly deposited in the bay, making the water shallow, which is ideal for reclamation but not for the increasingly large size of tankers and cargo ships. The depth was adequate at Tokyo, Osaka and Nagoya for small ships, but dredging is necessary for modern larger ones. Even with dredging only ships of 20,000 tons can use the ports, and space is limited and ports very congested. Outports have developed for larger ships. These ports have been built at the nearest point where there is deep water. Kobe, the outport for Osaka, serves the Hanshin industrial area and was the largest port in Japan until 1966. It lies where deep water comes close to the coast but mountains rise from a narrow coastal plain, leaving only a very narrow strip of land that can be built on.

Yokohama serves as the outport for Tokyo and the main port for the Keihin industrial area, and Yokkaichi is an outport for Nagoya with its own fast-growing industry.

There are many excellent deep sheltered harbours in Japan along the drowned sections of her coastline around the Inland Sea, in north-east Tohoku on the borders of the Kitakami Plateau and on the transverse coastline of north-west Kyushu, but these are not areas suitable for industrial development, as they are isolated from the largest plains by mountainous terrain and drowning has submerged what little plain there was and made the water too deep for deltas to build rapidly. Only in a few places, as at Nagasaki and Kure, are there plains which have been used to build up small industrial centres.

Two thirds of Japan's foreign trade is concentrated in the five main ports of Keihin and Hanshin. Kobe with 21% and Osaka with 11% in 1965 serve the Hanshin industrial area and the whole of Western Japan. Yokohama with 21%, Tokyo 8% and Kawasaki 4% serve Keihin and the northern half of Japan. The high concentration of trade is a direct reflection of Japan's highly concentrated industrial development. Only three other ports are of major importance all in the other two industrial areas. Nagoya with 4% and Yokkaichi with 3% serve Chukyo and the combined ports of Kitakyushu including Shimonoseki, Moji and Wakamatsu together handles 4% and serve Kanmon. Thus in spite of the very large number of small ports in Japan 81% of her trade is concentrated in a very small number of ports serving the main industrial areas.

As raw materials and fuel supplies for industry are Japan's main imports these come mainly to the three main ports serving industrial areas. Yokohama handled 21% of Japan's imports and Kobe and Osaka each 14%. Together these three ports receive half the imports. Raw materials for petro-chemical complexes and new seaboard steelworks on reclaimed land with deep water go increasingly direct to the plant. Exports are more concentrated with 33% passing through Kobe and 27% through Yokohama in 1965. There are more detail of ports on pages 248 and 268–279.

Japan's ports serve for both coastal and foreign trade. Her coastal trade is equal to her foreign trade and both are growing rapidly with the development of her industry. The greatly increased traffic has made her harbours inadequate both in depth and space. Port improvement plans are making some progress, but, like her other public facilities, Japan's ports are overburdened by her rapid industrial development. Japan's domestic trade is the concern of many small ports serving centres of population on small plains. Nowhere is far from the sea in Japan and the population is concentrated on plains near the sea, so that sea transport is important for heavy goods. Small 1,000–5,000-ton ships are used in coastal navigation. Sea traffic is becoming more important in domestic trade and 41% of domestic trade was carried by sea in 1966.

CHAPTER FOURTEEN

Regional Character

Japan may be divided for the purpose of regional analysis into regions which the Japanese tacitly recognize by giving them distinctive names. Each region has its own individuality, which is shown by characteristic features of terrain, climate, land use and degrees of economic development, but the boundaries between them are not clearly defined.

A simple division gives the three major regions of Hokkaido, distinctive because of its cold climate and recent settlement; central and south-western Japan, the subtropical area of early settlement that the foreigner thinks of as 'typical' Japan; with, between them, the intermediate area of Tohoku. The more complex southern area can be further sub-divided into the twelve main regions used in table 5 (overleaf) to bring out contrasts.

Kinki

Kinki is the ancient heartland of Japan. It was the political centre from AD 100 to 1602. It is characterized by its wealth of ancient shrines and temples, and many beautiful crafts, reminders of Japan's cultural heritage which make it one of the most popular areas for tourists. The *jori* grid pattern, especially noticeable in the Nara Basin, indicates its early settlement.

This highly complex area of faulted blocks has densely populated tectonic basins which support Japan's second most important industrial region, Hanshin. The Kinki is an area of growing population and expanding industry where incomes are high. Industry dominates the economy, employing 27% of the work force, which is higher than in any other region. Only 18% of the work force are farmers, as there are no great areas of plain. Average incomes are second only to those of Kanto, in spite of the relatively low incomes that are earned on the small farms. As the older of Japan's two great industrial areas Hanshin industries tend to be more labour-intensive and heavier than those of Keihin, and more representative of the second phase of industrial growth when Hanshin was the leading centre. Textiles, iron and steel, metals, shipbuilding, railway rolling stock and other heavy engineering and chemicals (especially inorganic chemicals) are all important, as are the many small industries making a wide variety of goods. There is less of the very large-scale industry with high capitalization and complex technology, including electrical engineering and other consumer engineering goods and petro-chemicals, that are so important in Keihin. Industrial centres are mainly concentrated in the Hanshin industrial complex along the sea,

	Income per household per month thousand yen 1964	*Per cent workforce in agri-culture 1965*	*Per cent workforce in manufacturing 1965*	*Industrial production thousand million yen*	*Population change 1955–65 million*
Hokkaido	55	16	12	2·6	+7·7
Tohoku (Aomori, Yamagata, Iwate, Fukushima, Akita)	47	42	11	2·8	−5·8
E. Kanto (Ibaragi, Gumma, Tochigi)	49	46	21	4·3	−0·6
W. Kanto (Saitama, Chiba, Tokyo, Kanagawa)	68	9	32	30·0	+36·2
Hokuriku (Niigata, Ishikawa, Toyama, Fukui)	57	34	22	3·6	−1·1
Tosan (Nagano, Gifu)	50	33	24	3·2	+0·2
Tokai (Shizuoka)	57	21	29	3·9	+1·0
Chukyo (Aichi, Mie)	57	18	35	10·7	+2·0
Kinki (Shiga, Nara, Hyogo, Wakayama, Osaka)	62	18	27	23·2	+2·3
San In (Tottori, Shimane)	45	40	11	0·4	−9·8
Setouchi (Okayama, Ehime, Hiroshima, Kagawa, Yamaguchi)	48	28	23	6·5	−1·4
S. Shikohu (Tokushima, Kochi)	48	35	14	0·8	−7·9
N. Kyushu (Fukuoka, Saga, Nagasaki, Oita)	47	28	14	5·0	−3·6
S. Kyushu (Miyasaki, Kagoshima)	45	45	10	0·8	7·8
Average	52	23	24	Total 27·7	10·0

TABLE 5 Regional contrasts

with Kyoto as the only other centre of importance (pp. 200 & 271), where textiles and engineering have now overshadowed the still important craft industry. There is a great deal of rural industry carried on in homes and small workshops, organized by Osaka merchants and often making parts that are assembled in Hanshin.

Farming in Kinki is on a very small scale, as farms have been many times divided during the long period of settlement. Some farms are worked extremely intensively, producing vegetables and animal products for the city market, but many members of farm families make industrial goods at home or travel to work in the cities (p. 94). There are three elements in the farming landscape. Firstly the small, flat, often poorly drained basin plains where rice is grown but irrigation water is short, as summer rainfall is relatively low in this rain-shadow area. Many small ponds and dams have been built to supply water, as they have in Nara (fig. 8). The land is so flat that flooding is a danger that makes winter cropping difficult. Secondly the many upland fields on the wide diluvial terraces and fans built out round the edge of each basin (fig. 7) are at several levels formed at various stages of uplift. Here the lower, finer terrace soils are used to grow tea – especially around Kyoto, where the tea produced is especially valued, and vegetables for the cities. The mulberries grown here have long been used to provide Kyoto's craft industries with silk, but these have now declined. Thirdly the

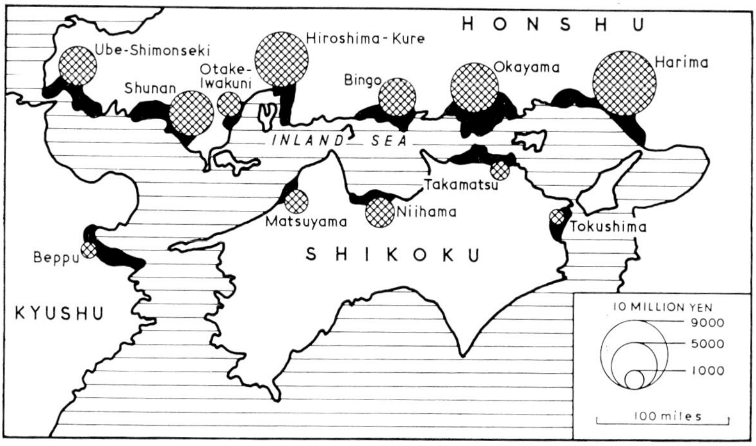

FIG. 157. Industrial areas on the Inland Sea (12).

higher coarser terraces which are less developed, as are the hills where the cutting of the forest over many generations to get wood for building and for fuel has led to the removal of the soil, increased the rate of run-off, and caused flooding on the paddyland and the spreading of coarse detritus.

Setouchi

Setouchi is characterized by its mountain nature, its ancient occupation and its highly developed industries on widely scattered small plains. It is an area of complex faulting, much like Kinki, with five main basins which have been drowned to form the Inland Sea. The Inland Sea unites rather than divides the area around it and is today one of the most important arteries of communication in Japan, as it has been from the time of the Yamato empire 2,000 years ago when the main centres of Yamato culture, was at the eastern end of it (fig. 29). With the hazards on land of flooded river, and forested mountain, now, as then, water communications made it easier to get from one side of the sea to the other than from the Inland Sea to the coasts of the Japan Sea and southern Shikoku. As a deep sheltered waterway it serves as a natural canal between the north Kyushu industrial area and Hanshin, with a remarkable number of scattered industrial towns on small densely populated plains along its northern and southern shores (fig. 157).

One of the main elements in its busy trade is the carrying of coal from north Kyushu fields to the industrial towns. Many of the raw materials that are imported from south-east Asia, India, Africa and Europe come through Shimonoseki Strait and use this route. Iron ore from India, tin from Malaya and engineering goods from Europe come this way, and the varied manufactured goods leave Japan by way of the Inland Sea. Smaller ships carry raw materials distributed from Kobe and industrial products from Hanshin industries, and collect industrial products from the many small coastal industrial towns for export through Kobe. There are frequent, regular ships carrying passengers and cargo plying between many small ports with natural harbours. Fishing boats from the hundreds of small fishing ports along the shores harvest its waters. The beauty of the island-dotted waters attracts tourists and nearly 2 million passengers were carried on pleasure cruises from Osaka in 1960.

Setouchi forms an important part of Japan's main industrial belt and its many small but important industrial towns produce about 8% of Japan's manufactures. Industrial towns have grown on many small plains, often on the coast, using the sea for the export of goods. On the north coast the towns are served by the ancient San Yo road and one of the few electrified railways. Both these are of prime importance in Japan's communication system. In spite of good communications through many natural harbours, space and difficult land communications are limiting factors to further industrial growth, and industry is not growing as fast here as it is in the industrial centres further east, in spite of many land reclamation schemes. Like Hanshin this region has its roots in the second phase of industrialization and includes textiles, and heavy engineering, but there is considerable development of the petro-chemical industry with synthetic fibres, plastics and other related industries on reclaimed land.

There are more and larger and still expanding industrial centres on the northern shore, where communications are easier. In the Harima industrial area near Kobe, Himeji is adding new heavy engineering and petro-chemical industries to older important iron and steel and heavy machinery, chemical and textile factories. In Okayama there are large reclamation projects south of the city on the shores of Kojima Bay and at Mizushima further west. Mizushima is growing with the establishment of an important petro-chemical complex with associated industries, especially synthetic fibres. In Hiroshima machinery is the main industry, especially with motor vehicles and shipbuilding. Large new areas are being reclaimed along the delta and the nearby coast to the south. Kure, which is not on a delta and so has deeper water, is a naval base with iron and steel, shipbuilding and metals but little land reclamation. Shunan west of Hiroshima, and Otake-Iwakuni in between, both have new petro-chemical complexes with associated industries.

Bingo is a smaller centre with more traditional labour-intensive textile, rubber, rayon and chemical industries. Ube is closely associated with Kitakyushu and can best be considered in that region.

Industry on the Shikoku coast is less developed with small centres and small factories. Industries are more labour-intensive and include textiles, clothing, food, small machinery and traditional craft industries making fans, craft paper and lacquer goods. Development is greatest in Ehime, where the Besshi Mining Company on Shisaka Island off Niihama smelts a variety of non-ferrous home and imported ores. Ore is also smelted at Tamano near Okayama. By-products of these industries have given rise to a local chemical industry which is being greatly expanded with the new Sumitomo petro-chemical complex at Niihama. Rayon and synthetic textiles are important associated industries.

All round the Inland Sea there are many small fishing ports where fishermen use small trawlers to catch fish within the Inland Sea and in nearby waters (p. 238). The sea is also used to produce salt and many small reclaimed polders along the coast are flooded to make saltings. The old method of slow evaporation has been replaced since the war by pumping the water over a high trellis that gives it maximum contact with air and sunshine and so hastens evaporation. The Inland Sea, which is the driest and sunniest area in Japan and with a tidal range of only about 10 feet, is well suited to this small industry. Production is small but this is Japan's only home supply of salt.

This is part of Ogasawara's Core Zone and its early settlement has left, as in the Kinki, its characteristic *jori* grid pattern, especially in Kagawa (p. 96). Farms are the smallest in Japan, but they are cultivated intensively with a great deal of intercropping, and many of the steep hillsides are terraced for subsistence upland crops or new orange orchards. Farming is influenced by the Hanshin market and fruit, vegetables, tobacco, dairy products and beef are produced on highly commercialized and profitable farms (p. 131). *Igusa* is a special crop (p. 149) in the area. In contrast with this is the subsistence farming on many of the terraced hills. Industry is spread through the region so that many farm family members can work in factories and local workshops.

San In

The Chugoku peninsula, excluding the borders of the Inland Sea, is one of the poorest and least populous areas of Japan. The grid of north-west to south-east and south-west to north-east faults has not produced tectonic basins as it has in the Kinki and in the Inland Sea area. The Tertiary hills have been subjected to drowning followed by uplift in stages, which has produced a succession of marine platforms. With little alluvium and poor lithosols on the hills the area has been little developed and remains largely forested, in spite of its proximity to the heartland. Farming is poor, with a variety of subsistence crops and considerable terracing. There is some cattle rearing for beef on the hills. The cattle are sold to the lowland farmers in San Yo, who use them as work animals and fatten them for the city market. Kobe is famed for its beef, but beef is costly and not yet widely eaten in Japan. There is little industrial development in Chugoku away from the Inland Sea, and food and wood-based industries on the coast in San In are the only ones of any importance. San In, 'shady side', is very isolated and poor with no large lowland area. It is similar to Hokuriku in its raw gloomy (if warmer) winter.

Southern Shikoku

Away from the borders of the Inland Sea with its densely peopled plains, Shikoku is a poor, backward, sparsely populated mountain area much like inland and northern Chugoku. The folded mountains have relics of shifting cultivation but are mainly forested. The only important industry is the Besshi mine. The small alluvial plain of Kochi on the south coast receives the brunt of the strong rain-bearing summer winds and of typhoons. It differs markedly from San In in being sheltered from cold winter winds, and vegetable growing is well developed. It is within the warmest area of Japan and the long summer allows a double crop of rice to be grown.

Northern Kyushu

Northern Kyushu is part of the Core Zone of Japan, and was one of the areas near Asia which was settled even before the foundation of the Yamato heartland in the Kinki. Structurally it is much like Chugoku, but there are tectonic basins with alluvial floors which are densely populated and intensively cultivated, in some places yielding two crops of rice a year. Fukuoka is one of the oldest cities in Japan and is both an educational and political centre for Kyushu and an industrial town, with many small- and medium-scale machinery and food industries which have grown up beside old craft industries.

Much more important is the main industrial area of Kanmon which, though much smaller than Japan's three main industrial areas and lagging behind them in its rate of growth, still produces 5% of Japan's industrial production. It was one of the main centres of industry in Japan's second phase of industrialization, but has been superseded in the third phase. Its industrial development depended on the Chikuho coalfield, which is part of one of the two largest in Japan. It produces 21% of Japan's coal and half of that produced in north Kyushu. It lies in the Onga Valley, which reaches the coast only 3 miles west of tectonic Dokai Bay, which has become the centre of industrial development. This means that coal could easily be transported by rail down the valley. It had the advantage of being near the main trade route through Shimonoseki Strait to the Inland Sea and the heart of Japan, and at the crossing place of the Strait for routes going east. The establishment of coal-based industries began with the founding, by the government, of the Yawata iron and steel works in 1901.

Second phase industries still dominate north Kyushu industry, with larger-scale iron and steel, coal-based chemicals, cement and heavy machinery. New modern industries have not developed here. North Kyushu now produces only 18% of Japan's pig iron and steel, because of the growth of the iron and steel industry in Hanshin and Keihin (pp. 201 & 279).

The industrial area lies in an almost continuous belt between Wakamatsu on Dokai Bay in the west, through Yawata and Tobata on the shores of the bay to Kokura and Moji on the narrow coastal plain to the east, and across the Shimonoseki Strait to Shimonoseki and Ube in western Chugoku. The five towns in north

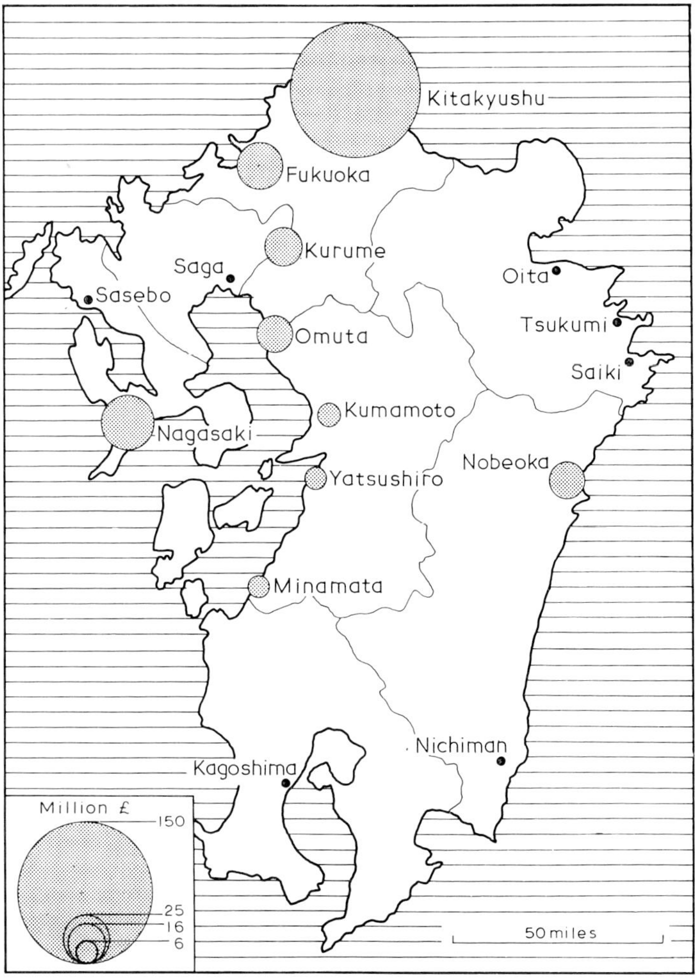

FIG. 158. The industrial towns of Kyushu (12).

Kyushu were in 1963 made into one city of almost a million inhabitants named Kitakyushu. The whole area from Wakamatsu to Ube can be conveniently called Kanmon. It is an area of huge plants whose heavy industry is characterized by its smoking chimneys, stock-piles of raw materials, and waste tips, with crowded housing stretching onto the hills. All is overcast with cloud in the gloomy winter. Communications are difficult. In the confined space between the hills and the sea roads and railway tracks take up much valuable land. Dokai Bay and Shimonoseki Strait divide the area into three distinct sections with poor communications between them. The 2-mile railway tunnel built in 1942 and the 1958 road tunnel pass under, and ferries cross the mile-wide Shimonoseki Strait. The new road suspension bridge across the mouth of Dokai Bay is helping to encourage development along the north coast of the bay.

There is some degree of specialization between the industrial towns in Kanmon. Those in the west of Kitakyushu have lighter industry. Moji has the best harbour in north Kyushu and is a leading port. Its industries are lighter than those of the area as a whole and include machinery, paper, ceramics and food. Kokura is an old-established castle town in a constricted area with a variety of iron and steel, paper, ceramics, textile and food industries, and is a fishing port. Tobata, Wakamatsu and Yawata on Dokai Bay have heavy industries, including the Yawata Iron and Steel Company works at Yawata and their new plant on reclaimed land at Tobata (pl. 45). There is much reclamation in progress on the shores of the Dokai Bay. Wakamatsu acts as the main port for this area. On the Chugoku side Shimonoseki is an important fishing port. The Ube coalfield produces 6% of Japan's coal, and Ube uses coal from the local coalfield to make chemicals. Railway equipment is an important industry.

The most important farming area in northern Kyushu is the Saga–Kumamoto Plain, where rice is the dominant crop and two crops can be grown each year. The plain is being extended by major reclamation projects on the shores of Ariake Bay (fig. 82). Some of the area has long been settled and there are relics of the *jori* pattern. Mount Aso has filled the western end of the Inland Sea and spread a liberal layer of acid volcanic ash over extensive diluvial terraces in Kumamoto. The slopes of Mount Aso provide pasture for cattle, and upland crops are grown on the poor soils of the diluvial terraces. Farm incomes are not high in north Kyushu, as farms are not very large and yields of rice are low, as the land has long been cultivated and lost its fertility. Crops are depleted by typhoons and by insect damage, as insects thrive in the warm climate with no cold winter to destroy them.

Outside the main industrial area there are several manufacturing towns apart from Fukuoka, which has already been mentioned. Nagasaki is the largest with a population of 405,000. It is a port with a very distinctive character, having been the main stronghold of Portuguese Christianization which has left a sizeable Christian population in the city and nearby areas. During the *closed period* in the Tokugawa era it was the only port open to Portuguese, Chinese and Dutch traders, and many western ideas came to Japan through Nagasaki. Industrially it is a Mitsubishi city with a complex of shipyards, marine and other engineering and metal works, all built by Mitsubishi Shipbuilding and Engineering Company. The shipyards are among the largest in Japan. Nagasaki has the advantage of one of the few sheltered deep-water harbours in Japan with coal from the nearby Sasebo and Karatsu fields, but its development has been hampered by its isolation from other centres of industry, its limited amount of flat land, and the decline of trade with China, in which Nagasaki played an important rôle before the war. Sasebo has the advantage of local coal and a less restricted site, and is growing faster than Nagasaki with shipbuilding as the main industry. A minor but well-known industry in the western peninsula is ceramics at Arita and Imari (p. 135).

There are three small industrial centres on Yatsushiro Bay. Omuta, using coal from the Miike coalfield, is a Mitsui city with chemicals dominating the industry; metals are also important. Kumamoto has food-processing works and Yatsushiro pulp and paper works.

The government's policy for the dispersal of industry will bring a new giant iron and steel and chemical complex to Tsurusaki on the deep water of the ria coast south of Oita. There is enough depth here to accommodate tankers of up to 100,000 tons, and the industry has the advantage of local surplus farm labour and plentiful water supply. Beppu to the north is a popular spa town with hundreds of hotels (p. 35).

Southern Kyushu

South Kyushu has always been isolated from the main stream of development in spite of being close to early centres of settlement, and has its own dialect, its individual customs and an independent outlook. It was a centre of insurrection in 1868 when its people played a leading rôle in the Meiji Restoration and remained semi-independent even after that. It is a frontier area like Tohoku, and like it was not settled until after the seventh century. Its isolation from north Kyushu by an inhospitable folded mountain block and by volcanoes, and its lack of alluvial plains, has not attracted settlement so its population is sparse. There is little industrialization and incomes are the lowest in Japan, only 72% of the national average. Industry employs only 18% of the work force, less than in any other area in Japan, while the farming percentage at 45 is the highest in the country, more than double the national average of 19%.

The northern part of south Kyushu is composed of an uplifted block of fold mountains much like southern Shikoku, and is the poorest and least populous area in Japan. It is largely forested but has some subsistence farms, often with shifting cultivation. The southern part is largely volcanic with many active volcanoes and broad ash uplands. The soil is poor and the yields of sweet potatoes and cereals, grown mainly for the farmers' own needs, are low. Like Tohoku it has been a horse-rearing area, but these are being replaced by beef cattle and pigs. It is warm enough for sugar and bananas to be grown and tobacco is an important crop. Recently vegetable and fruit growing have increased taking advantage of the warm winter (p. 103).

There is very little industry in the area. Kagoshima, the capital, has only food-processing industries. The only industrial centre is Nobeoka on the east coast, where hydroelectric power is used in the chemical and electro-chemical industries, whose products include rayon, synthetic fibres and plastics. Like Tsurusaki this is a product of the decentralization policy.

Nobi Plain and Chukyo

Chukyo, Japan's third largest industrial centre, lies in an area with an unusually large proportion of plain, much of which is very little above sea level. Chukyo industry is growing at a rate only exceeded by Keihin. It is an old textile and ceramic centre, where cotton, woollen and synthetic goods are made, and is rapidly becoming more important for its engineering and petro-chemical industries. Nagoya, the main centre, with nearly 2 million people is an expanding port. Yokkaichi, on the bay, is developing rapidly as an industrial centre in its own right. It will be one of Japan's leading petro-chemical centres with old-established textiles, ceramics and machinery as well. Other industrial towns in the area are remarkably specialized. Ichinomiya is the centre of the woollen industry, Seto produces china, Motomachi motor vehicles and Gifu craft products, including fans, lanterns, parasols and clothing. Toyohashi has more varied cotton, food, machinery, wood and metal industries (pp. 201 & 275).

The Nobi Plain is the core of an area of plain stretching west across the Nagara and Kiso rivers, with several smaller plains to the east along the coast. The great river valley has a huge area of carefully embanked polderland which is in great danger of flooding by tidal waves, as it was by the typhoon 'Georgia' in 1959 (pl. 13). Almost all the extensive low flat area is under rice, which is by far the most important crop, as very little land is dry enough to be cultivated for winter crops. This is the largest area of single-cropped paddyland on the Pacific coast south of 37°N. To the west and the east of the plain are areas of diluvium which were important mulberry-growing areas, but very little of this remains. Vegetables have replaced mulberries near Nagoya for the city market, but elsewhere cereals and other upland crops are grown.

There are smaller plains to the east surrounded by upland areas which extend on to two large peninsulas, and specialize in vegetable and flower growing. The Chita peninsula to the east has now been irrigated by water from the Kiso river. The Meiji irrigation canal from the Yahagi River irrigates West Mikawa and irrigation is planned for the Atsumi peninsula to the east.

Tokai

Tokai is a busy narrow coastal corridor between the high mountains of central Japan and the sea. It is an ancient routeway which, since 1600, has linked Kyoto, the former capital, and the trading centre of Osaka in the west with Tokyo, the political capital, in the east. Today Japan's most modern and busiest railway and its first expressway link the two great industrial centres of Hanshin and Keihin.

Its climate makes this the garden of Japan. Mandarin oranges are grown on south-facing slopes. Vegetables and dairy produce go to nearby Tokyo and tea is grown on diluvial terraces (p. 125). Although part of the industrial zone, it has no large industrial centres, but large factories are being built. The small port of Shimizu has a new petro-chemical complex and associated industries are developing. Other small towns have a variety of industries. Hamamatsu has cotton textiles and engineering. Shizuoka, Fuji, Yoshiwara, Fujinomiya and Numazu have food, paper, wood, chemical, metal and textile industries. Fuji, Hakone and the Izu peninsula are important tourist areas within easy access of Tokyo, with fine scenery and many spas.

Kanto

West Kanto is the leading industrial area in Japan, with 32% of Japan's industry in the main cities and 21% of her population. It is the fastest-growing industrial area with the densest and most prosperous and fastest-growing population. Incomes are a third above the national average. It contains the capital city, Tokyo, and Yokohama, which is the port for the whole of northern Japan. Industries which include engineering, chemicals and iron and steel, employ 32% of the work force in the area and are rapidly expanding, especially on newly reclaimed land along the coast of Tokyo Bay (pp. 200 & 263).

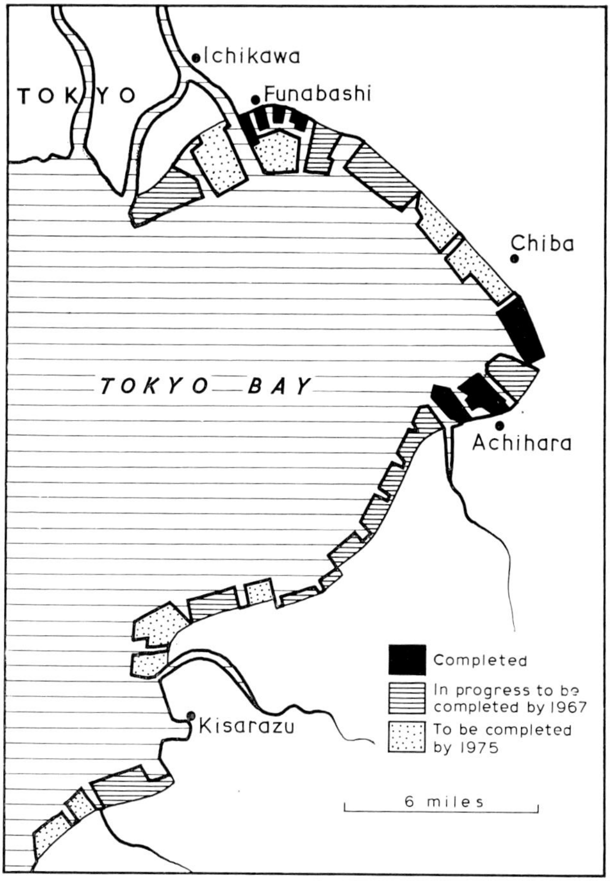

FIG. 159. Land reclamation for industry on Tokyo Bay (*Takeo Arisu*).

The Kanto Plain, the largest in Japan, is unusual because two-thirds of it is diluvium (p. 16). The area has been developed mainly since the Tokugawa capital was established in Tokyo in 1601.

Farming in the area only employs 9% of the work force and is very much influenced by the nature of the upland terrain and the proximity of Tokyo. The west has easy access to Tokyo and farming is relatively intensive. Rice is grown on well-drained alluvium and double cropping is the rule. On the upland valuable crops of vegetables are grown for the Tokyo market. Fodder crops are grown for dairy cows, pigs and chickens, and there are cash crops of soya beans, tea, tobacco and fruit. Half of Japan's mulberry acreage is in this area. In spite of the proximity of Tokyo much of the upland area remains as poor *genya*, as water is short, though some areas have recently been irrigated, notably the Sagamihara Plateau.

The east in contrast is much more backward, as it is isolated from Tokyo by the marshes of the lower Tone. Farming is much less intensive, as the paddyland is too wet for winter crops. Incomes are very much below those in the west. Though physiographically this is part of the Kanto area its stage of development is more akin to southern Tohoku than the rest of Kanto. It is developing more recently and more vegetables and tobacco are being grown and cattle reared for Tokyo.

Tosan

Tosan comprises the highest, most rugged and complex mountain area in Japan. It is the mountain node where the Honshu and Bonin mountain arcs meet and has been uplifted by tectonic movement, split by major faulting and subjected to widespread volcanic outpouring. The main tectonic line dividing northern from south-western Japan cuts through Tosan, from Itoigawa in Toyama on the Japan Sea coast to Mount Fuji and Suruga Bay in Shizuoka on the Pacific coast. East of this line runs the Fossa Magna, a faulted depression filled in parts by volcanic Mounts Myoko, Yatsu and Fuji.

This is an area with high rugged mountains cut by narrow valleys linking isolated populous basins. There are three basins along the foot of the main fault; from north to south the Matsumoto, Suwa and Kofu basins; and two, the Nagano and Ueda basins, near the eastern edge of the Fossa Magna. Each has a large amount of alluvial and diluvial material in the form of cones, fans and plains built out from the foot of the mountains. Each has a climate of more continental extremes than the neighbouring coast. There is much similarity in their development. The wide, well-drained diluvial terraces and lower mountain slopes were, in Tokugawa times, important cotton-producing areas, but foreign competition after the opening of Japan made them turn to mulberry growing and silkworm rearing. Mulberries did well on the poor soil and local towns were all important reeling centres. This formed the heart of Japan's silk-producing area. With the decline of the silk industry since 1930 farmers have had to find new crops yet again, and the mulberry area has been reduced to one-third. Each basin has its own specialities. The Kofu Basin has become the leading area for producing vines, both for table grapes and wine, and an important area for vegetables and melons, also growing cherries and persimmons. Nagano Basin has been very progressive and has become the most important apple-growing area after Aomori, with large areas of peaches, vegetables and flowers and the highest rice yields in Japan (p. 137), but farms are small and so incomes are not very high. The Suwa and Matsumoto basins have turned to vegetables and cereal crops and the Ina Basin to apples and pears.

The labour engaged in silk rearing has moved into a variety of light labour-intensive industries, many of them requiring as much manual dexterity as silk reeling. The Suwa Basin is highly industrialized and its light engineering and precision instrument industries have earned it the name of the Switzerland of Japan. Cameras, watches, electronic equipment and parts for autocycles are made in workshops and small factories, many of which sub-contract for firms in Tokyo. The Ina Basin has a similar range of industries and Nagano has machinery, publishing, food and textiles. Matsumoto has machinery, food and wood industries, and Ueda machinery, food and textiles.

Hokuriku

Hokuriku on the Japan Sea coast is characterized by its raw winter climate, its wet plains, its dependence on rice and its relative isolation. It was in the past the front door of Japan to China, but now that the Pacific trade has become dominant, and with no adequate port facilities on a shelving sandy coast, this area has become provincial. Its industry is developing with chemicals, paper and engineering. It has only 22% of its work force in industry.

It lies on a new coastal strip stretching from Niigata in the north to Fukui in the south and includes five plains, the largest of which are the Fukui–Kanazawa Plain, the Toyama Plain and the Niigata or Echigo Plain. The first

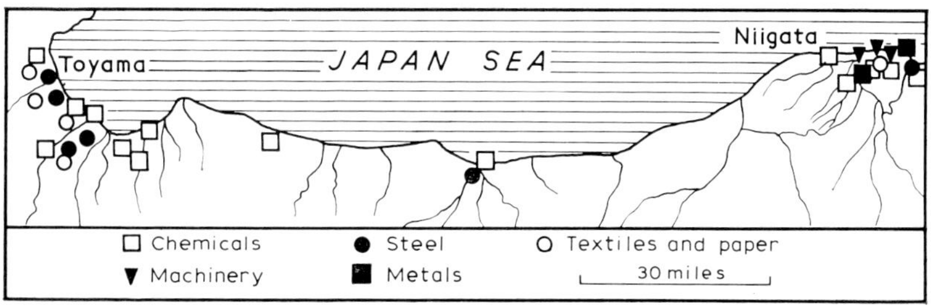

FIG. 160. Hokuriku industries (*Nippon no Chiri*, vol. 4).

and last have been formed by the infilling of lagoons behind a series of coastal sand bars. Rivers drain them poorly, as they meander across almost flat alluvium with high levées and much braiding and many changes of course. Linear villages line the levées and sandy ridges. The Toyama Plain differs in that it is composed of sloping fans of diluvium and alluvium.

Farming is almost completely dependent on rice, which covers as much as 81% of the cultivated area in Fukui, 82% in Ishikawa, 81% in Toyama and 80% in Niigata. Most of the farmland is alluvial paddyland except in Toyama, but even on the fans rice predominates. The cold winter with strong winds from Asia brings heavy rain and snow, which usually lies for two to three weeks. This makes it too cold and too wet for winter crops on the paddyfields in spite of the low latitude. It is very difficult to control water supply on the flat paddyland, which reduces the yields of rice which sometimes needs to be harvested by boat, and farm incomes are above average with a higher 34% of the work force in farming.

The oldest industrial area is in Fukui and Ishikawa, where the old-established silk industry has been adapted to modern needs and Fukui is now the leading producer of rayon in Japan. Associated with this are the chemical and textile machinery industries. The latter is particularly important in Kanazawa as well as Fukui and other machinery is also produced. The Niigata chemical industry is based on local and imported oil and abundant hydroelectric power (fig. 160). Machinery is also made and many wood products. Toyama is a new industrial area developed as a result of the government's dispersal-of-industry policy. It uses local limestone and hydroelectric power in the chemical, electro-chemical and electro-metallurgical industries, and there is paper and textile making. New land is being reclaimed from the sea for industries that include oil refining. This is one of the fastest-growing industrial areas in Japan outside the main industrial belt. A good supply of hydroelectric power is the great attraction.

Tohoku

Tohoku is part of the frontier zone of Japan, distant from the heartland and only settled from the south between the seventh and ninth centuries. With a low population density, declining towards the north, it is the least-developed area in Old Japan. It is a mountainous area whose basins are isolated from the sea and has no good ports, nor does it lend itself to industrialization. Farming is still the occupation of 42% of the work force. The birth rate is low and there is a declining population, with migration to Keihin and other industrial areas. Until recently this area has had many relics of feudalism and has been very backward. At the time of land reform there was a high proportion of tenancy and farmers have benefited greatly from becoming landowners. Tohoku has been one of the main areas to benefit from new varieties of rice and new methods of rice growing which have raised rice yields of 44 kilograms per hectare, which is well above the national average of 39 kilograms. This is very important to Tohoku farmers, as in the cold climate only 3% of paddyland can be cultivated in the winter and that only with green manure crops. Tohoku farming depends very heavily on rice, which forms 65% of the cultivated area and brings in 80% of incomes from farming. It produces 27% of Japan's rice with a great surplus, the west coast is the granary of Japan.

Farms are large in Tohoku, averaging between 3 and 4 acres, which is double that in the Core Zone, though only a third the size of Hokkaido farms. Farmers need a large area since few winter crops can be grown, as the whole area is beyond the northern limit of summer crops on the paddyland at about 37°N. Only half the upland area is cropped in winter and this is mainly in the warmer east, as the western side of Tohoku has deep snow in winter. The more isolated areas in Tohoku are still very backward, notably the Kitakami and Abukuma plateaux where farming is mainly for subsistence (p. 106).

Few specialized cash crops are grown in Tohoku other than rice, but Aomori grows 45% of Japan's apples, and silkworm rearing is important in the central areas of southern Tohoku. Stock rearing is poorly developed but horse rearing has been important, especially on the Kitakami Plateau, in the past but has declined. Dairy and beef cattle rearing is increasing, especially on the upland areas and near Keihin.

As the area has been settled relatively recently it is one of the most important areas for further reclamation. Among other projects the Sanbongihara Upland in the north-east is being developed for upland crops to feed dairy cattle, Hachiro Lake has been drained for paddyfields, and water control in the Kitakami Valley is increasing the cultivable area there.

Industry is poorly developed and employs only 11% of the work force compared with 24% for the nation as a whole. The mountainous nature of the country, the isolation and lack of ports and of major raw materials make industrialization difficult. There are supplies of coal, oil, iron, copper and lead, and the surplus food, chemical, engineering, lumbering and iron and steel industries are important. Mixed forests provide charcoal for heating. Tohoku is the leading producer.

Industrial towns are scattered, depending on the distribution of raw materials. At Kamaishi the Fuji Iron and Steel Company uses the largest supplies of iron ore in the country. Half Japan's small supply of oil is produced in Tohoku and it is used in the chemical plants in Akita. In the south the Fukushima–Koriyama and Yonezawa–Yamagata areas produce textiles, originally using local silk, and the former makes machinery using hydroelectric power. The Sendai–Shiogama industrial area produces rubber, steel and fish products and has been selected for further development. The Joban coalfield produces 7% of Japan's coal, which is used in the local chemical industry and by the large modern Hitachi electrical engineering works at Hitachi. This is the only modern large-scale industry in the area and is perhaps the herald of a new era of development spreading from the south, if the northward trend of industry illustrated in fig. 107 materializes and the government policy of decentralization is further implemented.

Hokkaido

Hokkaido differs from all other regions of Japan in its isolation from the old heartland, its recent development, and its different physical and climatic conditions. Because of this it has its own distinctive patterns of farming, settlement and industry.

Before the Meiji era there were only 58,000 people in Hokkaido, mainly

Japanese on the coast of the southern peninsula, which they had settled during the Tokugawa era after 1602. There were Ainu who never exceeded 30,000 in other areas. The Meiji government looked on Hokkaido as an area which needed to be developed as an outpost of mainland Japan to defend her from Russian encroachments from the north, and as an area which could provide resources in the form of food, fish, lumber and minerals for the mainland. Early military settlements along the Ishikari River were laid out with houses along a road and a square pattern that makes Hokkaido's landscape look so different today from the rest of Japan. After 1885 non-military colonization was subsidized and the population grew, increasing rapidly after 1890 to reach 1 million by 1900 and 3 million by the mid-thirties. With even more rapid increase through migration since 1945 the population reached 5 million by 1960. Hokkaido is the only prefecture in Japan outside the industrial belt with a net increase by migration between the 1955 and 1960 census, but her population density is still only a quarter of that of Japan as a whole. Rural settlement has been laid out on the American homesteading pattern, and most of the cities have been planned on a grid from the start, so that the grid pattern dominates Hokkaido's landscape even more strikingly than does the *jori* grid pattern around the Inland Sea, since this is limited only to the older areas of settlement.

Much about Hokkaido is modern compared with Old Japan. Wide straight city streets run throughout most of the town, as in Sapporo and Obihiro. In the centre are blocks of offices and shops. Corrugated iron is widely used, especially in farm buildings; her farmyards, with hip-roofed barns and silos, are very like those of the Middle West of USA and are stocked with well-fed, productive Holstein cows.

Because of the climate and newness of settlement the way of life in Hokkaido differs from that in Old Japan. Homes have solid walls, double sliding glass windows and wood-fired stoves to combat the long cold winter, when there is snow for six months, often several feet deep. At this time the trams in Sapporo run in deep snow trenches, and skiing is a favourite sport on the nearby mountains. The short summer is cool, and in places foggy. Cool summers and the lack of alluvial soil limit the growing of rice to only 20% of the cultivated area, which is under half of the 44% for all Japan. Upland soils form 80% of the total cultivated area and a rotation of pasture and fodder crops for dairy cows is accompanied by crops of beans, sugar beet, flax, rather than rice. The cold climate only allows one crop a year to be grown and poor soils make yields low, so that farms need to be much larger than in Old Japan. They average 9 acres which is four times the average in Japan. Farm incomes are the highest in Japan in spite of the fact that on such large farms and with stock to look after, there is little opportunity for other work to add to incomes. Hokkaido is the leading prefecture for dairy cows, horses, sheep, pasture and forage, beans, flax and sugar beet, but it is too cold for mulberries, oranges and tea. Though farming only employs 16% of the labour force (Japan 19%), 30% of industrial labour is engaged in processing farm produce.

The physical landscape makes a basic difference to the scenery, the relief is low and one misses the abrupt rocky mountain slopes, the narrow alluvial valleys, the tiny patchwork of fields and the many shrines of Old Japan. These are replaced by low hills, broad marine platforms, large diluvial terraces and marshy valley floors, larger fields and modern buildings. Much of Hokkaido is forested with mixed and coniferous forests. There is *genya* on the poorer volcanic soils and new volcanoes are bare, giving the Volcano Bay and Konsen landscapes a bleak appearance. The caldera scenery in the Toya and Akan National Parks is very beautiful and the associated volcanic activity exciting, but the long, straight, faulted coasts, often with a marine platform, look desolate.

Hokkaido's industry employs 12% of the work force compared with 16% in farming. It includes none of the traditional consumer, craft and textile elements, and is based on local raw materials. Farm products are processed in local market centres like Obihiro, making sugar and milk products, beer, *saké*, *shoyu* (soya sauce), *miso* (bean paste) and processing fish. Lumber forms the basis of a variety of small and large industries, making everything from chopsticks to furniture in small factories and workshops, and in paper making in large ones. Muroran on the south coast is an important centre for iron and steel production, producing 9% of Japan's pig iron and 4% of her steel. The industry is based on coal from the Ishikari field which makes up 44% of Japan's total production, and on local iron sand, but imported coking coal and iron ore are much more important than local supplies. Associated with the iron and steel works in Muroran is an oil refinery and cement works. Muroran is the main port for the Ishikari coalfield, exporting coal, iron and steel and lumber, and importing coking coal, iron ore and pig iron and oil. Fishing is one of the most important industries in Hokkaido, employing 5% of the work force and producing 20% of Japan's total catch. Cod, squid, mackerel, herring, salmon and crab are all important, and fish canning and processing is done both on board the mother ships and in Hakodate and smaller fishing ports.

Hokkaido has a high income per capita, the highest farm incomes in Japan and a growing population with as many as 58% living in towns. This contrasts strikingly with nearby prefectures in Tohoku, which is relatively backward with low incomes and a very high proportion (42%) of farmers and a declining population resulting from migration.

Within these regional limits there is little regional unity, as each region is divided by hills and mountains into many separate plains, each one often a centre of dense population. The plains have much in common in all parts of Japan. Each has an urban centre of varying size, surrounded by paddyland on an alluvial plain, upland, diluvial terraces and steep wooded mountains. Similar variations in the Japanese landscape are repeated throughout the country. The basins vary in their degree of development according to their accessibility especially to the sea, the availability of flat land for industrial development, their supply of raw materials and energy and their climate.

Glossary

Bonsai	dwarfed trees
Buraku	hamlet
Cho	approximately one hectare or $2\frac{1}{2}$ acres
Cho	a district of a town
Daimyo	a feudal lord
Geta	wooden shoes
Hatake	upland fields
Hibachi	a warming pot
Igusa	mat rush
Ikebana	flower arrangement
Jima	island
Jori	square field system established after 675
Kawa	river
Ken	prefecture
Kimono	Japanese dress
Kotatsu	heater
Machi	town
Meiji era	era beginning in 1868
Miso	soya bean paste
Mura	village
Nippon, Nihon	Japan
Noh	classical theatre
Nori	seaweed
Saké	rice wine
Samurai	warrior
Shi	city
Shinden	polder
Shoji	paper-covered sliding doors
Shoyu	soya sauce
Sukiyaki	a meat and vegetable dish
Tatami	straw mats
Tenjogawa	a river with levées
Tori	a shrine arch
Tsunami	a tidal wave caused by an earthquake
Yama	mountain
Zaibatsu	financial group

Bibliography

General

1 ACKERMAN E. A. *Japan's Natural Resources and their Relation to Japan's Economic Future.* University of Chicago Press, Chicago, 1953.
2 *Atlas of Japan.* Teikoku Shoin Co., Tokyo. Revised edition 1968.
3 GINSBERG, N. *Pattern of Asia.* Prentice Hall, New Jersey, 1958.
4 ISIDA, R. *Geography of Japan.* Kokusai Bunka Shinkokai, Tokyo, 1961.
5 *Japan Its Land, People and Culture.* Japan National Committee for UNESCO, Japanese Government, Tokyo, 1958.
6 *Kihan Nihon dai Chizu (Standard Atlas of Japan).* Teikoku Shoin Co., Tokyo, 1957.
7 *Proceedings of the International Geographical Union.* Regional Conference in Japan, 1957. Tokyo, 1959.
8 *Regional Geography of Japan.* International Geographical Union, Tokyo, 1957.
9 *Reports.* General Headquarters, Supreme Commander, Allied Powers. 1945 *et seq.*
10 *Shakai-Ka Chizu (Atlas of Social Studies).* Sanseido, Tokyo, 1957.
11 STORRY, R. *Japan.* Oxford University Press, 1965.
12 TREWARTHA, G. T. *Japan – Physical, Cultural and Regional Geography.* 2nd edition. Methuen, London, 1965.

Physiography

13 DAVIDSON, G. *The Japanese Earthquake of 1923.* Murby, London, 1931.
14 DERRUAU, M. 'Études sur quelques Volcans Explosifs Japonais', *Bulletin de l'Association de Geographes Français*, pp. 307–8. 1962.
15 *Geology and Mineral Resources of Japan.* Geological Survey of Japan. 2nd edition. Tokyo, 1960.
16 INOUE, E. 'Land Deformation in Japan', *Bulletin of the Geographical Survey Institute*, Vol. 6. Tokyo, 1960.
17 RUELLAN, F. *Le Kwansai. Étude Géomorphologique d'une région Japonaise.* Tours Arrault, Tours, 1940.
18 SUGIMURA, A. and NARUSE, Y. 'Changes in Sea Level in Southern Kanto', *Journal of Geology and Geography*, Vol. 25. Tokyo, 1954.
19 TAKAI, F. (ed.). *Geology of Japan.* University of California Press, 1963.
20 WATANABE, A. 'Landform divisions of Japan', *Bulletin of the Geographical Survey Institute*, Vol. 2, Part 1. Tokyo, 1950.
21 WATANABE, A. 'Major Geomorphological Divisions of the Coast of Japan', *Journal of Geography*, Vol. 66, No. 1. Tokyo, 1957.
Also 2, 4, 7, 8, 10, 12.

Climate

22 *Climatographic Atlas of Japan.* Japanese Government Central Meteorological Office, Tokyo, 1948.

23 OKADA, T. *Climate of Japan*. Japanese Government Central Meteorological Office. Tokyo, 1931.

24 SEKIGUTI, T. 'Progress of Climatology in Japan', *Bulletin of the American Meteorological Society*, Vol. 35. 1954.

25 TREWARTHA, G. T. *The Earth's Problem Climates*. Madison, Wisconsin, 1961.

Also 7 and 12.

Vegetation

26 *A World Geography of Forest Resources*. American Geographical Society. Ronald Press, New York, 1956.

27 *Forestry in Japan*. Japanese Government Ministry of Agriculture and Forestry. Tokyo, 1960.

Also 1, 7, 9, 10, 12.

Soil

28 SWANSON, C. L. W. 'Reconnaisance Soil Survey of Japan', *Proceedings. Soil Science Society of America*. 1946.

Also 1, 7, 10, 12.

History

29 ALLEN, G. C. *Short Economic History of Modern Japan, 1867–1937*. Revised edition. Allen & Unwin, London, 1962.

30 ALLEN, G. C. *Japan's Economic Recovery*. Oxford University Press, London, 1958.

31 ALLEN, G. C. and DONNITHORNE, A. *Western Enterprise in Far East Economic Development*. Allen & Unwin, London, 1954.

32 BEARDSLEY, R. 'Japan Before History', *Journal of Asian Studies*. Ann Arbor, 1955.

33 BEASLEY, W. G. *The Modern History of Japan*. Weidenfeld & Nicholson, London, 1963.

34 BORTON, H. *Japan's Modern Century*. Ronald, New York, 1955.

35 CLYDE, P. H. *The Far East*. 3rd edition. Prentice Hall, New Jersey, 1958.

36 FISHER, C. A. 'The Expansion of Japan', *Geographical Journal*, Vol. 116. 1950.

37 GROOT, G. J. *The Prehistory of Japan*. Colombia University Press, New York, 1951.

38 KIDDER, J. E. *Japan before Buddhism*. Thames & Hudson, London, 1959.

39 LOCKWOOD, W. W. *Economic Development of Japan, 1868–1938*. Oxford University Press, London, 1955.

40 MURDOCH, J. and YAMAGATA, I. *A History of Japan*. Routledge & Kegan Paul, London, 1949.

41 NORMAN, E. H. *Japan's Emergence as a Modern State*. Institute of Pacific Relations, New York, 1940.

42 OHKAWA, K. *Growth Rate of the Economy since 1878*. Kinokuniya, Book Store, Tokyo, 1957.

43 REISCHAUER, E. O. *Japan Past and Present.* Revised edition. Duckworth, London, 1964.

44 SANSOM, G. B. *Japan: A Short Cultural History.* Cresset, New York, 1953.

45 SANSOM, G. B. *History of Japan, 1334–1867* (3 vols.). Cresset, New York, 1958–64.

46 SANSOM, G. B. *The Western World and Japan.* Cresset, New York, 1950.

47 SCHUMPETER, E. B., ALLEN, G. C., GORDON, M. S. and PENROSE, E. F. *The Industrialisation of Japan and Manchukuo.* Macmillan, New York, 1940.

48 STORRY, R. *A History of Modern Japan.* Pelican, London, 1961.

Also 11.

Population

49 CROCKER, W. R. *The Japanese Population Problem.* Unwin, London, 1931.

50 DORE, R. P. 'Japan's Rural Fertility', *Population Studies.* London, 1953.

51 HIDAKA, T. 'Population Density of Japan', *Bulletin of the Geographical Survey Institute,* Vol. 5, Parts 1–2.

52 ISHII, R. *Population Pressure and Economic Life in Japan.* King, London, 1937.

53 KISS, G. *Le Problème de la Population au Japon.* Librairie des Science Politiques et Sociales, Paris, 1936.

54 KITAOKA, J. *Overpopulation and Family Planning.* Science Council of Japan, Tokyo, 1957.

55 NEUVY, P. 'L'Évolution Récente de la Population Japonaise', *Annals de Géographie,* Vol. 65. 1956.

56 OKASAKI, A. *Japan's Population Problems.* Ministry of Foreign Affairs, Tokyo, 1957.

57 OKASAKI, A. 'Le Problème et la Politique démographique au Japon', *Population,* Vol. 7. 1952.

58 PELZER, K. J. 'Japanese Migration and Colonization', Bowman, I., *Limits of Land Settlement.* Council on Foreign Relations, New York, 1937.

59 *Population Censuses of Japan* (including maps). Tokyo, 1955, 1960 and 1965.

60 *Population Problem Series.* Population Problems Research Council. 1950 *et seq.*

61 TAEUBER, I. B. *The Population of Japan.* Oxford University Press, London, 1958.

62 TAEUBER, I. B. and BEAL, E. G. 'The Dynamics of Population in Japan', *Millbank Memorial Fund Quarterly.* 1944.

63 TAEUBER, I. B. and NOTESTEIN, F. W. 'The Changing Fertility of the Japanese', *Population Studies,* Vol. I. London, 1947.

64 TAEUBER, I. B. 'Japan's Increasing People: Facts, Problems and Policies', *Pacific Affairs,* Vol. 23. March 1950.

65 TAEUBER, I. B. 'Recent Population Developments in Japan', *Pacific Affairs,* Vol. 29. 1956.

66 TAEUBER, I. B. 'Urbanisation and Population Change in the Development of Modern Japan', *Economic Development and Cultural Change,* No. 1, Part 2. University of Chicago. October 1960.

67 TAEUBER, I. B. 'Japan's Population: Miracle, Model or Case Study', *Foreign Affairs.* London, 1962.

Also 1, 7, 8, 12.

Settlement

68 CORNELL, J. B. and SMITH, R. J. 'Two Japanese Villages', *University of Michigan Occasional Papers*, No. 5. University of Michigan Press, 1955.
69 DAVIS, D. H. 'Type Occupance Patterns in Hokkaido', *Annals of the Association of American Geographers*, Vol. 24. 1934.
70 DAVIS, D. H. 'Present Status of Settlement in Hokkaido', *Geographical Review*, Vol. 24. 1934.
71 DORE, R. P. *City Life in Japan: a Study of a Tokyo Ward.* Routledge, London, 1958.
72 HALL, J. W. 'The Castle Town and Japan's Modern Urbanisation', *Journal of Asian Studies*, Vol. 15. Ann Arbor, 1955.
73 HALL, R. B. 'The Yamato Basin', *Annals of the Association of American Geographers*, Vol. 22. 1932.
74 HALL, R. B. 'Tokaido: Road and Region', *Geographical Review.* New York, Vol. 27. 1937.
75 HALL, R. B. 'Some Rural Settlement Forms in Japan', *Geographical Review*, Vol. 21. 1931.
76 HILL, D. M. *Rural Settlement Patterns in Yamaguchi Prefecture.* Geographical Essay Prize. Royal Geographical Society (typescript), 1950.
77 KIUCHI, S. 'Japanese Cities in the Realm of the East Asiatic Physical and Cultural Environment', *Journal of Geology and Geography*, Vol. 23. Tokyo, 1952.
78 KORNHAUSER, D. 'Urbanisation and Population Pressure in Japan', *Pacific Affairs*, Vol. 31. 1958.
79 LALANDE, G. 'La Ville de Tokyo'. *Revue Canadienne de Geographie*, Montreal. Vol 15. 1961.
80 MASAI, Y., and PHILBRICK, A. K. 'A Geographic Comparison of the Size of Great Cities, Examples from New York, Tokyo and London', *Journal of Geology and Geography*, Vol. 34. Tokyo, 1963.
81 MURATA, T. and KIUCHI, S. (ed.) *Geography of Tokyo and its Planning.* International Geographical Union, Tokyo, 1957.
82 TANIOKA, T. 'Systèms agraires: Le Jôri dans le Japon Ancien', *Annales – Économies, Sociétés, Civilisations*, No. 4. 1959.
83 YONEKURA, J. 'The Origin and Propagation of the Square Field System in the World', *Journal of Geography*, Vol. 61. Tokyo, 1952.
Also 1, 7, 8, 12.

Economic Geography

STATISTICAL

84 *Economic Survey of Japan.* Japanese Government: Economic Planning Agency. Japan Times. Annual.
85 *Hundred Year Statistics of the Japanese Economy.* Bank of Japan.
86 *Japanese Economic Statistics.* Japanese Government: Economic Planning Agency.
87 *Labour Force Survey.* Japanese Government: Bureau of Statistics. Annual.
88 *Monthly Statistics of Japan.* Japanese Government: Bureau of Statistics.

89 *Nippon*. Tsuneta Yano Memorial Society. Annual.
90 *Statistical Survey of the Economy of Japan*. Japanese Government: Ministry of Foreign Affairs. Annual.
91 *Statistical Year Book*. Japanese Government: Bureau of Statistics. Annual.

OTHER

92 AKI, K., TAURU, S., KUICHI, S. and TANAKA, K. *Nihon Keizai Chizu (Economic Atlas of Japan)*. Tokyo, 1954.
93 GINSBERG, N. and EYRE, J. D. *Key to the Economic Atlas of Japan*. University of Chicago Press, Chicago, 1959.
94 ALLEN, G. C. *Japan's Economic Expansion*. O.U.P., London, 1965.
95 COHEN, J. B. *Japan's Post War Economy*. Indiana University Press, 1958.
96 CORRESPONDENTS OF THE ECONOMIST. *Consider Japan*. Duckworth, London, 1963.
97 COWAN, C. D. (ed.). *The Economic Development of China and Japan*. Allen & Unwin, London, 1964.
98 *Economic Survey of Japan*. Japanese Government: Economic Planning Agency. Japan Times. Annual.
99 *Fuji Bank Bulletin*. Tokyo. Monthly.
100 HALL, R. B. JNR. *Japan: Industrial Power in Asia*. Van Nostrand, New Jersey and London, 1963.
101 HOLLERMAN, L. 'Japan's Place in the Scale of Economic Development', *Economic Development and Cultural Change*. University of Chicago, Jan. 1964.
102 *Japan*. Institute of World Economy, Tokyo. Annual.
103 *Japan Economic Year Book*. Oriental Economist, Tokyo. Annual.
104 KUZNETS, S., MOORE, W. E. and SPENGLER, J. J. *Economic Growth: Brazil, India and Japan*. Cambridge University Press, London, 1955.
105 MATSUMURA, Y. *Japan's Economic Growth, 1945–1960*. Tokyo News Service: 1961.
106 *Monthly Circular*. Mitsubishi Economic Research Institute, Tokyo.
107 *New Long Range Plans, 1958–1962 and 1961–1970*. Japanese Government, Economic Planning Agency. Japan Times, Tokyo, 1957 and 1961.
108 OKASAKI, A. *Histoire du Japon: L'Économie et la Population*. Press Universitaire de France, Paris, 1958.
109 OKITA, S. 'Savings and Economic Growth in Japan', *Economic Development and Cultural Change*. University of Chicago, 1957.
110 *Oriental Economist*. Tokyo. Monthly.
111 Oriental Economist *Yearbook*.
112 SAPIR, H. M. *Japan, China and the West*. National Economic Planning Agency, Washington, D.C., 1959.
113 *Survey of Japanese Finance and Industry*. Industrial Bank of Japan, Tokyo. Quarterly.
114 TANIBAYASHI, M. 'Prerequisites to the Expansion of Japan's Trade with South East Asia', *Asian Affairs*. Asia Kyokai, Vol. 2, Tokyo, Sept. 1957.
115 TANIBAYASHI, M. 'Trade with South East Asia', *Asian Affairs*. Asia Kyokai, Vol. 3, Tokyo, 1958.
116 *The Japanese Economy*. Economist Intelligence Unit, London, 1962.
Also 1, 7, 8, 12.

Agriculture

117 *Agricultural Development Series.* Agriculture, Forestry and Fisheries Productivity Conference. Tokyo. 1958 *et seq.*

118 *Agriculture in Japan.* Japan F.A.O. Association. Tokyo. 1955.

119 *An Introduction to Technical Developments in Japanese Agriculture.* Japan F.A.O. Association. Tokyo. 1959.

120 BEARDSLEY, R. K., HALL, J. W. and WARD, R. E. *Village Japan.* University of Chicago Press. Chicago. 1959.

121 *Census of Agriculture and Forestry in Japan.* Japanese Government: Ministry of Agriculture and Forestry, Tokyo. Five yearly.

122 DAVIS, D. H. 'Agricultural Occupation of Hokkaido', *Economic Geography*, Vol. 10. London, 1934.

123 DORE, R. P. *Land Reform in Japan.* Oxford University Press, London, 1959.

124 DORE, R. P. 'Beyond Land Reform', *Pacific Affairs*, Vol. 36. 1963.

125 DORE, R. P. 'Agricultural Improvement in Japan 1870–1900', *Economic Development and Cultural Change*, No. 1, Part 2. University of Chicago, 1960.

126 EMBREE, J. F. *A Japanese Village: Suye Mura.* Kegan Paul, Trench & Truber, London, 1944.

127 EYRE, J. D. 'Kojima Bay. Land Development', *Economic Geography*, Vol. 32. 1956.

128 EYRE, J. D. 'Japanese Inter Prefecture Rice Movements', *Economic Geography*, Vol. 38. 1962.

129 EYRE, J. D. 'Water Controls in a Japanese Irrigation System', *Geographical Review*, Vol. 45. 1955.

130 EYRE, J. D. 'Sources of Tokyo's Food Supply', *Geographical Review*, Vol. 49. 1959.

131 EYRE, J. D. 'Mountain Land Use in Northern Japan', *Geographical Review*, Vol. 52. 1962.

132 GRAD, A. J. *Land and Peasant in Japan.* Institute of Pacific Relations, New York, 1952.

133 HALL, R. B. 'Hand Tractors in Japanese Paddyfields', *Economic Geography*, Vol. 34. 1958.

134 HALL, R. B. 'Revolution in Asian Agriculture', *Journal of Geography*, Vol. 69. Tokyo, 1960.

135 *Japan's Agriculture and Forestry White Paper.* Japanese Government: Ministry of Agriculture and Forestry. Tokyo, 1957 and 1964.

136 KAKIUCHI, G. H. and MURAKAMI, S. 'Satsuma Oranges in Ocho-Mura', *Geographical Review*, Vol. 51. 1961.

137 *Kitakami Flood Control.* United Nations Economic Committee for Asia and the Far East. Flood Control Series, 1962.

138 MANCHESTER, C. H. 'Igusa', *Economic Geography*, Vol. 34. 1958.

139 MATSUO, T. *Rice and Rice Cultivation in Japan.* Institute of Asian Economic Affairs, Tokyo, 1961.

140 MORRISON, P. C. 'Viticulture in the Kofu Basin', *North Western University Studies in Geography*, Vol. 6. Evanston, Ill., 1962.

141 MOTOOKA, T. 'Changes in Land Use in Japanese Agriculture after the War', *Oriental Geographer*, Vol. 2, No. 2. Dacca, July, 1958.

142 *Multipurpose Projects.* Japanese Government: Ministry of Construction. Tokyo, 1954.

143 NAMUKI, M. 'The Farm Population, in the National Economy Before and After World War II', *Economic Development and Cultural Change*, No. 1, Part II. University of Chicago, 1960.

144 NASU, S. *Aspects of Japanese Agriculture.* Institute of Pacific Relations, New York, 1941.

145 OGASAWARA, Y. 'The Role of Rice and Rice Paddy Development', *Bulletin of the Geographical Institute*, Vol. 5, Part 4. Tokyo, 1958.

146 OGASAWARA, Y. 'Land Use of Japan', *Bulletin of the Geographical Institute*, Vol. 2, Part I. Tokyo, 1950.

147 OGURA, K. (ed.). *Agricultural Development in Modern Japan.* Japan FAO Association, Tokyo, 1963.

148 OHKAWA, K. and ROSOVSKY, H. 'The Role of Agriculture in Modern Japan's Economic Development', *Economic Development and Cultural Change*, No. 1, Part 2. University of Chicago, October 1960.

149 OKADA, Y. *An Analysis of Mechanisation of a Japanese Agricultural Village.* Niiike Mechanisation Production Committee, June 1960.

150 *Problems of Food and Agricultural Expansion in the Far East.* Food and Agriculture Organisation, Rome, 1955.

151 RAPER, A. F. and Others. *The Japanese Village in Transition.* General Headquarters Supreme Commander for Allied Powers, 1950.

152 *Resources Surveys.* General Headquarters Supreme Commander for Allied Powers, 1945 *et seq.*

153 SAITO, M. 'Japan's Agricultural Regions, with special reference to Part-time Households', *Journal of Geology and Geography*, Vol. 31. Tokyo, 1960.

154 SMITH, R. J. 'Co-operative Farms in a Japanese Agricultural Community', *University of Michigan Occasional Papers*, No. 3. 1952.

155 SMITH, T. C. *The Agrarian Origins of Modern Japan.* Stanford University Press, 1959.

156 *Statistical Year Book of Agriculture.* Food and Agriculture Organisation. Annual.

157 THOMPSON, J. H. 'Urban Agriculture in Southern Japan', *Economic Geography*, Vol. 33. 1957.

158 TOBATA, S. *An Introduction to the Agriculture of Japan.* Agriculture, Forestry and Fisheries Productivity Council, Tokyo, 1958.

159 *World Census of Agriculture In Japan.* Japanese Government: Ministry of Agriculture and Forestry. Tokyo, 1950.

Also 1, 4, 5, 6, 7, 9.

Fishing

160 MATHIESON R. S. 'Japan's Salmon Fisheries', *Economic Geography*, Vol. 34. 1958.

161 NORBECK, E. *Takashima: A Japanese Fishing Community.* University of Utah Press, 1954.

162 *Statistical Tables.* Japanese Government: Fisheries Agency. Annual.

Also 1, 3, 7, 8, 9, 12.

Industry and Trade

163 ABEGGLEN, J. C. *The Japanese Factory*. Massachusetts Institute of Technology, Boston, 1958.

164 ALLEN, G. C. *Japanese Industry: Its Recent Development and Present Condition*. Institution of Pacific Relations, New York, 1939.

165 ARUKAWA, Y. 'Small Wholesalers in Cotton Textile Marketing in Japan', *Annals of the School of Business Administration*, Vol. I. Kobe, 1957.

166 *Asian Affairs*. Asia Kyokai. Half-yearly.

167 *Bank Review*. Sumitomo. Osaka. Quarterly.

168 BEIKA, M. 'The Location of Industry', *Kobe Economic and Business Review*, Vol. I. 1953 *et seq*.

169 BORTON, H. *Japan between East and West*. Harper, New York, 1957.

170 *Cotton Industry Wages in Japan*. Toyo Spinning Company, 1955.

171 *Establishment Census*. Japanese Government: Bureau of Statistics. Periodic.

172 EYRE, J. D. 'Industrial Growth in the Suwa Basin', *Geographical Review*, Vol. 53. 1963.

173 EYRE, J. D. 'Patterns of Japanese Salt Production and Trade', *University of Michigan Occasional Papers*, No. 3. 1952.

174 EYRE, J. D. 'Tokyo's Influences in the Manufacturing Geography of Saitama Prefecture', *Economic Geography*, Vol. 53. 1963.

175 *Facts and Figures*. Japanese National Railways, Tokyo. Annual.

176 *Foreign Trade of Japan*. Japan External Trade Organisation. Annual.

177 HORNBECK, B. M. *Cotton and Chemical Fibres Competition in Japan*. United States Dept. of Agriculture, Foreign Agriculture Service. Foreign Agriculture Report 97. 1957.

178 ISHIDA, R. 'The Industrialisation of Japan. A Geographical Analysis', *Annals of the Hitotsubashi Academy*, Vol. 7. 1956.

179 *Japan's Iron and Steel Industry*. The JapanIron and Steel Federation. Annual.

180 *Statistical Yearbook*. The Japan Iron and Steel Federation, Tokyo. Annual.

181 *Japanese National Railways: A General Description*. Japanese National Railways, Tokyo, 1962.

182 *Japanese Industry*. Foreign Capital Research Society. Bank of Japan. Annual.

183 LEVINE, S. B. *Industrial Relations in Post War Japan*. University of Illinois, Louisana, 1958.

184 LEVINE, S. B. 'Management and Industrial Relations in Post War Japan', *Journal of Asian Studies*. Ann Arbor, 1955.

185 LEVINE, S. B. 'Industrial Relations in the New Japan', *Pacific Affairs*, Vol. 30. University of British Colombia, 1957.

186 LEVINE, S. B. 'Prospects of Japanese Labour', *Far Eastern Survey*, Vol. 22. American Institute of Pacific Relations, 1954.

187 MITCHELL, K. *Japan's Industrial Strength*. Institute of Pacific Relations, New York, 1942.

188 *Modernisation of Small Industry in Asia*. United Nations Economic Committee for Asia and the Far East, 1960.

189 *Monthly circular*. Mitsubishi Economic Research Institute, Tokyo. Monthly.

190 OKITA, S. 'Post War Structure of Japan's Foreign Trade', *Economia Internazionale*, Vol. 8. Geneva, 1960.

191 *Outline of Japanese Industry*. Asia Kyokai, 1955.

192 PEARSE, A. S. *Japan's Cotton Industry, 1955*. Cloister Press, Stockport, England, 1955.

193 *Principal Ports of Japan*. Japanese Government: Ministry of Transport. Port and Harbour Bureau. Periodic.

194 *Report of Research on the Effect of Modern Industry on Regional Communities*. Japan National Committee for UNESCO, 1957.

195 *Report of Study Group on Small Industry*. United Nations Economic Committee for Asia and the Far East, 1955.

196 *Research Monthly*. Industrial Bank of Japan, Tokyo. Monthly.

197 *Roads in Japan*. Japanese Government: Ministry of Construction Road Bureau. Annual.

198 SCALAPINO, R. A. 'The Forces Behind Development', Galenson, W., *Labour and Economic Development*. Wiley, New York, 1959.

199 SEKI, K. *Cotton Industry of Japan*. Japan Society for the Promotion of Science. Tokyo. 1956.

200 *Statistical Digest of Japanese Textile Industry*. Toyo Spinning Company. Annual.

201 *Statistics of Japanese Industrial Production*. Foreign Capital Research Society. Annual.

202 STEWART, J. R. *Japan's Textile Industry*. Report for ECAFE. Institute of Pacific Relations, New York, 1948.

203 TANIBAYASHI, M. 'Prerequisites to the expansion of Japan's Trade with South East Asia', *Asian Affairs*, Vol. 2. September 1957.

204 *The Electric Power Industry in Japan*. Overseas Electrical Industry Survey Institute. Annual.

205 *The Growth of Modern Industry and its Influence on the Local Community*. Japan Cultural Science Society, National Committee for UNESCO, 1955–7.

206 *The New Tokaido Line*. Japan National Railways, Tokyo, 1962.

207 *The Story of the Japanese Cotton Textile Industry*. All Japan Cotton Spinners Association, Osaka, 1957.

208 THOMPSON, J. H. and MIYAZAKI, N. 'A Map of Japan's Manufacturing', *Geographical Review*, Vol. 49. 1959.

209 *Trade and Industry of Japan*. Japan External Trade Organisation. Monthly.

210 WALTON, A. D. 'New Industrial Bases of Japan', *Advancement of Science*. London, May 1962–3.

211 WALTON, A. D. 'Japan's Synthetic Fibre Industry', *Geographical Review*, Vol. 3. 1961.

212 WALTON, A. D. 'The Founding of the Japanese Synthetic Textile Industry', *Journal of the Textile Institute*, Vol. 51. Manchester, 1960.

213 WALTON, A. D. 'Industrial Changes in Japan', *Journal of the Institute of Bankers*. London, December, 1962.

214 WALTON, A. D. 'The Japanese Cotton Textile Industry, 1945–1955', *Journal of the Textile Institute*, Vol. 19, No. 12. December 1958.

215 YAMANAKA, T. 'Prerequisites for Japanese Economy and Small/Medium Industry', *Annals of the Hitotsubashi Academy*, Vol. 5. 1957.

216 YAMANAKA, T. and KOBAYASHI, Y. *History and Structure of Japan's Small and Medium Scale Industry*. Science Council of Japan, 1957.

Also 1, 7, 8, 12.

Regional

217 HARRISON, J. A. *Japan's Northern Frontier*. University of Florida Press, 1953.

218 JONES, F. C. *Hokkaido: Its Present State of Development and Future Prospects*. Oxford University Press, London, 1958.

Also 8 and 12.

Addenda to the Second Edition

Physiography

219 SCHWIND, M. *Das Japanische Inselreich*. Band 1 Die Naturband schaft Gruter, Berlin, 1967.

History

220 REISCHAUER, E. O. and others. *East Asia: The Great Tradition*. Houghton Miffin, New York, 1960.

221 REISCHAUER, E. O. and others. *East Asia: the Modern Transformation*. Allen and Unwin, London, 1965.

Population and Settlement

222 HALL, P. *World Cities*. Weidenfeld & Nicholson, London, 1966.

223 *Japan National Commission for UNESCO*. An outlook of Studies on Population Problems in Japan. No. 6, 1964. NOZIRI, S. *Internal Migration of Rural Japan*. No. 7, 1965. UEDA, M. *Urban Concentration and Internal Migration in Japan*.

224 KONO, S. and SHIO, M. *Inter prefecture Migration in Japan 1960–61*. Asia. London, 1965.

225 WILKINSON, T. O. *The Urbanization of Japanese Labour 1868–1955*. University of Massachusetts Press, 1965.

Agriculture and Fisheries

226 ASHIKAWA, T. *Agriculture in Japan*. Japan F.A.O. Association, Tokyo, 1963.

227 HOYNDEN, Y. *The Co-operative Movement in Japan*, Vol. 1. Maruzan, Tokyo, 1958. *Agriculture and Fisheries Co-operatives in Japan*, Vol. 2. Azuma Shobo, 1962.

228 JOHNSON, B. F. Agriculture and Economic Development. The Relevance of the Japanese Experience. *Food Research Institute Studies*, Vol. IV, No. 3. Stanford University, 1966.

229 OGURA, T. *Agrarian Problems and Agricultural Policy: A Historical Sketch* Institute of Asian Economic Affairs, Tokyo, 1967.

230 BOGSTROM, G. *Japan's World Success in Fishing*. Fishing News (Books), London, 1964.

231 *The Third Fisheries Census in Japan.* Japanese Government: Ministry of Agriculture and Fisheries, 1963.
232 Overseas Technical Co-operation Agency. *Japanese Fisheries.* Tokyo, 1967.

Industry and Trade

233 BROADBRIDGE, S. A. *Industrial Dualism in Japan.* Cass, London, 1966.
234 COLLINS, H. E. The Japanese Coal and Steel Industries. *Steel Times.* London, January, 1967.
235 COOK, A. H. *Japanese Trade Unionism.* Cornell U.P., New York, 1966.
236 DRYSDALE, P. Japanese Australian Trade *in Australian National University, Papers on Modern Japan.* Canberra, 1968.
237 HOLLERMAN, L. *Japan's Dependence on the World Economy.* O.U.P., 1968.
238 *Japan Trade Guide.* Jiji Press, Tokyo. Annual.
239 LOCKWOOD, W. W. *The State and Economic Enterprise in Japan.* Princeton, U.P., 1965.
240 KOJIMA, K. *Japan's Trade Policies in Australian National University,* Papers on Modern Japan, Canberra, 1965.
241 *The Steel Industry of Japan.* The Japan Iron and Steel Federation Annual.

Selected List of Large-Scale Maps

(Obtainable from Edward Stanford, Long Acre, London, W.C.2)

219 *Great Map of Japan.* 1 : 500,000 Topographical map Nippon Koku Seisha 1963.

220 *Large-scale topographical maps.* Some especially useful sheets that are referred to in the text.

1 : 200,000 sheet	showing
Fukuoka	Kitakyushu
Kanazawa	Japan Sea coast
Kyoto and Osaka	Kyoto, Osaka, Kobe and basins of the Kinki
Muroran	Volcano Bay, elevated faulted coast and Muroran
Okayama	Inland Sea
Shizuoka and Kofu	Fuji Hakone volcanic features and Sagami Bay
Tokyo	Tokyo and Tokyo Bay

1 : 50,000	
Fukuoka sheet 1	Kitakyushu
Hachinohe 8	Iwate Plateau
Hiroshima 15	Iwakuni–Otake petro-chemicals area
Iida 2	Nagano and Ina Basins
Ise 2	Nagoya
Ise 5	Nobi Plain
Ishinomaki 1	Iwate rias and Kamaishi
Ishinomaki 14 and 15	Iwate coast and Matsushima
Kaimondake 1	Minamidani
Kofu 8, Shizuoka 1, 5, 6	Fuji Hakkone volcanic area
Kumamoto 9	Ariake Bay and reclamation
Kumamoto 3, Oita 15	Tanaka and Mount Aso
Kyoto 8, 12, 16 Wakayama 5, 9, 13	Kinki and Hanshin area
Kyoto 6, 9	Kyoto
Muroran 1, 9, 14	Lake Toya and Showashinzan
Muroran 2, Tomakomai 14	Muroran
Nagano 16	Suwa Basin
Nagano 4	Nagano
Nagasaki 4	Nagasaki
Obihiro 15	Obihiro
Okayama 1	Kojima Bay polders and Okayama
Okayama 10	Tomo and Inland Sea
Sapporo 5	Ebetsu–Hokkaido paddyland
Shan 7	Akan volcanic area
Shibetsu 14	Konsen reclamation
Shinjo 16	Yamagata Basin in W. Tohoku

Shizuoka 16	Kanaya River
Takahashi 4	Niiike
Takayama 3	Matsuyama Basin and glaciated mountains
Takayama 7	Japan Alps
Teisho 3	Incised Teisho River
Tokushima 15	Bocho in NE Shikoku and the Sanuki Plain dispersed settlement
Tokyo 2, 3, 6, 7, 8	Tokyo and Yokohama
Tokyo 11, 15	Mount Takeo
Toyama 6	Kurobe River and Japan Alps
Toyohashi 8	Hosoe
Tsusugisan 10	SE Shikoku incised Naka River
Utsonomiya 12	Sugaya
Wakayama 1	Nara and Basin
Yotsuka 13	Braided River Sakawa

1 : 25,000
Sheets are available for industrial areas and most of the coast and parts of Hokkaido.

221 *Land use maps*
1 : 200,000 available for Hokkaido. Geographical Survey Institute, Tokyo.
1 : 50,000 available for some other parts of Japan but not Hokkaido.

222 1 : 2,000,000. *Geology of Japan*. Japan Geological Survey 1964.

223 1 : 800,000 *series*. Three sets covering Japan with three sheets show population, land use and communication.

Index